*Everyman, I will go with thee,
and be thy guide*

D1363138

WITHDRAWN

SILVER POETS
OF THE SIXTEENTH CENTURY

Sir Thomas Wyatt, Henry Howard,
Sir Walter Ralegh, Sir Philip Sidney,
Mary Sidney, Michael Drayton and
Sir John Davies

Edited by
DOUGLAS BROOKS-DAVIES

EVERYMAN
J. M. DENT · LONDON
CHARLES E. TUTTLE
VERMONT

To Mary

Selection, Introduction and Notes © J.M.Dent 1992

All rights reserved

This title first published in Everyman 1947
New edition 1992
Updated 1994
Reissued 1997

J.M.Dent
Orion Publishing Group
Orion House, 5 Upper St Martin's Lane,
London WC2H 9EA
and
Charles E. Tuttle Co. Inc.
28 South Main Street,
Rutland, Vermont, 05701, USA

Typeset in Sabon by CentraCet Limited, Cambridge
Printed in Great Britain by
The Guernsey Press Co. Ltd, Guernsey, C.I.

British Library Cataloguing-in-Publication Data
is available upon request.

ISBN 0 460 87440 3

CONTENTS

v

Contents

NOTE ON THE AUTHORS
AND EDITOR

Sir Thomas Wyatt (1503–42)
Henry Howard, Earl of Surrey (c. 1517–47)
Sir Walter Ralegh (1552–1618)
Sir Philip Sidney (1554–86)
Mary Sidney, Countess of Pembroke (1561–1621)
Michael Drayton (1563–1631)
Sir John Davies (1569–1626)

Biographical details can be found at the front of the selection of
each poet's work.

Douglas Brooks-Davies was, until 1993, Senior Lecturer in
English Literature at the University of Manchester. He is currently Honorary Research Fellow there, and a freelance scholar.
His many publications include *Spenser's 'Faerie Queene': A
Critical Commentary on Books I and II* (1977); *The Mercurian
Monarch* (1983); *Pope's 'Dunciad' and the Queen of Night*
(1985); *Dickens's 'Great Expectations': A Critical Study* (1989);
Oedipal 'Hamlet' (1989); and a new annotated text of Spenser's
The Faerie Queene, Books I–III (Everyman, 1993). A major
contributor to *The Spenser Encyclopedia* (1990), he is currently
completing an edition of Spenser's minor poems.

CHRONOLOGY OF THE POETS' LIVES

Year	Age	Life
1503		Sir Thomas Wyatt born, at Allington Castle, Kent

CHRONOLOGY OF THE TIMES

Year	Literary Context	Historical Events
1503	William Dunbar, *The Thistle and the Rose* Works of Euripides first printed	Henry VII, first Tudor, reigning; chapel named after him begun in Westminster Abbey Leonardo da Vinci paints *Mona Lisa* Pope Pius III succeeded by Julius II
1504	Sannazaro, *Arcadia*	John Colet Dean of St Paul's
1505		Luther enters Augustinian friary Christ's College, Cambridge founded Erasmus returns to England John Knox born
1506	Reuchlin's Hebrew *Grammar* and *Dictionary*	Death of Columbus Macchiavelli establishes Florentine militia Bramante begins rebuilding of St Peter's, Rome Erasmus leaves England
1507	Dunbar, *Dance of the Seven Deadly Sins*	America named after Amerigo Vespucci
1508	Various works of Dunbar	Luther Professor of Divinity at Wittenberg University First book printed in Scotland
1509	Erasmus, *The Praise of Folly* Alexander Barclay, *The Ship of Fools* Stephen Hawes, *The Pastime of Pleasure*	Death of Henry VII; accession of Henry VIII, who marries Catherine of Aragon In Europe Pfefferkorn ordered by Holy Roman Emperor to destroy Jewish books The watch invented in Nuremberg by Henle Brasenose College, Oxford, St John's College, Cambridge founded

Year	Age	Life
1516	13	Wyatt's first court appearance; matriculates at St John's College, Cambridge
c. 1517		Henry Howard, Earl of Surrey born at Kenninghall Palace, Norfolk, son of Thomas Howard (Duke of Norfolk, 1524)
c. 1520	17	Wyatt marries Lord Cobham's daughter, Elizabeth Brooke
1521	18	Son, also Thomas Wyatt, born

Year	Literary Context	Historical Events
1510	Erasmus, *Institution of a Christian Prince*	Erasmus appointed Professor of Greek at Cambridge Colet founds St Paul's School
1513	Gavin Douglas writes *Aeneid* translation. Machiavelli, *The Prince* Skelton, *A Ballad of the Scottish King* Works of Plato, Pindar first printed	Scots, in alliance with France, defeated at Flodden; James IV killed Pope Leo X succeeds Julius II
1514	Alexander Barclay, *Eclogues* *Tacitus* printed	Fuggers permitted to sell indulgences in Germany Death of Bramante Peace declared between England and France
1516	Sir Thomas More, *Utopia* Ariosto, *Orlando Furioso* Erasmus's edition of New Testament	Corpus Christi College, Oxford founded
1517	Reuchlin, *On the Art of Cabbala*	Luther's 95 Theses affixed to door of Wittenberg Palace Church; start of Reformation
1518	Erasmus, *Familiar Colloquies* Works of Aeschylus printed	Luther interrogated at Augsburg
1519		Charles V elected Holy Roman Emperor Cortez begins conquest of Mexico Zwingli preaches as Protestant at Zurich
1520	Scottish New Testament	Luther excommunicated; publishes various Reformation pamphlets including *On the Freedom of a Christian* and *De captivitate Babylonica ecclesiae* Death of Raphael
1521	Major, *History of Scotland*. Henry VIII refutes Luther's *Babylonish Captivity* in *Golden Book*	Luther and followers outlawed by Edict of Worms Anabaptists at Wittenberg
1522	Luther's New Testament published Death of Douglas, Reuchlin	Leo X declares Henry VIII Defender of the Faith
1523	Lord Berners's translation of Froissart's *Chronicles*, Book 1	Pope Clement VII succeeds Leo X

Year	Age	Life
1525	22	Wyatt and wife separate; Wyatt's interest in Anne Boleyn (Surrey's first cousin) develops
1526	23	Wyatt on diplomatic mission to France with Sir Thomas Cheney; created Marshal of Calais
1527	24	Wyatt on mission to Pope with Sir John Russell
1530	13	Surrey becomes companion of Henry VIII's illegitimate son, Henry Fitzroy, Duke of Richmond
1532	29	Wyatt made Commissioner of the Peace in Essex; accompanies Henry VIII and Anne Boleyn to France.
	15	Surrey marries Lady Frances de Vere, daughter of Earl of Oxford; accompanies Henry VIII, Anne Boleyn, and the Duke of Richmond to France

Year	Literary Context	Historical Events
1524	Luther, first German hymn book Erasmus, *On the Freedom of the Will*	
1525	Luther (response to Erasmus), *On the Bondage of the Will* Tyndale's New Testament translation (burned 1526) Berner's Froissart, Books 3, 4	Cardinal Wolsey founds Cardinal College, Oxford (re-endowed as Christ Church, 1546) Suppression of free peasantry in Germany
1527	Castiglione, *The Courtier*	John Dee born Death of Machiavelli Rome sacked by Spaniards and Germans
1529	John Rastell, *The Pastime of People*	Luther and Zwingli at Marburg disagree about nature of Eucharist Fall of Wolsey Thomas More succeeds as Lord Chancellor; England establishes Reformation Parliament
1530	Sir David Lindsay, *The Complaint and Testament of the Papyngo* Rastell, *A New Book of Purgatory*	Death of Sannazaro and Wolsey Agricola, *De re metallica*
1531	Erasmus, edition of Aristotle Sir Thomas Elyot, *The Book Named the Governor* Cornelius Agrippa, *De occulta philosophia libri tres* (written 1510)	Henry VIII declared Head of the Church in England Charles V forbids Reformation doctrines in Netherlands
1532	First complete edition of Chaucer (by William Thynne) Robert Estienne's Latin dictionary Rabelais, *Pantagruel*	Thomas More resigns

Year	Age	Life
1533	30	Wyatt serves at Anne Boleyn's coronation
1535	32	Wyatt knighted
1536	33	Wyatt imprisoned in Tower of London, accused of having been Anne Boleyn's lover; released after Anne's execution (19 May)
	19	Surrey's first son, Thomas, born; the Duke of Richmond dies; Surrey and father active against the Pilgrimage of Grace rebellion
1537	20	Surrey suspected of sympathy with the rebels and imprisoned at Windsor; soon released
1537–40	34–37	Wyatt ambassador to court of Holy Roman Emperor Charles V in Spain; returns briefly to England in 1539

Year	Literary Context	Historical Events
1533	Skelton, *Magnificence* Sir Thomas More, *The Apology* Death of Ariosto	Henry VIII marries Anne Boleyn (executed 1536); marriage to Catherine of Aragon declared void; Henry excommunicated Cranmer Archbishop of Canterbury Thomas Cromwell Secretary of State Princess Elizabeth (later Elizabeth I) born, September
1534	Luther's Bible translation completed Rabelais, *Gargantua* Polydore Vergil's critical survey of British/Arthurian history and mythology, *Anglica historia* Lord Berners's translation of *Huon of Bordeaux* Elyot, *The Castle of Health*	Pope declares marriage to Catherine valid; England's final break with Rome with Act of Supremacy (Henry takes on papal powers in England) Jesuits founded Correggio dies Michelangelo begins Sistine Chapel *Last Judgement* Paul III becomes pope
1535	Coverdale's Bible translation Berners's translation of *The Golden Book of Marcus Aurelius*	English bishops reject papal authority; visitation of churches and monasteries ordered; Sir Thomas More and Bishop Fisher of Rochester executed
1536	Calvin, *Institutio religionis Christianae* Death of Erasmus	Anne Boleyn executed; Henry VIII marries Jane Seymour Dissolution of lesser monasteries in England; Pilgrimage of Grace rebellion in northern England English and Welsh systems of government unified; Cromwell appointed Lord Privy Seal Calvin to Geneva Sansovino begins St Mark's Library, Venice
1537		Lady Joanna Lumley (first known translator of a Greek play into English) born Death of Jane Seymour First Roman Catholic hymn book

Year	Age	Life
1540	37	Wyatt returns to England; his friend Thomas Cromwell executed 28 July
	23	Surrey's first cousin, Katharine Howard, marries Henry VIII
1541	38	Wyatt accused of treason
	24	Surrey created Knight of the Garter
1542	39	Wyatt receives royal pardon; dies at Sherborne, 11 October
	25	Surrey arrested after Katharine Howard's execution; released; fights with father in Scotland
1543	26	Surrey imprisoned for a month for riotous behaviour during Lent (see poem 'London, thou hast accused me'); on release, goes to continent to fight with Holy Roman Emperor, Charles V
1544	27	Surrey starts to build Italianate palace at Mount Surrey, Norfolk
1545	28	Surrey serves in France at siege of Montreuil
1546	29	Surrey loses battle at St Etienne; recalled to England; accused of treason

Year	Literary Context	Historical Events
1538		Roger Ascham appointed Reader in Greek at St John's College, Cambridge Becket's shrine at Canterbury destroyed and other shrines and relics
1539	Coverdale, *Ghostly Psalms* Works of Diodorus Siculus first printed	Dissolution of greater English monasteries; Henry VIII issues Six Articles
1540	Sir David Lindsay, *A Satire of the Three Estates* Gavin Douglas, *The Palace of Honour*	Henry marries Anne of Cleves, then Katharine Howard (executed 1542) Thomas Cromwell executed
1541	Clément Marot's French *Psalms* translation	Henry VIII assumes title of King of Ireland and Head of the Irish Church Wales represented in Parliament Loyola appointed first General of Jesuits Paracelsus dies
1542	Brinkelow, *Lamentation of a Christian against London* Hall, *Union of the Families of Lancaster and York*	Henry VIII marries Katherine Parr; Edward (later Edward VI) born; Mary Queen of Scots born, succeeds to throne on death of James V (regency) Magdalene College, Cambridge founded
1543		Copernicus's heliocentric theory published Holbein dies in London
1545	Ascham, *Toxophilus* Sir Thomas Elyot, *Defence of Good Women*	Council of Trent opens; Counter-Reformation begins; first complete edition of Luther's works
1546	John Heywood, *A Dialogue . . . of all the Proverbs in the English Tongue* John Bale, *Acts of English Votaries*	Ascham Public Orator, Cambridge University; Trinity College, Cambridge founded; Christ Church, Oxford re-endowed Peace between England and France First book in Welsh printed Death of Luther

Year	Age	Life
1547	30	Surrey executed, 19 January
1549		Wyatt's *Psalm* paraphrases published
1552		Sir Walter Ralegh born, Devon

Year	Literary Context	Historical Events
1547	*Certain Sermons or Homilies* (Bonner, Cranmer, etc.) William Baldwin, *Treatise of Philosophy*	Henry VIII dies; succession of Edward VI; Somerset made Protector; Henry VIII's Six Articles repealed Francis I dies; Henry II succeeds to French throne Council of Trent moves to Bologna
1548	Loyola, *Spiritual Exercises* Bale's history of British writers Hugh Latimer's 'Plough' Sermon	Religious guilds and chantries abolished in England by Chantries Act
1549	First *Book of Common Prayer* Joachim du Bellay, *Défense et illustration de la langue française* (Pléiade manifesto) Leland, *Journey* (edited by Bale) Anon, *The Complaint of Scotland*	Enclosures legalised Calvin and followers of Zwingli agree over Communion Council of Trent closed
1550	Ronsard, *Odes* Vasari, *Lives of the Painters* Alchemical *Rosarium philosophorum* Cranmer, *Defence of the Doctrine of the Sacrament* Harington's translation of Cicero's *Of Friendship*	Somerset deposed, succeeded by Northumberland Julius III becomes pope
1551	Estienne publishes first Bible divided into verses Gessner, *Historia animalium* (first modern animal taxonomy) Cranmer, *Answer to Stephen Gardner* Robinson's translation of More's *Utopia* Nicholas Breton born	Council of Trent (second session)
1552	Second Edwardian *Prayer Book* Calvin, *Concerning Predestination*	Somerset executed Eustachio discovers Eustachian tube and valve
1553	Gavin Douglas's *Aeneid* translation Thomas Wilson, *Art of Rhetoric* Anon, *Lazarillo de Tormes* (first picaresque novel) Death of Rabelais	Death of Edward VI; Lady Jane Grey proclaimed queen; accession of Mary Tudor (Catholic); arrest of Protestant bishops; restoration of Catholic bishops

Year	Age	Life
1554		Book 4 of Surrey's *Aeneid* translation published Sir Philip Sidney born at Penshurst Place, Kent, to Sir Henry Sidney and Lady Mary, sister to the Earl of Leicester
1557		Collection of Wyatt's and Surrey's lyrics published in *Tottel's Miscellany*; Tottel also publishes Surrey's *Aeneid* translation, Books 2 and 4, under the title *Certaine Bokes of Vergil's Æneis turned into English meter*
1561		Mary Sidney born at Ticknall Place, Worcestershire

Year	Literary Context	Historical Events
1554	John Foxe, *Commentarii* (first edition of what will be translated as *Acts and Monuments* (1563) Hermetic *Pimander* published	Lady Jane Gray executed; full restoration of Roman Catholicism in England; Mary I marries Philip of Spain Trinity College, Oxford founded
1555	Ronsard, *Hymns* Lord Berners, *Arthur of Little Britain* Death of Sir David Lindsay, Polydore Vergil	John Knox unites Scots Protestants; Bishops Latimer and Ridley burned at Oxford St John's College, Oxford founded
1556	Heywood, *Spider and Fly* First part of Genevan metrical psalter	Archbishop Cranmer burned; Cardinal Pole becomes Archbishop of Canterbury Philip II succeeds to Spanish throne Paul IV becoms pope Death of Loyola
1557	More, English *Works* Sir Thomas North, *Dial of Princes*	Incorporation of Stationers' Company Gonville and Caius College, Cambridge founded
1558	John Knox, *First Blast of the Trumpet against the Monstrous Regiment of Women* Du Bellay, *Antiquities of Rome* Marguerite de Navarre, *Heptameron*	Mary I dies; accession of Elizabeth I Cardinal Pole dies Cecil appointed Chief Secretary of State
1559	*Mirror for Magistrates* (first edition) Elizabethan *Prayer Book* George Chapman born	Elizabeth I crowned; Protestantism re-established with her assent to Act of Supremacy Henry II of France dies; succeeded by Francis II Pius IV becomes pope
1560	Geneva Bible Barker's translation of Xenophon's *Cyropaedia*	Francis II dies; succeeded by Charles IX (Catherine de' Medici regent)
1561	Scaliger, *Poetices libri septem* Stow's edition of Chaucer Castiglione's *The Courtier* translated by Hoby Norton's translation of Calvin's *Institution* Francis Bacon born	Knox establishes constitution of Scottish Church

Year	Age	Life

1563   Michael Drayton born at Hartshill, Warwickshire

1564   10   Philip Sidney at Shrewsbury School

1567   13   Philip Sidney at Christ Church, Oxford

1569   17   Ralegh in France, fighting for Protestant cause
              Sir John Davies born at Tisbury, Wiltshire

Year	Literary Context	Historical Events
1562	Sackville and Norton, *Gorboduc* Heywood, *Works* Latimer, 27 *Sermons* Sternhold and Hopkins, *Whole Book of Psalms* Jewel, *Apologia pro ecclesia anglicana*	John Hawkins starts Africa–America slave trade Huguenot wars in France after massacre of Protestants Council of Trent re-opens Middle Temple building begun
1563	Foxe, *Book of Martyrs* (Protestant martyrology) Sackville, *Induction to Mirror for Magistrates* Samuel Daniel born	Council of Trent finishes Escorial begun
1564	John Dee, *Monas hieroglyphica* Anne Bacon's translation of Jewel's *Apology* Scottish *Psalter* Shakespeare, Marlowe born	Death of Calvin, Michelangelo
1565	Arthur Golding's translation of Ovid's *Metamorphoses* 1–4 John Awdelay, *Fraternity of Vagabonds* Barnaby Googe's translation of Palingenius, *Zodiac of Life* Stow, *Summary of English Chronicles*	Hawkins's second South America voyage (1564–5)
1566	Nicholas Udall, *Ralph Roister Doister* (first English comedy) published	James VI of Scotland (future James I) born Death of Nostradamus, astrologer Pius V becomes pope
1567	Full text of Golding's Ovid published Matthew Parker's edition of an Aelfric homily Turberville's poems Drant's translation of Horace's *Art of Poetry*	Mary Queen of Scots abdicates Hawkins's third voyage (West Indies and Guinea)
1568	Heywood's interlude, *The Four P's* Bishops' Bible Skelton, *Works* Death of Ascham, Coverdale	Douai College (seminary for training English Catholic priests) founded Mary Queen of Scots flees to England

Year	Age	Life
1572	18	Philip Sidney's European tour with Earl of Lincoln; returns 1575
1575	14	Mary Sidney at court
1576	22	Philip Sidney made Royal Cupbearer
1577	23	Philip Sidney appointed ambassador to Holy Roman Emperor Rudolf II
	16	Mary Sidney marries Henry Herbert, second Earl of Pembroke; moves to the Pembroke home, Wilton House, Wiltshire, and, with Philip Sidney, establishes literary academy

Year	Literary Context	Historical Events
1570	Ascham, *The Schoolmaster* Foxe, *Ecclesiastical History* Castelvetro, *Poetica d'Aristotele*	Papal bull *Regnans in excelsis* excommunicates Elizabeth I Palladio, *Treatise on Architecture* John Dee's English *Euclid*
1571	Latimer, *Fruitful Sermons*	Cecil becomes Lord Burghley London Royal Exchange opened Turks capture Cyprus from Venetians Jesus College, Oxford founded
1572	William Tyndale, *Whole Works* Ronsard, *La Franciade* Camoens, *Lusiads* John Donne, Ben Jonson born	Drake attacks Spaniards in South America August 23–4, French Protestants murdered in Paris (St Bartholomew Massacre) Gregory XIII becomes pope Death of John Knox
1573	Tasso, *Aminta* George Gascoigne, *A Hundred Sundry Flowers*	Drake views Pacific from Panama
1574	Parker's translation of Asser's *Life of Alfred*	Henry III succeeds Charles IX as King of France
1575	Comedy *Gammer Gurton's Needle* published Turberville, *Art of . . . Hunting* Gascoigne, *Posies* Rolland, *Court of Venus* Tasso, *Gerusalemme Liberata* Ronsard, *Sonnets pour Hélène*	Elizabeth I offered (and declines) sovereignty of Netherlands New poor law Anabaptists burned in England
1576	London's first playhouse Gascoigne, *The Steel Glass* (satire) and other works Works of Xenophon first printed	Death of Lady Joanna Lumley and Titian
1577	Holinshed, *Chronicles* (first edition) Peacham, *Garden of Eloquence* Death of Gascoigne, Thomas Smith Robert Burton born	Drake's voyage round world begins

Year	Age	Life
1579	25	Philip Sidney opposes Queen Elizabeth's marriage negotiations with the French Duc d'Alençon
1580	28	Ralegh in Ireland fighting against the 'rebels'
	11	Davies enters Winchester College
1581	27	Philip Sidney completes 'old' *Arcadia* and *Defence of Poesy*; Penelope Devereux, daughter of the Earl of Essex, marries Lord Rich; Philip Sidney responds by writing *Astrophil and Stella*
1583	29	Philip Sidney knighted; marries Frances, daughter of Sir Francis Walsingham
1584	32	Ralegh becomes MP for Devon; knighted
	15	Davies matriculates at the Queen's College, Oxford

Year	Literary Context	Historical Events
1578	Lyly, *Euphues, or the Anatomy of Wit* Du Bartas, *La Semaine* Barnaby Rich, *Alarm to England* Rolland, *Seven Sages*	English College moved from Douai to Rheims
1579	North, *Plutarch's Lives* translation Spenser, *The Shepherds' Calendar* Gosson, *School of Abuse* (first edition)	The Duc d'Alençon courts Elizabeth I English College at Rome founded Irish 'rebellion' against English
1580	Lyly, *Euphues and His England* Last miracle play at Coventry Stow, *Chronicles of England*	Drake returns from circumnavigation of globe
1581	Tasso, *Gerusalemme Liberata* (revised) Richard Mulcaster, *Positions [on the] training up of Children*	Act against English Catholics Levant Company founded
1582	Hakluyt, *Voyages* Buchanan's Scots history, *Rerum Scoticarum historiae* Allen, *Brief History of the Martyrdom of XII Priests* Watson, *Hecatompathia* Gosson, *Plays Confuted*	Jesuit mission to China Gregorian calendar introduced into Catholic Europe
1583	Scaliger, *De emendatione temporum* Sir Thomas Smith, *De republica Anglorum* Stanyhurst's *Aeneid* translation, 1–4 Massinger born	Discovery of Throckmorton plot against Elizabeth in favour of Mary Queen of Scots Whitgift becomes Archbishop of Canterbury
1584	Peele, *The Arraignment of Paris* Bruno's visionary work of political and religious harmony, *Lo spaccio della bestia trionfante* published in London (followed by *De gli heroici furori*, 1585) Greene, *The Card of Fancy* James VI, *Essays . . . in the Divine Art of Poesy* Scott, *Discovery of Witchcraft*	Jesuits and seminary priests expelled from England by act of parliament

Chronology of the Poets' Lives

Year	Age	Life
1585	33	Ralegh attempts to settle Virginia; project abandoned 1586
	31	Philip Sidney working on 'new' *Arcadia*, the psalm translations, and other translations from the French; appointed Joint Master of the Ordnance, also Governor of Flushing
1586	32	Sidney's parents die; Philip Sidney dies at battle of Zutphen
	25	Mary Sidney devotes the next few years to editing and completing his work
1587	35	Ralegh made Captain of the Queen's Guard
	18	Davies enters the Middle Temple, London, to read law
1590		Philip Sidney's 'new' *Arcadia* published

Year	Literary Context	Historical Events
1585	Greene, *Planetomachia* Watson, *Amyntas*	Leicester's expedition to Netherlands Sixtus V becomes pope
1586	Camden, *Britannia* Warner's verse chronicle *Albion's England* (first edition) Knox, *History of the Reformation within Scotland* Rowland's translation of *Lazarillo de Tormes* John Ford born	Trial of Mary Queen of Scots Star Chamber decree that all published works must have ecclesiastical approval
1587	Marlowe, *Dr Faustus*, *Tamburlaine* acted Churchyard, *Worthiness of Wales* Day's translation of Longus, *Daphnis and Chloe* Tasso, *Discorsi dell'arte poetica* Death of Foxe	Mary Queen of Scots executed English expedition against Cadiz Pope declares Crusade against England
1588	Anti-episcopal *Marprelate Tracts* William Morgan's Welsh translation of Bible Lyly, *Endimion* Fraunce, *Arcadian Rhetoric* Greene, *Pandosto* Byrd, *Psalms, Sonnets and Songs*	Spanish Armada
1589	Puttenham, *Art of English Poesy* Greene, *Menaphon* Nashe, *Anatomy of Absurdity* Lodge, *Scylla's Metamorphosis*	Death of Catherine de' Medici Henry III killed; succeeded as King of France by Henry of Navarre Sidney Sussex College, Cambridge founded
1590	Marlowe, *Tamburlaine*, *Jew of Malta* Spenser, *Faerie Queene*, Books 1–3	Urban VII becomes pope (September); succeeded by Gregory XIV (October; until 1591)

Year	Age	Life
1591		Philip Sidney's *Astrophil and Stella* published
	28	Drayton's biblical verse translations, *The Harmony of the Church*, published
	39	Ralegh's *Report of the Truth of the Fight about the Isles of Azores* published
1592	40	Ralegh imprisoned in Tower of London after discovery of his secret marriage to Elizabeth Throckmorton
	31	Mary Sidney's translations of Robert Jarnier's play *Marc-Antoine* and of Philippe du Plessis Mornay's *Discourse of Life and Death* published
	23	Davies touring Europe
1593		Philip Sidney's 'new' *Arcadia* republished, together with books 3–5 of 'old' *Arcadia*, edited by Mary Sidney.
	30	Drayton's pastoral *Idea: The Shepherd's Garland* and *Piers Gaveston* published
1594	31	Drayton's sonnet sequence *Idea's Mirror* and *Matilda* published
1595	43	Ralegh's expedition to South America. Philip Sidney's *Defence of Poesy* published (edited by Mary Sidney)
	32	Drayton in service with the celebrated patron Lucy, Countess of Bedford; publishes *Endymion and Phoebe* after death of his patron Sir Henry Goodere (with whose daughter, Anne, he remained in love for the rest of his life)
	26	Davies called to the Bar; his *Epigrams* published
1596	44	Ralegh in expedition against Spaniards at Cadiz; publishes account of South American expedition, *Discoverie . . . of Guiana*
	33	Drayton's historical verse narrative *Mortimeriados* and *Robert, Duke of Normandy* published
	27	Davies's *Orchestra* published (written 1594)

Year	Literary Context	Historical Events
1591	Harington's translation of Ariosto, *Orlando Furioso* Shakespeare, 2 and 3 *Henry VI* George Ripley, *Compound of Alchemy* Peele, *Descensus Astraeae*	Death of Spanish mystic, St John of the Cross Innocent IX becomes pope (October–December) Trinity College, Dublin founded
1592	Shakespeare, 1 *Henry VI* Marlowe, *Edward II*, *Dr Faustus* Kyd, *Spanish Tragedy* Constable, *Diana* Daniel, *Delia* Nashe, *Pierce Penniless*	Presbyterianism established in Scotland Remains of Pompeii discovered Clement VIII becomes pope Death of Montaigne
1593	Marlowe, *Massacre at Paris* Shakespeare, *Venus and Adonis, Richard III, Comedy of Errors* Hooker, *Laws of Ecclesiastical Polity*, 1–4 Barnaby Barnes, *Parthenophil and Parthenophe* Lodge, *Phyllis* *The Phoenix Nest* anthology Herbert born Death of Marlowe	Act against Jesuits and other 'disloyal persons'; church attendance compulsory in England London plague
1594	Morley, *Madrigals* Nashe, *Unfortunate Traveller* Shakespeare, *Titus Andronicus, Taming of the Shrew, Two Gentlemen of Verona*	Tyrone 'rebels' in Ireland Death of Palestrina
1595	Shakespeare, *Love's Labour's Lost, Midsummer Night's Dream, Richard II* Spenser, *Amoretti and Epithalamion* Chapman, *Ovid's Banquet of Sense* Daniel, *Civil Wars*, 1–4 Barnfield, *Cynthia, with Certain Sonnets*	Robert Southwell (Jesuit poet) martyred
1596	Shakespeare, *Merchant of Venice, King John* Spenser, *Faerie Queene*, Books 4–6 Deloney, *Jack of Newbury*	English (led by Essex) attack Cadiz Thermometer invented by Galileo

Year	Age	Life
1597	45	Ralegh in expedition against Spaniards in the Azores.
	34	Drayton works as playwright for Philip Henslowe at Rose and Fortune Theatres, London, until 1602; Drayton's *England's Heroical Epistles*, first edition, published.
	28	Davies's *Gulling Sonnets*
1598		Philip Sidney's collected *Works* published, edited by Mary Sidney
1599	30	Davies's *Nosce Teipsum* and *Hymns of Astræa*
c. 1600		Davies's *All Ovid's Elegies*
1601	40	Mary Sidney's husband, the Earl of Pembroke, dies.
	32	Davies elected MP for Corfe Castle, Dorset
1602	33	Davies's *Ten Sonnets to Philomel*

Year	Literary Context	Historical Events
1597	Shakespeare, *Romeo and Juliet* Joseph Hall, *Virgidemiarum* (*Harvest of Rods*) Hooker, *Ecclesiastical Polity*, Book 5 James VI, *Demonology* Roger Bacon, *The Mirror of Alchemy*	Second Armada fails because of bad weather
1598	Part of Chapman's *Iliad* translation printed Jonson, *Every Man in His Humour* Marlowe/Chapman, *Hero and Leander* Shakespeare, *1 Henry IV, Much Ado about Nothing* John Stow, *Survey of London* Francis Meres, *Palladis Tamia, Wit's Reflections* Marston, *Pygmalion's Image*	Death of Philip II of Spain Toleration to Huguenots by Edict of Nantes
1599	Jonson, *Every Man out of His Humour* Shakespeare, *Henry V, Julius Caesar* James VI, *Basilikon doron* (defending kingly Divine Right) Death of Spenser	Oliver Cromwell born Juan de Mariana, *De rege et regis institutione* (defends tyrannicide) Essex appointed Deputy in Ireland Nazari's mystical alchemical work, *Della tramutatione metallica*
1600	Shakespeare, *As You Like It, Merry Wives of Windsor, Twelfth Night* Fairfax's translation of Tasso, *Jerusalem Delivered* Dekker, *Shoemaker's Holiday* Jonson, *Cynthia's Revels* *England's Helicon* anthology	East India Company founded James VI appoints bishops in Scotland Giordano Bruno burned by Inquisition for 'heresy' Another Tyrone 'rebellion' in Ireland
1601	Shakespeare, *Hamlet, Troilus and Cressida* Jonson, *The Poetaster* Thomas Campion, *Book of Airs*	Essex executed for attempted rebellion
1602	Marston, *Antonio's Revenge* Davison, *Poetical Rhapsody* Campanella, *City of the Sun*	Bodleian Library founded

Chronology of the Poets' Lives

Year	Age	Life
1603	51	On accession of James I, Ralegh arrested for treason, imprisoned in Tower of London and remains there, except for release to undertake Orinoco expedition in 1616, until his death. In Tower writes *The History of the World*, 1614.
	34	Davies appointed Solicitor-General for Ireland; knighted.
	40	Drayton's *The Barons' Wars*
1604	41	Drayton's *The Owl*
1606	43	Drayton's *Poems Lyric and Pastoral*
	37	Davies appointed Attorney-General for Ireland
1608	45	Drayton's unsuccessful attempt to manage Whitefriars Playhouse and Children of the King's Revels
	39	Davies's *A Contention betwixt a Wife, a Widow and a Maid*
1609	40	Davies marries Eleanor Audeley, later notorious and finally celebrated for her prophecies and spiritual revelations

Chronology of the Times

Year	Literary Context	Historical Events
1603	Shakespeare, *All's Well That Ends Well* Jonson, *Sejanus* Daniel, *Defence of Rhyme*	Elizabeth dies; James VI succeeds as James I, grants tolerance to Catholics
1604	Shakespeare, *Hamlet, Othello* Marston, *The Malcontent*	Hampton Court Conference: James approves new Bible translation; James proclaimed king of 'Great Britain, France and Ireland'; peace between England and Spain
1605	Jonson's *Volpone* acted (published 1607) Francis Bacon, *Advancement of Learning* Cervantes, *Don Quixote*, Part 1 Thomas Tymme's alchemical *Practice of Chymical Physic*	Gunpowder Plot Leo XI becomes pope; succeeded by Paul V
1606	Shakespeare, *King Lear, Macbeth* Death of John Lyly	Trade treaty between England and France Anti-Catholic act passed by Parliament
1607	Shakespeare, *Antony and Cleopatra* (written) Tourneur, *Revenger's Tragedy* published	English settlement in Virginia Tyrone flees to Rome; land in Ulster given to English and Scottish settlers
1608	Shakespeare, *Coriolanus, Timon of Athens* Milton born	Telescope invented by Lippersheim Death of John Dee
1609	Spenser, *Faerie Queene* with *Cantos of Mutability* Jonson, *Epicoene* Shakespeare, *Pericles, Sonnets, Troilus and Cressida* Fulke Greville, *Mustapha*	Moors expelled from Spain New charter for Virginia Congregation of Female Jesuits founded
1610	Beaumont and Fletcher, *Maid's Tragedy* Jonson, *The Alchemist* Shakespeare, *Cymbeline, Winter's Tale* (?written) Camden's *Britannia* translated by Philemon Holland	Bishops fully restored in Scotland Hudson Bay explored by Henry Hudson First import of tea to Netherlands

Year	Age	Life
1612	49	Drayton's *Poly-Olbion*, Part 1 dedicated to Prince Henry.
	43	Davies elected MP for Fermanagh; publishes *A Discovery of the True Causes why Ireland was never entirely subdued ... until His Majesty's Happy Reign*
1613	44	Davies elected Speaker of the Lower House in the Irish Parliament
1616	64	Ralegh's expedition to the Orinoco
1618	66	Ralegh executed, 29 October, at Westminster
1619	56	Drayton's *Idea*

Year	Literary Context	Historical Events
1611	Spenser's works in folio Authorised Version of Bible Chapman, *Iliad* translation Aemilia Lanyer's part-feminist *Salve Deus Rex Judaeorum* (Hail God, King of the Jews)	Kepler invents astronomical telescope
1612	Webster, *White Devil*	Prince Henry (James's heir) dies Last burning of heretics in England Bermudas colonised by Virginian settlers
1613	Shakespeare, *Henry VIII* Various masques celebrating the royal wedding (Campion, Chapman, Beaumont) Campion, *Two Books of Airs*	Globe Theatre burned down Marriage of James's daughter Princess Elizabeth to Frederick, Elector Palatine
1614	Jonson, *Bartholomew Fair* Chapman, *Odyssey* translation, Books 1–12	Logarithms invented by Napier Isaac Casaubon proves mystical *Hermetica* a forgery
1615	Chapman, *Odyssey*, Books 13–24 Camden, *Annals*, Part 1 Cervantes, *Don Quixote*, Part 2	
1616	Webster, *Duchess of Malfi* Jonson, *The Devil Is an Ass*, *The Underwood*; folio edition of Jonson's works Death of Shakespeare, Cervantes	Richelieu becomes French Secretary of State Death of Tyrone
1618	Michael Maier's alchemical *Atalanta fugiens*	Francis Bacon appointed Lord Chancellor Founding of English West Africa Company
1619	Drummond of Hawthornden, *Conversations with Ben Jonson* Beaumont and Fletcher, *A King and No King* Death of Samuel Daniel	Frederick (husband of Princess Elizabeth) elected King of Bohemia
1620	Francis Bacon, *Novum organum* Massinger, *The Virgin Martyr*	Pilgrim Fathers leave Plymouth in *Mayflower*; arrive December; found New Plymouth First African slaves imported to North America

Chronology of the Poets' Lives

Year	Age	Life
1621	60	Mary Sidney dies, 25 September, in London.
	52	Davies elected MP for Newcastle-under-Lyme
1622	59	Drayton's *Poly-Olbion*, Part 2
1626	57	November, Davies appointed Lord Chief Justice; December, Davies dies
1627	64	Drayton's *Nymphidia*, etc.
1630	67	Drayton's *The Muses' Elysium*
1631	68	Drayton dies

Year	Literary Context	Historical Events
1621	Burton, *Anatomy of Melancholy* Massinger, *The Duke of Milan, The Maid of Honour*	Gregory XV becomes pope
1622	Middleton and Rowley, *The Changeling*	James I dissolves Parliament
1623	Shakespeare, First Folio Death of Nicholas Breton	Prince Charles fails to secure Spanish marriage treaty Urban VIII becomes pope
1624	Massinger, *The Renegado* Herbert of Cherbury, *De veritate* (*On Truth*) Middleton, *Game at Chess*	Monopolies declared illegal by Parliament Virginia a Crown colony Dutch found New Amsterdam
1625	Massinger, *A New Way to Pay Old Debts*	Death of James I; Charles I succeeds; marries French Catholic Henrietta Maria
1626	Massinger, *The Roman Actor* Sandys's translation of Ovid's *Metamorphoses*	Irish College founded at Rome
1627	Bacon, *New Atlantis*	Propaganda College founded at Rome
1628		Harvey reveals double circulation of blood
1629		Parliament dissolved by Charles I English settle Massachusetts
1630		Congregation of English Ladies founded at Munich Pope disbands Congregation of Female Jesuits
1631	Petty's *Political Arithmetic* advocates state regulation of economic policy Herbert, *The Temple* Death of Donne	English colonisation of Leeward islands
1633	Donne's *Poems* published Prynne, *Histriomastix* Cowley, *Poetical Blossoms* Robert Fludd's alchemical *Key* (*Clavis philosophiae et alchymiae*)	Laud appointed Archbishop of Canterbury Charles I crowned King of Scotland
1634	Milton, *Comus*	
1637	Milton, *Lycidas* Death of Ben Jonson	Rebellion in Scotland after Charles tries to introduce new Prayer Book John Hampden and Ship money

Year	Age	Life

Year	Literary Context	Historical Events
1642	Browne, *Religio medici* Denham, *Cooper's Hill* Milton, *Apology for Smectymnus*	Civil War begins

INTRODUCTION

Old Hamlet's plea 'remember me' (*Hamlet*, I. v), uttered at the opening of the seventeenth century, is a fitting epitaph on the preceding hundred years or so, for during that period, imitating the impetus of European humanism, English nationalism had asserted itself by remembering: remembering (and re-membering) the pure church of Peter that had, it was thought by the reformers, been obscured by centuries of Roman Catholic corruption; remembering ancient literary forms (epic, epigram, satire, Ovidian epistle, etc.); and remembering, under the influence of Tudor propaganda, that the roots of British history drew their nourishment from the long-cold ashes of Troy. It was a period for which the past was so pressingly present that more than one writer was compelled to explain the closeness in terms of the Pythagorean doctrine (revived by the fifteenth-century Florentine humanist Pico della Mirandola and others) of metempsychosis, or soul-transference. Hence Edmund Spenser, in his great epic poem in praise of Queen Elizabeth I, writes of (and to) Chaucer's ghost:

> Then pardon, O most sacred happie spirit,
> That I thy labours lost may thus revive . . .;
> Ne dare I like, but through infusion sweete
> Of thine owne spirit, which doth in me survive . . .
> (*Faerie Queene*, IV. ii. 34)

The fact that this invocation occurs in the canto in which Spenser, continuing Chaucer's fragmentary *Squire's Tale*, begins his story of the three brothers, Priamond, Diamond and Triamond, who inherit each other's soul in turn, makes this more than just hyperbole: Spenser means exactly what he says. Similarly, Ralegh's sonnet on Sir Arthur Gorges' translation of Lucan (Ralegh, no. 26), concludes: 'Such was thy Lucan, whom so to translate,/Nature thy Muse, like Lucan's, did create' (where *translate* means *reincarnate* as well as *render into a different tongue*); and Mary Sidney, taking her brother Philip rather than an ancient writer as her authority, reincarnates him only slightly less explicitly when she seizes on him as her soul and muse combined, in dedicating the psalm translations to him: 'So dared my Muse with thine itself combine,/As mortal stuff with that which is divine' (Mary Sidney, no. 2 (1)). But in this most heartrending of sixteenth-century elegies, the optimism soon quails before the fact of her aloneness in a world now dominated by her brother's absence: 'Deep wounds enlarged, long festered in their gall,/Fresh-bleeding smart: not eye but heart tears fall . . .'.

It is not just Philip's soul passing across to his sister in the shape of a muse in this poem that identifies the fact of soul-transference with the act of literary translation; for another figure, this time from the remoter past, is present, revived, as well. Through Mary Sidney's grief we sense the tones, if not the words, of Dido, abandoned by Aeneas in Book 4 of Virgil's *Aeneid* as he is urged to leave her and establish empire in Italy. If one female voice haunts English verse of the sixteenth century as it is represented here it is, surely, that of Dido, who was remembered by Tudor poets with as much piety as Purcell's Dido could have wished when, at the end of the next century, she too pleaded, in her grieving refrain, 'remember me'. It was Henry Howard, Earl of Surrey, who made the Dido cult official by electing to translate Books 2 and 4 of the *Aeneid*, thereby creating his own version of Virgil's epic (and of Trojan–Roman history) by counterpointing the death of Troy and of Aeneas's wife, Creusa (the subject of Book 2) against the death of Dido (Book 4; Surrey, no. 42): for Surrey in this translation, it seems (and here he was rediscovering a truth conveyed in Ovid's *Heroides*), male history is parasitic upon female sacrifice. And this means in turn that the triumphant invention of blank verse in English – Surrey's achievement here as he attempted to convey something of the effect of ancient epic's dactylic hexameter (a verse line consisting of six metrical feet, each foot comprising three syllables, the first of which is long, the remaining two short) – is a curiously radical act. The new verse form rejects 'arms and the man' (Virgil's announced subject in *Aeneid* 1, a favourite book with the Renaissance that Surrey chose not to translate), espousing instead tales – Creusa's, Dido's – of womanly fortitude, endurance and revenge.

Dido haunts at least two of Surrey's other works, too: the remarkable act of female ventriloquism in 'O happy dames' (no. 19) as he imagines himself as a wife deprived of her husband:

> In ship, freight with rememberance
> Of thoughts and pleasures past,
> He sails, that hath in governance
> My life, while it will last . . .

and his 'Good ladies' (no. 20) with its beautiful:

> The fearful dreams I have, oft times they grieve me so
> That then I wake, and stand in doubt if they be true or no;
> Sometimes the roaring seas me seems do grow so high,
> That my sweet lord in danger great, alas, doth often lie;
> Another time the same doth tell me he is come,
> And playing, where I shall him find, with T. his little son . . .

Wyatt, despite his characteristic pose of male victim of the entanglements and decorums of *amour courtois*, was also fascinated by Dido. At the end of his life he turned to that obscure moment at the close of *Aeneid* 1 where Dido's court minstrel sings a cosmogony and starts to weave a long poem from it in the form of 'Iopas's Song', which begins: 'When Dido feasted first the wandering Trojan knight' (Wyatt, no. 110). Maybe Wyatt, the courtly lover who had dared love a queen, could not but remember Queen Dido's welcome to Aeneas – especially after his particular queen, Anne Boleyn, had been vilified and executed by Henry VIII. And doubtless Henry's treatment of Anne prompted the earlier translation of an epigram attributed to Ausonius, a fourth-century AD poet and rhetorician: 'Dido am I, the founder first of Carthage' (Wyatt, no. 35). For this epigram tellingly revises Virgil's account of Dido in the *Aeneid*, letting Dido narrate in her own voice the extent to which male propagandist poets distort the history of the individual in the name of the nation. Inspired by the female victims liberated by Ovid's *Heroides*, she points out that she didn't kill herself because she had been betrayed by Aeneas. On the contrary, she killed herself in an act of stoic decisiveness because, importuned by Iarbas, she wished to affirm her fidelity to her husband's memory. Thus the epigram releases a second Dido (like a phantom Helen) into sixteenth-century English poetry; and when Ralegh translated it as he sat in the Tower writing his *History of the World* he made her accuse Virgil even more directly of falsehood (Ralegh, no. 27 (15)):

> I am that Dido, which thou here dost see
> Cunningly framed in beauteous imagery:
> Like this I was, but had not such a soul
> As Maro feigned, incestuous and foul.
> Aeneas never with his Trojan host
> Beheld my face or landed on this coast.

If for Sidney in the *Defence of Poetry* (1595) poets feign laudably and inevitably in the name of a higher truth, for this Dido they lie culpably: 'Poets are liars, and for verse's sake/Will make the gods of human crimes partake'.

This kind of poetic revisionism – the construction of two Didos so that truth and falsehood, history and poetry can, in a form of feminist poetics, confront and accuse each other – is an aspect of the split at the heart of the sixteenth century. Expressing itself in so many ways, this split is seen at its diagrammatically simplest level in the argument (encapsulated in Marlowe's *Dr Faustus*) between aspirational humanism on the one hand and pessimistic Calvinism (which is, interestingly, essentially anti-feminist) on the other: between a humanity proud of its freedom to rise and be at one with the angels and a humanity bound by corruption and sin to accept its baseness before God and the justice of its probable damnation. To the extreme Protestant all that humanism stood for was a lie and, like the Catholicism from which it historically in part emerged, an icon to be smashed.

Wyatt and Ralegh, both in their ways humanist icon makers, also shared their century's iconoclasm; except that in their case the iconoclasm resulted not so much from reforming zeal as from experience of life at court. They were both courtiers and gained the privileges of being royal favourites, and both learned early the scepticism and pragmatism that the courtly life fostered. Both saw (and in Ralegh's case particularly, exploited) the human weakness that the monarch displayed. And this in turn encouraged a poetic double vision: if many of Wyatt's lyrics are fantasies uttered or sung to imagined (or real) beloveds in a courtly or aristocratic–domestic setting and cosily supportive of an idealised late mediaevalism, other of his poems iconoclastically expose the rawly cynical sexual politics of the Henrician court. While in the case of Ralegh, the nostalgic Marianism of the 'Walsingham' ballad (Ralegh, no. 16) and the poems in praise of Cynthia (which are among the most moving expressions of the iconic cult of Elizabeth) have, as their necessary obverse, the *Ocean to Cynthia* (Ralegh, no. 19), which is in effect a rewriting of those texts in the light of personal experience: his affair with an infinitely more mundane Elizabeth, Elizabeth Throckmorton, secret marriage to whom brought the queen's wrath, in the form of imprisonment in the Tower, forcibly down upon him.

What is especially interesting about the *Ocean to Cynthia* is that, as Ralegh writes this most riddling and poetically startling of fragments, prostrating himself before the offended Cynthia, he assumes the apologetic, despairing, yet self-justifying voice and posture adopted by Aeneas at that moment in *Aeneid* 6 when, encountering Dido's shade in the underworld, he tries to excuse himself to her and, hurt yet magnificent, she stalks away into the darkness. Ralegh's Aeneas role means, of course, that he perceives Cynthia as Dido, the proud and successful founder of Carthage, spurning the man who has so shabbily betrayed her, and that there is a close relationship between the *Ocean to Cynthia* and Ralegh's translation of the Ausonius epigram. It is as if his enforced meditation in the Tower as a result of the Throckmorton marriage on the wrongs performed by men on women (and vice versa) spawned, when he was imprisoned again, that further elaborate meditation on the uncertainty of the world's vanities and the capriciousness of tyrants, the *History of the World*, and in particular the revisionist Dido of Book 2's twenty-second chapter.

The Dido of Ralegh's Ausonius translation also reveals the way in which poets iconise the female in order to deny her. 'Cunningly framed in beauteous imagery' she may be, but if her soul has been abused by Virgil and others then evidently the iconisation of woman is a form of lip service licensing vilification. Ralegh's praise and exploitation of the queen led him to the risk (certainty) of exposure – the practice, in other words, of a double life built on abusive disregard of her fondness and need for him. It is his realisation of this that accounts for the writhing guilt and (Calvinist) sense of unworthiness and damnation that also permeate the *Ocean to Cynthia*. In another and more general sense these sorts of awareness dominate the sixteenth-century sonnet and lyric as a whole, permeating them with a poetics of doubleness. For whatever else the English adoption and adaptation of the sonnet form achieved, its main success lay in its dialogic confrontation between the guilty pull of sexual inclination on the one hand and idealising modes of portraying the feminine on the other.

Some sonneteers, supported by the cult of Elizabeth (which reached its climax in the 1590s, the heyday of the sonnet sequence), followed Petrarchan idealism – shot through as it was with Platonism, Mariolatry, and the metaphorical richness of the Song of Songs – fairly closely (examples include Spenser, Drayton, and Samuel Daniel). But it is noteworthy that the first 'Petrarchan' sequence in English, Sidney's *Astrophil and Stella* (written early 1580s, published 1591), which was in effect the 'only begetter' of the twenty or so that followed up to the publication of Shakespeare's *Sonnets* in 1609, was so radical in its approach to the problem of writing about woman and love. Structurally dialogic, with iconoclast confronting iconophile (as in Ralegh's reply to Marlowe's 'Passionate Shepherd'; Ralegh, nos 12a, b), the sonneteer interrupts his sonnets periodically with songs which voice the Petrarchan and pastoral norms of Orphic harmony and grief, of celebratory praise of the beloved, of her cruelty, and so on. The songs belong to the world of the *Arcadia* lyrics, with their Theocritean certainties and the ordered world they reflect. The sonnets themselves, though, from the moment in sonnet 1 when the humanist and Protestant–individualist ego asserts 'Fool, . . . look in thy heart and write', are essentially interrogative of the literary tradition that gave them birth and that is now marginalised into the songs and deprived of its rightful (14-line sonnet) structure. This means in turn that those conventionally Petrarchan sonnets that are admitted into the sequence (for example, the group around sonnet 9, 'Queen Virtue's court, which some call Stella's face') read curiously artificially, contextualised as they are by those other sonnets which so evidently reflect the writer's self-conscious awareness of the cultural situation that gave birth to the governing love metaphors in the first place: we encounter the conventions only after we have been reminded that, under a

Protestant regime, we should 'serve/The inner light'; that 'what we call Cupid's dart/An image is, which for ourselves we carve', etc. (sonnet 5).

Adrian Benjamin and Alastair Fowler were surely right to connect the sonnet total of *Astrophil and Stella*, 108, with the number of bowling stones in the game reputedly played by the suitors at the Ithacan court as Penelope awaited the return of her husband, Odysseus. For the game – called Penelope – is a ludic representation of deferral, the expression of desire and its frustration: even if a suitor hit the central stone (the Penelope) with his bowling stone, he never obtained the real Penelope; and neither did Astrophil–Philip obtain Lady Penelope Rich (see Alastair Fowler, *Triumphal Forms* (1970), ch. 9). It is, I think, no accident that Sir John Davies's *Orchestra* (1596) also remembers Penelope's court. The many followers of E. M. W. Tillyard's *Elizabethan World Picture* (1943) and his edition of the poem (1945) regarded (and regard) *Orchestra* as the epitome of supposed late sixteenth-century philosophical security, the affirmative utterance of stable cosmic, rhythmic and musical truths. But the setting should give us pause, as should the revised ending (see headnote on *Orchestra* in the notes, below), which leaves the poem, like Wyatt's 'Iopas's Song' and Ralegh's *Ocean to Cynthia*, a self-conscious fragment. Penelope is being wooed by the suitor Antinous with commonplaces. His is therefore a partial voice and her responses, few though they are, demand attention as well. So that whether the poem is about the Elizabethan succession question (urgent at the time Davies was working on the poem) or not, *Orchestra*, like *Astrophil and Stella*, draws attention to itself, too, as a dialogic process querying the terms it is employing. Paying lip service to the harmonies of the Pythagorean–Platonic universe, it has its queen for much of its length refusing them and suggesting that there is an alternative world view to that of the enclosed and self-referring one of dance that Antinous proposes. In other words, this Penelope, with her contradiction of the hectoring voice of male hegemony, has learned from Ausonius's Dido again.

Moreover, the fact that the poem's author long outlived Elizabeth means that its final revision into stated incompleteness (the 1622 title announces that the work is 'Not finished') leaves us with a final irony. *Orchestra* didn't only survive its immediate circumstances (most poems do that). It outlived almost immediately the myths that begot it so that the final text of 1622 informs us that the cult of Elizabeth was a socio-political construct and that this version of the poem 'knows' that it is posthumous to that cult. The Penelope of Homer's *Odyssey* affirmed her selfhood against the suitors in the absence of her husband; Astrophil lamented the presence of Penelope's husband and her consequential absence from him; the final twist occurs when Penelope herself is dead. 'Here are wanting some stanzas describing Queen Elizabeth' writes the Davies of 1622, nostalgically reawakening under King James a sense of the greatness of days gone by and, simultaneously, reminding us that myths too, like Pan, must die. There is a touching irony in the juxtaposition in the 1622 volume of the *Hymns of Astræa* and *Orchestra*: the latter, through its history of textual revision, doesn't only revise itself, it revises the *Hymns* as well just as surely as the *Ocean to Cynthia* revises Ralegh's earlier poems to the queen, and as Sidney's *Astrophil and Stella* queries the bases upon which the vast *Arcadia* is erected.

But, of course, Sir Philip Sidney didn't actually introduce Petrarch into England. As all the histories tell us, *Astrophil and Stella* marked the second Petrarchan renaissance (though they omit to tell us as often that in England as on the continent Petrarch didn't just denote *rime* alone so much as *rime* and *trionfi* (triumphs), and that the *trionfi*, too, are a form of metaphoric revision of the *rime*). The first Petrarch renaissance was pioneered by Wyatt and Surrey and was, in fact, as radical as Sidney's, though its literary quantity was smaller. The sonnets Wyatt and Surrey chose to translate are by no means the ones we might have expected. The lover of Laura is of course there; but so also is the politically astute Petrarch whom Wyatt (for instance) makes his own in 'Caesar, when that the traitor of Egypt' (Wyatt, no. 1, comparing the lover's feigning with the hypocrisy of rulers) and 'The pillar perished is' (no. 17), which is about the execution of his friend and patron, Thomas Cromwell, though *Tottel's Miscellany* (1557), in which it was first published, insisted it was a love poem. Indeed, Wyatt's plaintive lover is, in a large number of instances, not so much voicing indignation at a scornful mistress as he is outrage at the arbitrariness of a tyrannical monarch, and his Petrarchan sonnets, like his lyrics, often veil truths that would appear to have their more obvious home in the epigrams.

As for Surrey he, even more fascinatingly, used Petrarch in order to create his own myth of infatuation (that of Geraldine), so that for him, too, the sonnet was a means of enquiry into the processes of iconisation; and even a cursory inspection reveals a subtlety in his metaphrases of Petrarch superior to Wyatt's and, at times, even Sidney's. Consider his first sonnet, 'The soote season', apparently a 'translation' of Petrarch's *rime*, 310. For Tottel, with whom (again) it made its first public appearance, it was so obviously a translation that he gave it the title 'Description of Spring, wherin eche thing renewes, save onelie the lover'. But a more astute reader, while acknowledging Tottel's signal, might well query its appropriateness. Petrarch's sonnet is about himself as lover of the dead Laura. Surrey's, on the other hand, seems to be more generally ruminative and, in relation to its Petrarchan 'source', positively deviant. For one thing, Surrey introduces linguistic and metrical archaisms, so that for this pioneer the new sonnet form is accompanied, in this poem at least, by the late-mediaeval 'soote' and 'eke' and alliterative half lines (soote season ... bud and bloom; told her tale; spray now springs, etc.); which suggests perhaps that the sonnet is about the fact of literary newness and renewal and a meditation on the way innovation is obliged to remember forebears.

In this sense it is a genuinely humanist document: not an imitation of Petrarch so much as a courteous admission of all the literary dead into the thrustingly busy world of the living. Bees are, after all, images of the lyric poet for Plato in the *Ion*, so that 'The busy bee [who] her honey now she mings' is at once *mixing* her melody out of its various components (*melos* is the Greek word for honey) and *remembering* (another meaning of *ming*), on behalf of the poet himself, those literary ancestors without whom the literary present would be either impossible or meaningless.

Moreover, the nightingale may well be enjoying new growth of down and feather, but the line in which she appears ('The nightingale, with feathers new, she sings') 'translates' Petrarch's reference to Philomel ('e garrir Progne e pianger Filomena'; and warbling Procne and grieving Philomel), the nightingale whose name means *melody lover* and whose tale of rape at the hands of her brother-in-law Tereus was told in Ovid's *Metamorphoses* 6. He ripped out her tongue so that she could not tell anyone and, subsequently fleeing from him, she was metamorphosed into a nightingale so that she could evade capture. The nightingale's song is thus, mythologically speaking, an act of remembrance, a revisiting of the agony of her sexual violation which was then recapitulated in her bloody unvoicing. For the Renaissance she was a familiar image of the poet (Sidney remembers her in *Certain Sonnets*, 2, for instance). The question is, is Surrey remembering Philomel? Or is his failure to name her as Petrarch does a deliberate stifling of Philomel's tongue again or, at least, a delicate refusal to admit that the substance of poetry appears to be, according to Ovid, male sexual aggression and betrayal? And if it is either of these, how does the sonnet relate to Surrey's poetic *oeuvre* as a whole, intimately bound up as it was with what we know of his life as courtier, lover, and prisoner? What links it to the *Aeneid* translation with its extremely vocal Dido?

It is an almost impossible thing to introduce an anthology of verse by so many poets represented by so many poems. All, in the end, I wish to do is plead for their richness and fascination and remind you, as their readers, that they were written by human beings very like ourselves who wrote poems of dream and nightmare, sexual longing and frustration, of escapism, and of the greatest despair. Even Drayton's *Endymion and Phoebe*, superficially so remote from us with its elaborate mythological Neoplatonism, is, after all, a double text, simultaneously cult praise of Elizabeth and an utterance of sublimated longing and frustrated desire for his beloved (and unattainable) Anne Goodere. And more of these poems than we have, perhaps, recognised are about a universal concern that seems always likely to be with us: political persecution, tyranny, and imprisonment.

DOUGLAS BROOKS-DAVIES

NOTE ON THE
SELECTION AND TEXTS

Since *Silver Poets of the Sixteenth Century* was first published in 1947 there has been a vast shift in our understanding of the period and major textual work on Tudor poetry. The present anthology attempts to reflect both these factors while retaining the title and main strength of the original: the title because it has become so standard for students of the period that it seemed, to editor and publishers alike, unnecessary to alter it; the main strength – of wide coverage of the anthologised poets so that readers were confronted with extremely full selections – because it seems the most sensible and economical way of enabling readers to enter the period. To the expected major figures – Wyatt, Surrey, Ralegh and Sidney (all represented in new texts with considerable completeness) – I have added Mary Sidney (Lady Herbert), Countess of Pembroke, who is represented by what I regard as her best work; and Michael Drayton's epyllion *Endymion and Phoebe*, presented here for the first time in a modernised fully annotated form and a fascinating complement to the panegyrics on Queen Elizabeth written by Ralegh and Sir John Davies (whose *Hymns of Astraea* are printed here together with *Orchestra*).

Texts: represent current editorial opinion, but since this is not a textual edition, major substantive variants only are recorded in the notes. Spelling and punctuation have been modernised, though archaic words have been retained, as have archaic forms where they reflect pronunciation. Capitalisation has been preserved, and in many cases introduced, to signal the presence of personification (and hence allegory, psychomachia, etc.): e.g., Hope and Love and hope and love sometimes co-exist within the same text.

liii

ACKNOWLEDGEMENTS

The texts in this edition are based where possible on early printed editions: sources are detailed in the Notes. There is also an inevitable textual overlap with the original edition of *Silver Poets of the Sixteenth Century*, edited by Gerald Bullett and first published in 1947, which the Editor would like to acknowledge here. The Editor and Publishers also gratefully acknowledge the following:

SIR THOMAS WYATT
Substantive emendations are made from the Egerton MS 2711 and the Devonshire MS Add 17492 by permission of the British Library; from the Blage MS by permission of Trinity College Dublin; from the Parker MS 168 by permission of the Master and Fellows of Corpus Christi College, Cambridge; and from *The Arundel Harington Manuscript of Tudor Poetry*, ed. Ruth Hughey, 2 vols (Columbus, Ohio: Ohio State University Press, 1960).

HENRY HOWARD, EARL OF SURREY
Substantive emendations are made from BL MS Add 36529 by permission of the British Library; and from *The Arundel Harington Manuscript of Tudor Poetry* ed. Ruth Hughey.

SIR WALTER RALEGH
Non-printed sources used are the Hatfield MS (Cecil Papers 144), the BL MS Add 22602, the BL MS Harleian 6917, the BL MS Add 23229, the BL MS Add 27407, the MS Rawlinson Poetry 85 (Bodleian Library), the MS Malone 19 (Bodleian Library), the Drummond MS (National Library of Scotland); MS photographs are used from *The Queen and the Poet*, Walter Oakshott (London: Faber and Faber Ltd, 1960); variants are used from the Marsh MS 2.3.5.21 (Marsh's Library, Dublin), first transcribed by L. G. Black in *The Times Literary Supplement*, 23 May 1968.

SIR PHILIP SIDNEY
By permission of Oxford University Press various readings are adopted from *The Poems of Sir Philip Sidney*, ed. W. A. Ringler Jnr (Oxford: Clarendon Press, 1962), and *The Countess of Pembroke's Arcadia*, ed. Jean Robertson (Oxford: Clarendon Press, 1973).

MARY SIDNEY (HERBERT), COUNTESS OF PEMBROKE
Mary Sidney's translation of Petrarch's *Triumph of Death* is printed from the Petyt MS 538.43.1 by permission of the Masters of the Bench of the Inner Temple; 'To the angel spirit of Sir Philip Sidney' is modernised and repunctuated from the text in *The Poems of Sir Philip Sidney*, ed. W. A. Ringler Jnr, by permission of Oxford University Press; and psalm translations are used from *The Psalms of Sir Philip Sidney and the Countess of Pembroke*, ed. J. C. A. Rathmell (New York: The Stuart Editions, New York University Press, 1963).

SILVER POETS OF THE
SIXTEENTH CENTURY

SIR THOMAS WYATT

SIR THOMAS WYATT

Dates: 1503–42. Born at Allington Castle, Kent, son of Henry and Anne; first court appearance as Henry VIII's Sewer Extraordinary in 1516, in which year he also entered St John's College, Cambridge. Married Elizabeth Brooke (daughter of Lord Cobham) in 1520(?); she bore him a son, Thomas, in 1521. He separated from her in 1525, the year from which his interest in Anne Boleyn also probably dates. He accompanied Sir Thomas Cheney on a diplomatic mission to France in 1526 and, the following year, accompanied Sir John Russell on a similar mission to the papal court in Rome. He was made Marshal of Calais (1526–30) and Commissioner of the Peace in Essex (1532), accompanying Henry and Anne Boleyn (now the king's mistress) to Calais later the same year. (In January 1533 Anne married Henry; Wyatt served at her coronation in June.) In 1535 he was knighted, but in May 1536 he was imprisoned in the Tower, probably because he was suspected of having been one of Anne Boleyn's lovers (Henry was busy ridding himself of Anne after a miscarriage in January by accusing her of adultery). On 19 May Anne was executed and Wyatt was released from the Tower. His father died in November 1536.

From 1537–9 Wyatt was in Spain as Henry's ambassador to the court of the Holy Roman Emperor Charles V, returning to England in June 1539 via Lisbon. Later that year and until May 1540 he was again ambassador to Charles. His return to England was followed by the execution of his friend Thomas Cromwell (28 July). 1541 saw him accused of treason (a revival of charges originally levelled against him by Edmund Bonner in 1538 that, while ambassador, he had had dealings with Cardinal Pole and been rude about the king). Received a royal pardon and fully restored to favour (he was given various royal offices) in 1542, but became ill after welcoming Charles V's envoy at Falmouth and died at Sherborne on 11 October.

SONNETS

1

Caesar, when that the traitor of Egypt
With the honourable head did him present,
Covering his gladness, did represent
Plaint with his tears outward, as it is writ;
And Hannibal eke, when Fortune him shut   5
Clean from his reign and from his intent,
Laughed to his folk whom Sorrow did torment,
His cruel despite for to disgorge and quit:
So chanceth it oft that every passion
The mind hideth by colour contrary   10
With feigned visage, now sad, now merry;
Whereby, if I laughed any time or season,
It is for because I have none other way
To cloak my care but under sport and play.

2

Whoso list to hunt, I know where is an hind,
But as for me, hélas, I may no more.
The vain travail hath wearied me so sore,
I am of them that farthest cometh behind.
Yet may I by no means my wearied mind   5
Draw from the deer, but as she fleeth afore,
Fainting I follow. I leave off, therefore,
Since in a net I seek to hold the wind.
Who list her hunt, I put him out of doubt:
As well as I may spend his time in vain;   10
And graven with diamonds in letters plain
There is written her fair neck round about:
'*Noli me tangere* for Caesar's I am,
And wild for to hold though I seem tame.'

3

Was I never yet of your love grieved,
Nor never shall while that my life doth last:
But of hating myself that date is past,
And tears continual sore have me wearied.
I will not yet in my grave be buried,   5
Nor on my tomb your name yfixed fast

3

As cruel cause that did the spirit soon haste
From the unhappy bones by great sighs stirred.
Then if an heart of amorous faith and will
May content you without doing grief,   10
Please it you so to this to do relief:
If otherwise ye seek for to fulfil
Your disdain, ye err and shall not as ye ween:
And ye yourself the cause thereof hath been.

4

If amorous faith in heart unfeigned,
A sweet languor, a great lovely desire,
If honest will kindled in gentle fire,
If long error in a blind maze chained,
If in my visage each thought depainted,   5
Or else in my sparkling voice lower or higher
Which now fear, now shame, woefully doth tire,
If a pale colour which love hath stained,
If to have another than myself more dear,
If wailing or sighing continually   10
(With sorrowful anger feeding busily),
If burning afar off and freezing near
Are cause that by love myself I destroy:
Yours is the fault and mine the great annoy.

5

Farewell, Love and all thy laws, forever;
Thy baited hooks shall tangle me no more:
Senec and Plato call me from thy lore
To perfect wealth my wit for to endeavour.
In blind error when I did persevere,   5
Thy sharp repulse, that pricketh aye so sore,
Hath taught me to set in trifles no store
And 'scape forth, since Liberty is liever.
Therefore farewell: go trouble younger hearts,
And in me claim no more authority;   10
With idle youth go use thy property
And thereon spend thy many brittle darts:
For hitherto though I have lost all my time,
Me lusteth no longer rotten boughs to climb.

6

My heart I gave thee not to do it pain,
But to preserve it was to thee taken:
I served thee not to be forsaken,
But that I should be rewarded again.
I was content thy servant to remain,   5
But not to be paid under this fashion.
Now since in thee is none other reason,
Displease thee not if that I do refrain,
Unsatiate of my woe and thy desire,
Assured by craft to excuse thy fault.   10
But since it please thee to feign a default,
Farewell I say, parting from the fire:
For he that believeth bearing in hand,
Plougheth in water, and soweth in the sand.

7

There was never file half so well filed
To file a file for every smith's intent
As I was made a filing instrument
To frame other, while I was beguiled.
But Reason hath at my folly smiled,   5
And pardoned me since that I me repent
Of my lost years and time misspent;
For Youth did me lead, and Falsehood guiled.
Yet this trust I have of full great appearance:
Since that Deceit is ay returnable,   10
Of very force it is agreeable
That therewithal be done the recompense.
Then Guile beguiled plained should be never,
And the reward little trust forever.

8

I find no peace, and all my war is done;
I fear and hope; I burn and freeze like ice;
I fly above the wind yet can I not arise;
And nought I have, and all the world I seize on.
That looseth nor locketh, holdeth me in prison   5
And holdeth me not, yet can I 'scape no wise,
Nor letteth me live, nor die at my device,
And yet of death it giveth me occasion.

Without eyen I see, and without tongue I plain;
I desire to perish, and yet I ask health;   10
I love another, and thus I hate myself;
I feed me in sorrow, and laugh in all my pain:
Likewise displeaseth me both Death and Life –
And my delight is causer of this strife.

9

My galley charged with forgetfulness
Thorough sharp seas in winter nights doth pass
'Tween rock and rock, and eke mine enemy, alas,
That is my lord, steereth with cruelness,
And every oar a thought in readiness   5
As though that Death were light in such a case.
An endless wind doth tear the sail apace
Of forced sighs and trusty fearfulness:
A rain of tears, a cloud of dark disdain,
Hath done the wearied cords great hinderance,   10
Wreathed with Error and eke with Ignorance;
The stars be hid that led me to this pain.
Drowned is Reason that should me comfort,
And I remain, despairing of the port.

10

Avising the bright beams of these fair eyes,
Where he is that mine oft moisteth and washeth,
The wearied mind straight from the heart departeth
For to rest in his worldly paradise
And find the sweet bitter under this guise.   5
What webs he hath wrought well he perceiveth,
Whereby with himself on Love he plaineth,
That spurreth with fire and bridleth with ice.
Thus is it in such extremity brought:
In frozen thought now, and now it standeth in flame,   10
'Twixt misery and wealth, 'twixt earnest and game,
But few glad and many a diverse thought,
With sore repentance of his hardiness:
Of such a root cometh fruit fruitless.

11

How oft have I, my dear and cruel foe,
With those your eyes for to get peace and truce

Proffered you mine heart: but you do not use
Among so high things to cast your mind so low.
If any other look for it, as ye trow,   5
Their vain weak hope doth greatly them abuse;
And thus I disdain that that ye refuse:
It was once mine, it can no more be so.
If I then it chase, nor it in you can find
In this exile no manner of comfort,   10
Nor live alone, nor where he is called resort,
He may wander from his natural kind.
So shall it be great hurt unto us twain
And yours the loss and mine the deadly pain.

12

Like to these unmeasurable mountains
Is my painful life, the burden of ire:
For of great height be they, and high is my desire;
And I of tears, and they be full of fountains;
Under craggy rocks they have full barren plains,   5
Hard thoughts in me my woeful mind doth tire;
Small fruit and many leaves their tops do attire,
Small effect with great trust in me remains;
The boisterous winds oft their high boughs do blast,
Hot sighs from me continually be shed;   10
Cattle in them, and in me love is fed;
Immovable am I, and they are full steadfast;
Of the restless birds they have the tune and note,
And I always plaints that pass thorough my throat.

13

Unstable dream, according to the place,
Be steadfast once, or else at least be true:
By tasted sweetness make me not to rue
The sudden loss of thy false feigned grace.
By good respect in such a dangerous case   5
Thou broughtest not her into this tossing mew,
But madest my sprite live my care to renew,
My body in tempest her succour to embrace:
The body dead, the sprite had his desire;
Painless was the one, the other in delight.   10
Why then, alas, did it not keep it right,
Returning to leap into the fire,

And where it was at wish it could not remain?
Such mocks of dreams they turn to deadly pain.

14

You that in Love find luck and abundance
And live in lust and joyful jollity,
Arise for shame, do away your sluggardy:
Arise, I say, do May some observance!
Let me in bed lie dreaming in mischance, 5
Let me remember the haps most unhappy
That me betide in May most commonly,
As one whom Love list little to advance.
Sephame said true that my nativity
Mischanced was with the ruler of the May. 10
He guessed, I prove of that, the verity:
In May my wealth and eke my life, I say,
Have stood so oft in such perplexity.
Rejoice! Let me dream of your felicity.

15

If waker Care, if sudden pale colour,
If many sighs with little speech to plain,
Now Joy, now Woe, if they my cheer distain,
For hope of small, if much to fear therefore,
To haste, to slack my pace less or more, 5
Be sign of love, then do I love again.
If thou ask whom, sure since I did refrain
Brunet that set my wealth in such a roar,
The unfeigned cheer of Phyllis hath the place
That Brunet had: she hath and ever shall: 10
She from myself now hath me in her grace;
She hath in hand my wit, my will, and all:
My heart alone well worthy she doth stay
Without whose help scant do I live a day.

16

I abide and abide and better abide
(And after the old proverb) the happy day;
And ever my lady to me doth say:
'Let me alone and I will provide.'
I abide and abide and tarry the tide 5

8

And, with abiding, speed well ye may;
Thus do I abide, I wot, alway,
Neither obtaining nor yet denied.
Aye me, this long abiding
Seemeth to me, as who sayeth,
A prolonging of a dying death   10
Or a refusing of a desired thing:
Much were it better for to be plain
Than to say 'abide' and yet shall not obtain.

17

The pillar perished is whereto I leant,
The strongest stay of mine unquiet mind:
The like of it no man again can find
(From east to west still seeking though he went)
To mine unhap; for Hap away hath rent   5
Of all my joy the very bark and rind,
And I, alas, by Chance am thus assigned
Dearly to mourn till Death do it relent.
But since that thus it is by destiny,
What can I more but have a woeful heart,   10
My pen in plaint, my voice in woeful cry,
My mind in woe, my body full of smart,
And I myself myself always to hate
Till dreadful Death do ease my doleful state?

EPIGRAMS

18

Who hath heard of such cruelty before:
That, when my plaint remembered her my woe
That caused it, she, cruel more and more,
Wished each stitch as she did sit and sew
Had pricked mine heart for to increase my sore.   5
And, as I think, she thought it had been so,
For as she thought 'This is his heart indeed',
She pricked hard and made herself to bleed.

19

Alas, madame, for stealing of a kiss
Have I so much your mind then offended?

Have I then done so grievously amiss
That by no means it may be amended?
Then revenge you, and the next way is this: 5
Another kiss shall have my life ended;
For to my mouth the first my heart did suck:
The next shall clean out of my breast it pluck.

20

She sat and sewed that hath done me the wrong
Whereof I plain, and have done many a day;
And, whilst she heard my plaint in piteous song,
Wished my heart the sampler as it lay.
The blind master whom I have served so long,   5
Grudging to hear that he did hear her say,
Made her own weapon do her finger bleed,
To feel if pricking were so good in deed.

21

Sometime I fled the fire that me brent
By sea, by land, by water, and by wind,
And now I follow the coals that be quent
From Dover to Calais, against my mind:
Lo, how desire is both sprung and spent!   5
And he may see that whilom was so blind,
And all his labour now he laugh to scorn,
Meshed in the briers that erst was all to-torn.

22

The enemy of life, decayer of all kind,
That with his cold withers away the green,
This other night me in my bed did find,
And offered me to rid my fever clean:
And I did grant, so did Despair me blind.   5
He drew his bow with arrow sharp and keen
And struck the place where Love had hit before,
And drove the first dart deeper more and more.

23

Venomous thorns that are so sharp and keen
Sometime bear flowers fair and fresh of hue;
Poison oft-time is put in medicine

And causeth health in man for to renew;
Fire that purgeth all thing that is unclean   5
May heal, and hurt: and if these been true,
I trust sometime my harm may be my health
Since every woe is joined with some wealth.

24

In doubtful breast whilst motherly Pity
With furious Famine standeth at debate,
Saith the Hebrew mother: 'O child unhappy,
Return thy blood where thou hadst milk of late;
Yield me those limbs that I made unto thee,   5
And enter there where thou wert generate:
For of one body against all nature
To another must I make sepulture'.

25

Tagus farewell, that westward with thy streams
Turns up the grains of gold already tried:
With spur and sail for I go seek the Thames,
Gainward the sun that showeth her wealthy pride,
And to the town (which Brutus sought by dreams)   5
Like bended moon doth lend her lusty side:
My king, my country, alone for whom I live,
Of mighty Love the wings for this me give.

26

Of purpose Love chose first for to be blind,
For he with sight of that I behold
Vanquished had been against all godly kind:
His bow your hand and truss should have unfold,
And he with me to serve had been assigned,   5
But for he blind and reckless would him hold
And still by chance his deadly strokes bestow
With such as see I serve and suffer woe.

27

The fruit of all the service that I serve
Despair doth reap, such hapless hap have I;
But though he have no power to make me swerve,
Yet by the fire for cold I feel I die;

In paradise for hunger still I starve;   5
And in the flood for thirst to death I dry:
So Tantalus am I and in worse pain,
Amidst my help that helpless doth remain.

28

A lady gave me a gift she had not
And I received her gift I took not:
She gave it me willingly, and yet she would not;
And I received it, albeit I could not.
If she give it me, I force not;   5
And if she take it again, she cares not.
Construe what this is and tell not,
For I am fast sworn I may not.

29

Hate whom ye list for I care not;
Love whom ye list and spare not;
Do what ye list and fear not;
Say what ye list and dread not:
For as for me, I am not   5
But even as one that recketh not
Whether ye hate or hate not,
For in your love I dote not.
Wherefore I pray you forget not,
But love whom ye list and spare not.   10

30

All in thy sight my life doth whole depend:
Thou hidest thyself and I must die therefore.
But Since thou mayest so easily save thy friend,
Why dost thou stick to heal that thou madest sore?
Why do I die, since thou mayest me defend?   5
For if I die, then mayest thou live no more,
Since the one by the other doth live and feed the heart,
I with thy sight, thou also with my smart.

31

Stand whoso list upon the slipper top
Of court's estates, and let me here rejoice
And use me Quiet without let or stop,

Unknown in court that hath such brackish joys.
In hidden place so let my days forth pass   5
That, when my years be done withouten noise,
I may die aged after the common trace.
For him Death grippeth right hard by the crop
That is much known of other, and of himself, alas,
Doth die unknown, dazed with dreadful face.   10

32

Accused though I be without desert,
None can it prove, yet ye believe it true:
Nor never yet, since that ye had my heart,
Entended I to be false or untrue:
Sooner I would of Death sustain the smart   5
Than break one thing of that I promised you:
Accept therefore my service in good part.
None is alive that ill tongues can eschew;
Hold them as false, and let not us depart
Our friendship old in hope of any new: 10
Put not thy trust in such as use to feign,
Except thou mind to put thy friend to pain.

33

In court to serve, decked with fresh array,
Of sugared meats feeling the sweet repast,
The life in banquets and sundry kinds of play
Amid the press of lordly looks to waste,
Hath with it joined oft-times such bitter taste   5
That whoso joys such kind of life to hold
In prison joys, fettered with chains of gold.

34

Lux, my fair falcon, and your fellows all,
How well pleasant it were, your liberty!
Ye not forsake me that fair might ye befall.
But they that sometime liked my company,
Like lice away from dead bodies they crawl: 5
Lo, what a proof in light adversity!
But ye, my birds, I swear by all your bells
Ye be my friends, and so be but few else.

35

Dido am I, the founder first of Carthage,
That, as thou seest, mine own death do procure
To save my faith, and for no new love's rage
To flee Iarbas and keep my promise sure.
But see Fortune, that would in no other age   5
Mine honest will in perfect bliss assure:
For while I lived she made my day short,
And now with lies my shame she doth report.

SATIRES

36

Mine own John Poyntz, since ye delight to know
    The cause why that homeward I me draw
    And flee the press of courts whereso they go
Rather than to live thrall under the awe
    Of lordly looks, wrapped within my cloak,   5
    To will and lust learning to set a law:
It is not for because I scorn or mock
    The power of them to whom Fortune hath lent
    Charge over us, of right to strike the stroke;
But true it is that I have always meant   10
    Less to esteem them than the common sort,
    Of outward things that judge in their intent
Without regard what doth inward resort.
    I grant sometime that of glory the fire
    Doth touch my heart. Me list not to report   15
Blame by honour and honour to desire;
    But how may I this honour now attain
    That cannot dye the colour black a liar?
My Poyntz, I cannot frame my tune to feign,
    To cloak the truth for praise without desert   20
    Of them that list all vice for to retain.
I cannot honour them that sets their part
    With Venus and Bacchus all their life long,
    Nor hold my peace of them although I smart.
I cannot crouch nor kneel to do so great a wrong   25
    To worship them like God on earth alone
    That are as wolves these silly lambs among.
I cannot with my words complain and moan
    And suffer nought, nor smart without complaint,

Nor turn the word that from my mouth is gone.   30
I cannot speak and look like a saint,
    Use wiles for wit and make deceit a pleasure,
    And call craft counsel, for profit still to paint.
I cannot wrest the law to fill the coffer,
    With innocent blood to feed myself fat,   35
    And do most hurt where most help I offer.
I am not he that can allow the state
    Of high Caesar and damn Cato to die,
    That with his death did 'scape out of the gate
From Caesar's hands (if Livy do not lie)   40
    And would not live where liberty was lost,
    So did his heart the common wealth apply.
I am not he such eloquence to boast
    To make the crow singing as the swan,
    Nor call the lion of coward beasts the most   45
That cannot take a mouse as the cat can;
    And he that dieth for hunger of the gold,
    Call him Alexander, and say that Pan
Passeth Apollo in music many fold;
    Praise Sir Thopas for a noble tale   50
    And scorn the story that the knight told;
Praise him for counsel that is drunk of ale;
    Grin when he laugheth that beareth all the sway,
    Frown when he frowneth and groan when he is pale,
On others' lust to hang both night and day.   55
    None of these points would ever frame in me:
    My wit is nought; I cannot learn the way.
And much the less of things that greater be,
    That asken help of colours of device
    To join the mean with each extremity,   60
With the nearest virtue to cloak alway the vice
    And, as to purpose likewise it shall fall,
    To press the virtue that it may not rise:
As drunkenness good fellowship to call;
    The friendly foe with his double face   65
    Say he is gentle and courteous therewithal;
And say that Favel hath a goodly grace
    In eloquence; and cruelty to name
    Zeal of justice, and change in time and place;
And he that suffereth offence without blame   70
    Call him pitiful, and him true and plain
    That raileth reckless to every man's shame;

Say he is rude that cannot lie and feign;
    The lecher a lover; and tyranny
    To be the right of a prince's reign.   75
I cannot, I – no, no, it will not be!
    This is the cause that I could never yet
    Hang on their sleeves that weigh, as thou mayest see,
A chip of chance more than a pound of wit.
    This maketh me at home to hunt and to hawk,   80
    And in foul weather at my book to sit,
In frost and snow then with my bow to stalk.
    No man doth mark whereso I ride or go,
    In lusty leas at liberty I walk,
And of these news I feel nor weal nor woe,   85
    Save that a clog doth hang yet at my heel:
    No force for that, for it is ordered so
That I may leap both hedge and dike full well.
    I am not now in France to judge the wine,
    With savoury sauce the delicates to feel;   90
Nor yet in Spain where one must him incline,
    Rather than to be, outwardly to seem:
    I meddle not with wits that be so fine.
Nor Flanders' cheer letteth not my sight to deem
    Of black and white nor taketh my wit away   95
    With beastliness: they beasts do so esteem.
Nor I am not where Christ is given in prey
    For money, poison, and treason at Rome –
    A common practice used night and day.
But here I am in Kent and Christendom   100
    Among the Muses where I read and rhyme,
    Where if thou list, my Poyntz, for to come,
Thou shalt be judge how I do spend my time.

37

My mother's maids, when they did sew and spin,
    They sang sometime a song of the field mouse
    That, for because her livelood was but thin,
Would needs go seek her townish sister's house.
    She thought herself endured too much pain: 5
    The stormy blasts her cave so sore did souse
That when the furrows swimmed with the rain
    She must lie cold and wet in sorry plight
    And, worse than that, bare meat there did remain

To comfort her when she her house had dight –   10
    Sometime a barley corn, sometime a bean,
    For which she laboured hard both day and night
In harvest time whilst she might go and glean.
    And when her store was 'stroyed with the flood,
    Then wellaway, for she undone was clean.   15
Then was she fain to take, instead of food,
    Sleep (if she might) her hunger to beguile.
    'My sister,' quod she, 'hath a living good,
And hence from me she dwelleth not a mile.
    In cold and storm she lieth warm and dry   20
    In bed of down; the dirt doth not defile
Her tender foot; she laboureth not as I.
    Richly she feedeth, and at the rich man's cost;
    And for her meat she needs not crave nor cry.
By sea, by land, of the delicates the most   25
    Her cater seeks, and spareth for no peril.
    She feedeth on boiled bacon meat and roast
And hath thereof neither charge nor travail.
    And when she list, the liquor of the grape
    Doth glad her heart till that her belly swell.'   30
And at this journey she maketh but a jape:
    So forth she goeth, trusting of all this wealth
    With her sister her part so for to shape
That (if she might keep herself in health)
    To live a lady while her life doth last.   35
    And to the door now is she come by stealth
And with her foot anon she scrapeth full fast.
    The other for fear durst not well scarce appear,
    Of every noise so was the wretch aghast.
At last she asked softly who was there   40
    And, in her language as well as she could,
    'Peep,' quod the other, 'sister, I am here.'
'Peace,' quod the town mouse, 'why speakest thou so loud?'
    And by the hand she took her fair and well.
    'Welcome,' quod she, 'my sister, by the rood.'   45
She feasted her that joy it was to tell
    The fare they had; they drank the wine so clear
    And, as to purpose now and then it fell,
She cheered her with 'How sister, what cheer!'
    Amidst this joy befell a sorry chance   50
    That (wellaway) the stranger bought full dear
The fare she had: for as she looked askance,

Under a stool she spied two steaming eyes
In a round head with sharp ears. In France
Was never mouse so feared, for though the unwise   55
    Had not yseen such a beast before,
    Yet had Nature taught her after her guise
To know her foe and dread him evermore.
    The towny mouse fled – she knew whither to go.
    The other had no shift, but wondrous sore   60
Feared of her life. At home she wished her tho!
    And to the door, alas, as she did skip,
    The heaven it would, lo, and eke her chance was so,
At the threshold her silly foot did trip;
    And ere she might recover it again   65
    The traitor cat had caught her by the hip
And made her there against her will remain,
    That had forgotten her poor surety and rest
    For seeming wealth wherein she thought to reign.
Alas, my Poyntz, how men do seek the best   70
    And find the worst by error as they stray!
    And no marvel, when sight is so oppressed,
And blind the guide: anon, out of the way
    Goeth guide and all in seeking quiet life.
    O wretched minds, there is no gold that may   75
Grant that ye seek, no war, no peace, no strife.
    No, no, although thy head were hooped with gold,
    Sergeant with mace, halberd, sword, nor knife
Cannot repulse the care that follow should:
    Each kind of life hath with him his disease.   80
    Live in delight even as thy lust would,
And thou shalt find, when lust doth most thee please,
    It irketh straight and by itself doth fade.
    A small thing it is that may thy mind appease.
None of ye all there is that is so mad   85
    To seek grapes upon brambles or briers,
    Nor none (I trow) that hath his wit so bad
To set his hay for conies over rivers,
    Ne ye set not a drag-net for a hare.
    And yet the thing that most is your desire   90
Ye do mis-seek with more travail and care:
    Make plain thine heart that it be not knotted
    With hope or dread, and see thy will be bare
From all affects whom vice hath ever spotted;
    Thyself content with that is thee assigned   95

And use it well that is to thee allotted.
Then seek no more out of thyself to find
    The thing that thou hast sought so long before,
    For thou shalt feel it sitting in thy mind:
Mad if ye list to continue your sore.   100
    Let present pass, and gape on time to come,
    And deep yourself in travail more and more.
Henceforth, my Poyntz, this shall be all and sum:
    These wretched fools shall have nought else of me.
    But to the great God and to his high doom   105
None other pain pray I for them to be
    But, when the rage doth lead them from the right
    That, looking backward, Virtue they may see
Even as she is, so goodly fair and bright;
    And whilst they clasp their lusts in arms across,   110
    Grant them, good Lord (as thou mayest, of thy might)
To fret inward for losing such a loss.

38

A spending hand that alway poureth out
    Had need to have a bringer-in as fast;
    And on the stone that still doth turn about
There groweth no moss: these proverbs yet do last.
    Reason hath set them in so sure a place   5
    That length of years their force can never waste.
When I remember this and eke the case
    Wherein thou stands, I thought forthwith to write,
    Brian, to thee, who knows how great a grace
In writing is to counsel man the right.   10
    To thee, therefore, that trots still up and down
    And never rests, but running day and nigh
From realm to realm, from city, street, and town,
    Why dost thou wear thy body to the bones
    And mightest at home sleep in thy bed of down   15
And drink good ale (so nappy for the nonce),
    Feed thyself fat and heap up pound by pound?
    Likest thou not this? 'No.' Why? 'For swine so groins
In sty, and chaw the turds moulded on the ground,
    And drivel on pearls, the head still in the manger: 20
    So of the harp the ass doth hear the sound;
So sacks of dirt be filled up in the cloister
    That serves for less than do these fatted swine.

Though I seem lean and dry without moisture,
Yet will I serve my prince, my lord and thine,   25
   And let them live to feed the paunch that list,
   So I may feed to live, both me and mine.'
By God, well said! But what and if thou wist
   How to bring in as fast as thou dost spend?
   'That would I learn.' And it shall not be missed   30
To tell thee how. Now hark what I intend:
   Thou knowest well, first, whoso can seek to please
   Shall purchase friends where Truth shall but offend.
Flee therefore Truth: it is both Wealth and Ease.
   For though that Truth of every man hath praise,   35
   Full near that wind goeth Truth in great misease.
Use Virtue as it goeth nowadays,
   In word alone to make thy language sweet,
   And of the deed yet do not as thou says:
Else be thou sure thou shalt be far unmeet   40
   To get thy bread, each thing is now so scant.
   Seek still thy profit upon thy bare feet;
Lend in no wise (for fear that thou do want)
   Unless it be as to a dog a cheese;
   By which return be sure to win a cant   45
Of half at least: it is not good to lese.
   Learn at Kitson (that in a long white coat
   From under the stall without lands or fees
Hath leapt into the shop) who knoweth by rote
   This rule that I have told thee herebefore.   50
   Sometime also rich age beginneth to dote;
See thou when there thy gain may be the more.
   Stay him by the arm whereso he walk or go,
   Be near alway and, if he cough too sore,
When he hath spit, tread out and please him so.   55
   A diligent knave that picks his master's purse
   May please him so that he, withouten mo,
Executor is, and what is he the worse?
   But if so chance you get nought of the man,
   The widow may for all thy charge deburse.   60
A rivelled skin, a stinking breath, what then?
   A toothless mouth shall do thy lips no harm:
   The gold is good, and though she curse or ban,
Yet where thee list thou mayest lie good and warm:
   Let the old mule bite upon the bridle   65
   Whilst there do lie a sweeter in thine arm.

In this also see you be not idle:
 Thy niece, thy cousin, thy sister, or thy daughter,
 If she be fair, if handsome be her middle,
If thy better hath her love besought her,   70
 Advance his cause and he shall help thy need:
 It is but love; turn it to a laughter.
But 'ware, I say (so gold thee help and speed)
 That in this case thou be not so unwise
 As Pandar was in such a like deed;   75
For he, the fool, of conscience was so nice
 That he no gain would have for all his pain.
 Be next thyself, for friendship bears no prize.
Laughest thou at me? Why, do I speak in vain?
 'No, not at thee, but at thy thrifty gest: 80
 Wouldest thou I should, for any loss or gain,
Change that for gold that I have ta'en for best
 Next godly things: to have an honest name?
 Should I leave that? Then take me for a beast!'
Nay then, farewell; and if you care for shame,   85
 Content thee then with honest poverty,
 With free tongue what thee mislikes to blame,
And, for thy truth, sometime adversity.
 And therewithal this thing I shall thee give:
 In this world now, little prosperity,   90
And coin to keep as water in a sieve.

RONDEAUX

39

Behold, Love, thy power how she despiseth:
My great pain how little she regardeth.
The holy oath, whereof she taketh no cure,
Broken she hath, and yet she bideth sure
Right at her ease and little she dreadeth.   5
Weaponed thou art, and she unarmed sitteth:
To thee disdainful her life she leadeth,
To me spiteful without cause or measure:
 Behold, Love.

I am in hold: if pity thee moveth,   10
Go bend thy bow that stony hearts breaketh,
And with some stroke revenge the displeasure

Of thee and him that sorrow doth endure
And, as his lord, thee lowly entreateth.
   Behold, Love.   15

40

What 'vaileth Truth, or by it to take pain,
To strive by steadfastness for to attain
To be just, and true, and flee from doubleness,
Sithens all alike, where ruleth craftiness,
Rewarded is both false and plain?   5
Soonest he speedeth that most can feign:
True meaning heart is had in disdain.
Against deceit and doubleness
   What 'vaileth Truth?

Deceived is he by crafty train   10
That meaneth no guile, and doth remain
Within the trap without redress
But for to love, lo, such a mistress,
Whose cruelty nothing can refrain:
   What 'vaileth Truth?   15

41

Help me to seek for I lost it there,
And if that ye have found it, ye that be here,
And seek to convey it secretly,
Handle it soft and treat it tenderly,
Or else it will plain and then appair.   5
But rather restore it mannerly
Since that I do ask it thus honestly,
For to lose it it sitteth me too near:
   Help me to seek.

Alas, and is there no remedy,   10
But have I thus lost it wilfully?
Iwis it was a thing all too dear
To be bestowed and wist not where.
It was mine heart: I pray you heartily
   Help me to seek.   15

42

Go, burning sighs, unto the frozen heart:
Go break the ice which Pity's painful dart

Might never pierce; and if mortal prayer
In heaven may be heard, at last I desire
That Death or Mercy be end of my smart.   5
Take with thee pain (whereof I have my part)
And eke the flame from which I cannot start,
And leave me then in rest, I you require:
   Go, burning sighs.

I must go work, I see, by craft and art,   10
For Truth and Faith in her is laid apart:
Alas, I cannot therefore assail her
With pitiful plaint and scalding fire
That out of my breast doth strainably start:
   Go, burning sighs.   15

43

What no, perdie, ye may be sure!
Think not to make me to your lure
With words and cheer so contrarying
Sweet and sour counterweighing:
Too much it were still to endure: 5
Truth is tried where craft is in ure.
But though ye have had my heart's cure,
Trow ye I dote without ending?
   What no, perdie!

Though that with pain I do procure   10
For to forget that once was pure
Within my heart, shall still that thing,
Unstable, unsure, and wavering,
Be in my mind without recure?
   What no, perdie!   15

PETRARCHAN CANZONI

44

Mine old dear enemy, my froward master,
Afore that Queen I caused to be accited
Which holdeth the divine part of nature,
That like as gold in fire he might be tried.
Charged with dolour, there I me presented   5
With horrible fear, as one that greatly dreadeth
A wrongful death and Justice alway seeketh.

And thus I said: 'Once my left foot, Madame,
When I was young I set within his reign,
Whereby other than fierily burning flame   10
I never felt, but many a grievous pain.
Torment I suffered, anger and disdain,
That mine oppressed patience was past
And I mine own life hated at the last.

'Thus hitherto have I my time passed   15
In pain and smart. What ways profitable,
How many pleasant days, have me escaped
In serving this false liar so deceivable?
What wit have words so prest and forcible
That may contain my great mishappiness   20
And just complaints of his ungentleness?

'O small honey, much aloes and gall,
In bitterness have my blind life tasted.
His false sweetness (that turneth as a ball)
With the amorous dance have made me traced,   25
And where I had my thought and mind araced
From all earthly frailness and vain pleasure,
He took me from rest and set me in error.

'He hath made me regard God much less than I ought,
And to myself to take right little heed;   30
And for a woman have I set at nought
All other thoughts, in this only to speed;
And he was only counsellor of this deed,
Always whetting my youthly desire
On the cruel whetstone, tempered with fire.   35

'But, alas, where now had I ever wit
(Or else any other gift given me of nature)
That sooner shall change my wearied sprite
Than the obstinate will that is my ruler?
So robbeth my liberty with displeasure   40
This wicked traitor, whom I thus accuse,
That bitter life have turned me in pleasant use.

'He hath chased me thorough divers regions:
Thorough desert woods and sharp high mountains,
Thorough froward people and strait pressions,   45
Thorough rocky seas, over hills and plains,

With weary travail and laborous pains,
Always in trouble and in tediousness,
In all error and dangerous distress.

'But nother he nor she, my t'other foe,   50
For all my flight did ever me forsake,
That, though timely death hath been too slow
That as yet it hath me not overtake,
The heavenly goodness of pity do it slake
And not this, his cruel extreme tyranny,   55
That feedeth him with my care and misery.

'Since I was his hour rested I never,
Nor look for to do; and eke the wakey nights
The banished Sleep may no wise recover:
By deceit and by force over my sprites   60
He is ruler; and, since, there never bell strikes
Where I am that I hear not, my plaints to renew;
And he himself, he knoweth that that I say is true.

'For never worms have an old stock eaten
As he my heart, where he is alway resident,   65
And doth the same with death daily threaten:
Thence come the tears and the bitter torment,
The sighs, the words, and eke the languishment
That annoy both me and peradventure other:
Judge thou that knowest the one and the other.'   70

Mine adversary with grievous reproof
Thus he began: 'Hear, Lady, the other part,
That the plain truth (from which he draweth aloof)
This unkind man, shall show ere that I part.
In young age I took him from that art   75
That selleth words and maketh a clattering knight,
And of my wealth I gave him the delight.

'Now shameth he not on me for to complain
That held him evermore in pleasant game
From his desire that might have been his pain.   80
Yet only thereby I brought him to some frame
Which, as wretchedness, he doth greatly blame.
And toward Honour I quickened his wit
Where else as a dastard he might have sit.

'He knoweth that Atrides, that made Troy fret,   85
And Hannibal, to Rome so troublous,

Whom Homer honoured, Achilles that great,
And the African, Scipion the famous,
And many other by much virtue glorious,
Whose fame and honour did bring them above,   90
I did let fall in base dishonest love.

'And unto him, though he no deals worthy were,
I chose right the best of many a million,
That under the moon was never her peer
Of wisdom, womanhood, and discretion;   95
And of my grace I gave her such a fashion,
And eke such a way I taught her for to teach,
That never base thought his heart might have reach.

'Evermore thus to content his mistress,
That was his only frame of honesty,   100
I steered him still toward Gentleness
And caused him to regard Fidelity;
Patience I taught him in adversity:
Such virtues he learned in my great school,
Whereof he repenteth, the ignorant fool.   105

'These were the deceits and the bitter gall
That I have used, the torment and the anger,
Sweeter than for to enjoy any other in all.
Of right good seed ill fruit I gather
And so hath he that the unkind doth further.   110
I nourish a serpent under my wing
And of his nature now ginneth he to sting.

'And (for to tell at last my great service)
From thousand dishonesties I have him drawn,
That by my means in no manner of wise   115
Never vile pleasure him hath overthrown,
Where in his deed Shame hath him always gnawn,
Doubting report that should come to her ear:
Whom now he accuseth he wonted to fear.

'Whatsoever he hath of any honest custom,   120
Of her and me that holdeth he every whit.
But lo, there was never nightly phantom
So far in error as he is from his wit
To plain on us: he striveth with the bit
Which may rule him and do him pleasure and pain   125
And in one hour make all his grief remain.

'But one thing there is above all other:
I gave him wings wherewith he might fly
To Honour and Fame and (if he would) farther,
By mortal things, above the starry sky.   130
Considering the pleasure that an eye
Might give in earth by reason of his love,
What should that be that lasteth still above?

'And he the same himself hath said ere this;
But now forgotten is both that and I   135
That gave her him, his only wealth and bliss.'
And at this word, with deadly shright and cry,
'Thou gave her me,' quod I, 'but by and by
Thou took her straight from me: that woe worth thee!'
'Not I,' quod he, 'but price that is well worthy.'   140

At last both each for himself concluded,
I trembling, but he with small reverence:
'Lo, thus as we have now each other accused,
Dear Lady, we wait only thy sentence.'
She (smiling after this said audience)   145
'It liketh me,' quod she, 'to have heard your question,
But longer time doth ask resolution.'

45

In Spain

So feeble is the thread that doth the burden stay
Of my poor life, in heavy plight, that falleth in decay,
That, but it have elsewhere some aid or some succours,
The running spindle of my fate anon shall end his course.
Since the unhappy hour that did me to depart   5
From my sweet weal one only hope hath stayed my life apart,
Which doth persuade such words unto my sorry mind:
'Maintain thyself, O woeful sprite, some better luck to find;
For, though thou be deprived from thy desired sight,
Who can thee tell if thy return be for thy most delight?   10
Or who can tell thy loss if thou once mayest recover?
Some pleasant hour thy woe may wrap, and thee defend and
    cover.'
This is the trust that yet hath my life sustained,
And now, alas, I see it faint, and I by trust am trained.

The time doth fleet and I perceive the hours how they bend   15
So fast that I have scant the space to mark my coming end:
Westward the sun from out the east scant doth show his light
When in the west he hides him straight within the dark of
    Night,
And comes as fast where he began his path awry:
From east to west, from west to the east, so doth his journey   20
    lie.
The life so short, so frail, that mortal men live here,
So great a weight, so heavy charge, the body that we bear
That, when I think upon the distance and the space
That doth so far divide me from my dear desired face,
I know not how to attain the wings that I require   25
To lift my weight that it might fly to follow my desire;
Thus of that hope that doth my life something sustain,
Alas, I fear (and partly feel) full little doth remain.

Each place doth bring me grief where I do not behold
Those lively eyes which of my thoughts were wont the   30
    keys to hold:
Those thoughts were pleasant sweet whilst I enjoyed that grace;
My pleasure past, my present pain where I might well embrace.
But for because my want should more my woe increase,
In watch, in sleep, both day and night my will doth never cease
That thing to wish, whereof (since I did lose the sight)   35
I never saw the thing that might my faithful heart delight.
The uneasy life I lead doth teach me for to mete
The floods, the seas, the land and hills that doth them
    entermete
'Tween me and those shining lights that wonted to clear
My dark pangs of cloudy thoughts as bright as Phoebus'   40
    sphere;
It teacheth me also what was my pleasant state,
The more to feel by such record how that my wealth doth bate.

If such record, alas, provoke the inflamed mind
Which sprang that day that I did leave the best of me behind;
If Love forget himself (by length of absence let),   45
Who doth me guide, O woeful wretch, unto this baited net
Where doth increase my care? Much better were for me
As dumb as stone, all thing forgot, still absent for to be.
Alas, the clear crystal, the bright transparent glass,
Doth not bewray the colour hid which underneath it has,   50
As doth the accumbered sprite thoughtful throes discover

Of fierce delight, of fervent love, that in our hearts we cover.
Out by these eyes it showeth (that ever more delight
In plaint and tears to seek redress), and that both day and
night.

These new kinds of pleasures wherein most men rejoice,   55
To me they do redouble still of stormy sighs the voice;
For I am one of them whom plaint doth well content:
It sits me well mine absent wealth, me seems me, to lament,
And with my tears for to assay to charge mine eyes twain
Like as mine heart above the brink is fraughted full of pain.   60
And for because thereto of those fair eyes to treat
Do me provoke, I shall return, my plaint thus to repeat:
For there is nothing else that touches me so within,
Where they rule all – and I alone nought but the case or skin.
Wherefore I do return to them as well or spring   65
From whom descends my mortal woe above all other thing;
So shall mine eyes in pain accompany mine heart
That were the guides that did it lead of love to feel the smart.

The crisped gold that doth surmount Apollo's pride;
The lively streams of pleasant stars that under it doth glide   70
(Wherein the beams of love doth still increase their heat
Which yet so far touch me so near in cold to make me sweat);
The wise and pleasant talk, so rare or else alone,
That did me give the courteous gift that such had never none,
Be far from me, alas; and every other thing   75
I might forbear with better will than that that did me bring
With pleasant word and cheer redress of lingered pain,
And wonted oft in kindled will to Virtue me to train.
Thus am I driven to hear and hearken after news;
My comfort scant, my large desire in doubtful trust renews.   80

And yet, with more delight to moan my woeful case,
I must complain: those hands, those arms that firmly do
   embrace
Me from myself and rule the stern of my poor life,
The sweet disdains, the pleasant wraths, and eke the lovely
   strife
That wonted well to tune, in temper just and meet,   85
The rage that oft did make me err by furor undiscreet:
All this is hid me fro with sharp and cragged hills.
At other will my long abode my deep despair fulfils.
But if my hope sometime rise up by some redress,

It stumbleth straight for feeble faint, my fear hath such   90
   excess.
Such is the sort of hope, the less for more desire,
Whereby I fear and yet I trust to see that I require:
The resting place of Love where Virtue lives and grows,
Where I desire my weary life also may take repose.

My song, thou shalt attain to find that pleasant place   95
Where she doth live by whom I live; may chance thee have
   this grace:
When she hath read and seen the dread wherein I starve,
Between her breasts she shall thee put, there shall she thee
   reserve:
Then tell her that I come, she shall me shortly see;
If that for weight the body fail, this soul shall to her flee.   100

LYRICS

46

It may be good, like it who list,
But I do doubt. Who can me blame?
For oft assured, yet have I missed,
And now again I fear the same:
The windy words, the eyes' quaint game   5
Of sudden change maketh me aghast:
For dread to fall I stand not fast.

Alas, I tread an endless maze
That seeketh to accord two contraries,
And hope still, and nothing haze,   10
Imprisoned in liberties:
As one unheard and still that cries,
Always thirsty and yet nothing I taste:
For dread to fall I stand not fast.

Assured I doubt I be not sure;   15
And should I trust to such surety
That oft hath put the proof in ure
And never hath found it trusty?
Nay, sir, in faith it were great folly;
And yet my life thus I do waste: 20
For dread to fall I stand not fast.

47

Resound my voice, ye woods that hear me plain,
Both hills and vales causing reflection;
And rivers eke record ye of my pain,
Which hath ye oft forced by compassion
As judges to hear mine exclamation;   5
(Among whom pity, I find, doth remain):
Where I it seek, alas, there is disdain.

Oft ye rivers, to hear my woeful sound
Have stopped your course; and, plainly to express,
Many a tear by moisture of the ground   10
The earth hath wept to hear my heaviness
Which, causeless to suffer without redress,
The hugy oaks have roared in the wind,
Each thing (me thought) complaining in their kind.

Why then, hélas, doth not she on me rue?   15
Or is her heart so hard that no pity
May in it sink, my joy for to renew?
O stony heart, how hath this joined thee,
So cruel that art, cloaked with beauty?
No grace to me from thee there may proceed   20
But, as rewarded, Death for to be my meed.

48

In faith I wot not well what to say,
Thy chances been so wonderous,
Thou, Fortune, with thy diverse play
That causeth joy full dolorous
And eke the same right joyous: 5
Yet though thy chain hath me enwrapped,
Spite of thy hap, hap hath well happed.

Though thou me set for a wonder,
And seekest thy change to do me pain,
Men's minds yet may thou not order,   10
And honesty (and it remain)
Shall shine for all thy cloudy rain.
In vain thou seekest to have me trapped:
Spite of thy hap, hap hath well happed.

In hindering thou diddest further,   15
And made a gap where was a stile;

Cruel wills been oft put under:
Weening to lour, thou diddest smile.
Lord, how thyself thou diddest beguile
That in thy cares wouldest me have lapped!   20
But spite of thy hap, hap hath well happed.

49

Such hap as I am happed in
Had never man of truth, I ween:
At me Fortune list to begin
To show that never hath been seen —
A new kind of unhappiness.   5
Nor I cannot the thing I mean
   Myself express.

Myself express my deadly pain,
That can I well if that might serve;
But why I have not help again,   10
That know I not, unless I starve
For hunger still amidst my food:
So granted is that I deserve
   To do me good.

To do me good what may prevail?   15
For I deserve and not desire,
And still of cold I me bewail
And raked am in burning fire:
For though I have (such is my lot)
In hand to help that I require,   20
   It helpeth not.

It helpeth not but to increase
That that by proof can be no more:
That is the heat that cannot cease,
And that I have, to crave so sore.   25
What wonder is this greedy lust
To ask and have; and yet therefore
   Refrain I must.

Refrain I must, what is the cause?
Sure, as they say, 'So hawks be taught';   30
But in my case layeth no such clause
For with such craft I am not caught:
Wherefore I say, and good cause why,

With hapless hand no man hath raught
  Such hap as I.   35

50

They flee from me that sometime did me seek
With naked foot stalking in my chamber.
I have seen them gentle, tame, and meek
That now are wild and do not remember
That sometime they put themself in danger   5
To take bread at my hand; and now they range,
Busily seeking with a continual change.

Thanked be Fortune it hath been otherwise
Twenty times better, but once in special,
In thin array after a pleasant guise,   10
When her loose gown from her shoulders did fall
And she me caught in her arms long and small,
Therewithal sweetly did me kiss
And softly said: 'Dear heart, how like you this?'

It was no dream: I lay broad waking.
But all is turned thorough my gentleness
Into a strange fashion of forsaking;
And I have leave to go of her goodness
And she also to use newfangleness.
But since that I so kindly am served   20
I would fain know what she hath deserved.

51

There was never nothing more me pained,
Nor nothing more me moved,
As when my sweetheart her complained
That ever she me loved.
  Alas the while!   5

With piteous look she said and sighed:
'Alas what aileth me,
To love and set my wealth so light
On him that loveth not me?
  Alas the while!   10

'Was I not well void of all pain
When that nothing me grieved?
And now with sorrows I must complain

And cannot be relieved:
  Alas the while!   15

'My restful nights and joyful days
Since I began to love
Be take from me; all thing decays
Yet can I not remove:
  Alas the while!'   20

She wept and wrung her hands withal,
The tears fell in my neck;
She turned her face and let it fall,
Scarcely therewith could speak,
  Alas the while!   25

Her pains tormented me so sore
That comfort had I none,
But cursed my fortune more and more
To see her sob and groan:
  Alas the while!   30

52

Patience: though I have not
The thing that I require
I must of force, God wot,
Forbear my most desire,
For no ways can I find   5
To sail against the wind.

Patience, do what they will
To work me woe or spite;
I shall content me still
To think both day and night,   10
To think and hold my peace
Since there is no redress.

Patience withouten blame,
For I offended nought:
I know they know the same   15
Though they have changed their thought.
Was ever thought so moved
To hate that it hath loved?

Patience of all my harm,
For Fortune is my foe;   20

Patience must be the charm
To heal me of my woe:
Patience without offence
Is a painful Patience.

53

If Fancy would favour
As my deserving shall,
My love, my paramour,
Should love me best of all.

But if I cannot attain   5
The grace that I desire,
Then may I well complain
My service and my hire.

Fancy doth know how
To further my true heart   10
If Fancy might avow
With Faith to take part.

But Fancy is so frail
And flitting still so fast
That Faith may not prevail   15
To help me first nor last.

For Fancy at his lust
Doth rule all but by guess:
Whereto should I then trust
In Truth or Steadfastness?   20

Yet gladly would I please
The fancy of her heart
That may me only ease
And cure my care-full smart.

Therefore, my lady dear,   25
Set once your fantasy
To make some hope appear
Of steadfast remedy.

For if he be my friend
And undertake my woe,   30
My grief is at an end
If he continue so.

Else Fancy doth not right:
As I deserve and shall
To have you day and night   35
To love me best of all.

54

Marvel no more although
The songs I sing do moan;
For other life than woe
I never proved none,
And in my heart also   5
Is graven with letters deep
A thousand sighs and mo
A flood of tears to weep.

How may a man in smart
Find matter to rejoice?   10
How may a mourning heart
Set forth a pleasant voice?
Play who that can that part,
Needs must in me appear
How Fortune overthwart   15
Doth cause my mourning cheer.

Perdie, there is no man,
If he never saw sight,
That perfectly tell can
The nature of the light: 20
Alas, how should I then,
That never tasted but sour,
But do as I began,
Continually to lour?

But yet perchance some chance   25
May chance to change my tune;
And when such chance doth chance
Then shall I thank Fortune:
And if I have such chance
Perchance ere it be long –   30
For such a pleasant chance
To sing some pleasant song.

55

    'Ah, Robin,
     Jolly Robin,
   Tell me how thy leman doth,
And thou shall know of mine'.

'My lady is unkind, perdie!'   5
   'Alack, why is she so?'
'She loveth another better than me
   And yet she will say no'.

Response
I find no such doubleness:
   I find women true.
My lady loveth me doubtless   10
   And will change for no new.

Le plaintif
Thou art happy while that doth last
   But I say as I find:
That women's love is but a blast,   15
   And turneth like the wind.

Response
If that be true yet, as thou sayest,
   That women turn their heart,
Then speak better of them thou mayest
   In hope to have thy part.   20

Le plaintif
Such folks shall take no harm by love
   That can abide their turn,
But I, alas, can no way prove
   In love but lack and mourn.

Response
But if thou wilt avoid thy harm   25
   Learn this lesson of me:
At other fires thyself to warm
   And let them warm with thee.

56

To wish and want and not obtain,
To seek and sue ease of my pain:

Since all that ever I do is vain
  What may it avail me?

Although I strive both day and hour   5
Against the stream with all my power,
If Fortune list yet for to lour,
  What may it avail me?

If willingly I suffer woe,
If from the fire me list not go,   10
If then I burn to plain me so,
  What may it avail me?

And if the harm that I suffer
Be run too far out of measure,
To seek for help any further   15
  What may it avail me?

What though each heart that heareth me plain
Pitieth and plaineth for my pain:
If I no less in grief remain,
  What may it avail me?   20

Yea, though the want of my relief
Displease the causer of my grief,
Since I remain still in mischief,
  What may it avail me?

Such cruel chance doth so me threat   25
Continually inward to fret:
Then of release for to treat
  What may it avail me?

Fortune is deaf unto my call,
My torment moveth her not at all,   30
And though she turn as doth a ball
  What may it avail me?

For in Despair there is no rede;
To want of ear speech is no speed;
To linger still alive as dead,   35
  What may it avail me?

57

My hope, alas, hath me abused,
And vain rejoicing hath me fed:
Lust and joy have me refused

And care-full plaint is in their stead.
Too much advancing slacked my speed,　　5
Mirth hath caused my heaviness,
And I remain all comfortless.

Whereto did I assure my thought
Without displeasure steadfastly?
In Fortune's forge my joy was wrought,　　10
And is revolted readily.
I am mistaken wonderly;
For I thought nought but faithfulness,
Yet I remain all comfortless.

In gladsome cheer I did delight　　15
Till that delight did cause my smart
And all was wrong where I thought right;
For right it was that my true heart
Should not from truth be set apart
Since truth did cause my hardiness:　　20
Yet I remain all comfortless.

Sometime delight did tune my song
And led my heart full pleasantly,
And to myself I said among:
'My hap is coming hastily'.　　25
But it hath happed contrary:
Assurance causeth my distress,
And I remain all comfortless.

Then if my note now do vary
And leave his wonted pleasantness,　　30
The heavy burden that I carry
Hath altered all my joyfulness:
No pleasure hath still steadfastness,
But haste hath hurt my happiness
And I remain all comfortless.　　35

58

Once, as methought, Fortune me kissed
And bade me ask what I thought best
And I should have it as me list,
Therewith to set my heart in rest.

I asked nought but my dear heart　　5
To have for evermore mine own:

Then at an end were all my smart,
Then should I need no more to moan.

Yet for all that, a stormy blast
Had overturned this goodly day,   10
And Fortune seemed at the last
That to her promise she said nay.

But like as one out of despair
To sudden hope revived I:
Now Fortune sheweth herself so fair   15
That I content me wonderly.

My most desire my hand may reach,
My will is alway at my hand,
Me need not long for to beseech
Her that hath power me to command.   20

What earthly thing more can I crave?
What would I wish more at my will?
Nothing on earth more would I have
Save that I have, to have it still.

For Fortune hath kept her promise   25
In granting me my most desire:
Of my sufferance I have redress,
And I content me with my hire.

59

My lute, awake! Perform the last
Labour that thou and I shall waste,
And end that I have now begun;
For when this song is sung and past,
My lute, be still for I have done.   5

As to be heard where ear is none,
As lead to grave in marble stone,
My song may pierce her heart as soon:
Should we then sigh or sing or moan?
No, no, my lute, for I have done.   10

The rocks do not so cruelly
Repulse the waves continually
As she my suit and affection,
So that I am past remedy,
Whereby my lute and I have done.   15

Proud of the spoil that thou hast got
Of simple hearts thorough Love's shot
By whom, unkind, thou hast them won,
Think not he hath his bow forgot
Although my lute and I have done.   20

Vengeance shall fall on thy disdain
That makest but game on earnest pain:
Think not alone under the sun
Unquit to cause thy lovers plain,
Although my lute and I have done.   25

Perchance thee lie withered and old
The winter nights that are so cold,
Plaining in vain unto the moon.
Thy wishes then dare not be told:
Care then who list for I have done.   30

And then may chance thee to repent
The time that thou hast lost and spent
To cause thy lovers sigh and swoon;
Then shalt thou know beauty but lent,
And wish and want as I have done.   35

Now cease, my lute: This is the last
Labour that thou and I shall waste,
And ended is that we begun.
Now is this song both sung and past:
My lute, be still, for I have done.   40

60

If Chance assigned
Were to my mind
By very kind
Of destiny,
Yet would I crave   5
Nought else to have
But only life and liberty.

Then were I sure
I might endure
The displeasure   10
Of cruelty,
Where now I plain,

41

(Alas, in vain)
Lacking my life for liberty.

For without the one   15
The other is gone,
And there can none
It remedy:
If the one be past
The other doth waste,   20
And all for lack of liberty.

And so I drive,
As yet alive,
Although I strive
With misery,   25
Drawing my breath,
Looking for death
And loss of life for liberty.

But thou that still
Mayest at thy will   30
Turn all this ill
Adversity,
For the repair
Of my welfare
Grant me but life and liberty.   35

And if not so
Then let all go
To wretched woe
And let me die:
For the one or the other,   40
There is none other —
My death, or life with liberty.

61

I have sought long with steadfastness
To have had some ease of my great smart,
But nought availeth faithfulness
To grave within your stony heart.

But hap and hit or else hit not,   5
As uncertain as is the wind:
Right so it fareth by the shot
Of Love, alas, that is so blind.

Therefore I played the fool in vain
With pity when I first began   10
Your cruel heart for to constrain,
Since love regardeth no doleful man.

But of your goodness all your mind
Is that I should complain in vain;
This is the favour that I find: 15
Ye list to hear how I can plain.

But though I plain to please your heart,
Trust me I trust to temper it so
Not for to care which do revert:
All shall be one in wealth or woe.   20

For Fancy ruleth though Right say nay,
Even as the goodman kissed his cow:
None other reason can ye lay
But as who sayeth: 'I reck not how'.

62

Like as the swan towards her death
Doth strain her voice with doleful note,
Right so sing I with waste of breath:
'I die! I die! and you regard it not'.

I shall enforce my fainting breath   5
That all that hears this deadly note
Shall know that you doth cause my death:
I die! I die! and you regard it not.

Your unkindness hath sworn my death,
And changed hath my pleasant note   10
To painful sighs that stops my breath:
I die! I die! and you regard it not.

Consumeth my life, faileth my breath;
Your fault is forger of this note,
Melting in tears a cruel death: 15
I die! I die! and you regard it not.

My faith with me after my death
Buried shall be, and to this note
I do bequeath my weary breath
To cry: 'I died and you regarded not'.   20

63

In eternum I was once determed
For to have loved, and my mind affirmed
That with my heart it should be confirmed
   In eternum.

Forthwith I found the thing that I might like,   5
And sought with love to warm her heart alike
For, as me thought, I should not see the like
   In eternum.

To trace this dance I put myself in press:
Vain Hope did lead and bade I should not cease   10
To serve, to suffer, and still to hold my peace
   In eternum.

With this first rule I furthered me apace
That, as methought, my troth had taken place
With full assurance to stand in her grace   15
   In eternum.

It was not long ere I by proof had found
That feeble building is on feeble ground,
For in her heart this word did never sound:
   In eternum.   20

In eternum then from my heart I cast
That I had first determed for the best;
Now in the place another thought doth rest
   In eternum.

64

Heaven and earth, and all that hear me plain,
Do well perceive what care doth cause me cry,
Save you alone to whom I cry in vain:
'Mercy, madame, alas, I die, I die!'

If that you sleep, I humbly you require   5
Forbear a while and let your rigour slake
(Since that by you I burn thus in this fire):
To hear my plaint, dear heart, awake, awake!

Since that so oft ye have made me to wake
In plaint and tears and in right piteous case,   10
Displease you not if force do now me make
To break your sleep, crying 'Alas, alas!'

It is the last trouble that ye shall have
Of me, madame, to hear my last complaint:
Pity at least your poor unhappy slave,   15
For in despair, alas, I faint, I faint!

It is not now but long and long ago
I have you served as to my power and might
As faithfully as any man might do,
Claiming of you nothing of right, of right,   20

Save of your grace only to stay my life
That fleeth as fast as cloud afore the wind:
For since that first I entered in this strife
An inward death hath fret my mind, my mind.

If I had suffered this to you unware   25
Mine were the fault and you nothing to blame;
But since you know my woe and all my care,
Why do I die, alas? For shame, for shame!

I know right well my face, my look, my tears,
Mine eyes, my words, and eke my dreary cheer   30
Have cried my death full oft unto your ears:
Hard of belief it doth appear, appear.

A better proof I see that you would have
How I am dead: therefore when ye hear tell,
Believe it not although ye see my grave.   35
Cruel, unkind! I say: 'Farewell, farewell!'

65

Comfort thyself, my woeful heart,
Or shortly on thyself thee wreak,
For length redoubleth deadly smart:
Why sighs thou, heart, and wilt not break?

To waste in sighs were piteous death;   5
Alas, I find thee faint and weak;
Enforce thyself to lose thy breath:
Why sighs thou, then, and wilt not break?

Thou knowest right well that no redress
Is thus to pine; and for to speak,
Perdie, it is remediless: 10
Why sighs thou, then, and wilt not break?

It is too late for to refuse
The yoke when it is on thy neck;
To shake it off vaileth not to muse: 15
Why sighs thou then and wilt not break?

To sob and sigh it were but vain
Since there is none that doth it reck;
Alas, thou dost prolong thy pain:
Why sighs thou then and wilt not break?   20

Then in her sight, to move her heart,
Seek on thyself thyself to wreak
That she may know thou sufferedest smart:
Sigh there thy last and therewith break.

66

To cause accord or to agree
Two contraries in one degree
And in one point, as seemeth me,
To all man's wit it cannot be:
   It is impossible.   5

Of heat and cold when I complain
And say that heat doth cause my pain
When cold doth shake my every vein,
And both at once, I say again:
   It is impossible.   10

That man that hath his heart away,
If life liveth there, as men do say,
That he heartless should last one day
Alive and not to turn to clay,
   It is impossible.   15

'Twixt life and death, say what who saith,
There liveth no life that draweth breath,
They join so near; and eke i'faith
To seek for life by wish of death,
   It is impossible.   20

Yet Love, that all thing doth subdue,
Whose power there may no life eschew,
Hath wrought in me that I may rue
These miracles to be so true
   That are impossible.   25

67

Though this thy port and I thy servant true,
And thou thyself dost cast thy beams from high
From thy chief house, promising to renew
Both joy and eke delight, behold yet how that I,
Banished from my bliss, care-fully do cry: 5
'Help now, Cytherea, my lady dear,
My fearful trust *en voguant la galère*'.

Alas, the doubt that dreadful absence giveth:
Without thine aid assurance is there none.
The firm faith that in the water fleeteth   10
Succour thou, therefore: in thee it is alone.
Stay that with faith that faithfully doth moan
And thou also givest me both hope and fear:
Remember thou me *en voguant la galère*.

By seas and hills elonged from thy sight,   15
Thy wonted grace reducing to my mind,
In stead of sleep thus I occupy the night:
A thousand thoughts and many doubts I find,
And still I trust thou canst not be unkind,
Or else despair my comfort, and my cheer   20
Would flee forthwith *en voguant la galère*.

Yet, on my faith, full little doth remain
Of any hope whereby I may myself uphold;
For since that only words do me retain,
I may well think thy affection is but cold.   25
But since my will is nothing as I would,
But in thy hands it resteth whole and clear,
Forget me not *en voguant la galère*.

68

Process of time worketh such wonder
That water, which is of kind so soft,
Doth pierce the marble stone asunder
By little drops falling from aloft.

And yet an heart that seems so tender   5
Receiveth no drop of the stilling tears
That alway still cause me to render
The vain plaint that sounds not in her ears.

So cruel, alas, is nought alive,
So fierce, so froward, so out of frame,   10
But some way, some time, may so contrive
By means the wild to temper and tame.

And I that always have sought and seek
Each place, each time, for some lucky day,
This fierce tiger, less I find her meek   15
And more denied the longer I pray.

The lion in his raging furor
Forbears that sueth meekness for his boot;
And thou, alas, in extreme dolour
The heart so low thou treads under thy foot: 20

Each fierce thing, lo, how thou dost exceed
And hides it under so humble a face;
And yet the humble to help at need
Nought helpeth Time, Humbleness, nor place.

69

After great storms the calm returns
And pleasanter it is thereby;
Fortune likewise that often turns
Hath made me now the most happy.

The heaven that pitied my distress,   5
My just desire, and my cry
Hath made my languor to cease
And me also the most happy.

Whereto despaired ye, my friends?
My trust alway in Him did lie   10
That knoweth what my thought intends,
Whereby I live the most happy.

Lo, what can take Hope from that heart
That is assured steadfastly?
Hope therefore ye that live in smart,   15
Whereby I am the most happy.

And I that have felt of your pain
Shall pray to God continually
To make your hope your health retain,
And me also the most happy.   20

70

O goodly hand
Wherein doth stand
My heart distressed in pain:
Fair hand, alas,
In little space   5
My life that doth restrain!

O fingers slight,
Departed right,
So long, so small, so round,
Goodly begone   10
And yet alone
Most cruel in my wound.

With lilies white
And roses bright
Doth strive thy colour fair;   15
Nature did lend
Each finger's end
A pearl for to repair.

Consent at last
(Since that thou hast   20
My heart in thy demesne)
For service true
On me to rue
And reach me love again.

And if not so   25
Then with more woe
Enforce thyself to strain
This simple heart,
That suffereth smart,
And rid it out of pain.   30

71

If in the world there be more woe
Than I have in my heart,
Whereso it is, it doth come fro
And in my breast there doth it grow
For to increase my smart.   5
Alas, I am receipt of every care,
And of my life each sorrow claims his part.

Who list to live in quietness
By me let him beware,
For I by high disdain   10
Am made without redress,
And unkindness, alas, hath slain
My poor true heart all comfortless.

72

What means this? When I lie alone
I toss, I turn, I sigh, I groan,
My bed me seems as hard as stone:
    What means this?

I sigh, I plain continually,   5
The clothes that on my bed do lie
Always methink they lie awry:
    What means this?

In slumbers oft for fear I quake,
For heat and cold I burn and shake,   10
For lack of sleep my head doth ache:
    What means this?

A mornings then when I do rise
I turn unto my wonted guise;
All day after muse and devise: 15
    What means this?

And if, perchance, by me there pass
She unto whom I sue for grace
The cold blood forsaketh my face:
    What means this?   20

But if I sit near her by
With loud voice my heart doth cry,
And yet my mouth is dumb and dry:
    What means this?

To ask for help no heart I have,   25
My tongue doth fail what I should crave;
Yet inwardly I rage and rave:
    What means this?

Thus have I passed many a year
And many a day, though nought appear   30

But most of that that most I fear:
  What means this?

73

When first mine eyes did view and mark
Thy fair beauty to behold,
And when mine ears listened to hark
The pleasant words that thou me told,
I would, as then I had, been free   5
From ears to hear and eyes to see.

And when my lips gan first to move,
Whereby my heart to thee was known,
And when my heart did talk of love
To thee that hast true love down thrown,   10
I would my lips and tongue also
Had then been dumb, no deal to go.

And when my hands have handled ought
That thee hath kept in memory,
And when my feet have gone and sought   15
To find and get thy company,
I would each hand a foot had been
And I each foot a hand had seen.

And when in mind I did consent
To follow this my fancy's will,
And when my heart did first relent   20
To taste such bait my life to spill,
I would my heart had been as thine
Or else thy heart had been as mine.

74

The joy so short alas, the pain so near,
The way so long, the departure so smart:
The first sight, alas, I bought too dear
That so suddenly now from hence must part.
The body gone, yet remain shall the heart   5
With her, which for me salt tears did rain,
And shall not change till that we meet again.

Though time doth pass, yet shall not my love;
Though I be far, always my heart is near;
Though other change, yet will not I remove;   10

Though other care not, yet love I will and fear;
Though other hate, yet will I love my dear;
Though other will of lightness say adieu,
Yet will I be found steadfast and true.

When other laugh, alas then do I weep;   15
When other sing, then do I wail and cry;
When other run, perforced I am to creep;
When other dance, in sorrow I do lie;
When other joy, for pain well near I die,
Thus brought from wealth, alas, to endless pain,   20
That undeserved, causeless to remain.

75

The knot, which first my heart did strain
When that your servant I became,
Doth bind me still for to remain
Always your own, as now I am;
And if ye find that I do feign,   5
With just judgement myself I damn
   To have disdain.

If other thought in me do grow
But still to love you steadfastly,
If that the proof do not well show   10
That I am yours assuredly,
Let every wealth turn me to woe
And you to be continually
   My chiefest foe.

If other love or new request   15
Do seize my heart but only this,
Or if within my wearied breast
Be hid one thought that mean amiss,
I do desire that mine unrest
May still increase, and I to miss   20
   That I love best.

If in my love there be one spot
Of false deceit or doubleness,
Or if I mind to slip this knot
By want of faith or steadfastness,   25
Let all my service be forgot,
And when I would have chief redress,
   Esteem me not.

But if that I consume in pain
With burning sighs and fervent love,   30
And daily seek none other gain
But with my deed these words to prove,
Methink of right I should obtain
That ye would mind for to remove
   Your great disdain.   35

And for the end of this my song
Unto your hands I do submit
My deadly grief and pains so strong
Which in my heart be firmly shut:
And when ye list, redress my wrong,   40
Since well ye know this painful fit
   Hath last too long.

76

Since Love will needs that I shall love,
Of very force I must agree;
And since no chance may it remove
In wealth and in adversity,
I shall alway myself apply   5
To serve and suffer patiently.

Though for goodwill I find but hate
And cruelty my life to waste,
And though that still a wretched state
Should pine my days unto the last,   10
Yet I profess it willingly
To serve and suffer patiently.

For since my heart is bound to serve
(And I not ruler of mine own)
Whatso befall till that I starve,   15
By proof full well it shall be known
That I shall still myself apply
To serve and suffer patiently.

Yea, though my grief find no redress,
But still increase before mine eyes;   20
Though my reward be cruelness
With all the harm hap can devise,
Yet I profess it willingly
To serve and suffer patiently.

Yea, though Fortune her pleasant face   25
Should show to set me up aloft,
And straight my wealth for to deface
Should writhe away as she doth oft,
Yet would I still myself apply
To serve and suffer patiently.   30

There is no grief, no smart, no woe
That yet I feel, or after shall,
That from this mind may make me go:
And whatsoever me befall,
I do profess it willingly   35
To serve and suffer patiently.

77

Perdie, I said it not,
Nor never thought to do:
As well as I ye wot
I have no power thereto;
And if I did, the lot   5
That first did me enchain
Do never slack the knot
But straiter to my pain;

And if I did, each thing
That may do harm or woe   10
Continually may wring
My heart whereso I go.
Report may always ring
Of shame of me for aye
If in my heart did spring   15
The word that ye do say:

If I said so, each star
That is in heaven above
May frown on me to mar
The hope I have in love;   20
And if I did, such war
As they brought out of Troy
Bring all my life afar
From all this lust and joy;

And if I did so say,   25
The beauty that me bound

Increase from day to day
More cruel to my wound;
With all the moan that may
To plaint may turn my song;   30
My life may soon decay,
Without redress, by wrong.

If I be clear fro thought
Why do ye then complain?
Then is this thing but sought   35
To turn me to more pain.
Then that that ye have wrought
Ye must it now redress:
Of right therefore ye ought
Such rigour to repress.   40

And as I have deserved,
So grant me now my hire:
Ye know I never swerved,
Ye never found me liar:
For Rachel have I served,   45
For Leah cared I never;
And her I have reserved
Within my heart for ever.

78

LOVER: It burneth yet, alas, my heart's desire.
LADY: What is the thing that hath inflamed thy heart?
LOVER: A certain point, as fervent as the fire.
LADY: The heat shall cease if that thou wilt convert.
LOVER: I cannot stop the fervent raging ire.   5
LADY: What may I do if thyself cause thy smart?
LOVER: Hear my request, alas, with weeping cheer.
LADY: With right good will: say on, lo, I thee hear.

LOVER: That thing would I that maketh two content.
LADY: Thou seekest, perchance, of me that I may not. 10
LOVER: Would God thou wouldest, as thou mayest well,
   assent.
LADY: That I may not: thy grief is mine, God wot.
LOVER: But I it feel, whatso thy words have meant.
LADY: Suspect me not: my words be not forgot.
LOVER: Then say, alas, shall I have help or no?   15
LADY: I see no time to answer yea, but no.

LOVER: Say yea, dear heart, and stand no more in doubt.
LADY: I may not grant a thing that is so dear.
LOVER: Lo, with delays thou drives me still about.
LADY: Thou wouldest my death, it plainly doth appear.   20
LOVER: First may my heart his blood and life bleed out.
LADY: Then for my sake, alas, thy will forbear.
LOVER: From day to day thus wastes my life away.
LADY: Yet, for the best, suffer some small delay.

LOVER: Now, good, say yea: do once so good a deed.   25
LADY: If I said yea, what should thereof ensue?
LOVER: An heart in pain, of succour so should speed;
   'Twixt yea and nay my doubt shall still renew:
   My sweet, say yea and do away this dread.
LADY: Thou wilt needs so: be it so, but then be true.   30
LOVER: Nought would I else, nor other treasure none.

Thus hearts be won by love, request, and moan.

79

Blame not my lute, for he must sound
Of this or that as liketh me;
For lack of wit the lute is bound
To give such tunes as pleaseth me:
Though my songs be somewhat strange   5
And speaks such words as touch thy change,
   Blame not my lute.

My lute, alas, doth not offend,
Though that perforce he must agree
To sound such tunes as I intend   10
To sing to them that heareth me:
Then though my songs be somewhat plain
And toucheth some that use to feign,
   Blame not my lute.

My lute and strings may not deny   15
But as I strike they must obey;
Break not them then so wrongfully
But wreak thyself some wiser way,
And, though the songs which I indite
Do quit thy change with rightful spite,   20
   Blame not my lute.

Spite asketh spite and changing change
And falsed faith must needs be known;

The fault so great, the case so strange,
Of right it must abroad be blown: 25
Then since that by thine own desert
My songs do tell how true thou art,
   Blame not my lute.

Blame but thyself that hast misdone
And well deserved to have blame: 30
Change thou thy way so evil begun,
And then my lute shall sound that same.
But if till then my fingers play
By thy desert their wonted way,
   Blame not my lute.   35

Farewell, unknown, for though thou break
My strings in spite with great disdain,
Yet have I found out for thy sake
Strings for to string my lute again.
And if perchance this foolish rhyme   40
Do make thee blush at any time,
   Blame not my lute.

80

That time that Mirth did steer my ship
Which now is fraught with heaviness,
And Fortune bote not then the lip
But was defence of my distress,
Then in my book wrote my mistress: 5
'I am yours, you may well be sure,
And shall be while my life doth dure'.

But she herself which then wrote that
Is now mine extreme enemy:
Above all men she doth me hate,   10
Rejoicing of my misery;
But though that for her sake I die
I shall be hers, she may be sure,
As long as my life doth endure.

It is not Time that can wear out   15
With me that once is firmly set:
While Nature keeps her course about
My love from her no man can let
Though never so sore they me threat:

Yet am I hers, she may be sure,   20
And shall be while that life doth dure.

And once I trust to see that day
(Renewer of my joy and wealth)
That she to me these words shall say:
'In faith, welcome to me myself,   25
Welcome, my joy, welcome, my health,
For I am thine, thou mayest be sure,
And shall be while that life doth dure'.

Ho me, alas, what words were these?
In covenant I might find them so!   30
I reck not what smart or disease,
Torment or trouble, pain or woe
I suffered so that I might know
That she were mine, I might be sure,
And should be while that life doth dure.   35

81

The restful place (reviver of my smart),
The labour's salve (increasing my sorrow),
The body's ease (and troubler of my heart),
Quieter of mind (and my unquiet foe),
Forgetter of pain (remembering my woe),   5
The place of sleep (wherein I do but wake),
Besprent with tears, my bed, I thee forsake.

The frost, the snow, may not redress my heat,
Nor yet no heat abate my fervent cold:
I know nothing to ease my pains meet;   10
Each cure causeth increase by twenty fold,
Reviving cares upon my sorrows old:
Such overthwart affects they do me make,
Besprent with tears, my bed for to forsake.

Yet helpeth it not: I find no better ease   15
In bed or out. This most causeth my pain:
Where most I seek how best that I may please,
My lost labour, alas, is all in vain:
Yet that I gave I cannot call again.
No place from me my grief away can take;   20
Wherefore with tears, my bed, I thee forsake.

82

Deem as ye list: upon good cause
I may and think of this or that,
But what or why myself best knows
Whereby I think and fear not;
But thereunto I may well think   5
The doubtful sentence of this clause:
I would it were not as I think;
I would I thought it were not.

For if I thought it were not so,
Though it were so, it grieved me not: 10
Unto my thought it were as though
I hearkened though I hear not.
At that I see I cannot wink,
Nor from my thought so let it go:
I would it were not as I think;   15
I would I thought it were not.

Lo, how my thought might make me free
Of that perchance it needeth not:
Perchance none doubt the dread I see;
I shrink at that I bear not;   20
But in my heart this word shall sink
Unto the proof may better be:
I would it were not as I think;
I would I thought it were not.

If it be not, show no cause why   25
I should so think, then care I not;
For I shall so myself apply
To be that I appear not:
That is as one that shall not shrink
To be your own until I die,   30
And, if it be not as I think,
Likewise to think it is not.

83

I know not where my heavy sighs to hide:
My sorrowful heart is so vexed with pain
I wander forth as one without a guide
That seeketh to find a thing parted in twain,
And so forth run that scant can turn again.   5

Thus time I pass and waste full piteously,
For death it is out of thy sight to be.

I scantly know from whom comes all my grief,
But that I waste as one doth in sickness;
And cannot tell which way comes my mischief,   10
For all I taste to me is bitterness;
And of my health I have no sickerness,
Nor shall not have till that I do thee see:
It is my death out of thy sight to be.

I live in earth as one that would be dead,   15
And cannot die: alas, the more my pain!
Famished I am, and yet always am fed:
Thus contrary all thing doth me constrain
To laugh, to mourn, to walk, to joy, to plain,
And shall do still: there is no remedy   20
Until the time that in thy sight I be.

There nis sickness but health it doth desire,
Nor poverty but riches like to have,
Nor ship in storm but steering doth require
Harbour to find so that she may her save.   25
And I, alas, nought in this world do crave
Save that thou list on him to have mercy
Whose death it is out of thy sight to be.

84

And wilt thou leave me thus?
Say nay, say nay, for shame,
To save thee from the blame
Of all my grief and grame:
And wilt thou leave me thus?   5
  Say nay, say nay!

And wilt thou leave me thus
That hath loved thee so long
In wealth and woe among?
And is thy heart so strong   10
As for to leave me thus?
  Say nay, say nay!

And wilt thou leave me thus
That hath given thee my heart
Never for to depart,   15

Neither for pain nor smart?
And wilt thou leave me thus?
  Say nay, say nay!

And wilt thou leave me thus
And have no more pity   20
Of him that loveth thee?
Hélas, thy cruelty!
And wilt thou leave me thus?
  Say nay, say nay!

85

I see that Chance hath chosen me
Thus secretly to live in pain
And to another given the fee
Of all my loss to have the gain:
By chance assigned, thus do I serve,   5
And other have that I deserve.

Unto myself sometime alone
I do lament my woeful case:
But what availeth me to moan
Since Truth and Pity hath no place   10
In them to whom I sue and serve,
And other have that I deserve?

To seek by mean to change this mind,
Alas, I prove it will not be;
For in my heart I cannot find
Once to refrain, but still agree   15
(As bound by force) alway to serve:
And other have that I deserve.

Such is the fortune that I have:
To love them most that love me least,   20
And to my pain to seek and crave
The thing that other have possessed.
So thus in vain alway I serve,
And other have that I deserve.

And till I may appease the heat   25
(If that my hap will hap so well)
To wail my woe my heart shall fret
Whose pensive pain my tongue can tell.

Yet thus unhappy must I serve,
And other have that I deserve.   30

86

Is it possible
That so high debate,
So sharp, so sore, and of such rate,
Should end so soon and was begun so late?
  Is it possible?   5

Is it possible
So cruel intent,
So hasty heat and so soon spent,
From love to hate, and thence for to relent?
  Is it possible?   10

Is it possible
That any may find
Within one heart so diverse mind
To change or turn as weather and wind?
  Is it possible?   15

Is it possible
To spy it in an eye
That turns as oft as chance on die,
The truth whereof can any try?
  Is it possible?   20

It is possible
For to turn so oft,
To bring that lowest that was most aloft,
And to fall highest yet to light soft:
  It is possible.   25

All is possible
Whoso list believe:
Trust therefore first and after prove,
As men wed ladies by licence and leave,
  All is possible.   30

87

Quondam was I in my lady's grace
I think, as well as now be you;
And when that you have trod the trace

Then shall you know my words be true,
    That *quondam* was I.   5

Quondam was I: she said for ever;
That 'ever' lasted but a short while.
Promise made not to dissever,
I thought she laughed – she did but smile:
    Then *quondam* was I.   10

Quondam was I: he that full oft lay
In her arms with kisses many one.
It is enough that this I may say:
Though among the mo now I be gone,
    Yet *quondam* was I.   15

Quondam was I: yet she will you tell
That, since the hour she was first born,
She never loved none half so well
As you. But what although she had sworn?
    Sure *quondam* was I.   20

88

Ah, my heart, ah, what aileth thee
To set so light my liberty,
Making me bond when I was free:
Ah, my heart, ah, what aileth thee?

When thou were rid from all distress,   5
Void of all pain and pensiveness –
To choose again a new mistress,
Ah, my heart, ah, what aileth thee?

When thou were well, thou could not hold;
To turn again, that were too bold: 10
Thus to renew my sorrows old,
Ah, my heart, ah, what aileth thee?

Thou knowest full well that but of late
I was turned out of Love's gate:
And now to guide me to this mate,   15
Ah, my heart, ah, what aileth thee?

I hoped full well all had been done
But now my hope is ta'en and won:
To my torment to yield so soon,
Ah, my heart, ah, what aileth thee?   20

89

Forget not yet the tried intent
Of such a truth as I have meant;
My great travail so gladly spent
   Forget not yet.

Forget not yet when first began
The weary life ye know since when,
The suit, the service none tell can:
   Forget not yet.

Forget not yet the great assays,
The cruel wrong, the scornful ways,
The painful patience in denays:
   Forget not yet.

Forget not yet, forget not this:
How long ago hath been and is
The mind that never meant amiss:
   Forget not yet.

Forget not then thine own approved
The which so long hath thee so loved
Whose steadfast faith yet never moved:
   Forget not this.

90

I am as I am, and so will I be,
But how that I am none knoweth truly:
Be it evil, be it well, be I bond, be I free,
I am as I am, and so will I be.

I lead my life indifferently,
I mean nothing but honestly;
And though folks judge full diversely,
I am as I am, and so will I die.

I do not rejoice nor yet complain:
Both Mirth and Sadness I do refrain,
And use the mean since folks will feign;
Yet I am as I am, be it pleasure or pain.

Diverse do judge as they do trow,
Some of pleasure and some of woe;
Yet for all that, nothing they know,
But I am as I am wheresoever I go.

But since that judgers do thus decay
Let every man his judgement say:
I will it take in sport and play
For I am as I am whosoever say nay.   20

Who judgeth well, well God him send;
Who judgeth evil, God them amend:
To judge the best therefore intend,
For I am as I am, and so will I end.

Yet some there be that take delight   25
To judge folks' thought for envy and spite;
But whether they judge me wrong or right
I am as I am, and so do I write,

Praying you all that this do read
To trust it as you do your creed   30
And not to think I change my weed,
For I am as I am however I speed.

But how that is I leave to you:
Judge as ye list, false or true.
Ye know no more than afore ye knew,   35
Yet I am as I am whatever ensue.

And from this mind I will not flee,
But to you all that misjudge me
I do protest, as ye may see,
That I am as I am and so will I be.   40

91

What should I say
Since Faith is dead
And Truth away
From you is fled?
Should I be led   5
With doubleness?
Nay, nay, mistress!

I promised you;
And you promised me
To be as true   10
As I would be:
But since I see
Your double heart,
Farewell, my part.

Thought for to take   15
It is not my mind,
But to forsake
One so unkind;
And as I find
So will I trust: 20
Farewell, unjust.

Can ye say nay
But that you said
That I alway
Should be obeyed?   25
And thus betrayed
Ere that I wist!
Farewell, unkissed.

92

I must go walk the woods so wild
And wander here and there
In dread and deadly fear;
For where I trust I am beguiled,
And all for your love, my dear.   5

I am banished from my bliss
By craft and false pretence,
Faultless, without offence;
And of return no certain is,
And all for your love, my dear.   10

Banished am I, remediless,
To wilderness alone,
Alone to sigh and moan;
And of relief all comfortless,
And all for your love, my dear.   15

My house shall be the greenwood tree,
A tuft of brakes my bed:
And this my life I lead
As one that from his joy doth flee,
And all for your love, my dear.   20

The running streams shall be my drink,
Acorns shall be my food:

Nought else shall do me good
But on your beauty for to think,
And all for your love, my dear. 25

And when the deer draw to the green,
Makes me think on a roe:
How I have seen ye go
Above the fairest, fairest beseen!
And all for your love, my dear. 30

But where I see in any cote
Two turtles sit and play,
Rejoicing all the day,
Alas, I think: this have I lost,
And all for your love, my dear. 35

No bird, no bush, no bough I see
But bringeth to my mind
Something whereby I find
My heart far wandered, far fro me,
And all for your love, my dear. 40

The tune of birds when I do hear,
My heart doth bleed, alas,
Remembering how I was
Wont for to hear your ways so clear;
And all for your love, my dear. 45

My thought doth please me for the while:
While I see my desire
Nought else I do require.
So with my thought I me beguile,
And all for your love, my dear. 50

Yet I am further from my thought
Than earth from heaven above,
And yet for to remove
My pain, alas, availeth nought;
And all for your love, my dear. 55

And where I lie secret, alone,
I mark that face anon
That stayeth my life, as one
That other comfort can get none:
And all for your love, my dear. 60

The summer days that be so long
I walk and wander wide,
Alone, without a guide,
Always thinking how I have wrong;
And all for your love, my dear.   65

The winter nights that are so cold
I lie amid the storms,
Unwrapped, in pricking thorns,
Remembering my sorrows old:
And all for your love, my dear.   70

A woeful man such desert life
Becometh best of all:
But woe might them befall
That are the causers of this strife,
And all for your love, my dear.   75

93

V. Innocentia
Veritas Viat Fides
Circumdederunt me inimici mei

Who list his wealth and ease retain,
Himself let him unknown contain:
Press not too fast in at that gate
Where the return stands by disdain,
For sure, *circa Regna tonat*.   5

The high mountains are blasted oft
When the low valley is mild and soft;
Fortune with Health stands at debate;
The fall is grievous from aloft,
And sure, *circa Regna tonat*.   10

These bloody days have broken my heart:
My lust, my youth did them depart,
And blind desire of estate.
Who hastes to climb seeks to revert:
Of truth, *circa Regna tonat*.   15

The bell tower showed me such sight
That in my head sticks day and night:
There did I learn out of a grate,
For all favour, glory, or might,
That yet *circa Regna tonat*.   20

By proof, I say, there did I learn
Wit helpeth not defence to earn
Of innocency to plead or prate:
Bear low, therefore, give God the stern,
For sure, *circa Regna tonat.*   25

94

Like as the bird in the cage enclosed,
The door unsparred and the hawk without,
'Twixt death and prison piteously oppressed,
Whether for to choose standeth in doubt:
Certes so do I, which do seek to bring about   5
Which should be best by determination:
By loss of life liberty, or life by prison.

O, mischief by mischief to be redressed!
Where pain is the best there lieth little pleasure:
By short death out of danger yet to be delivered,   10
Rather than with painful life, thraldom, and dolour,
For small pleasure much pain to suffer:
Sooner therefore to choose (methinketh it wisdom)
By loss of life liberty than life by prison.

By length of life yet should I suffer,   15
Awaiting time and Fortune's chance.
Many things happen within an hour;
That which me oppressed may me advance.
In Time is trust, which, by Death's grievance,
Is utterly lost: then were it not reason   20
By death to choose liberty, and not life by prison?

But death were deliverance, and life length of pain.
Of two ills (let see) now choose the best:
This bird to deliver, you that hear her plain,
Your advice, you lovers, which shall be best: 25
In cage in thraldom, or by hawk to be oppressed?
And which for to choose make plain conclusion:
By loss of life liberty, or life by prison.

95

My pen, take pain a little space
To follow that which doth me chase
And hath in hold my heart so sore;

69

But when thou hast this brought to pass,
My pen, I prithee, write no more.   5

Remember oft thou hast me eased
And all my pains full well appeased;
But now I know (unknown before)
That where I trust I am deceived,
And yet, my pen, thou canst no more.   10

A time thou haddest, as other have,
To write which way my hope to crave.
That time is past: withdraw therefore;
Since we do lose that other save,
As good leave off and write no more.   15

In worth to use another way,
Not as we would, but as we may,
For once my loss is past restore
And my desire is my decay:
My pen, yet write a little more.   20

To love in vain whoever shall,
Of worldly pain it passeth all,
As in like case I find. Wherefore
To hold so fast and yet to fall?
Hélas, my pen, now write no more.   25

Since thou hast taken pain this space
To follow that which doth me chase
And hath in hold my heart so sore,
Now hast thou brought my mind to pass:
My pen, I prithee, write no more.   30

96

For want of will in woe I plain
Under colour of soberness,
Renewing with my suit my pain,
My wanhope with your steadfastness:
Awake, therefore, of gentleness.   5
Regard at length, I you require,
The swelting pains of my desire.

Betimes who giveth willingly
Redoubled thanks aye doth deserve;
And I that sue unfeignedly   10

In fruitless hope, alas, do starve.
How great my cause is for to swerve
(And yet how steadfast is my suit)
Lo, here ye see: where is the fruit?

As hound that hath his keeper lost   15
Seek I your presence to obtain
In which my heart delighteth most
And shall delight, though I be slain.
You may release my band of pain:
Loose then the care that makes me cry   20
For want of help, or else I die.

I die, though not incontinent,
By process yet consumingly,
As waste of fire which doth relent,
If you as wilful will deny: 25
Wherefore cease of such cruelty
And take me wholly in your grace
Which lacketh will to change his place.

97

Pain of all pain, the most grievous pain
Is to love heartily and cannot be loved again.

Love with unkindness is causer of heaviness,
Of inward sorrow and sighs painful.
Whereas I love is no redress   5
To no manner of pastime: the sprites so dull
With privy mournings and looks rueful,
The body all wearish, the colour pale and wan,
More like a ghost than like a living man

When Cupido hath inflamed the heart's desires   10
hTo love thereas is disdain;
Of good or ill the mind oblivious,
Nothing regarding but love to attain;
Always imagining by what mean or train
It may be at rest thus in a moment   15
Now here, now there, being never content;

Tossing and turning when the body would rest,
With dreams oppressed and visions fantastical;
Sleeping or waking, love is ever pressed,
Sometime to weep, sometime to cry and call,   20

Bewailing his fortune and life bestial,
Now in hope of recure and now in despair:
This is a sorry life to live alway in care!

Record of Terence in his comedies poetical:
In love is jealousy and injuries many one,   25
Anger and debate with mind sensual,
Now war, now peace, musing all alone,
Sometime all mort and cold as any stone.
This causeth unkindness of such as cannot skill
Of true love, assured with heart and good will.   30

Lucrece the Roman, for love of her lord
And because perforce she had commit adultery
With Tarquinus, as the story doth record,
Herself did slay with a knife most piteously
Among her nigh friends, because that she   35
So falsely was betrayed: lo, this was the guerdon
Whereas true love hath no dominion.

To make rehearsal of old antiquity
What needeth it? We see by experience
Among lovers it chanceth daily   40
Displeasure and variance for none offence;
But if true love might give sentence
That unkindness and disdain should have no place
But true heart for true love, it were a great grace.

O Venus, lady, of love the goddess,   45
Help all true lovers to have love again:
Banish from thy presence disdain and unkindness;
Kindness and pity to thy service retain.
For true love, once fixed in the cordial vein
Can never be revulsed by no manner of art,   50
Unto the soul from the body depart.

98

Spite hath no power to make me sad,
Nor scornfulness to make me plain:
It doth suffice that once I had,
And so to leave it is no pain.

Let them frown on that least doth gain;   5
Who did rejoice must needs be glad;
And though with words thou weenest to reign,
It doth suffice that once I had.

Since that in checks thus overthwart
And coyly looks thou dost delight,   10
It doth suffice that mine thou wert
Though change hath put thy faith to flight.

Alas, it is a peevish spite
To yield thyself and then to part,
But since thou settest thy faith so light   15
It doth suffice that mine thou wert.

And since thy love doth thus decline
And in thy heart such hate doth grow,
It doth suffice that thou wert mine,
And with goodwill I quit it so.   20

Sometime my friend, farewell, my foe –
Since thou change I am not thine:
But for relief of all my woe
It doth suffice that thou wert mine.

Praying you all that hears this song   25
To judge no wight, nor none to blame,
It doth suffice she doth me wrong
And that herself doth know the same.

And though she change, it is no shame:
Their kind it is and hath been long.   30
Yet I protest she hath no name:
It doth suffice she doth me wrong.

99

It was my choice, it was no chance,
That brought my heart in other's hold,
Whereby it hath had sufferance
Longer, perdie, than Reason would.
Since I it bound where it was free,   5
Methinks, iwis, of right it should
    Accepted be.

Accepted be without refuse,
Unless that Fortune hath the power
All right of love for to abuse;   10
For (as they say) one happy hour
May more prevail than right or might:

If Fortune then list for to lour
  What 'vaileth right?

What 'vaileth right if this be true? 15
Then trust to Chance and go by guess;
Then whoso loveth may well go sue
Uncertain Hope for his redress:
Yet some would say assuredly
Thou mayest appeal for thy release 20
  To Fantasy.

To Fantasy pertains to choose:
All this I know, for Fantasy
First into love did me induce;
But yet I know as steadfastly 25
That if love have no faster knot
So nice a choice slips suddenly:
  It lasteth not.

It lasteth not that stands by change:
Fancy doth change, Fortune is frail; 30
Both these to please, the way is strange.
Therefore, methinks, best to prevail,
There is no way that is so just
As Truth to lead though t'other fail,
  And thereto trust. 35

100

Sometime I sigh, sometime I sing,
Sometime I laugh, sometime mourning
(As one in doubt) this is my saying:
Have I displeased you in anything?

Alack, what aileth you to be grieved? 5
Right sorry am I that ye be moved.
I am your own if truth be proved,
And by your displeasure as one mischieved.

When ye be merry, then am I glad;
When ye be sorry, then am I sad; 10
Such grace or fortune I would I had
You for to please however I were bestad.

When ye be merry why should I care?
Ye are my joy and my welfare.

I will you love, I will not spare 15
Into your presence as far as I dare.

All my poor heart and my love true
While life doth last I give it you,
And you to serve with service due
And never to change you for no new. 20

101

So unwarely was never no man caught
With steadfast look upon a goodly face
As I of late; for suddenly methought
My heart was torn out of his place.

Thorough mine eye the stroke from hers did slide: 5
Directly down unto my heart it ran,
In help whereof the blood thereto did glide
And left my face both pale and wan.

Then was I like a man for woe amazed
Or like the bird that flyeth into fire; 10
For while that I upon her beauty gazed
The more I burnt in my desire.

Anon the blood start in my face again,
Inflamed with heat that it had at my heart,
And brought therewith throughout in every vein 15
A quaking heat with pleasant smart.

Then was I like the straw when that the flame
Is driven therein by force and rage of wind:
I cannot tell, alas, what I shall blame
Nor what to seek nor what to find. 20

But well I wot the grief holds me so sore
In heat and cold, betwixt hope and dread,
That but her help to health doth me restore,
The restless life I may not lead.

102

Sufficed not, madame, that you did tear
My woeful heart; but thus also to rent
The weeping paper that to you I sent
Whereof each letter was written with a tear:

Could not my present pains, alas, suffice   5
Your greedy heart, and that my heart doth feel
Torments that prick more sharper than the steel,
But new and new must to my lot arise?

Use then my death: so shall your cruelty,
Spite of your spite, rid me from all my smart,   10
And I no more such torments of the heart
Feel as I do. This shalt thou gain thereby.

103

Pass forth, my wonted cries,
Those cruel ears to pierce,
Which in most hateful wise
Doth still my plaints reverse;
Do you, my tears, also   5
So wet her barren heart
That Pity there may grow
And Cruelty depart.

For though hard rocks among
She seems to have been bred,   10
And with tigers full long
Been nourished and fed,
Yet shall that nature change
If Pity once win place,
Whom as unknown and strange   15
She now away doth chase.

And as the water soft
Without forcing of strength
Where that it falleth oft
Hard stones doth pierce at length,   20
So in her stony heart
My plaints at length shall grave,
And rigour set apart,
Cause her grant that I crave.

Wherefore, my plaints, present   25
Still so to her my suit
As it (through her assent)
May bring to me some fruit.
And as she shall me prove,
So bid her me regard   30

And render love for love,
Which is a just reward.

104

Absence absenting causeth me to complain,
My sorrowful complaints abiding in distress,
And departing most privy increaseth my pain:
Thus live I uncomforted, wrapped all in heaviness.

In heaviness I am wrapped, devoid of all solace;   5
Neither pastime nor pleasure can revive my dull wit;
My sprites be all taken and Death doth me menace
With his fatal knife the thread for to kit.

For to kit the thread of this wretched life
And shortly bring me out of this case: 10
I see it availeth not; yet must I be pensive
Since Fortune from me hath turned her face.

Her face she hath turned with countenance contrarious
And clean from her presence she hath exiled me,
In sorrow remaining as a man most dolorous,   15
Exempt from all pleasure and worldly felicity.

All worldly felicity now am I private
And left in desert most solitarily,
Wandering all about as one without mate:
My death approacheth; alas, what remedy?   20

What remedy, alas, to rejoice my woeful heart,
With sighs suspiring most ruefully?
Now welcome! I am ready to depart:
Farewell all pleasure; welcome pain and smart.

105

Farewell, all my welfare,
My shoe is trod awry.
Now may I cark and care
To sing lullay-by-by.
Alas, what shall I do thereto?   5
There is no shift to help me now.

Who made it such offence
To love for love again?
God wot that my pretence

Was but to ease his pain,   10
For I had ruth to see his woe:
Alas, more fool, why did I so?

For he from me is gone
And makes thereat a game,
And hath left me alone   15
To suffer sorrow and shame.
Alas, he is unkind, doubtless,
To leave me thus all comfortless.

It is a grievous smart
To suffer pains and sorrow,   20
But most grieved my heart
He laid his faith to borrow;
And falsed hath his faith and truth,
And he forsworn by many an oath.

All ye lovers, perdie,   25
Hath cause to blame his deed
Which shall example be
To let you of your speed:
Let never seely woman again
Trust to such words as men can feign.   30

For I unto my cost
Am warning to you all
That they whom you trust most
Soonest deceive you shall.
But complaint cannot redress   35
Of my great grief the great excess.

106

If thou wilt mighty be, flee from the rage
Of cruel will and see thou keep thee free
From the foul yoke of sensual bondage;
For though thy empire stretch to Indian sea
And for thy fear trembleth the farthest Thulee,   5
If thy desire have over thee the power,
Subject then art thou, and no governor.

If to be noble and high thy mind be moved,
Consider well thy ground and thy beginning;
For he that hath each star in heaven fixed   10
And gives the Moon her horns and her eclipsing,

Alike hath made thee noble in his working,
So that wretched no way thou may be
Except foul Lust and Vice do conquer thee.

All were it so thou had a flood of gold,   15
Unto thy thirst yet should it not suffice;
And though with Indian stones a thousand fold
More precious than can thyself devise
Ycharged were thy back, thy covetise
And busy biting yet should never let   20
Thy wretched life, ne do thy death profit.

107

Alone, musing,
Remembering
The woeful life that I do lead,
Then sore sighing,
I lie crying   5
As one for pain near dead.

The unkindness
Of my mistress
In great distress hath me brought;
Yet disdaineth she   10
To take pity,
And setteth my heart right nought.

Who would have thought
She would have wrought
Such sorrow unto my heart,   15
Seeing that I
Endeavoured me
From her never to depart?

108

Absence, alas,
Causeth me pass
From all solace
To great grievance;
Yet though that I   5
Absent must be
I trust that she
Hath remembrance.

Where I her find
Loving and kind,   10
There my poor mind
Eased shall be.
And for my part,
My love and heart
Shall not revert   15
Though I should die.

Beauty, Pleasure,
Riches, treasure,
Or to endure
In prison strong   20
Shall not me make
Her to forsake
Though I should lack
Her never so long.

For once trust I,   25
Ere that I die,
For to espy
The happy hour,
At liberty
With her to be   30
That pities me
In this dolour.

109

Horrible of hue, hideous to behold,
Care-full of countenance, his hair all clustered,
With dead droppy blood that down his face rolled,
Pale, painful, and piteously pierced,
His heart in sunder sorrowfully shivered,   5
Methought a man, thus marvellously murdered,
This night to me came and care-fully cried:

'O man misfortunate, more than any creature,
That painfully yet lives more pain to perceive,
What hardened hath thy heart this harm to suffer?   10
Thy doubtful hope, it do thee but deceive:
No good nor grace to glad thee shalt receive.
By pain from thy pain then pain to procure,
More bitter it were than Death to endure.

'Follow me,' saith he, 'hold here my hand.   15
Too long is Death in tears to groan:
The sea shall sooner quench the brand
Of the desire that hath thee thus undone
Or sooner send thee to a deadly swoon:
Hold in thy hand the haft here of this knife   20
And with the blade boldly bereave thy life.

'Come off,' quod he. 'I come,' quod I;
Then therewith (as methought)
My breast I pierced painfully.
My heart right soon I it raught,   25
But, lord, alas, it was for nought,
For with that stroke I did awake:
My heart for sorrow yet feel I quake.

110

Iopas's Song [unfinished]

When Dido feasted first the wandering Trojan knight
Whom Juno's wrath with storms did force in Libyc sands to
    light,
That mighty Atlas did teach (the supper lasting long)
With crisped locks, on golden harp, Iopas sang in his song:
'That same,' quod he, 'that we the world do call and name,   5
Of heaven and earth with all contents it is the very frame,
Or thus: of heavenly powers, by more power kept in one;
Repugnant kinds, in mids of whom the earth hath place alone,
Firm, round, of living things the mother, place, and nurse,
Without the which in equal weight this heaven doth hold   10
    his course,
And it is called by name the first moving heaven.
The firmament is next, containing other seven:
Of heavenly powers that same is planted full and thick
As shining lights, which we call stars, that therein cleave and
    stick.
With great swift sway the first, and with his restless source   15
Carryeth itself and all those eight in even continual course;
And of this world so round within that rolling case
There be two points that never move, but firmly keep their
    place:
The t'one we see alway, the t'other stands object
Against the same, dividing just the round by line direct   20

Which by imagination drawn from t'one to t'other
Toucheth the centre of the earth: way there is none other.
And these been called the poles, described by stars not bright:
Arctic the t'one northward we see, Antarctic t'other hight.
The line that we devise from t'one to t'other so   25
As axle is upon the which the heavens about doth go,
Which of water nor earth, of air nor fire have kind:
Therefore the substance of those same were hard for man to
      find.
But they been uncorrupt, simple and pure, unmixed,
And so we say been all those stars that in those same been   30
      fixed,
And eke those erring seven in circles as they stray,
So called because against that first they have repugnant way
And smaller byways too, scant sensible to man –
Too busy work for my poor harp, let sing them he that can.
The widest (save the first) of all these nine above   35
One hundred year doth ask of space for one degree to move,
Of which degrees we make, in the first moving heaven,
Three hundred and three score in parts justly divided even.
And yet there is another between those heavens two
Whose moving is so sly, so slack, I name it not for now.   40
The seventh heaven, or the shell next to the starry sky,
All those degrees that gathereth up with aged pace so sly
And doth perform the same (as elders' count hath been)
In nine and twenty years complete and days almost sixteen,
Doth carry in his bout the star of Saturn old,   45
A threatener of all living things with drought and with his cold.
The sixth whom this contains doth stalk with younger pace,
And in twelve year doth somewhat more than t'other's voyage
      was;
And this in it doth bear the star of Jove benign,
'Tween Saturn's malice and us men friendly defending sign.   50
The fifth beareth bloody Mars that, in three hundred days
And twice eleven, with one full year hath finished all those
      ways.
A year doth ask the fourth, and hours thereto six,
And in the same the day his eye, the Sun, therein he sticks.
The third, that governed is by that that governeth me   55
And love for love and for no love provokes as oft we see,
In like space doth perform that course that did the t'other.
So doth the next to the same that second is in order,
But it doth bear the star that called is Mercury

That many a crafty secret step doth tread as calcars try.   60
That sky is last, and first next us, those ways hath gone
In seven and twenty common days and eke the third of one,
And beareth with his sway the diverse Moon about,
Now bright, now brown, now bent, now full, and now her
   light is out.
Thus have they of their own two movings all those seven: 65
One wherein they be carried still each in his several heaven,
Another of himselves where their bodies been led
In byways and in lesser rounds, as I afore have said:
Save, of them all, the Sun doth stray least from the straight;
The starry sky hath but one course, that we have called the   70
   eight.
And all these movings eight are meant from west to the east
Although they seem to climb aloft (I say) from east to west;
But that is but by force of the first moving sky
In twice twelve hours from east to the east that carrieth them
   by and by.
But mark we well also these movings of these seven   75
Be not about that axletree of the first moving heaven;
For they have their two poles directly t'one to t'other . . .'

HENRY HOWARD,
EARL OF SURREY

HENRY HOWARD, EARL OF SURREY

Dates: 1517(?)–47. The eldest child of the strongly Catholic Thomas Howard and Lady Elizabeth Stafford (daughter of the Duke of Buckingham), Surrey was born at Kenninghall Palace, Norfolk, and received the courtesy title Earl of Surrey when his paternal grandfather died in 1524 and his father assumed the title 3rd Duke of Norfolk.

In 1530 Surrey became companion and close friend of Henry VIII's young illegitimate son, Henry Fitzroy, Duke of Richmond, at Windsor, and in 1532, after marrying Lady Frances de Vere, daughter of the Earl of Oxford, he accompanied his first cousin Anne Boleyn, the king, and the Duke of Richmond to France, staying there for over a year as a member of the entourage of Francis I. 1536 saw the birth of his first son, Thomas, the execution of Anne Boleyn, the death of the Duke of Richmond (who was buried at one of the Howard homes, Thetford Abbey), and Surrey's service with his father against the Pilgrimage of Grace rebellion which protested against the king's dissolution of the monasteries. Surrey was suspected of being in sympathy with the rebels, and was imprisoned in 1537 at Windsor for striking Sir Edward Seymour, brother of Henry's new queen, Jane Seymour, after Seymour had repeated the charge within the precincts of Hampton Court. He was soon released, and led a relatively uneventful life until the king married Surrey's other first cousin, Catherine Howard (1540), whereupon Surrey was made Knight of the Garter (April, 1541).

After Catherine's execution in 1542, Surrey was again arrested, this time for challenging a courtier and, later the same year, fought in Scotland with his father. In 1543 he was imprisoned for riotous behaviour during Lent, then proceeded to the continent to fight with the Holy Roman Emperor, Charles V. In 1544 he started to build an Italianate renaissance palace at Mount Surrey, Norfolk (subsequently completely destroyed), and in 1545 served in France at the siege of Montreuil, eventually being put in charge of Boulogne. In 1546 he lost a minor battle at St Etienne, was recalled to England three months later (March), accused of treason, and beheaded on 19 January 1547.

SONNETS

1

The soote season, that bud and bloom forth brings,
With green hath clad the hill and eke the vale;
The nightingale, with feathers new, she sings,
And turtle to her make hath told her tale.
Summer is come, for every spray now springs;   5
The hart hath hung his old head on the pale;
The buck in brake his winter coat he flings;
The fishes fleet with new repaired scale;
The adder all her slough away she slings;
The swift swallow pursueth the flies small;   10
The busy bee her honey now she mings:
Winter is worn that was the flowers' bale.
And thus I see among these pleasant things
Each care decays, and yet my sorrow springs.

2

In Cyprus springs, whereas dame Venus dwelt,
A well so hot that, whoso tastes the same,
Were he of stone, as thawed ice should melt
And kindled find his breast with secret flame;
Whose moist poison dissolved hath my hate.   5
This creeping fire my cold limbs so oppressed
That in the heart that harboured freedom late
Endless despair long thraldom hath impressed.
One eke so cold in frozen ice is found
Whose chilling venom of repugnant kind   10
The fervent heat doth quench of Cupid's wound
And with the spot of change infects the mind,
Whereof my dear hath tasted to my pain:
My service thus is grown into disdain.

3

Alas, so all things now do hold their peace,
Heaven and earth disturbed in no thing:
The beasts, the air, the birds their song do cease;
The Night's chair the stars about doth bring.
Calm is the sea, the waves work less and less: 5
So am not I, whom love, alas, doth wring,

Bringing before my face the great increase
Of my desires, whereat I weep and sing
In joy and woe, as in a doubtful ease.
For my sweet thoughts sometime do pleasure bring,   10
But by and by the cause of my disease
Gives me a pang that inwardly doth sting,
When that I think what grief it is again
To live and lack the thing should rid my pain.

4

Love, that doth reign and live within my thought,
And built his seat within my captive breast,
Clad in the arms wherein with me he fought
Oft in my face he doth his banner rest.
But she that taught me love and suffer pain,   5
My doubtful hope and eke my hot desire
With shamefast look to shadow and refrain,
Her smiling grace converteth straight to ire.
And coward Love then to the heart apace
Taketh his flight, where he doth lurk and plain   10
His purpose lost, and dare not show his face.
For my lord's guilt thus faultless bide I pain,
Yet from my lord shall not my foot remove:
Sweet is the death that taketh end by love.

5

Set me whereas the Sun doth parch the green,
Or where his beams may not dissolve the ice;
In temperate heat where he is felt and seen;
With proud people, in presence sad and wise;
Set me in base, or yet in high degree;   5
In the long night, or in the shortest day;
In clear weather, or where mists thickest be;
In lost youth, or when my hairs be grey;
Set me in earth, in heaven, or yet in hell,
In hill, in dale, or in the foaming flood;   10
Thrall, or at large, alive whereso I dwell,
Sick, or in health, in ill fame or in good:
Yours will I be, and with that only thought
Comfort myself when that my hope is nought.

6

From Tuscan came my lady's worthy race:
Fair Florence was sometime her ancient seat;
The western isle, whose pleasant shore doth face
Wild Cambria's cliffs, did give her lively heat.
Fostered she was with milk of Irish breast;   5
Her sire an earl, her dame of prince's blood;
From tender years in Britain she doth rest
With a king's child, where she tastes ghostly food.
Hunsdon did first present her to mine eyen:
Bright is her hue, and Geraldine she hight;   10
Hampton me taught to wish her first for mine,
And Windsor, alas, doth chase me from her sight.
Beauty of kind, her virtues from above:
Happy is he that may obtain her love.

7

The golden gift that Nature did thee give,
To fasten friends and feed them at thy will
With form and favour, taught me to believe
How thou art made to show her greatest skill,
Whose hidden virtues are not so unknown   5
But lively dooms might gather at the first
Where Beauty so her perfect seed hath sown,
Of other graces follow needs there must.
Now certes, lady, since all this is true,
That from above thy gifts are thus elect,   10
Do not deface them then with fancies new,
Nor change of minds let not thy mind infect:
But mercy him thy friend that does thee serve,
Who seeks alway thine honour to preserve.

8

I never saw you, madame, lay apart
Your cornet black, in cold nor yet in heat,
Sith first you knew of my desire so great
Which other fancies chased clean from my heart.
Whiles to myself I did the thought reserve   5
That so unware did wound my woeful breast,
Pity I saw within your heart did rest;
But since ye knew I did you love and serve,

Your golden tress was clad alway in black,
Your smiling looks were hid thus evermore,   10
All that withdrawn that I did crave so sore.
So doth this cornet govern me alack,
In summer sun, in winter breath of frost;
Of your fair eyes whereby the light is lost.

9

The fancy (which that I have served long)
That hath alway been enemy to mine ease,
Seemed of late to rue upon my wrong,
And bade me fly the cause of my misease.
And I forthwith did press out of the throng,   5
That thought by flight my painful heart to please
Some other way, till I saw faith more strong.
And to myself I said: 'Alas, those days
In vain were spent, to run the race so long.'
And with that thought I met my guide, that plain   10
Out of the way wherein I wandered wrong
Brought me amidst the hills in base Boulogne:
Where I am now, as restless to remain,
Against my will, full pleased with my pain.

10

Brittle beauty, that Nature made so frail,
Whereof the gift is small, and short the season,
Flowering today, tomorrow apt to fail,
Tickle treasure, abhorred of reason,
Dangerous to deal with, vain, of none avail,   5
Costly in keeping, past not worth two peason,
Slipper in sliding as is an eel's tail,
Hard to obtain, once gotten not geason.
Jewel of jeopardy that peril doth assail
False and untrue, enticed oft to treason,   10
Enemy to youth: that most may I bewail.
Ah, bitter sweet, infecting as the poison,
Thou farest as fruit that with the frost is taken:
Today ready ripe, tomorrow all to — shaken.

11

When Windsor walls sustained my wearied arm,
My hand my chin, to ease my restless head,
Each pleasant spot revested green with warm:
The blossomed boughs with lusty Very spread,
The flowered meads, the wedded birds so late,   5
Mine eyes discovered. Then did to mind resort
The jolly woes, the hateless short debate,
The rakehell life that 'longs to love's disport.
Wherewith (alas) mine heavy charge of care
Heaped in my breast breaks forth against my will,   10
And smoky sighs that overcast the air:
My vapoured eyes such dreary tears distil
The tender spring to quicken where they fall,
And I half bent to throw me down withal.

12

The Assyrians' king in peace, with foul desire
And filthy lusts that stained his regal heart,
In war that should set princely hearts afire
Vanquished did yield for want of martial art.
The dint of swords from kisses seemed strange,   5
And harder than his lady's side his targe;
From glutton feasts to soldier's fare a change;
His helmet far above a garland's charge.
Who scarce the name of manhood did retain,
Drenched in sloth and womanish delight,   10
Feeble of spirit, impatient of pain,
When he had lost his honour and his right,
Proud time of wealth, in storms appalled with dread,
Murdered himself to show some manful deed.

13

Diverse thy death do diversely bemoan:
Some, that in presence of that lively head
Lurked, whose breasts Envy with hate had sown,
Yield Caesar's tears upon Pompeius' head;
Some, that watched with the murderer's knife,   5
With eager thirst to drink thy guiltless blood,
Whose practice brake by happy end of life,
Weep envious tears to hear thy fame so good.

But I, that knew what harboured in that head,
What virtues rare were tempered in that breast,   10
Honour the place that such a jewel bred,
And kiss the ground whereas thy corse doth rest
With vapoured eyes, from whence such streams avail
As Pyramus did on Thisbe's breast bewail.

14

The great Macedon that out of Persia chased
Darius, of whose huge power all Asia rang,
In the rich ark Dan Homer's rhymes he placed,
Who feigned gests of heathen princes sang.
What holy grave, what worthy sepulture,   5
To Wyatt's Psalms should Christians then purchase?
Where he doth paint the lively faith and pure,
The steadfast hope, the sweet return to grace
Of just David by perfect penitence;
Where rulers may see in a mirror clear   10
The bitter fruit of false concupiscence:
How Jewry bought Uriah's death full dear.
In princes' hearts God's scourge imprinted deep
Might them awake out of their sinful sleep.

15

Norfolk sprang thee, Lambeth holds thee dead,
Clere of the County of Cleremont though hight;
Within the womb of Ormonde's race thou bred,
And sawest thy cousin crowned in thy sight.
Shelton for love, Surrey for Lord thou chase   5
(Ay me, while life did last that league was tender)
Tracing whose steps thou sawest Kelsall blaze,
Laundersey burnt, and battered Bullen render:
At Muttrell gates, hopeless of all recure,
Thine Earl half dead gave in thy hand his will;   10
Which cause did thee this pining death procure,
Ere summers four times seven thou couldst fulfill.
Ah Clere, if love had booted, care, or cost,
Heaven had not won, nor Earth so timely lost.

SONGS AND ELEGIES

16

When raging love with extreme pain
Most cruelly distrains my heart;
When that my tears, as floods of rain,
Bear witness of my woeful smart;
When sighs have wasted so my breath   5
That I lie at the point of death:

I call to mind the navy great
That the Greeks brought to Troy town,
And how the boisterous winds did beat
Their ships, and rent their sails adown,   10
Till Agamemnon's daughter's blood
Appeased the gods that them withstood;

And how that in those ten years' war
Full many a bloody deed was done,
And many a lord that came full far   15
There caught his bane, alas, too soon,
And many a good knight overrun,
Before the Greeks had Helen won.

Then think I thus: 'Sith such repair,
So long time war of valiant men,   20
Was all to win a lady fair,
Shall I not learn to suffer then,
And think my life well spent to be
Serving a worthier wight than she?'

Therefore I never will repent,   25
But pains, contented, still endure:
For like as when, rough winter spent,
The pleasant spring straight draweth in ure,
So, after raging storms of care,
Joyful at length may be my fare.   30

17

Give place, ye lovers, here before
That spent your boasts and brags in vain:
My lady's beauty passeth more
The best of yours, I dare well sayen,

Than doth the sun the candle light,   5
Or brightest day the darkest night;

And therefore hath a troth as just
As had Penelope the fair,
For what she sayeth ye may it trust
As it by writing sealed were,   10
And virtues hath she many moe
Than I with pen have skill to show.

I could rehearse, if that I would,
The whole effect of Nature's plaint
When she had lost the perfect mould   15
(The like to whom she could not paint):
With wringing hands how she did cry,
And what she said, I know it, I.

I know she swore with raging mind,
Her kingdom only set apart,   20
There was no loss by law of kind
That could have gone so near her heart:
And this was chiefly all her pain,
She could not make the like again.

Sith Nature thus gave her the praise   25
To be the chiefest work she wrought,
In faith, methink some better ways
On your behalf might well be sought
Than to compare (as ye have done)
To match the candle with the sun.   30

18

Since Fortune's wrath envieth the wealth
Wherein I reigned, by the sight
Of that that fed mine eyes by stealth
With sour, sweet, dread and delight,
Let not my grief move you to moan,   5
For I will weep and wail alone.

Spite drave me into Boreas' reign
(Where hoary frosts the fruits do bite)
When hills were spread and every plain
With stormy winter's mantle white: 10
And yet, my dear, such was my heat,
When others freeze then did I sweat.

And now though on the Sun I drive,
Whose fervent flame all things decays,
His beams in brightness may not strive   15
With light of your sweet golden rays,
Nor from my breast this heat remove
The frozen thoughts graven by love.

Ne may the waves of the salt flood
Quench that your beauty set on fire;   20
For though mine eyes forbear the food
That did relieve the hot desire,
Such as I was such will I be,
Your own: what would ye more of me?

19

O happy dames, that may embrace
The fruit of your delight,
Help to bewail the woeful case
And eke the heavy plight
Of me, that wonted to rejoice   5
The fortune of my pleasant choice:
Good ladies, help to fill my mourning voice.

In ship, freight with rememberance
Of thoughts and pleasures past,
He sails, that hath in governance   10
My life, while it will last;
With scalding sighs, for lack of gale,
Furthering his hope, that is his sail
Toward me, the sweet port of his avail.

Alas, how oft in dreams I see   15
Those eyes that were my food,
Which sometime so delighted me
That yet they do me good;
Wherewith I wake with his return
Whose absent flames did make me burn: 20
But when I find the lack, Lord how I mourn.

When other lovers in arms across
Rejoice their chief delight,
Drowned in tears to mourn my loss
I stand the bitter night   25
In my window, where I may see

Before the winds how the clouds flee:
Lo, what a mariner Love hath made me!

And in green waves when the salt flood
Doth rise by rage of wind,   30
A thousand fancies in that mood
Assail my restless mind:
Alas, now drencheth my sweet foe,
That with the spoil of my heart did go,
And left me; but, alas, why did he so?   35

And when the seas wax calm again,
To chase from me annoy,
My doubtful hope doth cause me plain:
So dread cuts off my joy.
Thus is my wealth mingled with woe,   40
And of each thought a doubt doth grow:
Now he comes: will he come? Alas, no, no.

20

Good ladies, you that have your pleasure in exile,
Step in your foot, come take a place, and mourn with me
    awhile;
And such as by their lords do set but little price,
Let them sit still, it skills them not what chance come on the
    dice.
But you whom love hath bound, by order of desire,   5
To love your lords, whose good deserts none other
    would require,
Come you yet once again, and set your foot by mine,
Whose woeful plight, and sorrows great no tongue may well
    define.
My lord and love, alas, in whom consists my wealth,
Hath Fortune sent to pass the seas, in hazard of his health.   10
Whom I was wont t'embrace with well contented mind
Is now amid the foaming floods, at pleasure of the wind.
There God him well preserve, and safely me him send,
Without which hope my life, alas, were shortly at an end;
Whose absence yet (although my hope doth tell me plain   15
With short return he comes anon) yet ceaseth not my pain.
The fearful dreams I have, oft times they grieve me so
That then I wake, and stand in doubt if they be true or no;
Sometime the roaring seas me seems do grow so high,

That my sweet lord in danger great, alas, doth often lie;   20
Another time the same doth tell me he is come,
And playing, where I shall him find, with T. his little son;
So forth I go apace to see that lifesome sight,
And with a kiss methinks I say: 'Now welcome home, my
    knight;
Welcome, my sweet, alas, the stay of my welfare: 25
Thy presence bringeth forth a truce betwixt me and my care.'
Then lively doth he look, and salueth me again,
And saith: 'My dear, how is it now that you have all this pain?'
Wherewith the heavy cares that heaped are in my breast
Break forth and me discharge clean of all my great unrest.   30
But when I me awake, and find it but a dream,
The anguish of my former woe beginneth more extreme,
And me tormenteth so that unneath may I find
Some hidden where to steal the grief of my unquiet mind.
Thus every way you see with absence how I burn,   35
And for my wound no cure there is but hope of some return;
Save when I think by sour, how sweet is felt the more,
It doth abate some of my pains that I abode before;
And then unto my self I say: 'When that we two shall meet,
But little time shall seem this pain, that joy shall be so sweet.' 40
Ye winds, I ye conjure, in chiefest of your rage,
That you my lord me safely send, my sorrows to assuage;
And that I may not long abide in such excess,
Do your good will to cure a wight that liveth in distress.

21

When Summer took in hand the Winter to assail
With force of might and virtue great his stormy blasts to quail,
And when he clothed fair the Earth about with green,
And every tree new garmented, that pleasure was to seen,
Mine heart gan new revive, and changed blood did stir   5
Me to withdraw my winter woe that kept within the door.
'Abroad,' quod my desire, 'assay to set thy foot
Where thou shalt find a savour sweet, for sprung is every root;
And to thy health, if thou were sick in any case,
Nothing more good than in the spring the air to feel a space. 10
There shalt thou hear and see all kinds of birds ywrought
Well tune their voice with warble small, as Nature hath them
    taught.'
Thus pricked me my lust the sluggish house to leave,

And for my health I thought it best such counsel to receive.
So on a morrow forth, unwist of any wight,   15
I went to prove how well it would my heavy burden light.
And when I felt the air so pleasant round about,
Lord, to myself how glad I was that I had gotten out!
There might I see how Ver had every blossom hent,
And eke the new betrothed birds ycoupled how they went.   20
And in their songs methought they thanked Nature much
That by her licence all that year to love, their hap was such,
Right as they could devise to choose them feres throughout;
With much rejoicing to their lord thus flew they all about.
Which when I gan resolve, and in my head conceive,   25
What pleasant life, what heaps of joy, these little birds receive,
And saw in what estate I, weary man, was brought
By want of that they had at will, and I reject at nought:
Lord, how I gan in wrath unwisely me demean!
I cursed Love, and him defied: I thought to turn the stream.   30
But when I well beheld he had me under awe
I asked mercy for my fault that so transgressed his law:
'Thou blinded god,' quod I, 'forgive me this offence:
Unwittingly I went about to malice thy pretence.'
Wherewith he gave a beck, and thus methought he swore: 35
'Thy sorrow ought suffice to purge thy fault, if it were more.'
The virtue of which sound mine heart did so revive
That I (methought) was made as whole as any man alive.
But here I may perceive mine error, all and some,
For that I thought that so it was, yet was it still undone;   40
And all that was no more but mine empressed mind,
That faint would have some good relief of Cupid well assigned.
I turned home forthwith, and might perceive it well
That he aggrieved was right sore with me for my rebell.
My harms have ever since increased more and more,   45
And I remain, without his help, undone for evermore.
A mirror let me be unto ye lovers all:
Strive not with Love, for if ye do, it will ye thus befall.

22

In Winter's just return, when Boreas 'gan his reign,
And every tree unclothed fast, as Nature taught them plain,
In misty morning dark, as sheep are then in hold,
I hied me fast, it sat me on, my sheep for to unfold.
And as it is a thing that lovers have by fits,   5

Under a palm I heard one cry as he had lost his wits,
Whose voice did ring so shrill in uttering of his plaint,
That I amazed was to hear how Love could him attaint.
'Ah, wretched man,' quod he, 'come, Death, and rid this woe:
A just reward, a happy end, if it may chance thee so.   10
Thy pleasures past have wrought thy woe without redress;
If thou hadst never felt no joy, thy smart had been the less.'
And, reckless of his life, he gan both sigh and groan:
A rueful thing methought it was to hear him make such moan.
'Thou cursed pen,' said he, 'woe worth the bird thee bare: 15
The man, the knife, and all that made thee, woe be to
     their share.
Woe worth the time and place where I so could indite,
And woe be it yet once again, the pen that so can write.
Unhappy hand, it had been happy time for me
If, when to write thou learned first, unjointed hadst thou be.' 20
Thus cursed he himself, and every other wight,
Save her alone whom Love him bound to serve both day and
     night.
Which when I heard (and saw) how he himself fordid,
Against the ground with bloody strokes himself even there to
     rid,
Had been my heart of flint, it must have melted tho;   25
For in my life I never saw a man so full of woe.
With tears for his redress I rashly to him ran,
And in my arms I caught him fast, and thus I spake him than:
'What woeful wight art thou, that in such heavy case
Torments thyself with such despite, here in this desert place?' 30
Wherewith, as all aghast, fulfilled with ire and dread,
He cast on me a staring look, with colour pale and dead:
'Nay, what art thou,' quoth he, 'that in this heavy plight
Dost find me here, most woeful wretch, that life hath in despite?'
'I am,' quoth I, 'but poor, and simple in degree: 35
A shepherd's charge I have in hand, unworthy though I be.'
With that he gave a sigh, as though the sky should fall,
And loud (alas) he shrieked oft, and 'Shepherd' gan he call,
'Come, hie thee fast at once, and print it in thy heart,
So thou shalt know, and I shall tell thee, guiltless how
     I smart.'   40
His back against the tree, sore feebled all with faint,
With weary sprite he stretched him up, and thus he told his
     plaint:
'Once in my heart,' quoth he, 'it chanced me to love

Such one in whom hath Nature wrought, her cunning for to
    prove.
And sure I cannot say, but many years were spent   45
With such good will so recompensed, as both we were content.
Whereto then I me bound, and she likewise also,
The Sun should run his course awry ere we this faith forgo.
Who joyed then but I? who had this worldes bliss?
Who might compare a life to mine, that never thought   50
    on this?
But dwelling in this truth, amid my greatest joy,
Is me befallen a greater loss than Priam had of Troy.
She is reversed clean, and beareth me in hand
That my deserts have given her cause to break this faithful
    band,
And for my just excuse availeth no defence.   55
Now knowest thou all; I can no more. But, Shepherd, hie
    thee hence,
And give him leave to die that may no longer live:
Whose record, lo, I claim to have, my death I do forgive.
And eke, when I am gone, be bold to speak it plain,
Thou hast seen die the truest man that ever love did pain.'   60
Wherewith he turned him round, and gasping oft for breath,
Into his arms a tree he raught, and said, 'Welcome my death!
Welcome a thousandfold, now dearer unto me
Than should, without her love to live, an emperor to be.'
Thus in this woeful state he yielded up the ghost,   65
And little knoweth his lady what a lover she hath lost.
Whose death when I beheld, no marvel was it (right
For pity though my heart did bleed) to see so piteous sight.
My blood from heat to cold oft changed wondrous sore:
A thousand troubles there I found I never knew before.   70
'Tween dread and dolour so my sprites were brought in fear,
That long it was ere I could call to mind what I did there.
But as each thing hath end, so had these pains of mine:
The Furies passed, and I my wits restored by length of time.
Then as I could devise, to seek I thought it best   75
Where I might find some worthy place for such a corse to rest.
And in my mind it came, from thence not far away
Where Cressid's love, king Priam's son, the worthy Troilus lay.
By him I made his tomb, in token he was true,
And as to him belonged well, I covered it with blue.   80
Whose soul by angel's power departed not so soon
But to the heavens, lo, it fled, for to receive his doom.

23

Too dearly had I bought my green and youthful years
If, in mine age, I could not find when craft for love appears;
And seldom though I come in court among the rest,
Yet can I judge in colours dim as deep as can the best.
Where grief torments the man that suffereth secret smart,   5
To break it forth unto some friend it easeth well the heart;
So stands it now with me for my beloved friend:
This case is thine for whom I feel such torment of my mind,
And for thy sake I burn so in my secret breast
That till thou know my whole disease my heart can   10
    have no rest.
I see how thine abuse hath wrested so thy wits
That all it yields to thy desire, and follows thee by fits.
Where thou hast loved so long, with heart and all thy power,
I see thee fed with feignèd words, thy freedom to devour.
I know (though she say nay, and would it well withstand)   15
When in her grace thou held thee most, she bare thee but in
    in hand.
I see her pleasant cheer in chiefest of thy suit;
When thou art gone I see him come that gathers up the fruit.
And eke in thy respect I see the base degree
Of him to whom she gave the heart that promised was   20
    to thee.
I see (what would you more?) stood never man so sure
On woman's word, but wisdom would mistrust it to endure.

24

If Care do cause men cry, why do not I complain?
If each man do bewail his woe, why show not I my pain?
Since that amongst them all I dare well say is none
So far from weal, so full of woe, or hath more cause to moan.
For all things having life sometime have quiet rest: 5
The bearing ass, the drawing ox, and every other beast,
The peasant and the post, that serve at all assays,
The ship-boy and the galley-slave, have time to take their ease,
Save I, alas, whom Care of force doth so constrain
To wail the day and wake the night continually in pain,   10
From pensiveness to plaint, from plaint to bitter tears,
From tears to painful plaint again; and thus my life it wears.
No thing under the sun that I can hear or see
But moveth me for to bewail my cruel destiny.

For where men do rejoice, since that I cannot so, 15
I take no pleasure in that place, it doubleth but my woe.
And when I hear the sound of song or instrument,
Methink each tune there doleful is and helps me to lament.
And if I see some have their most desired sight,
Alas, think I, each man hath weal save I, most woeful wight! 20
Then, as the stricken deer withdraws himself alone,
So do I seek some secret place where I may make my moan.
There do my flowing eyes show forth my melting heart,
So that the streams of those two wells right well declare my
    smart;
And in those cares so cold I force myself a heat 25
(As sick men in their shaking fits procure themselves to sweat)
With thoughts that for the time do much appease my pain;
But yet they cause a farther fear, and breed my woe again:
Methink within my thought I see right plain appear
My heart's delight, my sorrow's leech, mine earthly 30
    goddess here,
With every sundry grace that I have seen her have.
Thus I within my woeful breast her picture paint and grave,
And in my thought I roll her beauties to and fro:
Her laughing cheer; her lively look; my heart that pierced so;
Her strangeness when I sued her servant for to be; 35
And what she said, and how she smiled, when that she
    pitied me.
Then comes a sudden fear, that riveth all my rest,
Lest absence cause forgetfulness to sink within her breast:
For when I think how far this earth doth us divide,
Alas, meseems Love throws me down; I feel how that I slide. 40
But then I think again, why should I thus mistrust
So sweet a wight, so sad and wise, that is so true and just?
For loth she was to love, and wavering is she not;
The farther off the more desired: thus lovers tie their knot.
So in despair and hope plunged am I both up and down, 45
As is the ship with wind and wave when Neptune list to frown.
But as the watery showers delay the raging wind,
So doth Good Hope clean put away Despair out of my mind
And bids me for to serve and suffer patiently,
For what wot I the after weal that Fortune wills to me? 50
For those that care do know and tasted have of trouble,
When passed is their woeful pain each joy shall seem them
    double,
And bitter sends she now, to make me taste the better

The pleasant sweet when that it comes, to make it seem the
   sweeter.
And so determine I to serve until my death;   55
Yea, rather die a thousand times than once to false my faith.
And if my feeble corpse through weight of woeful smart
Do fail or faint, my will it is that still she keep my heart.
And when this carcass here to earth shall be refared,
I do bequeath my wearied ghost to serve her afterward.   60

25

Wrapped in my careless cloak, as I walk to and fro,
I see how Love can show what force there reigneth in his bow;
And how he shooteth eke a hardy heart to wound;
And where he glanceth by again, that little hurt is found.
For seldom it is seen he woundeth hearts alike: 5
The one may rage when t'other's love is often far to seek.
All this I see, with more; and wonder thinketh me
How he can strike the one so sore, and leave the other free.
I see that wounded wight that suffereth all this wrong,
How he is fed with yeas and nays, and liveth all too long.   10
In silence though I keep such secrets to myself,
Yet do I see how she sometimes doth yield a look by stealth,
As though it seemed, 'Iwis, I will not lose thee so,'
When in her heart so sweet a thought did never truly grow.
Then say I thus: Alas, that man is far from bliss   15
That doth receive for his relief none other gain but this.
And she that feeds him so (I feel and find it plain)
Is but to glory in her power that over such can reign.
Nor are such graces spent but when she thinks that he,
A wearied man, is fully bent such fancies to let flee.   20
Then, to retain him still, she wrasteth new her grace,
And smileth, lo, as though she would forthwith the
   man embrace.
But when the proof is made to try such looks withal,
He findeth then the place all void, and freighted full of gall.
Lord, what abuse is this! Who can such women praise   25
That for their glory do devise to use such crafty ways?
I, that among the rest do sit and mark the row,
Find that in her is greater craft than is in twenty moe:
When tender years, alas, with wiles so well are sped,
What will she do when hoary hairs are powdered in
   her head?'   30

26

Girt in my guiltless gown, as I sit here and sew,
I see that things are not indeed as to the outward show.
And whoso list to look, and note things somewhat near,
Shall find, where plainness seems to haunt, nothing but craft
    appear.
For with indifferent eyes myself can well discern   5
How some to guide a ship in storms stick not to take the stern
Whose skill and cunning tried in calm to steer a barge
(They would soon show, you should soon see) it were too great
    a charge.
And some I see again sit still and say but small
That can do ten times more than they say they can do all;   10
Whose goodly gifts are such, the more they understand
The more they seek to learn and know and take less charge in
    hand.
And, to declare more plain, the time flits not so fast
But I can bear right well in mind the song now sung and past,
The author whereof came, wrapped in a crafty cloak,   15
In will to force a flaming fire where he could raise no smoke.
If power and will had met, as it appeareth plain,
The truth nor right had ta'en no place, their virtues had been
    vain.
So that you may perceive, and I may safely see,
The innocent that guiltless is condemned should have be.   20
Much like untruth to this the story did declare,
Where the elders laid to Susan's charge meet matter to
    compare.
They did her both accuse, and eke condemn her too,
And yet no reason, right nor truth did lead them so to do.
And she, thus judged to die, toward her death went forth   25
Fraughted with faith, a patient pace, taking her wrong in
    worth.
But He that doth defend all those that in him trust,
Did raise a Childe for her defence to shield her from the unjust.
And Daniel chosen was then of this wrong to weet
How, in what place, and eke with whom, she did this crime   30
commit.
He caused the elders part the one from the other's sight,
And did examine one by one and charged them both say right.
'Under a mulberry tree it was,' first said the one;

The next named a pomegranate tree, whereby the truth was
  known.
Then Susan was discharged, and they condemned to die,   35
As right requires and they deserve that framed so foul a lie.
And He that her preserved, and let them of their lust,
Hath me defended hitherto, and will do still I trust.

27

The Sun hath twice brought forth the tender green
And clad the earth in lively lustiness;
Once have the winds the trees despoiled clean,
And now again begins their cruelness,
Since I have hid under my breast the harm   5
That never shall recover healthfulness.
The Winter's hurt recovers with the warm;
The parched green restored is with shade:
What warmth, alas, may serve for to disarm
The frozen heart that mine in flame hath made?   10
What cold again is able to restore
My fresh green years that wither thus and fade?
Alas, I see nothing hath hurt so sore
But Time sometime reduceth a return:
Yet Time my harm increaseth more and more,   15
And seems to have my cure always in scorn.
Strange kind of death in life that I do try,
At hand to melt, far off in flame to burn;
And like as Time list to my cure apply,
So doth each place my comfort clean refuse.   20
Each thing alive that seeth the heaven with eye
With cloak of night may cover and excuse
Himself from travail of the day's unrest,
Save I (alas) against all others use,
That then stir up the torment of my breast   25
To curse each star as causer of my fate.
And when the Sun hath eke the dark repressed
And brought the day, it doth nothing abate
The travail of my endless smart and pain.
For then (as one that hath the light in hate)   30
I wish for night, more covertly to plain,
And me withdraw from every haunted place
Lest in my cheer my chance should 'pear too plain;
And in my mind I measure, pace by pace,

To seek the place where I my self had lost   35
That day that I was tangled in that lace
In seeming slack that knitteth ever most.
But never yet the travail of my thought
Of better state could catch a cause to boast;
For if I find sometime that I have sought   40
Those stars by whom I trusted of the port,
My sails do fall, and I advance right nought,
As anchored fast; my spirits do all resort
To stand aghast and sink in more and more
The deadly harm which she doth take in sport.   45
Lo, if I seek, how I do find my sore!
And if I fly, I carry with me still
The venomed shaft which doth his force restore
By haste of flight. And I may plain my fill
Unto my self, unless this care-full song   50
Print in your heart some parcel of my will:
For I, alas, in silence all too long
Of mine old hurt yet feel the wound but green.
Rue on my life, or else your cruel wrong
Shall well appear, and by my death be seen.   55

28

Such wayward ways hath Love, that most part in discord
Our wills do stand, whereby our hearts but seldom do accord.
Deceit is his delight, and to beguile and mock
The simple hearts which he doth strike with froward, diverse
   stroke.
He makes the one to rage with golden burning dart,   5
And doth allay with leaden cold again the other's heart.
Hot gleams of burning fire and easy sparks of flame
In balance of unequal weight he pondereth by aim.
From easy ford, where I might wade and pass full well,
He me withdraws, and doth me drive into the deep dark   10
   hell;
And me withholds where I am called and offered place,
And wills me that my mortal foe I do beseech of grace.
He lets me to pursue a conquest well near won,
To follow where my pains were lost ere that my suit begun.
Lo, by these rules I know how soon a heart can turn   15
From war to peace, from truce to strife, and so again return:
I know how to convert my will in other's lust;
Of little stuff unto my self to weave a web of trust;

And how to hide my harm with soft, dissembled cheer,
When in my face the painted thoughts would outwardly   20
  appear.
I know how that the blood forsakes the face for dread,
And how by shame it stains again the cheek with flaming red;
I know under the green the serpent how he lurks;
The hammer of the restless forge I know eke how it works;
I know, and can by rote, the tale that I would tell   25
(But oft the words come forth awry of him that loveth well);
I know in heat and cold the lover how he shakes,
In singing how he can complain, in sleeping how he wakes
To languish without ache, sickless for to consume,
A thousand things for to devise resolving all in fume.   30
And though he list to see his lady's face full sore,
Such pleasures as delight his eye do not his health restore.
I know to seek the track of my desired foe,
And fear to find that I do seek. But chiefly this I know:
That lovers must transform into the thing beloved,   35
And live (alas, who could believe?) with sprite from life
  removed.
I know in hearty sighs and laughters of the spleen
At once to change my state, my will, and eke my colour clean;
I know how to deceive myself withouten help,
And how the lion chastised is by beating of the whelp.   40
In standing near my fire I know how that I freeze:
Far off I burn, in both I waste, and so my life I lese.
I know how love doth rage upon a yielding mind,
How small a net may take and mesh a hart of gentle kind;
Or else with seldom sweet to season heaps of gall,   45
Revived with a glimpse of grace old sorrows to let fall.
The hidden trains I know and secret snares of love;
How soon a look may print a thought that never will remove.
That slipper state I know, those sudden turns from wealth,
That doubtful hope, that certain woe, and sure despair of   50
  health.

29

Each beast can choose his fere according to his mind,
And eke can show a friendly cheer, like to their beastly kind.
A lion saw I late, as white as any snow,
Which seemed well to lead the race, his port the same did
  show.

Upon the gentle beast to gaze it pleased me, 5
For still methought he seemed well of noble blood to be.
And as he pranced before, still seeking for a make
(As who would say 'There is none here, I trow, will me
    forsake')
I might perceive a wolf as white as whalës bone;
A fairer beast of fresher hue beheld I never none, 10
Save that her looks were fierce and froward eke her grace:
Toward the which this gentle beast gan him advance apace,
And with a beck full low he bowed at her feet
In humble wise, as who would say 'I am too far unmeet'.
But such a scornful cheer wherewith she him rewarded 15
Was never seen, I trow, the like, to such as well deserved.
With that she start aside well near a foot or twain,
And unto him thus gan she say with spite and great disdain:
'Lion,' she said, 'if thou hadst known my mind beforn,
Thou hadst not spent thy travail thus, nor all thy pain 20
    forlorn.
Do way! I let thee weet thou shalt not play with me:
Go range about, where thou mayest find some meeter fere for
    thee.'
Forthwith he beat his tail, his eyes began to flame;
I might perceive his noble heart much moved by the same.
Yet saw I him refrain, and eke his wrath assuage, 25
And unto her thus gan he say, when he was past his rage:
'Cruel, you do me wrong to set me thus so light;
Without desert, for my good will, to show me such despite.
How can ye thus entreat a lion of the race,
That with his paws a crowned king devoured in the place, 30
Whose nature is to prey upon no simple food,
As long as he may suck the flesh and drink of noble blood?
If you be fair and fresh, am I not of your hue?
And for my vaunt I dare well say my blood is not untrue,
For you yourself have heard, it is not long ago 35
Since that, for love, one of the race did end his life in woe
In tower both strong and high, for his assured truth,
Whereas in tears he spent his breath, alas, the more the ruth.
This gentle beast likewise, whom nothing could remove,
But willingly to lose his life for loss of his true love. 40
Other there be whose life, to linger still in pain,
Against their will preserved is that would have died right fain.
But now I do perceive that nought it moveth you
My good intent, my gentle heart, nor yet my mind so true,

But that your will is such to lure me to the trade   45
As other some full many years to trace by craft you made.
And thus behold our kinds how that we differ far:
I seek my foes, and you your friends do threaten still with war:
I fawn where I am fed, you flee that seeks to you;
I can devour no yielding prey, you kill where you subdue;   50
My kind is to desire the honour of the field,
And you with blood to slake your thirst on such as to you
    yield:
Wherefore I would you wist, that for your coy looks
I am no man that will be trained nor tangled by such hooks.
And though some list to bow where blame full well they   55
    might,
And to such beasts a currant fawn that should have travail
    bright,
I will observe the law that Nature gave to me
To conquer such as will resist, and let the rest go free.
And as a falcon free, that soareth in the air,
Which never fed on hand or lure, that for no stale doth care, 60
While that I live and breathe such shall my custom be,
In wildness of the woods to seek my prey where pleaseth me;
Where many one shall rue that never made offence:
Thus your refuse against my power shall bode them no defence.
In the revenge whereof I vow and swear thereto   65
A thousand spoils I shall commit I never thought to do;
And if to light on you my hap so good shall be,
I shall be glad to feed on that that would have fed on me.
And thus farewell, unkind, to whom I bent too low:
I would you wist the ship is safe that bare his sail so low.   70
Since that a lion's heart is for a wolf no prey,
With bloody mouth go slake your thirst on simple sheep, I say,
With more despite and ire than I can now express,
Which to my pain though I refrain, the cause you well may
    guess:
As for because my self was author of this game,   75
It boots me not that, by my wrath, I should disturb the same.

30

O loathsome place, where I
Have seen and heard my dear,
When in my heart her eye
Hath made her thought appear,

By glimpsing with such grace   5
As Fortune it ne would
That lasten any space
Between us longer should.

As Fortune did advance
To further my desire,   10
Even so hath Fortune's chance
Thrown all amidst the mire;
And that I have deserved
With true and faithful heart
Is to his hands reserved   15
That never felt the smart.

But happy is that man
That 'scaped hath the grief
That Love well teach him can,
By wanting his relief.   20
A scourge to quiet minds
It is, who taketh heed,
A common plage that binds,
A travail without meed.

This gift it hath also: 25
Whoso enjoys it most,
A thousand troubles grow
To vex his wearied ghost.
And last it may not long –
The truest thing of all   30
(And sure the greatest wrong)
That is within this thrall.

But since thou, desert place,
Canst give me no account
Of my desired grace   35
That I to have was wont:
Farewell! Thou hast me taught
To think me not the first
That Love hath set aloft
And casten in the dust.   40

31

Laid in my quiet bed, in study as I were,
I saw within my troubled head a heap of thoughts appear.

And every thought did show so lively in mine eyes,
That now I sighed, and then I smiled, as cause of thought did
  rise:
I saw the little boy, in thought how oft that he   5
Did wish of God to 'scape the rod, a tall young man to be;
The young man, eke, that feels his bones with pains oppressed,
How he would be a rich old man, to live and lie at rest;
The rich old man, that sees his end draw on so sore,
How he would be a boy again, to live so much the more.   10
Whereat full oft I smiled, to see how all these three,
From boy to man, from man to boy, would chop and change
  degree.
And, musing thus, I think the case is very strange
That man from wealth to live in woe doth ever seek to change.
Thus thoughtful as I lay I saw my withered skin,   15
How it doth show my dinted jaws, the flesh was worn so thin.
And eke my toothless chaps, the gates of my right way
That opes and shuts as I do speak, do thus unto me say:
'Thy white and hoarish hairs, the messengers of age,
That show like lines of true belief that this life doth assuage, 20
Bid thee lay hand and feel them hanging on thy chin;
The which do write two ages past, the third now coming in.
Hang up therefore the bit of thy young wanton time,
And thou that therein beaten art, the happiest life define.'
Whereat I sighed and said: 'Farewell, my wonted joy;   25
Truss up thy pack, and trudge from me to every little boy,
And tell them thus from me, their time most happy is,
If, to their time, they reason had to know the truth of this.'

32

So cruel prison how could betide, alas,
  As proud Windsor, where I, in lust and joy,
With a king's son my childish years did pass,
  In greater feast than Priam's sons of Troy;

Where each sweet place returns a taste full sour: 5
  The large green courts, where we were wont to hove,
With eyes cast up unto the maidens' tower,
  And easy sighs, such as folk draw in love.

The stately sales; the ladies bright of hue;
  The dances short; long tales of great delight,   10
With words and looks that tigers could but rue,
  Where each of us did plead the other's right;

The palm play, where, despoiled for the game,
With dazed eyes oft we by gleams of love
Have missed the ball and got sight of our dame,   15
To bait her eyes which kept the leads above;

The gravelled ground, with sleeves tied on the helm,
On foaming horse, with swords and friendly hearts,
With cheer as though the one should overwhelm,
Where we have fought and chased oft with darts;   20

With silver drops the meads yet spread for ruth,
In active games of nimbleness and strength
Where we did strain, trailed by swarms of youth,
Our tender limbs, that yet shot up in length;

The secret groves, which oft we made resound   25
Of pleasant plaint and of our ladies' praise,
Recording soft what grace each one had found,
What hope of speed, what dread of long delays;

The wild forest, the clothed holts with green,
With reins availed and swift ybreathed horse,   30
With cry of hounds and merry blasts between,
Where we did chase the fearful hart a force;

The void walls eke, that harboured us each night,
Wherewith (alas) revive within my breast
The sweet accord, such sleeps as yet delight,   35
The pleasant dreams, the quiet bed of rest,

The secret thoughts imparted with such trust,
The wanton talk, the diverse change of play,
The friendship sworn, each promise kept so just,
Wherewith we passed the winter nights away.   40

And with this thought the blood forsakes my face,
The tears berain my cheek of deadly hue
The which, as soon as sobbing sighs, alas,
Upsupped have, thus I my plaint renew:

'O place of bliss, renewer of my woes,   45
Give me accompt where is my noble fere,
Whom in thy walls thou didst each night enclose,
To other lief, but unto me most dear.'

Echo, alas, that doth my sorrow rue,
Returns thereto a hollow sound of plaint.   50

Thus I, alone, where all my freedom grew,
In prison pine with bondage and restraint,

And with remembrance of the greater grief
To banish the less I find my chief relief.

33

W. resteth here, that quick could never rest;
Whose heavenly gifts increased by disdain
And virtue sank the deeper in his breast:
Such profit he by envy could obtain.

A head where Wisdom mysteries did frame;   5
Whose hammers beat still in that lively brain
As on a stithe, where that some work of fame
Was daily wrought, to turn to Britain's gain.

A visage stern and mild, where both did grow
Vice to contemn, in Virtue to rejoice;   10
Amid great storms, whom Grace assured so
To live upright, and smile at Fortune's choice.

A hand that taught what might be said in rhyme,
That reft Chaucer the glory of his wit;
A mark the which (unperfected for Time)   15
Some may approach but never none shall hit.

A tongue that served in foreign realms his king,
Whose courteous talk to Virtue did inflame
Each noble heart; a worthy guide to bring
Our English youth by travail unto Fame.   20

An eye whose judgment none affect could blind,
Friends to allure, and foes to reconcile;
Whose piercing look did represent a mind
With virtue fraught, reposed, void of guile.

A heart where dread was never so impressed   25
To hide the thought that might the truth advance;
In neither Fortune lost nor yet repressed,
To swell in wealth, or yield unto mischance.

A valiant corse where Force and Beauty met,
Happy – alas, too happy – but for foes;   30
Lived, and ran the race that Nature set;
Of manhood's shape, where she the mould did lose.

But to the heavens that simple soul is fled,
Which left, with such as covet Christ to know,
Witness of faith that never shall be dead;   35
Sent for our health, but not received so.

Thus, for our guilt, this jewel have we lost;
The earth his bones, the heavens possess his ghost.

ETHICAL AND RELIGIOUS POEMS

34

My Ratclif, when thy reckless youth offends,
Receive thy scourge by others' chastisement;
For such calling, when it works none amends,
Then plagues are sent without advertisement.
Yet Solomon said, the wronged shall recure;
But Wyatt said true, the scar doth aye endure.

35

Of thy life, Thomas, this compass well mark:
Not aye with full sails the high seas to beat,
Ne by coward dread, in shunning storms dark,
On shallow shores thy keel in peril freat.
Whoso gladly halseth the golden mean,   5
Void of dangers advisedly hath his home,
Not with loathsome muck as a den unclean,
Nor palace-like, whereat Disdain may glome.
The lofty pine the great wind often rives;
With violenter sway fallen turrets steep;   10
Lightnings assault the high mountains and clives.
A heart well stayed, in overthwartes deep
Hopeth amends; in sweet doth fear the sour.
God, that sendeth, withdraweth winter sharp:
Now ill, not aye thus. Once Phoebus to lower   15
With bow unbent shall cease, and frame to harp
His voice. In strait estate appear thou stout;
And so wisely, when lucky gale of wind
All thy puffed sails shall fill, look well about;
Take in a reef: haste is waste, proof doth find.   20

36

Martial, the things for to attain
The happy life be these, I find:
The riches left, not got with pain;
The fruitful ground; the quiet mind:
The equal friend; no grudge nor strife;   5
No charge of rule nor governance;
Without disease the healthful life;
The household of continuance:
The mean diet, no delicate fare;
Wisdom joined with simplicity;   10
The night discharged of all care,
Where wine may bear no sovereignty;
The chaste wife wise, without debate;
Such sleeps as may beguile the night;
Contented with thine own estate,   15
Neither wish Death nor fear his might.

37

London, hast thou accused me
Of breach of laws, the root of strife,
Within whose breast did boil to see
So fervent hot thy dissolute life,
That even the hate of sins, that grow   5
Within thy wicked walls so rife,
For to break forth did convert so
That terror could it not repress?
The which, by words since preachers know
What hope is left for to redress,   10
By unknown means it liked me
My hidden burden to express,
Whereby it might appear to thee
That secret sin hath secret spite.
From Justice rod no fault is free;   15
But that all such as work unright
In most quiet are next ill rest.
In secret silence of the night
This made me (with a reckless breast)
To wake thy sluggards with my bow: 20
A figure of the Lord's behest,
Whose scourge for sin the Scriptures show;
That, as the fearless thunderclap

By sudden flame at hand we know,
Of pebble stones the soundless rap   25
The dreadful plague might make thee see
Of God's wrath, that doth thee enwrap;
That Pride might know (from conscience free)
How lofty works may her defend;
And Envy find, as he hath sought,   30
How others seek him to offend;
And Wrath taste of each cruel thought
The just shape higher in the end;
And idle Sloth, that never wrought,
To heaven his spirit lift may begin;   35
And greedy Lucre live in dread
To see what hate ill got goods win;
The lechers, ye that Lust do feed,
Perceive what secrecy is in sin;
And gluttons' hearts for sorrow bleed,   40
Awakened when their fault they find.
In loathsome vice each drunken wight
To stir to God: this was my mind.
Thy windows had done me no spite,
But proud people that dread no fall,   45
Clothed with falsehood and unright,
Bred in the closures of thy wall.
But, wrested to wrath in fervent zeal,
Thou hast to strife my secret call:
Endured hearts no warning feel.   50
O shameless Whore! Is dread then gone
By such thy foes as meant thy weal?
Oh member of false Babylon,
The shop of craft, the den of ire:
Thy dreadful doom draws fast upon.   55
Thy martyrs' blood, by sword and fire,
In heaven and earth for justice call:
The Lord shall hear their just desire;
The flame of wrath shall on thee fall;
With famine and pest lamentably   60
Stricken shall be thy lechers all;
Thy proud towers and turrets high,
Enemies to God, beat stone from stone;
Thine idols burnt that wrought iniquity;
When none thy ruin shall bemoan,   65
But render unto the right wise Lord,

That so hath judged Babylon,
Immortal praise with one accord.

38

When reckless youth in an unquiet breast,
Set on by wrath, revenge and cruelty,
After long war patience had oppressed,
And justice wrought by princely equity:
My Denny, then mine error, deep impressed   5
Began to work despair of liberty,
Had not David, the perfect warrior, taught
That of my fault thus pardon should be sought.

39

Psalm 88

Oh Lord upon whose will dependeth my welfare,
To call upon thy holy name since day nor night I spare,
Grant that the just request of this repentant mind
So pierce thine ears that in thy sight some favour it may find.
My soul is fraughted full with grief of follies past,   5
My restless body doth consume and death approacheth fast,
Like them whose fatal thread thy hand hath cut in twain,
Of whom there is no further bruit, which in their graves
  remain.
Oh Lord, thou hast cast me headlong to please my foe,
Into a pit all bottomless, whereas I plain my woe: 10
The burden of thy wrath it doth me sore oppress,
And sundry storms thou hast me sent of terror and distress.
The faithful friends are fled and banished from my sight,
And such as I have held full dear have set my friendship light;
My durance doth persuade of freedom such despair   15
That (by the tears that bain my breast) mine eyesight doth
  appair.
Yet did I never cease thine aid for to desire,
With humble heart and stretched hands for to appease thy ire.
Wherefore dost thou forbear, in the defence of thine,
To show such tokens of thy power, in sight of Adam's line,   20
Whereby each feeble heart with Faith might so be fed
That in the mouth of thy elect thy mercies might be spread?
The flesh that feedeth worms cannot thy love declare,
Nor such set forth thy Faith as dwell in the land of Despair.

In blind endured hearts light of thy lively name   25
Cannot appear, as cannot judge the brightness of the same;
Nor blasted may thy name be by the mouth of those
Whom Death has shut in silence, so as they may not disclose.
The lively voice of them that in thy word delight
Must be the trump that must resound the glory of thy might: 30
Wherefore I shall not cease, in chief of my distress,
To call on thee till that the sleep my wearied limbs oppress;
And in the morning eke (when that the sleep is fled)
With floods of salt repentant tears to wash my restless bed.
Within this care-full mind, burdened with care and grief,   35
Why dost thou not appear, Oh Lord, that shouldest be his
    relief?
My wretched state behold, whom Death shall straight assail,
Of one from youth afflicted still, that never did but wail.
The dread, lo, of thine ire hath trod me under feet;
The scourges of thine angry hand hath made Death seem   40
    full sweet:
Like to the roaring waves the sunken ship surround,
Great heaps of care did swallow me and I no succour found;
For they whom no mischance could from my love divide
Are forced, for my greater grief, from me their face to hide.

40

The sudden storms that heave me to and fro
Had well near pierced Faith, my guiding sail,
For I, that on the noble voyage go
To succour Truth, and Falsehood to assail,
Constrained am to bear my sails full low   5
And never could attain some pleasant gale;
For unto such the prosperous winds do blow
As run from port to port to seek avail.
This bred Despair, whereof such doubts did grow
That I gan faint, and all my courage fail: 10
But now, my Blage, mine error well I see:
Such goodly light King David giveth me.

41

The storms are past, these clouds are overblown,
And humble cheer great rigour hath repressed.
For the default is set a pain foreknown,
And patience graft in a determined breast.

And in the heart where heaps of grief were grown 5
The sweet revenge hath planted mirth and rest;
No company so pleasant as mine own.
. . . .
Thraldom at large hath made this prison free;
Danger well past, remembered, works delight. 10
Of lingering doubts such hope is sprung pardie,
That nought I find displeasant in my sight;
But when my glass presenteth unto me
The cureless wound that bleedeth day and night,
To think, alas, such hap should granted be 15
Unto a wretch that hath no heart to fight,
To spill that blood that hath so oft been shed
For Britain's sake, alas, and now is dead.

42

Translations from the *Aeneid*, Books 2 and 4

Book 2 *(lines 1–44; 340–428; 681–828; 966–1068)*

They whisted all, with fixed face attent,
When prince Aeneas from the royal seat
Thus gan to speak: O Queen, it is thy will
I should renew a woe cannot be told,
How that the Greeks did spoil and overthrow 5
The Phrygian wealth and wailful realm of Troy,
Those ruthful things that I myself beheld,
And whereof no small part fell to my share:
Which to express, who could refrain from tears?
What Myrmidon? or yet what Dolopes? 10
What stern Ulysses' waged soldier?
And lo, moist night now from the welkin falls,
And stars declining counsel us to rest.
But since so great is thy delight to hear
Of our mishaps and Troyès last decay 15
(Though to record the same my mind abhors
And plaint eschews) yet thus will I begin:
   The Greeks' chieftain, all irked with the war
Wherein they wasted had so many years
And oft repulsed by fatal Destiny, 20
A huge horse made, high raised like a hill,
By the divine science of Minerva
(Of cloven fir compacted were his ribs)

For their return a fained sacrifice:
The fame whereof so wandered it at point.   25
In the dark bulk they closed bodies of men
Chosen by lot, and did enstuff by stealth
The hollow womb with armed soldiers.

   There stands in sight an isle, hight Tenedon,
Rich and of fame while Priam's kingdom stood: 30
Now but a bay, and road unsure for ship.
Hither them secretly the Greeks withdrew,
Shrouding themselves under the desert shore.
And, weening we they had been fled and gone
And with that wind had fet the land of Greece,   35
Troyè discharged her long continued dole:
The gates cast up, we issued out to play,
The Greekish camp desirous to behold,
The places void, and the forsaken coasts:
Here Pyrrhus' band; there fierce Achilles pight;   40
Here rode their ships; there did their battles join.
Astonied, some the scatheful gift beheld,
Behight by vow unto the chaste Minerve,
All wondering at the hugeness of the horse.

           *   *   *

   It was the time when, granted from the gods,   340
The first sleep creeps most sweet in weary folk.
Lo, in my dream, before mine eyes, methought,
With rueful cheer I saw where Hector stood
(Out of whose eyes there gushed streams of tears)
Drawn at a cart as he of late had been,   345
Distained with bloody dust, whose feet were bowlen
With the strait cords wherewith they haled him.
Ay me, what one! that Hector how unlike,
Which erst returned clad with Achilles' spoils,
Or when he threw into the Greekish ships   350
The Trojan flame: so was his beard defiled,
His crisped locks all clustered with his blood,
With all such wounds, as many he received
About the walls of that his native town!
Whom frankly thus methought I spake unto,   355
With bitter tears and doleful deadly voice:
'O Troyan light! O only hope of thine!
What lets so long thee stayed? or from what coasts,
Our most desired Hector, dost thou come?

Whom, after slaughter of thy many friends,   360
And travail of the people and thy town,
All-wearied, lord, how gladly we behold!
What sorry chance hath stained thy lively face?
Or why see I these wounds, alas so wide?'
He answered nought, nor in my vain demands   365
Abode, but from the bottom of his breast
Sighing he said: 'Flee, flee, O goddess' son,
And save thee from the fury of this flame.
Our enemies now are masters of the walls,
And Troyè town now falleth from the top: 370
Sufficeth that is done for Priam's reign.
If force might serve to succour Troyè town,
This right hand well mought have been her defence.
But Troyè now commendeth to thy charge
Her holy reliques, and her privy gods.   375
Them join to thee, as fellows of thy fate.
Large walls rear thou for them; for so thou shalt,
After time spent in the overwandered flood.'
This said, he brought forth Vesta in his hands,
Her fillets eke, and everlasting flame.   380
   In this mean while with diverse plaint the town
Throughout was spread; and louder more and more
The din resounded, with rattling of arms.
Although mine old father Anchises' house
Removed stood, with shadow hid of trees,   385
I waked: therewith to the house-top I clamb,
And hearkening stood I: like as when the flame
Lights in the corn by drift of boisterous wind,
Or the swift stream that driveth from the hill
Roots up the fields and presseth the ripe corn   390
And ploughed ground, and overwhelms the grove,
The silly herdman all astonied stands,
From the high rock while he doth hear the sound.
   Then the Greeks' faith, then their deceit appeared.
Of Deiphobus the palace large and great   395
Fell to the ground, all overspread with flash;
His next neighbour Ucalegon afire:
The Sygean seas did glister all with flame.
Upsprang the cry of men and trumpets' blast.
Then, as distraught, I did my armour on,   400
Ne could I tell yet whereto arms availed.
But with our feres to throng out from the press

Toward the tower our hearts brent with desire:
Wrath pricked us forth, and unto us it seemed
A seemly thing to die armed in the field.   405
   Wherewith Panthus, 'scaped from the Greekish darts,
Otreus' son, Phoebus' priest, brought in hand
The sacred reliques and the vanquished gods,
And in his hand his little nephew led;
And thus, as frantic, to our gates he ran.   410
'Panthus,' quod I, 'in what estate stand we?
Or for refuge what fortress shall we take?'
Scarce spake I this, when wailing thus he said:
'The latter day and fate of Troy is come,
The which no plaint or prayer may avail.   415
Troyans we were, and Troyè was sometime,
And of great fame the Teucrian glory erst:
Fierce Jove to Greece hath now transposed all;
The Greeks are lords over this fired town.
Yonder huge horse that stands amid our walls   420
Sheds armed men, and Sinon, victor now,
With scorn of us doth set all things on flame.
And, rushed in at our unfolded gates,
Are thousands moe than ever came from Greece.
And some with weapons watch the narrow streets,   425
With bright swords drawn, to slaughter ready bent.
And scarce the watches of the gate began
Them to defend, and with blind fight resist.'

* * *

   But lo, Polites, one of Priam's sons,
Escaped from the slaughter of Pyrrhus,
Comes fleeing through the weapons of his foes,
Searching, all wounded, the long galleries
And the void courts; whom Pyrrhus, all in rage,   685
Followed fast to reach a mortal wound;
And now in hand well near strikes with his spear.
Who, fleeing forth till he came now in sight
Of his parents, before their face fell down
Yielding the ghost, with flowing streams of blood.   690
Priamus then, although he were half dead,
Might not keep in his wrath, nor yet his words,
But crieth out: 'For this thy wicked work,
And boldness eke such thing to enterprise,
If in the heavens any justice be,   695

That of such things takes any care or keep,
According thanks the gods may yield to thee
And send thee eke thy just deserved hire,
That made me see the slaughter of my child,
And with his blood defile the father's face.   700
But he, by whom thou feignest thyself begot,
Achilles, was to Priam not so stern:
For lo, he tendering my most humble suit
The right and faith, my Hector's bloodless corpse
Rendered, for to be laid in sepulture,   705
And sent me to my kingdom home again.'
Thus said the aged man, and therewithal
Forceless he cast his weak unwieldy dart
Which, repulsed from the brass where it gave dint,
Without sound hung vainly in the shieldès boss.   710
Quod Pyrrhus: 'Then thou shalt this thing report:
On message to Pelide my father go:
Show unto him my cruel deeds, and how
Neoptolem is swerved out of kind.
Now shalt thou die,' quod he. And with that word   715
At the altar him trembling gan he draw
Wallowing through the bloodshed of his son;
And his left hand all clasped in his hair,
With his right arm drew forth his shining sword,
Which in his side he thrust up to the hilts.   720
Of Priamus this was the fatal fine,
The woeful end that was allotted him,
When he had seen his palace all on flame
With ruin of his Troyan turrets eke.
That royal prince of Asia (which of late   725
Reigned over so many peoples and realms)
Like a great stock now lieth on the shore;
His head and shoulders parted been in twain,
A body now without renown and fame.
    Then first in me entered the grisly fear.   730
Dismayed I was. Wherewith came to my mind
The image eke of my dear father, when
I thus beheld the king of equal age
Yield up the sprite with wounds so cruelly.
Then thought I of Creusa left alone,   735
And of my house in danger of the spoil,
And the estate of young Iulus eke.
I looked back to seek what number then

123

I might discern about me of my feres;
But wearied they had left me all alone: 740
Some to the ground were lopen from above,
Some in the flame their irked bodies cast.

   There was no moe but I left of them all
When that I saw in Vesta's temple sit
Dame Helen, lurking in a secret place 745
(Such light the flame did give as I went by
While here and there I cast mine eyen about)
For she in dread lest that the Troians should
Revenge on her the ruin of their walls,
And of the Greeks the cruel wreaks also, 750
The fury eke of her forsaken make,
The common bane of Troy, and eke of Greece,
Hateful she sat beside the altars hid.
Then boiled my breast with flame and burning wrath
To revenge my town unto such ruin brought, 755
With worthy pains on her to work my will.
Thought I: 'Shall she pass to the land of Spart
All safe, and see Mycene her native land,
And like a queen return with victory
Home to her spouse, her parents, and children, 760
Followed with a train of Troyan maids,
And served with a band of Phrygian slaves;
And Priam eke with iron murdered thus,
And Troyè town consumed all with flame
Whose shore hath been so oft forbathed in blood? 765
No! no! for though on women the revenge
Unseemly is (such conquest hath no fame),
To give an end unto such mischief yet
My just revenge shall merit worthy praise
And quiet eke my mind, for to be wroke 770
On her which was the causer of this flame,
And satisfy the cinder of my feres.'

   With furious mind while I did argue thus,
My blessed mother then appeared to me,
Whom erst so bright mine eyes had never seen, 775
And with pure light she glistered in the night,
Disclosing her in form a goddess like,
As she doth seem to such as dwell in heaven.
My right hand then she took and held it fast,
And with her rosy lips thus did she say: 780
'Son, what fury hath thus provoked thee

To such untamed wrath? what ragest thou?
Or where is now become the care of us?
Wilt thou not first go see where thou hast left
Anchises, thy father fordone with age?   785
Doth Creusa live, and Ascanius thy son?
Whom now the Greekish bands have round beset,
And were they not defenced by my cure,
Flame had them raught and enemies' sword ere this.
Not Helen's beauty hateful unto thee,   790
Nor blamed Paris yet, but the gods' wrath
Reft you this wealth, and overthrew your town.
Behold! and I shall now the cloud remove
Which overcast thy mortal sight doth dim,
Whose moisture doth obscure all things about: 795
And fear not thou to do thy mother's will,
Nor her advice refuse thou to perform.
Here, where thou seest the turrets overthrown,
Stone beat from stone, smoke rising mix with dust,
Neptunus there shakes with his mace the walls   800
And eke the loose foundations of the same,
And overwhelms the whole town from his seat;
And cruel Juno with the foremost here
Doth keep the gate that Scea cleped is,
Near wood for wrath, whereas she stands, and calls   805
In harness bright the Greeks out of their ships.
And in the turrets high behold where stands
Bright shining Pallas all in warlike weed,
And with her shield, where Gorgon's head appears;
And Jupiter, my father, distributes   810
Availing strength and courage to the Greeks:
Yet overmore, against the Troyan power,
He doth provoke the rest of all the gods.
Flee then, my son, and give this travail end;
Ne shall I thee forsake, in safeguard till   815
I have thee brought unto thy father's gate.'
This did she say: and therewith gan she hide
Herself in shadow of the close night.
    Then dreadful figures gan appear to me,
And great gods eke aggrieved with our town.   820
I saw Troyè fall down in burning gledes,
Neptunus' town clean razed from the soil.
Like as the elm forgrown in mountains high,
Round hewen with axe, that husbandmen

With thick assaults strive to tear up, doth threat;   825
And hacked beneath trembling doth bend his top,
Till yold with strokes, giving the latter crack,
Rent from the height, with ruin it doth fall.

*   *   *

   And now we gan draw near unto the gate,
Right well escaped the danger, as methought,
When that at hand a sound of feet we heard.
My father then, gazing throughout the dark,
Cried on me, 'Flee, son! They are at hand.'   970
With that bright shields and sheen armours I saw.
But then, I know not what unfriendly god
My troubled wit from me bereft for fear:
For while I ran by the most secret streets,
Eschewing still the common haunted track,   975
From me (caitiff) alas bereaved was
Creusa then, my spouse, I wot not how,
Whether by fate, or missing of the way,
Or that she was by weariness retained.
But never sith these eyes might her behold;   980
Nor did I yet perceive that she was lost,
Ne never backward turned I my mind,
Till we came to the hill whereas there stood
The old temple dedicate to Ceres.
   And when that we were there assembled all,   985
She was only away, deceiving us,
Her spouse, her son, and all her company.
What god or man did I not then accuse,
Near wood for ire, or what more cruel chance
Did hap to me, in all Troy's overthrow?   990
Ascanius to my feres I then betook,
With Anchises, and eke the Troyan gods,
And left them hid within a valley deep.
And to the town I gan me hie again,
Clad in bright arms, and bent for to renew   995
Adventures past, to search throughout the town,
And yield my head to perils once again.
   And first the walls and dark entry I sought
Of the same gate whereat I issued out,
Holding backward the steps where we had come   1000
In the dark night, looking all round about:
In every place the ugsome sights I saw,

The silence self of night aghast my sprite.
From hence again I passed unto our house,
If she by chance had been returned home.   1005
The Greeks were there, and had it all beset:
The wasting fire, blown up by drift of wind,
Above the roof in blazing flame sprang up,
The sound whereof with fury pierced the skies.
To Priam's palace and the castle then   1010
I made; and there at Juno's sanctuary
In the void porches, Phoenix, Ulysses eke,
Stern guardians stood, watching of the spoil.
The riches here were set, reft from the brent
Temples of Troy: the tables of the gods,   1015
The vessels eke that were of massy gold,
And vestures spoiled, were gathered all in heap.
The children orderly, and mothers pale for fright,
Long ranged on a row stood round about.
   So bold was I to show my voice that night,   1020
With clepes and cries to fill the streets throughout,
With Creusa's name in sorrow, with vain tears,
And oftensithes the same for to repeat.
The town restless with fury as I sought,
The unlucky figure of Creusa's ghost,   1025
Of stature more than wont, stood 'fore mine eyen.
Abashed then I woxe: therewith my hair
'Gan start right up, my voice stack in my throat,
When with such words she gan my heart remove:
'What helps to yield unto such furious rage,   1030
Sweet spouse?' quod she. 'Without will of the gods
This chanced not, ne lawful was for thee
To lead away Creusa hence with thee:
The king of the high heaven suffereth it not.
A long exile thou art assigned to bear,   1035
Long to furrow large space of stormy seas:
So shalt thou reach at last Hesperian land,
Where Lydian Tiber with his gentle stream
Mildly doth flow along the fruitful fields.
There mirthful wealth, there kingdom is for thee,   1040
There a king's child prepared to be thy make.
For thy beloved Creusa stint thy tears;
For now shall I not see the proud abodes
Of Myrmidons, nor yet of Dolopes:
Ne I, a Troyan lady and the wife   1045

127

Unto the son of Venus the goddess,
Shall go a slave to serve the Greekish dames.
Me here the god's great mother holds.
And now farewell, and keep in father's breast
The tender love of thy young son and mine.'   1050
   This having said, she left me all in tears
And minding much to speak; but she was gone,
And subtly fled into the weightless air.
Thrice raught I with mine arms to accoll her neck:
Thrice did my hands' vain hold the image escape,   1055
Like nimble winds, and like the flying dream.
So, night spent out, return I to my feres;
And there wondering I find together swarmed
A number of mates, mothers, and men,
A rout exiled, a wretched multitude,   1060
From each-where flock together, pressed to pass
With heart and goods to whatsoever land
By sliding seas me listed them to lead.
And now rose Lucifer above the ridge
Of lusty Ide and brought the dawning light.   1065
The Greeks held the entries of the gates beset;
Of help there was no hope. Then gave I place,
Took up my sire, and hasted to the hill.

Book 4 *(lines 1–70; 702–46; 859–943)*

But now the wounded queen with heavy care
Throughout the veins she nourished the playe,
Surprised with blind flame; and to her mind
Gan eke resort the prowess of the man
And honour of his race; while in her breast   5
Imprinted stack his words and picture's form;
Ne to her limbs Care granteth quiet rest.
   The next morrow with Phoebus' lamp the earth
Alightened clear, and eke the dawning day
The shadows dank gan from the pole remove,   10
When all unsound her sister of like mind
Thus spake she to: 'O sister Anne, what dreams
Be these that me tormented thus affray?
What new guest this that to our realm is come?
What one of cheer! how stout of heart in arms!   15
Truly I think (nor vain is my belief)
Of goddish race some offspring should he be:

128

Cowardry notes hearts swerved out of kind.
He driven, lord, with how hard destiny!
What battles eke achieved did he recount!   20
But that my mind is fixed unmoveably
Never with wight in wedlock aye to join
Sith my first love me left by Death dissevered,
If genial brands and bed me loathed not,
To this one guilt perchance yet might I yield.   25
Anne (for I grant, sith wretched Sychaeus' death,
My spouse, and house with brother's slaughter stained,
This only man hath made my senses bend
And pricked forth the mind that 'gan to slide)
Now feelingly I taste the steps of mine old flame.
But first I wish the earth me swallow down
With thunder, or the mighty lord me send
To the pale ghosts of hell and darkness deep,
Ere I thee stain, Shamefastness, or thy laws.
He that with me first coupled took away   35
My love with him, enjoys it in his grave.'
     Thus did she say, and with surprised tears
Bained her breast. Whereto Anne thus replied:
'O sister, dearer beloved than the light,
Thy youth alone in plaint still wilt thou spill,   40
That children sweet ne Venus' gift wilt know?
Cinders, thinkest thou, mind this? or graved ghosts?
Time of thy dole, thy spouse new dead, I grant
None might thee move: no, not the Libyan king,
Nor yet of Tyre, Iarbas set so light,   45
And other princes more whom the rich soil
Of Afric breeds in honours triumphant.
Wilt thou also gainstand thy liked love?
Comes not to mind upon whose land thou dwellest?
On this side, lo the Getule town behold,   50
A people bold, unvanquished in war;
And the undaunted Numides compass thee,
Also the Sirtes, unfriendly harbour;
On the other hand, a desert realm for thirst,
The Barceans, whose fury stretcheth wide.   55
What shall I touch the wars that move from Tyre?
Or yet thy brother's threats?
By God's purveyance it blew, and Juno's help,
The Troyans' ships, I think, to run this course.
Sister, what town shalt thou see this become!   60

Through such ally how shall our kingdom rise!
And by the aid of Troyan arms how great!
How many ways shall Carthage's glory grow!
Thou only now beseech the gods of grace
By sacrifice: which ended, to thy house   65
Receive him, and forge causes of abode;
Whiles winter frets the seas, and watery Orion,
The ships shaken, unfriendly the season.'
   Such words enflamed the kindled mind with love,
Loosed all shame, and gave the doubtful hope.   70

         *   *   *

   It was then night. The sound and quiet sleep
Had through the earth the wearied bodies caught;
The woods, the raging seas, were fallen to rest
When that the stars had half their course declined;   705
The fields whist; beasts and fowls of diverse hue,
And what so that in the broad lakes remained
Or yet among the bushy thicks of briar
Laid down to sleep by silence of the night,
'Gan 'suage their cares, mindless of travels past.   710
Not so the sprite of this Phoenician:
Unhappy she, that on no sleep could chance,
Nor yet night's rest enter in eye or breast.
Her cares redouble. Love doth rise and rage again,
And overflows with swelling storms of wrath.   715
Thus thinks she then; this rolls she in her mind:
'What shall I do? shall I now bear the scorn
For to assay mine old wooers again
And humbly yet a Numid spouse require
Whose marriage I have so oft disdained?   720
The Troyan navy and Teucrian vile commands
Follow shall I, as though it should avail
That whilom by my help they were relieved?
Or for because with kind and mindful folk
Right well doth sit the passed thankful deed?   725
Who would me suffer (admit this were my will)
Or me, scorned, to their proud ships receive?
Oh woe-begone: full little knowest thou yet
The broken oaths of Laomedon's kind!
What then? alone on merry mariners   730
Shall I wait? or board them with my power
Of Tyrians assembled me about,

And such as I with travail brought from Tyre
Drive to the seas and force them sail again?
But rather die, even as thou hast deserved,   735
And to this woe with iron give thou end.
And thou, sister, first vanquished with my tears,
Thou in my rage with all these mischiefs first
Didst burden me and yield me to my foe.
Was it not granted me, from spousals free,   740
Like to wild beasts to live without offence,
Without taste of such cares? Is there no faith
Reserved to the cinders of Sychaeus?'
   Such great complaints brake forth out of her breast
Whilst Aeneas, full minded to depart,   745
All things prepared, slept in the poop on high.

*   *   *

   But trembling Dido eagerly now bent
Upon her stern determination,   860
Her bloodshot eyes rolling within her head,
Her quivering cheeks flecked with deadly stain,
Both pale and wan to think on death to come,
Into the inward wards of her palace
She rusheth in, and clamb up as distraught   865
The burial stack, and drew the Troyan sword,
Her gift sometime, but meant to no such use.
Where when she saw his weed and well known bed,
Weeping a while, in study gan she stay,
Fell on the bed, and these last words she said: 870
'Sweet spoils, while God and Destinies it would,
Receive this sprite and rid me of these cares.
I lived and ran the course Fortune did grant,
And under earth my great ghost now shall wend.
A goodly town I built, and saw my walls,   875
Happy, alas too happy, if these coasts
The Troyan ships had never touched aye.'
   This said, she laid her mouth close to the bed.
'Why then,' quoth she, 'unwroken shall we die?
But let us die, for thus and in this sort   880
It liketh us to seek the shadows dark.
And from the seas the cruel Troyan's eyes
Shall well discern this flame, and take with him
Eke these unlucky tokens of my death.'
   As she had said, her damsels might perceive   885

131

Her with these words fall pierced on a sword,
The blade imbrued and hands besprent with gore.
The clamour rang unto the palace top,
The bruit ran throughout all the astonied town.
With wailing great and women's shrill yelling   890
The roofs gan roar, the air resound with plaint,
As though Carthage or the ancient town of Tyre
With press of entered enemies swarmed full,
Or when the rage of furious flame doth take
The temple tops and mansions eke of men.   895
   Her sister Anne, spriteless for dread to hear
This fearful stir, with nails gan tear her face.
She smote her breast and rushed through the rout
And her, dying, she clepes thus by her name:
'Sister, for this with craft did you me bourd?   900
The stack, the flame, the altars, bred they this?
What shall I first complain, forsaken wight?
Loathest thou in death thy sister's fellowship?
Thou shouldest have called me to like destiny:
One woe, one sword, one hour might end us both.   905
This funeral stack built I with these hands,
And with this voice cleped to our native gods,
And cruel so absentest me from thy death?
Destroyed thou hast, sister, both thee and me,
Thy people eke, and princes born of Tyre.   910
Give here: I shall with water wash her wounds,
And suck with mouth her breath, if ought be left'.
   This said, unto the high degrees she mounted,
Embracing fast her sister now half dead
With wailful plaint, whom in her lap she laid,   915
The black swart gore wiping dry with her clothes.
But Dido striveth to lift up again
Her heavy eyen, and hath no power thereto:
Deep in her breast that fixed wound doth gape.
Thrice leaning on her elbow 'gan she raise   920
Herself upward, and thrice she overthrew
Upon the bed, ranging with wandering eyes
The skies for light, and wept when she it found.
   Almighty Juno, having ruth by this
Of her long pains and eke her lingering death,   925
From heaven she sent the goddess Iris down,
The throwing spirit and jointed limbs to loose:
For that neither by lot of Destiny

Nor yet by kindly Death she perished,
But wretchedly, before her fatal day, 930
And kindled with a sudden rage of flame,
Proserpine had not from her head bereft
The golden hair, nor judged her to hell.
The dewy Iris thus, with golden wings
(A thousand hues showing against the sun), 935
Amid the skies then did she fly adown
On Dido's head whereas she gan alight:
'This hair', quod she, 'to Pluto consecrate,
Commanded I reave and thy spirit unloose
From this body'. And when she thus had said, 940
With her right hand she cut the hair in twain
And therewith all the kindly heart gan quench
And into wind the life forthwith resolve.

SIR WALTER RALEGH

SIR WALTER RALEGH

Dates: 1552–1618. Born in Devon, younger son of country gentleman Walter Ralegh. Spent a year at Oriel College, Oxford; fought for the Protestant cause in France, 1569, and, after a spell at London's Middle Temple (probably used by him as a finishing school rather than for legal training), returned to fighting, this time against the Irish 'rebels'. Gained Elizabeth I's attention first for his comments on her Irish policy, then became her favourite (MP for Devon, 1584; knighted the same year; Vice-Admiral for Devon and Cornwall; Lieutenant of Cornwall and Warden of the Stannaries (tin mines); Captain of the Queen's Guard, 1587) until his affair with, and secret marriage to, Elizabeth Throckmorton, one of the queen's maids of honour, upon the discovery of which he was thrown into the Tower (1592). Released after a month or so, Ralegh, who had masterminded attempts to settle Virginia in the 1580s, turned his attention to Guiana in an expedition of 1595, in an effort to discover El Dorado. He regained some of his influence with the queen in the five years before her death in 1603; but his rivalry with Essex ensured the enmity of James I upon his accession to the throne.

In mid-1603 he was arrested on charges of alleged treason with Spain and stripped of his honours and possessions, and spent much of his subsequent twelve years in the Tower writing the *History of the World* and, among other things, developing his interest in alchemy and medicine. He also gained the friendship of the firmly Protestant Prince Henry, James's elder son who died in 1612. Released in 1616 to venture again to Guiana (an expedition which ended disastrously), he returned to imprisonment and, on 29 October 1618, execution in Old Palace Yard, Westminster.

VARIOUS POEMS

1

Walter Ralegh of the Middle Temple, in commendation of 'The Steel Glass'

Sweet were the sauce would please each kind of taste;
The life likewise were pure that never swerved;
For spiteful tongues in cankered stomachs placed
Deem worst of things which best (percase) deserved.
But what for that? This medicine may suffice: 5
To scorn the rest, and seek to please the wise.

Though sundry minds in sundry sort do deem,
Yet worthiest wights yield praise for every pain;
But envious brains do nought, or light, esteem
Such stately steps as they cannot attain: 10
For whoso reaps renown above the rest
With heaps of hate shall surely be oppressed.

Wherefore to write my censure of this book:
This Glass of Steel unpartially doth show
Abuses all, to such as in it look,   15
From prince to poor, from high estate to low.
As for the verse, who list like trade to try,
I fear me much, shall hardly reach so high.

2

An epitaph upon the right Honourable Sir Philip Sidney Knight: Lord Governor of Flushing

To praise thy life or wail thy worthy death
And want thy wit (thy wit high, pure, divine)
Is far beyond the power of mortal line,
Nor any one hath worth that draweth breath;

Yet rich in zeal (though poor in learning's lore),   5
And friendly care (obscured in secret breast),
And love (that envy in thy life suppressed),
Thy dear life done, and death hath doubled more;

And I, that in thy time and living state
Did only praise thy virtues in my thought,   10
As one that, seeled, the rising sun hath sought,
With words and tears now wail thy timeless fate.

Drawn was thy race aright from princely line,
Nor less than such – by gifts that Nature gave,
The common mother that all creatures have –   15
Doth virtue show, and princely lineage shine.

A king gave thee thy name. A kingly mind –
That God thee gave, who found it now too dear
For this base world, and hath resumed it near,
To sit in skies and sort with powers divine.   20

Kent thy birth-days, and Oxford held thy youth;
The heavens made haste and stayed nor years nor time:
The fruits of age grew ripe in thy first prime:
Thy will, thy words; thy words, the seals of truth.

Great gifts and wisdom rare employed thee thence   25
To treat from kings with those more great than kings:
Such hope men had to lay the highest things
On thy wise youth, to be transported hence.

Whence to sharp wars sweet Honour did thee call,
Thy country's love, religion, and thy friends   30
(Of worthy men the marks, the lives, and ends)
And her defence, for whom we labour all.

There didst thou vanquish shame and tedious age,
Grief, sorrow, sickness, and base Fortune's might:
Thy rising day saw never woeful night,   35
But passed with praise from off this worldly stage.

Back to the camp by thee that day was brought,
First thine own death; and after, thy long fame;
Tears to the soldiers; the proud Castilian's shame;
Virtue expressed; and Honour truly taught.   40

What hath he lost that such great grace hath won?
Young years for endless years, and hope unsure
Of Fortune's gifts for wealth that still shall dure:
Oh happy race, with so great praises run!

England doth hold thy limbs, that bred the same;   45
Flanders thy valour, where it last was tried;
The camp thy sorrow, where thy body died;
Thy friends, thy want; the world, thy virtue's fame;

Nations, thy wit; our minds lay up thy love;
Letters, thy learning; thy loss, years long to come;   50

In worthy hearts sorrow hath made thy tomb;
Thy soul and spirit enrich the heavens above.

Thy liberal heart embalmed in grateful tears,
Young sighs, sweet sighs, sage sighs, bewail thy fall;
Envy, her sting, and Spite hath left her gall;   55
Malice herself a mourning garment wears.

That day their Hannibal died, our Scipio fell
(Scipio, Cicero, and Petrarch of our time)
Whose virtues, wounded by my worthless rhyme,
Let angels speak, and heaven thy praises tell.

3

A farewell to false Love

Farewell, false Love, the oracle of lies,
A mortal foe and enemy to rest,
An envious boy, from whom all cares arise,
A bastard vile, a beast with rage possessed,
A way of error, a temple full of treason,   5
In all effects contrary unto Reason:

A poisoned serpent covered all with flowers,
Mother of sighs and murderer of repose,
A sea of sorrows from whence are drawn such showers
As moisture lend to every grief that grows,   10
A school of guile, a net of deep deceit,
A gilded hook that holds a poisoned bait:

A fortress foiled, which Reason did defend,
A siren song, a fever of the mind,
A maze wherein affection finds no end,   15
A ranging cloud that runs before the wind,
A substance like the shadow of the sun,
A goal of grief for which the wisest run:

A quenchless fire, a nurse of trembling fear,
A path that leads to peril and mishap,   20
A true retreat of sorrow and despair,
An idle boy that sleeps in Pleasure's lap,
A deep mistrust of that which certain seems,
A hope of that which Reason doubtful deems:

Sith, then, thy trains my younger years betrayed   25
And for my faith ingratitude I find,

And sith repentance hath my wrongs bewrayed,
Whose course was ever contrary to kind,
False Love, Desire, and Beauty frail, adieu:
Dead is the root whence all these fancies grew.   30

4

Fortune hath taken away

Fortune hath taken away my love,
My life's soul and my soul's heaven above;
Fortune hath taken away my princess,
My world's joy, and my true fancy's mistress.

Fortune hath taken thee away from me;   5
Fortune hath taken all by taking thee;
Dead to all joys, I only live to woe:
So is Fortune become my fancy's foe.

In vain my eyes, in vain ye waste your tears;
In vain my sighs, the smokes of my despairs;   10
In vain you search the Earth and heaven above;
In vain you seek, for Fortune keeps my love.

Then will I leave my love in Fortune's hand;
Then will I leave my love in worldlings' band,
And only love the sorrow due to me: 15
Sorrow, henceforth, that shall my princess be;

And only joy that Fortune conquers kings.
Fortune, that rules the Earth and earthly things
Hath taken my love in spite of Virtue's might:
So blind a goddess did never Virtue right.   20

With Wisdom's eyes had but blind Fortune seen,
Then had my love my love for ever been.
But, love, farewell: though Fortune conquer thee
No fortune base, nor frail, shall alter me.

5

The excuse

Calling to mind mine eye long went about
To entice my heart to seek to leave my breast,
All in a rage I thought to pull it out,
By whose device I lived in such unrest:

What could it say to purchase so my grace?   5
Forsooth, that it had seen my mistress' face.

Another time I likewise call to mind
My heart was he that all my woe had wrought,
For he my breast, the fort of Love, resigned,
When of such wars my fancy never thought: 10
    What could it say, when I would him have slain,
    But he was yours and had forgot me clean?

At length, when I perceived both eye and heart
Excused themselves as guiltless of mine ill,
I found my self was cause of all my smart,   15
And told my self: my self now slay I will.
    But when I found my self to you was true,
    I loved my self, because my self loved you.

6

Praised be Diana's fair and harmless light

Praised be Diana's fair and harmless light;
Praised be the dews wherewith she moists the ground;
Praised be her beams, the glory of the night;
Praised be her power, by which all powers abound;

Praised be her nymphs, with whom she decks the woods;   5
Praised be her knights, in whom true honour lives;
Praised be that force by which she moves the floods:
Let that Diana shine, which all these gives.

In heaven Queen she is among the spheres;
In aye she mistress-like makes all things pure;   10
Eternity in her oft-change she bears;
She Beauty is: by her the fair endure.

Time wears her not, she doth his chariot guide;
Mortality below her orb is placed;
By her the virtue of the stars down slide;   15
In her is Virtue's perfect image cast.

    A knowledge pure it is her worth to know:
    With Circes let them dwell that think not so.

7

Like to a hermit poor

Like to a hermit poor in place obscure
I mean to spend my days of endless doubt,
To wail such woes as time cannot recure,
Where none but Love shall ever find me out.

My food shall be of care and sorrow made;   5
My drink nought else but tears fallen from mine eyes;
And for my light in such obscured shade
The flames shall serve which from my heart arise.

A gown of grey my body shall attire,
My staff of broken hope whereon I'll stay,   10
Of late repentance linked with long desire
The couch is framed whereon my limbs I'll lay:

  And at my gate Despair shall linger still,
  To let in Death when Love and Fortune will.

8

Farewell to the Court

Like truthless dreams, so are my joys expired,
And past return are all my dandled days;
My love misled, and fancy quite retired:
Of all which past, the sorrow only stays.

My lost delights, now clean from sight of land,   5
Have left me all alone in unknown ways;
My mind to woe, my life in Fortune's hand:
Of all which past, the sorrow only stays.

As in a country strange without companion,
I only wail the wrong of Death's delays,   10
Whose sweet spring spent, whose summer well nigh done
(Of all which past, the sorrow only stays),

  Whom care forewarns, ere age and winter cold,
  To haste me hence, to find my fortune's fold.

9

A vision upon this conceit of *The Faerie Queene*

Methought I saw the grave where Laura lay,
Within that temple where the vestal flame
Was wont to burn; and passing by that way
To see that buried dust of living fame
(Whose tomb fair love and fairer virtue kept)   5
All suddenly I saw the Faery Queen,
At whose approach the soul of Petrarch wept;
And from thenceforth those graces were not seen,
For they this Queen attended, in whose stead
Oblivion laid him down on Laura's hearse: 10
Hereat the hardest stones were seen to bleed,
And groans of buried ghosts the heavens did pierce,
    Where Homer's spirit did tremble all for grief,
    And cursed the access of that celestial thief.

10

Another of the same

The praise of meaner wits this work like profit brings,
As doth the cuckoo's song delight when Philumena sings.
If thou hast formed right true Virtue's face herein,
Virtue herself can best discern to whom they written bin:
If thou hast Beauty praised, let her sole looks divine   5
Judge if aught therein be amiss, and mend it by her eyne:
If Chastity want aught, or Temperance her due,
Behold her princely mind aright, and write thy Queen anew.
Meanwhile she shall perceive how far her virtues soar
Above the reach of all that live, or such as wrote of yore,   10
And thereby will excuse and favour thy good will,
Whose virtue cannot be expressed but by an angel's quill.
    Of me no lines are loved nor letters are of price,
    Of all which speak our English tongue, but those of thy device.

11

The advice

Many desire, but few or none deserve
To win the fort of thy most constant will:
Therefore take heed, let fancy never swerve

But unto him that will defend thee still:
    For this be sure, the fort of fame once won,   5
    Farewell the rest, thy happy days are done.

Many desire, but few or none deserve
To pluck the flowers and let the leaves to fall:
Therefore take heed, let fancy never swerve,
But unto him that will take leaves and all: 10
    For this be sure, the flower once plucked away,
    Farewell the rest, thy happy days decay.

Many desire, but few or none deserve
To cut the corn, not subject to the sickle:
Therefore take heed, let fancy never swerve,   15
But constant stand, for mowers' minds are fickle:
    For this be sure, the crop being once obtained,
    Farewell the rest, the soil will be disdained.

12(a)

The passionate shepherd to his love
(by Christopher Marlowe)

Come live with me, and be my love,
And we will all the pleasures prove
That hills and valleys, dales and fields,
Woods, or steepy mountain yields.

And we will sit upon the rocks,   5
And see the shepherds feed their flocks
By shallow rivers, to whose falls
Melodious birds sing madrigals.

And I will make thee beds of roses,
And a thousand fragrant posies,   10
A cap of flowers, and a kirtle,
Embroidered all with leaves of myrtle,

A gown made of the finest wool
Which from our pretty lambs we pull,
Fair-lined slippers for the cold,   15
With buckles of the purest gold,

A belt of straw and ivy buds,
With coral clasps and amber studs:
And if these pleasures may thee move,
Come live with me, and be my love.   20

The shepherd swains shall dance and sing
For thy delight each May morning:
If these delights thy mind may move,
Then live with me, and be my love.

12(b)

The nymph's reply to the shepherd
(by Sir Walter Ralegh)

If all the world and love were young,
And truth in every shepherd's tongue,
These pretty pleasures might me move,
To live with thee, and be thy love.

Time drives the flocks from field to fold,   5
When rivers rage, and rocks grow cold,
And Philomel becometh dumb,
The rest complains of cares to come.

The flowers do fade, and wanton fields
To wayward Winter reckoning yields: 10
A honey tongue, a heart of gall,
Is fancy's spring, but sorrow's fall.

Thy gowns, thy shoes, thy beds of roses,
Thy cap, thy kirtle, and thy posies,
Soon break, soon wither, soon forgotten;   15
In folly ripe, in reason rotten.

The belt of straw and ivy buds,
Thy coral clasps and amber studs:
All these in me no means can move
To come to thee, and be thy love.   20

But could youth last, and love still breed,
Had joys no date, nor age no need,
Then these delights my mind might move,
To live with thee, and be thy love.

13

A poesy to prove affection is not love

Conceit begotten by the eyes
Is quickly born and quickly dies;
For while it seeks our hearts to have,

Meanwhile there Reason makes his grave:
For many things the eyes approve,   5
Which yet the heart doth seldom love.

For as the seeds in springtime sown
Die in the ground ere they be grown,
Such is Conceit, whose rooting fails,
As child that in the cradle quails,   10
Or else within the mother's womb
Hath his beginning and his tomb.

Affection follows Fortune's wheels
And soon is shaken from her heels;
For, following beauty or estate   15
Her liking still is turned to hate:
For all affections have their change,
And Fancy only loves to range.

Desire himself runs out of breath
And, getting, doth but gain his death: 20
Desire nor reason hath nor rest
And, blind, doth seldom choose the best:
Desire attained is not desire,
But as the cinders of the fire.

As ships in port desired are drowned,   25
As fruit once ripe then falls to ground,
As flies that seek for flames are brought
To cinders by the flames they sought:
So fond Desire, when it attains,
The life expires, the woe remains.   30

And yet some poets fain would prove
Affection to be perfect love,
And that Desire is of that kind,
No less a passion of the mind:
As if wild beasts and men did seek   35
To like, to love, to choose alike.

14

Sir Walter Ralegh to the Queen

Our passions are most like to floods and streams:
The shallow murmur, but the deep are dumb.
So, when affections yield discourse, it seems

The bottom is but shallow whence they come.
    They that are rich in words must needs discover   5
    That they are poor in that which makes a lover.

Wrong not, dear Empress of my heart,
    The merit of true passion
With thinking that he feels no smart
    That sues for no compassion;   10
Since if my plaints serve not to prove
    The conquest of your beauty,
It comes not from defect of love,
    But from excess of duty.

For, knowing that I sue to serve   15
    A saint of such perfection
As all desire, but none deserve,
    A place in her affection,
I rather choose to want relief
    Than venture the revealing: 20
Where glory recommends the grief,
    Despair distrusts the healing.

Thus those desires that aim too high
    For any mortal lover,
When Reason cannot make them die   25
    Discretion will them cover.
Yet when discretion doth bereave
    The plaints that they should utter,
Then your discretion may perceive
    That Silence is a suitor.   30

Silence in love bewrays more woe
    Than words though never so witty:
A beggar that is dumb, you know,
    Deserveth double pity.
Then misconceive not, dearest heart,   35
    My true though secret passion:
He smarteth most that hides his smart
    And sues for no compassion.

15

A poem of Sir Walter Ralegh's

Nature, that washed her hands in milk
    And had forgot to dry them,

Instead of earth took snow and silk
  At Love's request to try them,
If she a mistress could compose   5
To please Love's fancy out of those.

Her eyes he would should be of light,
  A violet breath and lips of jelly,
Her hair not black, nor over-bright,
  And of the softest down her belly: 10
As for her inside, he'd have it
Only of wantonness and wit.

At Love's entreaty such a one
  Nature made; but with her beauty
She hath framed a heart of stone,   15
  So as Love by ill destiny
Must die for her whom Nature gave him
Because her darling would not save him.

But Time, which Nature doth despise
  And rudely gives her love the lie,
Makes hope a fool and sorrow wise,   20
  His hands doth neither wash nor dry,
But being made of steel and rust
Turns snow and silk and milk to dust.

The light, the belly, lips, and breath   25
  He dims, discovers, and destroys:
With those he feeds but fills not, Death,
  Which sometimes were the food of joys:
Yea, Time doth dull each lively wit,
And dries all wantonness with it.   30

Oh cruel Time, which takes in trust
  Our youth, our joys, and all we have,
And pays us but with age and dust;
  Who, in the dark and silent grave,
When we have wandered all our ways,   35
Shuts up the story of our days.

16

As you came from the holy land

As you came from the holy land
  Of Walsingham,

Met you not with my true love
    By the way as you came?

How shall I know your true love   5
    That have met many one
As I went to the holy land
    That have come, that have gone?

She is neither white nor brown
    But as the heavens fair,   10
There is none hath a form so divine
    In the earth or the air.

Such an one did I meet, good sir,
    Such an angelic face,
Who like a queen, like a nymph, did appear   15
    By her gait, by her grace.

She hath left me here all alone,
    All alone as unknown,
Who sometimes did me lead with herself,
    And me loved as her own.   20

What's the cause that she leaves you alone
    And a new way doth take,
Who loved you once as her own
    And her joy did you make?

I have loved her all my youth,   25
    But now old, as you see:
Love likes not the falling fruit
    From the withered tree.

Know that Love is a careless child
    And forgets promise past;   30
He is blind, he is deaf when he list,
    And in faith never fast.

His desire is a dureless content
    And a trustless joy:
He is won with a world of despair   35
    And is lost with a toy.

Of womenkind such indeed is the love,
    Or the word *love* abused,
Under which many childish desires
    And conceits are excused.   40

But true love is a durable fire
   In the mind ever burning;
Never sick, never old, never dead,
   From itself never turning.

17

If Cynthia be a queen

If Cynthia be a queen, a princess, and supreme,
Keep these among the rest, or say it was a dream:
For those that like, expound, and those that loathe, express
Meanings according as their minds are moved more or less.
For writing what thou art, or showing what thou were,   5
Adds to the one disdain, to the other but despair:
   Thy mind of neither needs, in both seeing it exceeds.

18

My body in the walls captived

My body in the walls captived
Feels not the wounds of spiteful Envy;
But my thralled mind, of liberty deprived,
Fast fettered in her ancient memory,
Doth nought behold but Sorrow's dying face.   5
Such prison erst was so delightful
As it desired no other dwelling place;
But Time's effects, and Destinies despiteful,
Have changed both my keeper and my fare.
Love's fire and Beauty's light I then had store,   10
But now, close kept as captives wonted are,
That food, that heat, that light I find no more.
   Despair bolts up my doors and I, alone,
   Speak to dead walls: but those hear not my moan.

19

THE VITH AND LAST BOOK OF THE OCEAN TO CYNTHIA

Sufficeth it to you, my joys interred,
In simple words that I my woes complain —
You that then died when first my fancy erred,
Joys under dust that never live again.
If to the living were my Muse addressed,   5

Or did my mind her own spirit still inhold,
Were not my living passion so repressed
As to the dead, the dead did these unfold,
Some sweeter words, some more becoming verse,
Should witness my mishap in higher kind;　　　　10
But my love's wounds, my fancy in the hearse,
The idea but resting of a wasted mind,
The blossoms fallen, the sap gone from the tree,
The broken monuments of my great desires:
From these so lost what may the affections be?　　15
What heat in cinders of extinguished fires?
Lost in the mud of those high-flowing streams
Which through more fairer fields their courses bend,
Slain with self-thoughts, amazed in fearful dreams,
Woes without date, discomforts without end,　　　20
From fruitful trees I gather withered leaves,
And glean the broken ears with miser's hands,
Who sometime did enjoy the weighty sheaves;
I seek fair flowers amid the brinish sand.
All in the shade, even in the fair Sun days,　　　25
Under those healthless trees I sit alone,
Where joyful birds sing neither lovely lays
Nor Philomen recounts her direful moan.
No feeding flocks, no shepherd's company,
That might renew my dolorous conceit,　　　　30
While happy then, while love and fantasy
Confined my thoughts on that fair flock to wait;
No pleasing streams fast to the Ocean wending
(The messengers sometimes of my great woe)
But all on Earth, as from the cold storms bending,　35
Shrink from my thoughts in high heavens and below.
O hopeful love, my object and invention!
O true desire, the spur of my conceit!
O worthiest spirit, my mind's impulsion!
O eyes transpiercant, my affection's bait!　　　40
O princely form, my fancy's adamant,
Divine conceit, my pain's acceptance!
O all in one, O heaven on earth transparent,
The seat of joys and love's abundance!
Out of that mass of miracles my Muse　　　　45
Gathered those flowers, to her pure senses pleasing;
Out of her eyes (the store of joys) did choose
Equal delights, my sorrows counterpoising.

Her regal looks my rigorous sithes suppressed;
Small drops of joys sweetened great worlds of woes; 50
One gladsome day a thousand cares redressed:
Whom Love defends, what fortune overthrows?
When she did well, what did there else amiss?
When she did ill, what empires could have pleased?
No other power effecting woe or bliss, 55
She gave, she took, she wounded, she appeased.

The honour of her love Love still devising
(Wounding my mind with contrary conceit)
Transferred itself sometime to her aspiring,
Sometime the trumpet of her thought's retreat, 60
To seek new worlds, for gold, for praise, for glory,
To try desire, to try love severed far.
When I was gone she sent her memory
More strong than were ten thousand ships of war
To call me back, to leave great honour's thought, 65
To leave my friends, my fortune, my attempt,
To leave the purpose I so long had sought
And hold both cares and comforts in contempt.
Such heat in ice, such fire in frost remained,
Such trust in doubt, such comfort in despair: 70
Much like the gentle lamb, though lately weaned,
Plays with the dug though finds no comfort there.
But as a body violently slain
Retaineth warmth although the spirit be gone
And, by a power in Nature, moves again 75
Till it be laid below the fatal stone;
Or as the Earth, even in cold winter days,
Left for a time by her life-giving Sun,
Doth by the power remaining of his rays
Produce some green (though not as it hath done); 80
Or as a wheel forced by the falling stream,
Although the course be turned some other way,
Doth for a time go round upon the beam
Till, wanting strength to move, it stands at stay:
So my forsaken heart, my withered mind 85
(Widow of all the joys it once possessed,
My hopes clean out of sight) with forced wind
To kingdoms strange, to lands far-off addressed,
Alone, forsaken, friendless on the shore,
With many wounds, with Death's cold pangs embraced, 90

Writes in the dust (as one that could no more,
Whom Love and Time and Fortune had defaced)
Of things so great, so long, so manifold,
With means so weak, the soul even then departing,
The weal, the woe, the passages of old,   95
And worlds of thoughts described by one last sithing:
As if, when after Phoebus is descended
And leaves a light much like the past day's dawning,
And, every toil and labour wholly ended,
Each living creature draweth to his resting,   100
We should begin by such a parting light
To write the story of all ages past,
And end the same before the approaching night.
Such is again the labour of my mind,
Whose shroud, by sorrow woven now to end,   105
Hath seen that ever-shining Sun declined
So many years that so could not descend,
But that the eyes of my mind held her beams
In every part transferred by love's swift thought:
Far off or near, in waking or in dreams,   110
Imagination strong their lustre brought.
Such force her angelic appearance had
To master distance, time, or cruelty;
Such art to grieve, and after to make glad;
Such fear in love, such love in majesty.   115
My weary limbs her memory embalmed,
My darkest ways her eyes make clear as day:
What storms so great but Cynthia's beams appeased?
What rage so fierce that love could not allay?

Twelve years entire I wasted in this war,   120
Twelve years of my most happy younger days;
But I in them, and they, now wasted are:
Of all which past, the sorrow only stays.
So wrote I once and my mishap foretold,
My mind still feeling sorrowful success   125
Even as, before a storm, the marble cold
Doth by moist tears tempestuous times express:
So felt my heavy mind my harms at hand
Which my vain thought in vain sought to recure.
At middle day my sun seemed under land   130
When any little cloud did it obscure,
And as the icicles in a winter's day,

Whenas the Sun shines with unwonted warm,
So did my joys melt into secret tears,
So did my heart dissolve in wasting drops;   135
And as the season of the year outwears,
And heaps of snow from off the mountain tops
With sudden streams the valleys overflow,
So did the time draw on my more despair:
Then floods of sorrow and whole seas of woe   140
The banks of all my hope did overbear
And drowned my mind in depths of misery.
Sometime I died, sometime I was distract,
My soul the stage of fancy's tragedy;
Then furious madness, where true reason lacked,   145
Wrote what it would, and scourged mine own conceit.
Oh heavy heart, who can thee witness bear?
What tongue, what pen, could thy tormenting treat
But thine own mourning thoughts which present were?
What stranger mind believe the meanest part,   150
What altered sense conceive the weakest woe
That tore, that rent, that pierced thy sad heart?
And as a man distract, with treble might,
Bound in strong chains doth strive and rage in vain
Till, tired and breathless, he is forced to rest,   155
Finds by contention but increase of pain
And fiery heat inflamed in swollen breast,
So did my mind in change of passion
From woe to wrath, from wrath return to woe,
Struggling in vain from love's subjection.   160
Therefore all lifeless, and all helpless bound,
My fainting spirits sunk, and heart appalled,
My joys and hopes lay bleeding on the ground
That, not long since, the highest heaven scaled.
I hated life and cursed destiny: 165
The thoughts of passed times like flames of hell
Kindled afresh within my memory
The many dear achievements that befell
In those prime years and infancy of love,
Which to describe were but to die in writing.   170
Ah, those I sought, but vainly, to remove,
And vainly shall, by which I perish living.
And though strong Reason hold before mine eyes
The images and forms of worlds past,
Teaching the cause why all those flames that rise   175

From forms external can no longer last
Than that those seeming beauties hold in prime,
Love's ground, his essence, and his empery,
All slaves to age and vassals unto Time,
Of which repentance writes the tragedy: 180
But this my heart's desire could not conceive,
Whose love outflew the fastest flying time,
A beauty that can easily deceive
The arrest of years, and creeping age outclimb.
A spring of beauties which Time ripeth not 185
(Time that but works on frail mortality);
A sweetness which woe's wrongs outwipeth not,
Whom Love hath chose for his divinity;
A vestal fire that burns but never wasteth,
That loseth nought by giving light to all, 190
That endless shines eachwhere, and endless lasteth;
Blossoms of pride that can nor vade nor fall:
These were those marvellous perfections,
The parents of my sorrow and my envy,
Most deathful and most violent infections: 195
These be the tyrants that in fetters tie
Their wounded vassals, yet nor kill nor cure,
But glory in their lasting misery,
That as her beauties would our woes should dure,
These be the effects of powerful empery. 200

Yet have these wounders want, which want compassion,
Yet hath her mind some marks of human race,
Yet will she be a woman for a fashion,
So doth she please her virtues to deface.
And like as that immortal power doth seat 205
An element of waters to allay
The fiery sunbeams that on earth do beat,
And temper by cold night the heat of day,
So hath Perfection (which begat her mind)
Added thereto a change of fantasy 210
And left her the affections of her kind,
Yet free from every evil but cruelty.

But leave her praise; speak thou of nought but woe;
Write on the tale that Sorrow bids thee tell;
Strive to forget; and care no more to know: 215
Thy cares are known by knowing those too well.
Describe her now as she appears to thee,

Not as she did appear in days foredone:
In love those things that were no more may be,
For fancy seldom ends where it begun.   220

And as a stream, by strong hand bounded in
From Nature's course where it did sometime run,
By some small rent or loose part doth begin
To find escape till it a way hath won,
Doth then all unawares in sunder tear   225
The forced bounds, and raging run at large
In the ancient channels as they wonted were,
Such is of women's love the care-full charge
Held and maintained with multitude of woes;
Of long erections such the sudden fall: 230
One hour diverts, one instant overthrows,
For which our lives, for which our fortunes' thrall,
So many years those joys have dearly bought,
Of which when our fond hopes do most assure,
All is dissolved, our labours come to nought,   235
Nor any mark thereof there doth endure:
No more than when small drops of rain do fall
Upon the parched ground by heat updried:
No cooling moisture is perceived at all,
Nor any show or sign of wet doth bide.   240
But as the fields, clothed with leaves and flowers,
The banks of roses smelling precious sweet,
Have but their beauty's date and timely hours
And then defaced by Winter's cold and sleet
(So far as neither fruit nor form of flower   245
Stays for a witness what such branches bare,
But as Time gave, Time did again devour,
And changed our rising joy to falling care)
So of affection which our youth presented,
When she that from the sun reaves power and light   250
Did but decline her beams as discontented,
Converting sweetest days to saddest night:
All droops, all dies, all trodden under dust,
The person, place, and passages forgotten,
The hardest steel eaten with softest rust,   255
The firm and solid tree both rent and rotten.
Those thoughts (so full of pleasure and content)
That in our absence were affection's food,
Are razed out and from the fancy rent;

In highest grace and heart's dear care that stood,   260
Are cast for prey to hatred; and to scorn
Our dearest treasures and our heart's true joys;
The tokens hung on breast and kindly worn
Are now elsewhere disposed or held for toys;
And those which then our jealousy removed,   265
And others for our sakes then valued dear,
The one forgot, the rest are dear beloved,
When all of ours doth strange or vile appear.
Those streams seem standing puddles which before
We saw our beauties in, so were they clear.   270
Belphoebe's course is now observed no more:
That fair resemblance weareth out of dáte.
Our Ocean seas are but tempestuous waves,
And all things base that blessed were of late.
And as a field, wherein the stubble stands   275
Of harvest past, the ploughman's eye offends,
He tills again, or tears them up with hands,
And throws to fire as foiled and fruitless ends,
And takes delight another seed to sow:
So doth the mind root up all wonted thought   280
And scorns the care of our remaining woes;
The sorrows which themselves for us have wrought
Are burnt to cinders by new-kindled fires,
The ashes are dispersed into the air,
The sighs, the groans, of all our past desires   285
Are clean outworn, as things that never were.

With youth is dead the hope of Love's return,
Who looks not back to hear our after-cries:
Where he is not, he laughs at those that mourn;
Whence he is gone, he scorns the mind that dies;   290
When he is absent, he believes no words;
When Reason speaks, he careless stops his ears;
Whom he hath left he never grace affords,
But bathes his wings in our lamenting tears.

Unlasting passion, soon outworn conceit   295
Whereon I built, and on so dureless trust:
My mind had wounds (I dare not say deceit)
Were I resolved her promise was not just.
Sorrow was my revenge, and woe my hate;
I powerless was to alter my desire: 300
My love is not of time or bound to date;

My heart's internal heat and living fire
Would not, or could, be quenched with sudden showers.
My bound respect was not confined to days;
My vowed faith not set to ended hours: 305
I love the bearing and not-bearing sprays
Which now to others do their sweetness send:
The incarnate, snow-driven white, and purest azure,
Who from high heaven doth on their fields descend,
Filling their barns with grain, and towers with treasure.   310
Erring or never erring, such is love,
As while it lasteth scorns the account of those
Seeking but self-contentment to improve,
And hides, if any be, his inward woes,
And will not know, while he knows his own passion,   315
The often and unjust perseverance
In deeds of love, and state, and every action
From that first day and year of their joy's entrance.

But I, unblessed and ill-born creature,
That did embrace the dust her body bearing,   320
That loved her both by fancy and by nature,
That drew even with the milk in my first sucking
Affection from the parent's breast that bare me,
Have found her as a stranger so severe,
Improving my mishap in each degree.   325
But love was gone: so would I my life were!
A Queen she was to me, no more Belphoebe;
A lion then, no more a milk-white dove:
A prisoner in her breast I could not be;
She did untie the gentle chains of love.   330
Love was no more the love of hiding
All trespass and mischance for her own glory:
It had been such – it was still for the elect –
But I must be the example in love's story;
This was of all forepast the sad effect.   335
But thou, my weary soul and heavy thought,
Made by her love a burden to my being,
Dost know my error never was forethought,
Or ever could proceed from sense of loving.
Of other cause if then it had proceeding   340
I leave the excuse, sith judgment hath been given:
The limbs divided, sundered and a-bleeding,
Cannot complain the sentence was uneven.

This did that Nature's wonder, Virtue's choice,
The only paragon of Time's begetting,   345
Divine in words, angelical in voice,
That spring of joys, that flower of Love's own setting,
The Idea remaining of those golden ages,
That beauty braving heavens, and earth embalming,
Which after worthless worlds but play on stages: 350
Such didst thou her long since describe, yet sithing
That thy unable spirit could not find aught
In heaven's beauties or in earth's delight
For likeness fit to satisfy thy thought.
But what hath it availed thee so to write? —   355
She cares not for thy praise who knows not theirs;
It's now an idle labour and a tale
Told out of time that dulls the hearer's ears;
A merchandise whereof there is no sale.
Leave them, or lay them up with thy despairs: 360
She hath resolved, and judged thee long ago:
Thy lines are now a murmuring to her ears,
Like to a falling stream which, passing slow,
Is wont to nourish sleep and quietness.
So shall thy painful labours be perused   365
And draw on rest, which sometime had regard;
But those her cares thy errors have excused,
Thy days fordone have had their day's reward.
So her hard heart, so her estranged mind,
In which above the heavens I once reposed,   370
So to thy error have her ears inclined,
And have forgotten all thy past deserving,
Holding in mind but only thine offence,
And only now affecteth thy depraving,
And thinks all vain that pleadeth thy defence.   375
Yet greater fancy beauty never bred,
A more desire the heart blood never nourished:
Her sweetness an affection never fed
Which more in any age hath ever flourished.
The Mind and Virtue never have begotten   380
A firmer love since Love on earth had power
(A love obscured, but cannot be forgotten,
Too great and strong for Time's jaws to devour)
Containing such a faith as ages wound not,
Care (wakeful ever of her good estate),   385
Fear (dreading loss, which sithes and joys not),

A memory of the joys her grace begat,
A lasting gratefulness for those comforts past,
Of which the cordial sweetness cannot die.
These thoughts, knit up by faith, shall ever last;   390
These Time assays, but never can untie.
Whose life once lived in her pearl-like breast,
Whose joys were drawn but from her happiness,
Whose heart's high pleasure and whose mind's true rest
Proceeded from her fortune's blessedness,   395
Who was intentive, wakeful, and dismayed,
In fears, in dreams, in feverous jealousy,
Who long in silence served and obeyed
With secret heart and hidden loyalty
(Which never change to sad adversity,   400
Which never age, or Nature's overthrow,
Which never sickness, or deformity,
Which never wasting care, or wearing woe –
If subject unto these she could have been. . . .

Which never words, or wits malicious,   405
Which never honour's bait, or world's fame,
Achieved by attempts adventurous)
Or aught beneath the sun, or heaven's frame,
Can so dissolve, dissever, or destroy –
The essential love, of no frail parts compounded   410
(Though of the same now buried be the joy,
The hope, the comfort, and the sweetness ended):
But that the thoughts and memories of these
Work a relapse of passion, and remain
Of my sad heart the sorrow-sucking bees.   415
The wrongs received, the scorns, persuade in vain,
And though these medicines work desire to end
And are in others the true cure of liking,
The salves that heal Love's wounds and do amend
Consuming woe and slake our hearty sithing,   420
They work not so in thy mind's long disease:
External fancy Time alone recureth,
All whose effects do wear away with ease.
Love of delight, while such delight endureth,
Stays by the pleasure but no longer stays;   425
But in my mind so is her love enclosed,
And is therefore not only the best part,

But into it the essence is disposed:
O Love – the more my woe – to it thou art
Even as the moisture in each plant that grows,   430
Even as the sun unto the frozen ground,
Even as the sweetness to the incarnate rose,
Even as the centre in each perfect round,
As water to the fish, to men as air,
As heat to fire, as light unto the sun –   435
O Love, it is but vain to say thou were:
Ages and times cannot thy power outrun.
Thou art the soul of that unhappy mind
Which, being by Nature made an idle thought,
Began even then to take immortal kind   440
When first her virtues in thy spirits wrought.
From thee, therefore, that mover cannot move
Because it is become thy cause of being:
Whatever error may obscure that love,
Whatever frail effect of mortal living,   445
Whatever passion from distempered heart,
What absence, Time, or injuries effect,
What faithless friends, or deep dissembled art
Present to feed her most unkind suspect.
Yet as the air in deep caves under ground   450
Is strongly drawn when violent heat hath rent
Great clefts therein, till moisture do abound,
And then the same, imprisoned and up-pent,
Breaks out in earthquakes, tearing all asunder,
So in the centre of my cloven heart   455
(My heart, to whom her beauties were such wonder)
Lies the sharp poisoned head of that love's dart,
Which, till all break and all dissolve to dust,
Thence drawn it cannot be, or therein known;
There, mixed with my heart blood, the fretting rust   460
The better part hath eaten and outgrown.
But what of those, or these, or what of aught
Of that which was, or that which is, to treat?
What I possess is but the same I sought:
My love was false, my labours were deceit.   465
Nor less than such they are esteemed to be,
A fraud bought at the price of many woes,
A guile whereof the profits unto me:
Could it be thought premeditate for those?
Witness those withered leaves left on the tree,   470

The sorrow-worren face, the pensive mind:
The external shows what may the internal be:
Cold Care hath bitten both the root and rind.

But stay, my thoughts, make end; give Fortune way:
Harsh is the voice of Woe and Sorrow's sound;   475
Complaints cure not; and tears do but allay
Griefs for a time, which after more abound.
To seek for moisture in the Arabian sand
Is but a loss of labour and of rest;
The links which Time did break of hearty bands   480
Words cannot knit, or wailings make anew;
Seek not the sun in clouds when it is set.
On highest mountains where those cedars grew,
Against whose banks the troubled Ocean beat,
And were the marks to find thy hoped port,   485
Into a soil far off themselves remove
(On Sestos' shore, Leander's late resort,
Hero hath left no lamp to guide her love)
Thou lookest for light in vain, and storms arise:
She sleeps thy death that erst thy danger sithed.   490
Strive then no more, bow down thy weary eyes —
Eyes which to all these woes thy heart have guided.
She is gone, she is lost, she is found, she is ever fair:
Sorrow draws weakly where Love draws not too;
Woe's cries sound nothing but only in Love's ear.   495
Do then by dying what life cannot do;
Unfold thy flocks, and leave them to the fields
To feed on hills, or dales, where likes them best
Of what the summer or the springtime yields;
For Love and Time hath given thee leave to rest.   500
Thy heart (which was their fold) now in decay
By often storms, and winter's many blasts
All torn and rent, become misfortune's prey;
False hope, my shepherd's staff, now age hath brast;
My pipe, which Love's own hand gave my desire   505
To sing her praises and my woe upon,
Despair hath often threatened to the fire,
As vain to keep now all the rest are gone.
Thus home I draw as Death's long night draws on;
Yet, every foot, old thoughts turn back mine eyes;   510
Constraint me guides, as old age draws a stone
Against the hill, which over-weighty lies

For feeble arms or wasted strength to move;
My steps are backward, gazing on my loss,
My mind's affection and my soul's sole love,   515
Not mixed with Fancy's chaff or Fortune's dross.
To God I leave it, who first gave it me,
And I her gave, and she returned again,
As it was hers. So let His mercies be
Of my last comforts the essential mean.   520
    But be it so, or not, the effects are past:
    Her love hath end; my woe must ever last.

The end of the Books, of the Ocean's love to Cynthia,
and the beginning of the 22 Book, entreating of Sorrow

My day's delights, my springtime joys fordone,
Which in the dawn and rising sun of youth
Had their creation and were first begun,
Do in the evening and the winter sad
Present my mind, which takes my time's account,   5
The grief remaining of the joy it had.
My times that then ran o'er themselves in these,
And now run out in others' happiness,
Bring unto those new joys, and new-born days.
So could she not, if she were not the Sun,   10
Which sees the birth and burial of all else,
And holds that power with which she first begun,
Leaving each withered body to be torn
By Fortune, and by times tempestuous,
Which by her virtue once fair fruit have borne;   15
Knowing she can renew, and can create
Green from the ground, and flowers even out of stone,
By virtue lasting over time and date,
Leaving us only woe which, like the moss,
Having compassion of unburied bones,   20
Cleaves to mischance and unrepaired loss.
For tender stalks –

LATER POEMS

20 Now we have present made

Now we have present made
To Cynthia, Phoebe, Flora,
Diana and Aurora,
Beauty that cannot vade:

A flower of Love's own planting,   5
A pattern kept by Nature
For beauty, form and stature
When she would frame a darling.

She as the valley of Peru,
Whose summer ever lasteth;   10
Time-conquering-all she mastereth
By being always new.

As elemental fire
(Whose food and flame consumes not),
Or as the passion ends not   15
Of Virtue's true desire:

So her celestial frame
And quintessential mind,
Which heavens together bind,
Shall ever be the same.   20

Then to her servants leave her –
Love, Nature and Perfection:
Princess of world's affection,
O praises but deceive her.

If Love could find a quill   25
Drawn from an angel's wing,
Or did the Muses sing
That pretty wanton's will,

Perchance he could indite
To please all other sense: 30
But love's and woe's expense
Sorrow can only write.

21

The lie

Go, soul, the body's guest,
　Upon a thankless errand:
Fear not to touch the best,
　The truth shall be thy warrant:
Go, since I needs must die,   5
　And give the world the lie.

Say to the Court it glows
   And shines like rotten wood;
Say to the Church it shows
   What's good and doth no good: 10
If Church and Court reply,
   Then give them both the lie.

Tell Potentates they live
   Acting but others' action,
Not loved unless they give,   15
   Not strong but by a faction:
If Potentates reply,
   Give Potentates the lie.

Tell men of high condition,
   That manage the estate,   20
Their purpose is ambition,
   Their practice only hate:
And if they once reply,
   Then give them all the lie.

Tell them that brave it most,   25
   They beg for more by spending,
Who in their greatest cost
   Seek nothing but commending:
And if they make reply,   30
   Then give them all the lie.

Tell Zeal it wants devotion;
   Tell Love it is but Lust;
Tell Time it metes but motion;
   Tell flesh it is but dust:
And wish them not reply,   35
   For thou must give the lie.

Tell Age it daily wasteth;
   Tell Honour how it alters;
Tell Beauty how she blasteth;
   Tell Favour how it falters: 40
And as they shall reply,
   Give every one the lie.

Tell Wit how much it wrangles
   In tickle points of niceness;
Tell Wisdom she entangles   45
   Herself in over-wiseness:

And when they do reply,
   Straight give them both the lie.

Tell Physic of her boldness;
   Tell Skill it is prevention;
Tell Charity of coldness;
   Tell Law it is Contention:
And as they do reply
   So give them still the lie.

Tell Fortune of her blindness;
   Tell Nature of decay;
Tell Friendship of unkindness;
   Tell Justice of delay:
And if they will reply,
   Then give them all the lie.

Tell Arts they have no soundness,
   But vary by esteeming;
Tell schools they want profoundness
   And stand too much on seeming:
If Arts and schools reply,
   Give Arts and schools the lie.

Tell Faith it's fled the city;
   Tell how the country erreth;
Tell Manhood shakes off pity;
   Tell Virtue least preferreth:
And if they do reply,
   Spare not to give the lie.

So when thou hast, as I
   Commanded thee, done blabbing,
Although to give the lie
   Deserves no less than stabbing,
Stab at thee he that will,
   No stab thy soul can kill.

50

55

60

65

70

75

22

A Prognostication upon cards and dice

Before the sixth day of the next new year,
Strange wonders in this kingdom shall appear:
Four kings shall be assembled in this isle,
Where they shall keep great tumult for awhile:

Many men then shall have an end of crosses,   5
And many likewise shall sustain great losses;
Many that now full joyful are and glad
Shall at that time be sorrowful and sad;
Full many a Christian's heart shall quake for fear
The dreadful sound of trump when he shall hear;   10
Dead bones shall then be tumbled up and down
In every city and in every town.
By day or night this tumult shall not cease,
Until an herald shall proclaim a peace:
An herald strange, the like was never born,   15
Whose very beard is flesh and mouth is horn.

23

Sir Walter Ralegh to his son

Three things there be that prosper up apace
And flourish, whilst they grow asunder far;
But on a day they meet all in one place,
And when they meet they one another mar;
And they be these: the wood, the weed, the wag.   5
The wood is that which makes the gallow tree,
The weed is that which strings the hangman's bag,
The wag (my pretty knave) betokeneth thee.
Mark well, dear boy: whilst these assemble not,
Green springs the tree, hemp grows, the wag is wild;   10
But when they meet, it makes the timber rot,
It frets the halter, and it chokes the child.
    Then bless thee, and beware, and let us pray
    We part not with thee at this meeting day.

24

The passionate man's pilgrimage

Give me my scallop-shell of quiet,
My staff of faith to walk upon,
My scrip of joy, immortal diet,
My bottle of salvation,
My gown of glory, Hope's true gage,   5
And thus I'll take my pilgrimage.

Blood must be my body's balmer:
No other balm will there be given

Whilst my soul, like a white palmer,
Travels to the land of heaven, 10
Over the silver mountains,
Where spring the nectar fountains:
And there I'll kiss
The bowl of bliss,
And drink my eternal fill 15
On every milken hill.
My soul will be a-dry before,
But after it will ne'er thirst more.

And by the happy blissful way
More peaceful pilgrims I shall see, 20
That have shook off their gowns of clay,
And go apparelled fresh like me.
I'll bring them first
To slake their thirst,
And then to taste those nectar suckets, 25
At the clear wells
Where sweetness dwells,
Drawn up by saints in crystal buckets.

And when our bottles and all we
Are filled with immortality, 30
Then the holy paths we'll travel
Strewed with rubies thick as gravel,
Ceilings of diamonds, sapphire floors,
High walls of coral, and pearly bowers.

From thence to heaven's bribeless hall, 35
Where no corrupted voices brawl,
No conscience molten into gold,
Nor forged accusers bought and sold,
No cause deferred, nor vain-spent journey:
For there Christ is the king's attorney, 40
Who pleads for all without degrees,
And he hath angels, but no fees.

When the grand twelve million jury
Of our sins and sinful fury
'Gainst our souls black verdicts give, 45
Christ pleads his death, and then we live:
Be thou my speaker, taintless pleader,
Unblotted lawyer, true proceeder:

Thou movest salvation even for alms,
Not with a bribed lawyer's palms.   50

And this is my eternal plea
To him that made heaven, earth, and sea:
Seeing my flesh must die so soon
And want a head to dine next noon,
Just at the stroke, when my veins start and spread,   55
Set on my soul an everlasting head;
Then am I ready, like a palmer fit,
To tread those blest paths which before I writ.

25

On the life of man

What is our life? a play of passion;
Our mirth, the music of division:
Our mothers' wombs the tiring houses be,
Where we are dressed for this short comedy;
Heaven the judicious sharp spectator is,   5
That sits and marks still who doth act amiss;
Our graves that hide us from the searching sun
Are like drawn curtains when the play is done:
Thus march we playing to our latest rest;
Only we die in earnest, that's no jest.   10

26

To the translator of Lucan

Had Lucan hid the truth to please the time
He had been too unworthy of thy pen,
Who never sought, nor ever cared to climb
By, flattery, or seeking worthless men.
For this thou hast been bruised: but yet those scars   5
Do beautify no less than those wounds do
Received in just and in religious wars
(Though thou hast bled by both, and bearest them too).
Change not: to change thy fortune 'tis too late:
Who with a manly faith resolves to die   10
May promise to himself a lasting state,
Though not so great, yet free from infamy.
     Such was thy Lucan, whom so to translate,
     Nature thy Muse, like Lucan's, did create.

27

Verse translations from *The History of the World*

(1)

Virgil, *Aeneid*, 6, 724–7 (from Book 1, ch. 1.6)

The heaven, the earth, and all the liquid main,
The moon's bright globe, and stars Titanian,
A spirit within maintains: and their whole mass
A mind, which through each part infused doth pass,
Fashions, and works, and wholly doth transpierce   5
All this great body of the universe.

(2)

Catullus, *Poems*, 5. 4–6 (from Book 1, ch. 2.5)

> The sun may set and rise
> But we (contrariwise)
> Sleep after our short light
> One everlasting night.

(3)

Juvenal, *Satires*, 15. 9–11 (from Book 1, ch. 6.3)

The Egyptians think it sin to root up, or to bite
Their leeks or onions, which they serve with holy rite:
O happy nations, which of their own sowing
Have store of gods in every garden growing.

(4)

Orpheus to Musaeus, fragment 1 from Justin Martyr,
Hortatory Address to the Greeks, ch. 15 (from Book 1, ch. 6.7)

Then marking this my sacred speech, but truly lend
Thy heart, that's Reason's sphere, and the right way ascend,
And see the world's sole king. First, he is simply one,
Begotten of himself, from whom is born alone
All else, in which he is still; nor could it ere befall   5
A mortal eye to see him once: yet he sees all.

(5)

Sedulius, 1.226–31 (from Book 1, ch. 10.7)

Ah wretched they that worship vanities
And consecrate dumb idols in their heart,
Who their own Maker (God on high) despise,
And fear the work of their own hands and art.
What fury, what great madness, doth beguile   5
Men's minds? that man should ugly shapes adore,
Of birds, or bulls, or dragons, or the vile
Half-dog half-man on knees for aid implore?

(6)

Aeschylus, *Prometheus Bound*, 456–61 (from Book 2, ch. 6.4)

But Fortune governed all their works till when
I first found out how stars did set and rise –
A profitable art to mortal men;
And others of like use I did devise
As: letters to compose in learned wise
I first did teach; and first did amplify
The mother of the Muses, Memory.

(7)

Lucan, *Pharsalia*, 3. 220–1 (from Book 2, ch. 8.1)

Phoenicians first (if Fame may credit have)
In rude characters dared our words to 'grave.

(8)

Ovid, *Amores*, 2. 3. 43–4 (from Book 2, ch. 13.3)

Here Tantalus in water seeks for water, and doth miss
The fleeting fruit he catcheth at: his long tongue brought him
this.

(9)

Horace, *Satires*, 1. 1. 68–70 (from Book 2, ch. 13.3)

The thirsting Tantalus doth catch at streams that from him flee.
Why laughest thou? the name but changed, the tale is told of
thee.

(10)

Horace, *Odes*, 3. 16. 1–11 (from Book 2, ch. 13.4)

The brasen tower with doors close barred,
And watchful bandogs frightful guard,
  Kept safe the maidenhead
  Of Danae from secret love,
Till smiling Venus and wise Jove   5
  Beguiled her father's dread:
For, changed into a golden shower,
The god into her lap did pour
  Himself, and took his pleasure.
Through guards and stony walls to break   10
The thunderbolt is far more weak
  Than is a golden treasure.

(11)

Lucretius, *de rerum Naturae*, 5. 325–8 (from Book 2, ch. 13.7)

If all this world had no original,
But things have ever been as now they are,
Before the siege of Thebes or Troy's last fall,
Why did no poet sing some elder war?

(12)

Virgil, *Aeneid*, 3. 104–12 (from Book 2, ch. 14.1)

In the main sea the isle of Crete doth lie:
Where Jove was born, thence is our progeny.
There is mount Ida: there, in fruitful land,
An hundred great and goodly cities stand.
Thence (if I follow not mistaken Fame)   5
Teucer the eldest of our grandsires came
To the Rhaetean shores and reigned there
Ere yet fair Ilion was built, and ere
The towers of Troy; their dwelling place they sought
In lowest vale. Hence Cybel's rites were brought;   10
Hence Corybantian Cymbales did remove;
And hence the name of our Idaean grove.

(13)

Virgil, *Aeneid*, 3. 163–8 (from Book 2, ch. 16.1)

Hesperia the Grecians call the place:
An ancient fruitful land, a warlike race.
Œnotrians held it; now the later progeny
Gives it their captain's name, and calls it Italy.
This seat belongs to us, hence Dardanus,   5
Hence came the author of our stock, Iasius.

(14)

Horace, *Odes*, 4.9 25–8 (from Book 2, ch. 14.1)

Many by valour have deserved renown
   Ere Agamemnon, yet lie all oppressed
Under long night unwept for and unknown:
   For with no sacred poet were they blest.

(15)

Ausonius, *Epigrams*, 118 (from Book 2, ch. 22.6)

I am that Dido, which thou here dost see
Cunningly framed in beauteous imagery:
Like this I was, but had not such a soul
As Maro feigned, incestuous and foul.
Aeneas never with his Trojan host   5
Beheld my face or landed on this coast.
But flying proud Iarbas' villainy,
Not moved by furious love or jealousy,
I did with weapon chaste, to save my fame,
Make way for death untimely, ere it came.   10
This was my end. But first I built a town,
Revenged my husband's death, lived with renown.
Why did'st thou stir up Virgil, envious Muse,
Falsely my name and honour to abuse?
Readers, believe historians, not those   15
Which to the world Jove's thefts and vice expose.
Poets are liars, and for verse's sake
Will make the gods of human crimes partake.

(16)

Claudian, *Against Eutropius*, 1. 321–3 (Book 4, ch. 2.15)

Over the Medes and light Sabaeans reigns
This female sex; and under arms of queens
Great part of the barbarian land remains.

LAST POEMS

28

Possible first draft of the petition to Queen Anne

My day's delight, my springtime joys foredone,
Which in the dawn and rising sun of youth
Had their creation and were first begun,

Do in the evening and the winter sad
Present my mind, which takes my time's account,   5
The grief remaining of the joy it had.

For as no fortune stands, so no man's love
Stays by the wretched and disconsolate:
All old affections from new sorrows move.

Moss to unburied bones, ivy to walls,   10
Whom life and people have abandoned
Till the one be rotten, stays, till the other falls:

But friendships, kindred, and love's memory
Dies sole, extinguished hearing or beholding
The voice of woe or face of misery,   15

Who, being in all like those winter showers,
Do come uncalled but then forbear to fall
When parching heat hath burnt leaves and flowers.

And what we sometime were we seem no more:
Fortune hath changed our shapes and Destiny   20
Defaced our very form we had before,

For did in cinders any heat remain
Of those clear fires of love and friendliness,
I could not call for right and call in vain.

Or had Truth power, the guiltless could not fall,   25
Malice, Vainglory, and Revenge triumph:
But Truth alone cannot encounter all.

All love and all desert of former times
Malice hath covered from my sovereign's eyes
And largely laid abroad supposed crimes,   30

Burying the former with their memory,
Teaching offence to speak before it go,
Disguising private hate with public duty.

But Mercy is fled to God that Mercy made,
Compassion dead, Faith turned to Policy,   35
Which knows not those which sit in Sorrow's shade.

Cold walls, to you I speak: but you are senseless;
Celestial powers, you heard, but have determined
And shall determine to the greatest happiness.

To whom then shall I cry, to whom shall wrong   40
Cast down her tears or hold up folded hands?
To her to whom remorse doth most belong,

To her that is the first and may alone
Be called Empress of the Britons:
Who should have mercy if a queen have none?   45

Who should resist strong hate, fierce injury,
Or who relieve the oppressed state of Truth?
Who is companion else to powerful Majesty

But you, great, godliest, powerful princess,
Who have brought glory and posterity   50
Unto this widow land and people hopeless?

29

Sir Walter Ralegh's petition to the Queen. 1618

Oh had Truth power the guiltless could not fall,
Malice win glory, or Revenge triumph:
But Truth alone cannot encounter all.

Mercy is fled to God which Mercy made,
Compassion dead, Faith turned to Policy,   5
Friends know not those who sit in Sorrow's shade.

For what we sometime were we are no more:
Fortune hath changed our shape, and Destiny
Defaced the very form we had before.

All love and all desert of former times   10
Malice hath covered from my sovereign's eyes,
And largely laid abroad supposed crimes.

But kings call not to mind what vassals were,
But know them now, as Envy hath descrived them:
So can I look on no side from despair.   15

Cold walls, to you I speak: but you are senseless;
Celestial powers, you hear, but have determined
And shall determine to the greatest happiness.

Then unto whom shall I unfold my wrong,
Cast down my tears, or hold up folded hands?   20
To her to whom remorse doth most belong,

To her who is the first and may alone
Be justly called the Empress of the Britons:
Who should have mercy if a queen have none?

Save those that would have died for your defence: 25
Save him whose thoughts no treason ever tainted;
For, lo, destruction is no recompense.

If I have sold my duty, sold my faith
To strangers, which was only due to one,
Nothing I should esteem so dear as death.   30

But if both God and Time shall make you know
That I your humblest vassal am oppressed,
Then cast your eyes on undeserved woe

That I and mine may never mourn the miss
Of her we had, but praise our living Queen,   35
Who brings us equal, if not greater, bliss.

30

By Sir W. R. which he writ the night before his execution

> Even such is Time, which takes in trust
> Our youth, our joys, and all we have,
> And pays us but with age and dust;
> Who, in the dark and silent grave,
> When we have wandered all our ways,   5
> Shuts up the story of our days:
> But from which earth and grave and dust
> The Lord shall raise me up, I trust.

31

Sir W. Ralegh, on the snuff of a candle the night before
he died.

> Cowards fear to die, but courage stout,
> Rather than live in snuff, will be put out.

SIR PHILIP SIDNEY

SIR PHILIP SIDNEY

Dates: 1554–86. Born at Penshurst Place, Kent, eldest child of Sir Henry Sidney and Lady Mary (sister of the Earl of Leicester). Philip II of Spain was his godfather. Educated at Shrewsbury School from 1564 then at Christ Church, Oxford (1567). Undertook a European tour in 1572 with the Earl of Lincoln, during which he met the Protestant diplomat Hubert Languet. Returned to London June, 1575; made Royal Cupbearer, 1576; ambassador to the Holy Roman Emperor Rudolph II, 1577. Opposed Elizabeth I's projected marriage to the Duke of Alencon (1579) and received dedication of Spenser's *Shepherds' Calendar* the same year. 1581 saw the completion of the 'old' *Arcadia* (possibly begun 1577) and the *Defence of Poesy*. The following year Penelope Devereux, daughter of the first Earl of Essex (who had died in 1576 expressing the wish that his daughter should marry Sidney), married Lord Rich. Sidney then began *Astrophil and Stella* about her.

He was knighted in 1583 and in September of the same year married Frances, daughter of Sir Francis Walsingham, the queen's Secretary of State. 1585 saw work on the 'new' *Arcadia*, the psalm translations, and translations of Du Plessis Mornay's *De la vérité de la religion chrestienne* and Du Bartas's *La semaine ou création du monde*. Appointed Joint Master of the Ordnance (July 1585) then Governor of the Netherlands town of Flushing (his uncle, the Earl of Leicester, was in charge of the troops sent to support the Dutch in their revolt against occupying Spanish forces). In 1586 his mother and father died, as did Sidney himself, of an infection which developed after a musket wound to the thigh outside Zutphen. 1590 saw the publication of the 'new' *Arcadia* (republished 1593 together with Books 3–5 of the 'old' *Arcadia*). Two editions of the *Defence of Poesy* were published in 1595, one entitled *An Apology for Poetry*; his collected works were first published in 1598. See MARY SIDNEY.

POEMS FROM THE *ARCADIA*

1

Song Contest: Lalus and Dorus
('Come Dorus, come')

Lalus.   Come Dorus, come, let songs thy sorrows signify;
     And if for want of use thy mind ashamed is,
     That very shame with Love's high title dignify.
        No style is held for base where Love well named is:
     Each ear sucks up the words a true love scattereth,   5
     And plain speech oft than quaint phrase better framed is.

Dorus.   Nightingales seldom sing, the pie still chattereth;
     The wood cries most before it throughly kindled be;
     Deadly wounds inward bleed, each slight sore mattereth;
        Hardly they herd, which by good hunters singled be;   10
     Shallow brooks murmur most, deep silent slide away;
     Nor true love loves those loves with others mingled be.

Lalus.   If thou wilt not be seen, thy face go hide away;
     Be none of us, or else maintain our fashion:
     Who frowns at others' feasts doth better bide away.   15
        But if thou hast a love, in that love's passion,
     I challenge thee, by show of her perfection,
     Which of us two deserveth most compassion.

Dorus.   Thy challenge great, but greater my protection:
     Sing then, and see (for now thou hast inflamed me)   20
     Thy health too mean a match for my infection.
        No, though the heavens for high attempts have blamed
        me,
     Yet high is my attempt. O Muse, historify
     Her praise, whose praise to learn your skill hath framed me.

Lalus.   Muse, hold your peace; but thou, my god Pan,   25
        glorify
     My Kala's gifts, who with all good gifts filled is.
     Thy pipe, O Pan, shall help, though I sing sorrily:
        A heap of sweets she is, where nothing spilled is,
     Who though she be no bee, yet full of honey is;
     A lily field, with plough of rose which tilled is;   30
        Mild as a lamb, more dainty than a coney is;
     Her eyes my eyesight is, her conversation
     More glad to me than to a miser money is.

What coy account she makes of estimation!
How nice to touch! How all her speeches peized be!   35
A nymph thus turned, but mended in translation.

Dorus.   Such Kala is: but ah, my fancies raised be
In one whose name to name were high presumption,
Since virtues all, to make her title, pleased be.
     O happy gods, which by inward assumption   40
Enjoy her soul, in body's fair possession,
And keep it joined, fearing your seat's consumption.
     How oft with rain of tears skies make confession
Their dwellers rapt with sight of her perfection,
From heavenly throne to her heaven use digression.   45
     Of best things then what world can yield confection
To liken her? Deck yours with your comparison:
She is herself of best things the collection.

Lalus.   How oft my doleful sire cried to me, 'tarry son',
When first he spied my love! How oft he said to me   50
'Thou art no soldier fit for Cupid's garrison.
     My son, keep this, that my long toil hath laid to me:
Love well thine own: methinks wool's whiteness passeth all;
I never found long love such wealth hath paid to me.'
     This wind he spent; but when my Kala glasseth all   55
My sight in her fair limbs, I then assure myself,
Not rotten sheep, but high crowns she surpasseth all.
     Can I be poor, that her gold hair procure myself?
Want I white wool, whose eyes her white skin garnished?
Till I get her, shall I to keep inure myself?   60

Dorus.   How oft, when Reason saw love of her   harnished
With armour of my heart, he cried, 'O vanity,
To set a pearl in steel so meanly varnished!
     Look to thyself; reach not beyond humanity;
Her mind, beams, state far from thy weak wings
                              banished;   65
And love which lover hurts is inhumanity.'
     Thus Reason said; but she came, Reason vanished;
Her eyes so mastering me, that such objection
Seemed but to spoil the food of thoughts long famished.
     Her peerless height my mind to high erection   70
Draws up; and if Hope-failing end Life's pleasure,
Of fairer Death how can I make election?

Lalus.   Once my well-waiting eyes espied my treasure,

With sleeves turned up, loose hair, and breasts enlarged,
Her father's corn (moving her fair limbs) measure.   75
  'O,' cried I, 'of so mean work be discharged:
Measure my case, how by thy beauty's filling
With seed of woes my heart brim-full is charged.
  Thy father bids thee save, and chides for spilling;
Save then my soul, spill not my thoughts well heaped,   80
No lovely praise was ever got by killing.'
  These bold words she did hear, this fruit I reaped:
That she, whose look alone might make me blessed,
Did smile on me, and then away she leaped.

Dorus.   Once, O sweet once, I saw, with dread   85
    oppressed,
Her whom I dread; so that with prostrate lying
Her length the earth in Love's chief clothing dressed.
  I saw that riches fall, and fell a-crying:
'Let not dead earth enjoy so dear a cover,
But deck therewith my soul for your sake dying: 90
  Lay all your fear upon your fearful lover,
Shine eyes on me, that both our lives be guarded;
So I your sight, you shall yourselves recover.'
  I cried, and was with open rays rewarded.
But straight they fled, summoned by cruel Honour: 95
Honour, the cause desert is not regarded.

Lalus.   This maid thus made for joys, O Pan, bemoan
    her,
That without love she spends her years of love:
So fair a field would well become an owner.
  And if enchantment can a hard heart move,   100
Teach me what circle may acquaint her sprite
Affection's charms in my behalf to prove.
  The circle is my round-about-her sight;
The power I will invoke dwells in her eyes;
My charm should be: she haunt me day and night.   105

Dorus.   Far other care, O Muse, my sorrow tries,
Bent to such one in whom myself must say:
Nothing can mend one point that in her lies.
  What circle then in so rare force bears sway?
Whose sprite all sprites can spoil, raise, damn or save, 110
No charm holds her, but well possess she may.
  Possess she doth, and makes my soul her slave,

My eyes the bands, my thoughts the fatal knot:
No thralls like them that inward bondage have.

Lalus.   Kala, at length conclude my lingering lot;   115
Disdain me not, although I be not fair.
Who is an heir of many hundred sheep
Doth beauties keep which never sun can burn,
Nor storms do turn: fairness serves oft to wealth.
Yet all my health I place in your good will,   120
Which if you will (O do) bestow on me,
Such as you see, such still you shall me find,
Constant and kind: my sheep your food shall breed,
Their wool your weed; I will you music yield
In flowery field; and, as the day begins,   125
With twenty gins we will the small birds take,
And pastimes make, as Nature things hath made.
But when in shade we meet of myrtle boughs,
Then Love allows our pleasure to enrich,
The thought of which doth pass all worldly pelf.   130

Dorus.   Lady, yourself, whom neither name I dare,
And titles are but spots to such a worth,
Hear plaints come forth from dungeon of my mind:
The noblest kind rejects not others' woes.
I have no shows of wealth: my wealth is you,   135
My beauty's hue your beams, my health your deeds;
My mind for weeds your virtue's livery wears.
My food is tears; my tunes waymenting yield;
Despair my field; the flowers spirit's wars;
My day new cares; my gins my daily sight,   140
In which do light small birds of thoughts o'erthrown;
My pastimes none: time passeth on my fall;
Nature made all, but me of dolours made.
I find no shade but where my sun doth burn:
No place to turn; without, within, it fries;   145
Nor help by life or death who living dies.

Lalus.   But if my Kala this my suit denies,
Which so much reason bears,
Let crows pick out mine eyes, which saw too much:
If still her mind be such,   150
My earthly mould doth melt in watery tears.

    Dorus.   My earthy mould doth melt in watery tears,
    And they again resolve

To air of sighs, sighs to the heart's fire turn,
Which doth to ashes burn: 155
So doth my life within itself dissolve.

Lalus.   So doth my life within itself dissolve,
That I am like a flower
New plucked from the place where it did breed,
Life showing, dead indeed: 160
Such force hath Love above poor Nature's power.

Dorus.   Such force hath Love above poor Nature's power
That I grow like a shade
Which, being nought, seems somewhat to the eyne
While that one body shine.   165
O, he is marred that is for others made.

Lalus.   O, he is marred that is for others made:
Which thought doth mar my piping declaration,
Thinking how it hath marred my shepherd's trade.
    Now my hoarse voice doth fail this occupation,   170
And others long to tell their love's condition:
Of singing take to thee the reputation.

Dorus.   Of singing take to thee the reputation,
New friend of mine: I yield to thy ability;
My heart doth seek another estimation.   175
    But ah, my Muse, I would thou hadst facility
To work my goddess so by thy invention
On me to cast those eyes, where shine nobility.
    Seen and unknown; heard, but without attention.

2

Against Cupid ('Poor painters oft')

Poor painters oft with silly poets join
To fill the world with strange but vain conceits;
One brings the stuff, the other stamps the coin,
Which breeds nought else but gloses of deceits.
    Thus painters Cupid paint, thus poets do: 5
    A naked god, young, blind, with arrows two.

Is he a god, that ever flies the light?
Or naked he, disguised in all untruth?
If he be blind, how hitteth he so right?
How is he young, that tamed old Phoebus' youth?   10

But arrows two, and tipped with gold or lead?
Some hurt accuse a third with horny head.

No, nothing so: an old false knave he is,
By Argus got on Io, then a cow,
What time for her Juno her Jove did miss,   15
And charge of her to Argus did allow.
   Mercury killed his false sire for this act;
   His dam, a beast, was pardoned beastly fact.

With father's death, and mother's guilty shame,
With Jove's disdain at such a rival's seed,   20
The wretch, compelled, a runagate became,
And learned what ill a miser state doth breed:
   To lie, feign, glose, to steal, pry and accuse,
   Nought in himself, each other to abuse.

Yet bears he still his parents' stately gifts,   25
A horned head, cloven foot, and thousand eyes,
Some gazing still, some winking wily shifts,
With large long ears where never rumour dies.
   His horned head doth seem the heaven to spite;
   His cloven foot doth never tread aright.   30

Thus half a man, with man he daily haunts,
Clothed in the shape which soonest may deceive:
Thus half a beast, each beastly vice he plants
In those weak hearts that his advice receive.
   He prowls each place still in new colours decked,   35
   Sucking one's ill another to infect.

To narrow breasts he comes all wrapped in gain;
To swelling hearts he shines in honour's fire;
To open eyes all beauties he doth rain;
Creeping to each with flattering of desire.   40
   But for that Love's desire most rules the eyes,
   Therein his name, there his chief triumph lies.

Millions of years this old drivel Cupid lives,
While still more wretch, more wicked he doth prove;
Till now at length that Jove him office gives   45
(At Juno's suit, who much did Argus love)
   In this our world a hangman for to be
   Of all those fools that will have all they see.

3

In vain, mine eyes

In vain, mine eyes, you labour to amend
    With flowing tears your fault of hasty sight,
Since to my heart her shape you so did send
    That her I see, though you did lose your light.

In vain, my heart, now you with sight are burned,   5
    With sighs you seek to cool your hot desire,
Since sighs, into mine inward furnace turned,
    For bellows serve to kindle more the fire.

Reason, in vain (now you have lost my heart)
    My head you seek, as to your strongest fort,   10
Since there mine eyes have played so false a part
    That to your strength your foes have sure resort:
        And since in vain I find were all my strife,
        To this strange death I vainly yield my life.

4

Let not old age

Let not old age disgrace my high desire,
    O heavenly soul, in human shape contained:
Old wood inflamed doth yield the bravest fire,
    When younger doth in smoke his virtue spend.

Ne let white hairs, which on my face do grow,   5
    Seem to your eyes of a disgraceful hue,
Since whiteness doth present the sweetest show,
    Which makes all eyes do honour unto you.

Old age is wise, and full of constant truth;
    Old age well stayed from ranging humour lives;   10
Old age hath known whatever was in youth;
    Old age o'ercome the greater honour gives:
        And to old age since you yourself aspire,
        Let not old age disgrace my high desire.

5

My sheep are thoughts

My sheep are thoughts, which I both guide and serve;
Their pasture is fair hills of fruitless love;

On barren sweets they feed, and feeding starve:
I wail their lot, but will not other prove.
My sheephook is Wanhope, which all upholds;   5
My weeds, Desire, cut out in endless folds.
   What wool my sheep shall bear, while thus they live,
   In you it is, you must the judgement give.

6

You living powers

You living powers enclosed in stately shrine
Of growing trees, you rural gods that wield
Your sceptres here: if to your ears divine
A voice may come which troubled soul doth yield,
   This vow receive, this vow, O gods, maintain: 5
   My virgin life no spotted thought shall stain.

Thou purest stone, whose pureness doth present
My purest mind; whose temper hard doth show
My tempered heart: by thee my promise sent
Unto myself let after-livers know.   10
   No fancy mine, nor others' wrong suspect
   Make me, O virtuous Shame, thy laws neglect.

O Chastity, the chief of heavenly lights,
Which makes us most immortal shape to wear,
Hold thou my heart, establish thou my sprites: 15
To only thee my constant course I bear.
   Till spotless soul unto thy bosom fly,
   Such life to lead, such death I vow to die.

7

Over these brooks

Over these brooks, trusting to ease mine eyes
(Mine eyes, even great in labour with their tears),
I laid my face: my face wherein there lies
Clusters of clouds which no sun ever clears.
   In watery glass my watery eyes I see: 5
   Sorrows ill eased, where sorrows painted be.

My thoughts, imprisoned in my secret woes,
With flamy breaths do issue oft in sound:
The sound to this strange air no sooner goes

But that it doth with Echo's force rebound   10
   And make me hear the plaints I would refrain:
   Thus outward helps my inward griefs maintain.

Now in this sand I would discharge my mind,
And cast from me part of my burdenous cares:
But in the sands my pains foretold I find,   15
And see therein how well the writer fares.
   Since stream, air, sand, mine eyes and ears conspire,
   What hope to quench, where each thing blows, the fire?

8

Apollo great

Apollo great, whose beams the greater world do light,
And in our little world dost clear our inward sight,
Which ever shines, though hid from earth by earthly shade,
Whose lights do ever live, but in our darkness fade:
Thou God, whose youth was decked with spoil of Python's   5
   skin
(So humble knowledge can throw down the snakish sin),
Latona's son, whose birth in pain and travail long
Doth teach to learn the good what travails do belong;
In travail of our life (a short but tedious space)
While brickle hour-glass runs guide thou our panting race: 10
Give us foresightful minds; give us minds to obey
What foresight tells; our thoughts upon thy knowledge stay.
Let so our fruits grow up that Nature be maintained:
But so our hearts keep down, with Vice they be not stained.
Let this assured hold our judgements ever take,   15
That nothing wins the heaven but what doth earth forsake.

9

As I behind a bush did sit

Histor
    As I behind a bush did sit
    I silent heard more words of wit
    Than erst I knew: but first did plain
    The one, which t'other would refrain.

Plangus Boulon
Plangus. Alas, how long this pilgrimage doth last!   5
   What greater ills have now the heavens in store

To couple coming harms with sorrows past?
Long since my voice is hoarse, and throat is sore,
   With cries to skies, and curses to the ground:
   But more I plain, I feel my woes the more.   10
Ah where was first that cruel cunning found
   To frame of earth a vessel of the mind,
   Where it should be to self-destruction bound?
What needed so high sprites such mansions blind?
   Or, wrapped in flesh, what do they here obtain,   15
   But glorious name of wretched human-kind?
Balls to the stars, and thralls to Fortune's reign;
   Turned from themselves, infected with their cage,
   Where death is feared and life is held with pain.
Like players placed to fill a filthy stage,   20
   Where change of thoughts one fool to other shows,
   And all but jests, save only Sorrow's rage.
The child feels that; the man that feeling knows,
   With cries first born (the presage of his life)
   Where wit but serves to have true taste of woes.   25
A shop of shame, a book where blots be rife
   This body is: this body so composed
   As in itself to nourish mortal strife.
So diverse be the elements disposed
   In this weak work that it can never be   30
   Made uniform to any state reposed.
Grief only makes his wretched state to see
   (Even like a top which nought but whipping moves)
   This man, this talking beast, this walking tree.
Grief is the stone which finest judgement proves;   35
   For who grieves not hath but a blockish brain,
   Since cause of grief no cause from life removes.

Boulon. How long wilt thou with moanful music stain
   The cheerful notes these pleasant places yield,
   Where all good haps a perfect state maintain?   40

Plangus. Cursed be good haps, and cursed be they that build
   Their hopes on haps, and do not make Despair
   For all these certain blows the surest shield.
Shall I, that saw Erona's shining hair
   Torn with her hands, and those same hands of snow   45
   With loss of purest blood themselves to tear,
Shall I, that saw those breasts where beauties flow,
   Swelling with sighs, made pale with mind's disease,

And saw those eyes (those suns) such showers to show,
Shall I, whose ears her mournful words did seize   50
  (Her words in syrup laid of sweetest breath),
  Relent those thoughts which then did so displease?
No, no; Despair my daily lesson saith,
  And saith, although I seek my life to fly,
  Plangus must live to see Erona's death.   55
Plangus must live some help for her to try
  Though in despair, so Love enforceth me;
  Plangus doth live, and shall Erona die?
Erona die? O heaven (if heaven there be)
  Hath all thy whirling course so small effect?   60
  Serve all thy starry eyes this shame to see?
Let dolts in haste some altars fair erect
  To those high powers which idly sit above,
  And virtue do in greatest need neglect.

Boulon. O man, take heed how thou the gods do move   65
  To causeful wrath which thou canst not resist:
  Blasphemous words the speaker vain do prove.
Alas, while we are wrapped in foggy mist
  Of our self-love (so passions do deceive)
  We think they hurt when most they do assist.   70
To harm us worms should that high Justice leave
  His nature? nay, himself? for so it is.
  What glory from our loss can he receive?
But still our dazzled eyes their way do miss,
  While that we do at his sweet scourge repine,   75
  The kindly way to beat us to our bliss.
If she must die, then hath she passed the line
  Of loathsome days, whose loss how canst thou moan,
  That dost so well their miseries define?
But such we are, with inward tempest blown   80
  Of winds quite contrary in waves of will:
  We moan that lost, which had we did bemoan.

Plangus. And shall she die? shall cruel fire spill
  Those beams that set so many hearts on fire?
  Hath she not force even Death with love to kill?   85
Nay, even cold Death, inflamed with hot desire
  Her to enjoy (where joy itself is thrall),
  Will spoil the earth of his most rich attire.
Thus Death becomes a rival to us all,
  And hopes with foul embracements her to get,   90

In whose decay Virtue's fair shrine must fall.
O Virtue weak, shall Death his triumph set
    Upon thy spoils, which never should lie waste?
    Let Death first die; be thou his worthy let.
By what eclipse shall that sun be defaced?   95
    What mine hath erst thrown down so fair a tower?
    What sacrilege hath such a saint disgraced?
The world the garden is, she is the flower
    That sweetens all the place; she is the guest
    Of rarest price, both heaven and earth her bower.   100
And shall (O me) all this in ashes rest?
    Alas, if you a Phoenix new will have
    Burnt by the Sun, she first must build her nest.
But well you know the gentle Sun would save
    Such beams so like his own, which might have might   105
    In him, the thoughts of Phaëthon's dam to grave.
Therefore, alas, you use vile Vulcan's spite,
    Which nothing spares, to melt that virgin wax
    Which while it is, it is all Asia's light.
O Mars, for what doth serve thy armed axe?   110
    To let that witold beast consume in flames
    Thy Venus' child, whose beauty Venus lacks?
O Venus (if her praise no envy frames
    In thy high mind) get her thy husband's grace:
    Sweet speaking oft a currish heart reclaims.   115
O eyes of mine, where once she saw her face,
    Her face which was more lively in my heart;
    O brain, where thought of her hath only place;
O hand, which touched her hand when we did part;
    O lips, that kissed that hand with my tears sprent;   120
    O tongue, then dumb, not daring tell my smart;
O soul, whose love in her is only spent,
    What ever you see, think, touch, kiss, speak, or love,
    Let all for her, and unto her be bent.

Boulon. Thy wailing words do much my spirits move,   125
    They uttered are in such a feeling fashion
    That Sorrow's work against my will I prove.
Methinks I am partaker of thy passion,
    And in thy case do glass mine own debility:
    Self-guilty folk most prone to feel compassion.   130
Yet Reason saith, Reason should have ability
    To hold these worldly things in such proportion

As let them come or go with even facility.
But our desire's tyrannical extortion
 Doth force us there to set our chief delightfulness 135
 Where but a baiting place is all our portion.
But still, although we fail of perfect rightfulness,
 Seek we to tame these childish superfluities:
 Let us not wink though void of purest sightfulness;
For what can breed more peevish incongruities 140
 Than man to yield to female lamentations?
 Let us some grammar learn of more congruities.

Plangus. If through mine ears pierce any consolations
 By wise discourse, sweet tunes, or poet's fiction;
 If aught I cease these hideous exclamations, 145
While that my soul, she, she lives in affliction,
 Then let my life long time on earth maintained be
 To wretched me the last worst malediction.
Can I, that know her sacred parts, restrained be
 From any joy; know Fortune's vile displacing her, 150
 In moral rules let raging woes contained be?
Can I forget, when they in prison placing her,
 With swelling heart in spite and due disdainfulness
 She lay for dead, till I helped with unlacing her?
Can I forget from how much mourning plainfulness 155
 With diamond in window glass she graved,
 'Erona die, and end this ugly painfulness'?
Can I forget in how strange phrase she craved
 That quickly they would her burn, drown, or smother,
 As if by Death she only might be saved? 160
Then let me eke forget one hand from other;
 Let me forget that Plangus I am called;
 Let me forget I am son to my mother:
But if my memory thus must be thralled
 To that strange stroke which conquered all my senses, 165
 Can thoughts still thinking so rest unappalled?

Boulon. Who still doth seek against himself offences
 What pardon can avail? Or who employs him
 To hurt himself, what shields can be defences?
Woe to poor man: each outward thing annoys him 170
 In diverse kinds; yet as he were not filled,
 He heaps in inward grief that most destroys him.
Thus is our thought with pain for thistles tilled;
 Thus be our noblest parts dried up with Sorrow;

Thus is our mind with too much minding spilled.   175
One day lays up stuff of grief for the morrow;
   And whose good haps do leave him unprovided,
   Condoling cause of friendship he will borrow.
Betwixt the good and shade of good divided
   We pity deem that which but weakness is: 180
   So are we from our high creation slided.
But Plangus, lest I may your sickness miss
   Or rubbing, hurt the sore, I here do end:
   The ass did hurt when he did think to kiss.

Histor. Thus did they say, and then away did wend: 185
   High time for me, for scattered were my sheep
   While I their speech in my rude rhyming penned.
Yet for that night my cabin did them keep
   While Plangus did a story strange declare;
   But, hoarse and dry, my pipes I now must spare.   190

10

Echo song ('Fair rocks, goodly rivers')

Philisides	*Echo*

Fair rocks, goodly rivers, sweet woods, when
   shall I see Peace? **Peace.**
Peace? What bars me my tongue? Who is it
   that comes me so nigh? **I.**

O, I do know what guest I have met: it is Echo. **'Tis Echo.**
Well met, Echo, approach; then tell me thy will
   too. **I will too.**
Echo, what do I get yielding my sprite to my
   grieves? **Grieves.**   5
What medicine may I find for a pain that
   draws me to death? **Death.**
O poisonous medicine! What worse to me can
   be than it? **It.**
In what state was I then, when I took this
   deadly disease? **Ease.**
And what manner a mind which had to that
   humour a vein? **Vain.**
Hath not reason enough vehemence the desire
   to reprove? **Prove.**   10

Oft prove I; but what salve, when Reason
    seeks to be gone?   One.

O, what is it, what is it, that may be a salve to
    my love?   Love.

What do lovers seek for, long seeking for to
    enjoy?   Joy.

What be the joys for which to enjoy they went
    to the pains?   Pains.

Then to an earnest love what doth best victory
    lend?   End.   15

End? But I can never end: Love will not give
    me the leave.   Leave.

How be the minds disposed that can not taste
    thy physic?   Sick.

Yet say again thy advice for the ills that I told
    thee.   I told thee.

Doth the infected wretch of his ill the extremity
    know?   No.

But if he know not his harms, what guides hath
    he whilst he be blind?   Blind.   20

What blind guides can he have that leans to a
    fancy?   A fancy.

Can Fancy want eyes, or he fall that steppeth
    aloft?   Oft.

What causes first made these torments on me
    to light?   Light.

Can then a cause be so light that forceth a man
    to go die?   Aye.

Yet tell what light thing I had in me to draw
    me to die?   Eye.   25

Eyesight made me to yield, but what first
    pierced to mine eyes?   Eyes.

Eyes hurters, eyes hurt; but what from them to
    me falls?   Falls.

But when I first did fall, what brought most fall
    to my heart?   Art.

Art? What can be that art which thou dost
    mean by thy speech?   Speech.

What be the fruits of speaking art? What grows
    by the words?   Words.   30

O much more than words: those words served
    more me to bless.   Less.

O when shall I be known, where most to be

known I do long? | **Long.**

Long be thy woes for such news; but how
recks she my thoughts? | **Orts.**

Then, then what do I gain, since unto her will I
do wind? | **Wind.**

Wind, tempest and storms; yet in end what
gives she desire? | **Ire.** 35

Silly reward! Yet among women hath she of
virtue the most. | **Most.**

What great name may I give to so heavenly a
woman? | **A woe-man.**

Woe but seems to me joy, that agrees to my
thought so. | **I thought so.**

Think so, for of my desired bliss it is only the
course. | **Curse.**

Cursed be thyself for cursing that which leads
me to joys. | **Toys.** 40

What be the sweet creatures, where lowly
demands be not heard? | **Hard.**

Hard to be got, but got, constant, to be held
like steels. | **Eels.**

How be they held unkind? Speak, for th'hast
narrowly pried. | **Pride.**

Whence can pride come there, since springs of
beauty be thence? | **Thence.**

Horrible is this blasphemy unto the most holy. | **O lie.** 45

Thou liest, false Echo: their minds as Virtue be
just. | **Just.**

Mockest thou those diamonds, which only be
matched by the gods? | **Odds.**

Odds? What odds is there, since them to the
heavens I prefer? | **Err.**

Tell yet again me the names of these fair
formed to do evils. | **Devils.**

Devils? If in hell such devils do abide, to the
hells I do go. | **Go.** 50

11

O sweet woods

- - - - ◡ - - ◡ ◡

O sweet woods, the delight of solitariness!
O how much I do like your solitariness!

Where man's mind hath a freed consideration
Of goodness to receive lovely direction;
Where senses do behold the order of the heavenly host,   5
And wise thoughts do behold what the creator is.
Contemplation here holdeth his only seat,
Bounded with no limits, borne with a wing of hope,
Climbs even unto the stars; Nature is under it.
Nought disturbs thy quiet, all to thy service yield,   10
Each sight draws on a thought (thought, mother of Science),
Sweet birds kindly do grant harmony unto thee;
Fair trees' shade is enough fortification,
Nor danger to thyself, if be not in thyself.

O sweet woods, the delight of solitariness!   15
O how much I do like your solitariness!
Here nor Treason is hid, veiled in Innocence,
Nor Envy's snaky eye finds any harbour here,
Nor flatterers' venomous insinuations,
Nor cunning humorists' puddled opinions,   20
Nor courteous ruin of proffered usury,
Nor time prattled away, cradle of Ignorance,
Nor causeless Duty, nor cumber of Arrogance,
Nor trifling title of Vanity dazzleth us,
Nor golden manacles stand for a paradise: 25
Here Wrong's name is unheard, Slander a monster is.
Keep thy sprite from Abuse, here no Abuse doth haunt.
What man grafts in a tree dissimulation?

O sweet woods, the delight of solitariness!
O how well I do like your solitariness!   30
Yet dear soil, if a soul enclosed in a mansion
As sweet as violets, fair as a lily is,
Straight as cedar, a voice stains the canary birds,
Whose shade Safety doth hold, Danger avoideth her:
Such wisdom, that in her lives Speculation;   35
Such goodness, that in her Simplicity triumphs;
Where Envy's snaky eye winketh or else dieth,
Slander wants a pretext, Flattery gone beyond:
O, if such a one have bent to a lonely life
Her steps, glad we receive, glad we receive her eyes,   40
And think not she doth hurt our solitariness:
For such company decks such solitariness.

12

Phoebus farewell

Phoebus farewell, a sweeter saint I serve.
The high conceits thy heavenly wisdoms breed
My thoughts forget: my thoughts which never swerve
From her in whom is sown their freedom's seed,
And in whose eyes my daily doom I read.   5

Phoebus farewell, a sweeter saint I serve.
Thou art far off, thy kingdom is above:
She heaven on earth with beauties doth preserve.
Thy beams I like, but her clear rays I love;
Thy force I fear, her force I still do prove.   10

Phoebus, yield up thy title in my mind.
She doth possess, thy image is defaced;
But if thy rage some brave revenge will find
On her, who hath in me thy temple razed,
Employ thy might that she my fires may taste: 15
    And how much more her worth surmounteth thee,
    Make her as much more base by loving me.

13

Since that the stormy rage

Since that the stormy rage of passions dark
(Of passions dark, made dark by beauty's light)
With rebel force hath closed in dungeon dark
My mind ere now led forth by Reason's light:

Since all the things which give mine eyes their light   5
Do foster still the fruits of fancies dark,
So that the windows of my inward light
Do serve to make my inward powers dark:

Since, as I say, both mind and senses dark
Are hurt, not helped, with piercing of the light   10
(While that the light may show the horrors dark,
But cannot make resolved darkness light)
    I like this place where, at the least, the dark
    May keep my thoughts from thought of wonted light.

14

How is my sun

How is my sun, whose beams are shining bright,
Become the cause of my dark ugly night?
Or how do I, captived in this dark plight,
Bewail the case, and in the cause delight?

My mangled mind huge horrors still do fright,   5
With sense possessed, and claimed by Reason's right,
Betwixt which two in me I have this fight,
Where whoso wins, I put myself to flight.

Come, cloudy fears, close up my dazzled sight;
Sorrow, suck up the marrow of my might;   10
Due sighs, blow out all sparks of joyful light;
Tire on, Despair, upon my tired sprite:
    An end, an end, my dulled pen cannot write,
    Nor mazed head think, nor faltering tongue recite.

And hard underneath the sonnet, were these words written:

15

This cave is dark

This cave is dark, but it had never light.
    This wax doth waste itself, yet painless dies.
        These words are full of woes, yet feel they none.

I darkened am, who once had clearest sight.
    I waste my heart, which still new torment tries.   5
        I plain with cause, my woes are all mine own.

    No cave, no wasting wax, no words of grief,
    Can hold, show, tell, my pains without relief.

16

My true love hath my heart

My true love hath my heart, and I have his,
By just exchange, one for the other given.
I hold his dear, and mine he cannot miss:
There never was a better bargain driven.

His heart in me keeps me and him in one; 5
My heart in him his thoughts and senses guides;
He loves my heart, for once it was his own:
I cherish his, because in me it bides.

His heart his wound received from my sight;
My heart was wounded with his wounded heart: 10
For as from me on him his hurt did light,
So still, methought, in me his hurt did smart:
　　Both, equal hurt, in this change sought our bliss:
　　My true love hath my heart, and I have his.

17

O words which fall

O words which fall like summer dew on me,
O breath more sweet than is the growing bean,
O tongue in which all honeyed liquors be,
O voice that doth the thrush in shrillness stain,
　　Do you say still: this is her promise due, 5
　　That she is mine, as I to her am true.

Gay hair, more gay than straw when harvest lies,
Lips red and plum, as cherry's ruddy side,
Eyes fair and great, like fair great ox's eyes,
O breast in which two white sheep swell in pride: 10
　　Join you with me to seal this promise due,
　　That she be mine, as I to her am true.

But thou, white skin, as white as cruds well pressed,
So smooth as, sleekstone-like, it smoothes each part;
And thou dear flesh, as soft as wool new dressed, 15
And yet as hard as brawn made hard by art:
　　First four but say, next four their saying seal,
　　But you must pay the gage of promised weal.

18

Lock up, fair lids

Lock up, fair lids, the treasure of my heart:
Preserve those beams, this age's only light:
To her sweet sense, sweet Sleep, some ease impart,
Her sense too weak to bear her spirit's might.

And while, O Sleep, thou closest up her sight   5
(Her sight where Love did forge his fairest dart),
O harbour all her parts in easeful plight:
Let no strange dream make her fair body start.

But yet, O dream, if thou wilt not depart
In this rare subject from thy common right,   10
But wilt thyself in such a seat delight,

Then take my shape, and play a lover's part:
Kiss her from me, and say unto her sprite,
'Till her eyes shine, I live in darkest night'.

19

When two suns do appear

When two suns do appear
Some say it doth betoken wonders near,
As prince's loss or change:
Two gleaming suns of splendour like I see
And, seeing, feel in me   5
Of prince's heart quite lost the ruin strange.

But now each where doth range
With ugly cloak the dark envious Night,
Who, full of guilty spite
Such living beams should her black seat assail,   10
Too weak for them our weaker sight doth veil.

'No', says fair Moon, 'my light
Shall bar that wrong, and though it not prevail
Like to my brother's rays, yet those I send
Hurt not the face, which nothing can amend.'   15

20

What tongue can her perfections tell

What tongue can her perfections tell
In whose each part all pens may dwell?
Her hair fine threads of finest gold
In curled knots man's thought to hold,
But that her forehead says, 'In me   5
A whiter beauty you may see.'
Whiter indeed: more white than snow
Which on cold Winter's face doth grow.

That doth present those even brows
Whose equal lines their angles bows,   10
Like to the Moon when, after change,
Her horned head abroad doth range,
And arches be to heavenly lids
Whose wink each bold attempt forbids.
For the black stars those spheres contain,   15
The matchless pair even praise doth stain:
No lamp whose light by art is got,
No sun which shines and seeth not,
Can liken them, without all peer,
Save one as much as other clear,   20
Which only thus unhappy be
Because themselves they cannot see.

    Her cheeks with kindly claret spread,
Aurora-like new out of bed,
Or like the fresh queen-apple's side   25
Blushing at sight of Phoebus' pride.

    Her nose, her chin, pure ivory wears,
No purer than the pretty ears,
So that therein appears some blood,
Like wine and milk that mingled stood;   30
In whose incirclets if you gaze
Your eyes may tread a lover's maze,
But with such turns the voice to stray
No talk untaught can find the way.
The tip no jewel needs to wear: 35
The tip is jewel of the ear.

        But who those ruddy lips can miss
Which, blessed, still themselves do kiss?
Rubies, cherries, roses new,
In worth, in taste, in perfect hue,   40
Which never part but that they show
Of precious pearl the double row,
The second sweetly-fenced ward
Her heavenly-dewed tongue to guard,
Whence never word in vain did flow.   45

        Fair under these doth stately grow
The handle of this pleasant work,
The neck, in which strange graces lurk:
Such be, I think, the sumptuous towers
Which skill doth make in princes' bowers.   50

        So good assay invites the eye

202

A little downward to espy
The lovely clusters of her breasts,
Of Venus' babe the wanton nests,
Like pommels round of marble clear   55
Where azured veins well mixed appear,
With dearest tops of porphyry.
    Betwixt these two a way doth lie,
A way more worthy Beauty's fame
Than that which bears the Milky name.   60
This leads unto the joyous field
Which only still doth lilies yield;
But lilies such whose native smell
The Indian odours doth excel.
Waist it is called, for it doth waste   65
Men's lives until it be embraced.
    There may one see (and yet not see)
Her ribs in white all armed be,
More white than Neptune's foamy face
When struggling rocks he would embrace.   70
    In those delights the wandering thought
Might of each side astray be brought
But that her navel doth unite,
In curious circle, busy Sight:
A dainty seal of virgin wax   75
Where nothing but impression lacks.
    Her belly there glad sight doth fill,
Justly entitled Cupid's hill:
A hill most fit for such a master,
A spotless mine of alabaster: 80
Like alabaster fair and sleek,
But soft and supple, satin-like.
In that sweet seat the boy doth sport;
Loth, I must leave his chief resort;
For such an use the world hath gotten   85
The best things still must be forgotten.
    Yet never shall my song omit
Her thighs (for Ovid's song more fit)
Which flanked with two sugared flanks
Lift up their stately swelling banks   90
That Albion cliffs in whiteness pass,
With haunches smooth as looking glass.
    But bow all knees: now of her knees
My tongue doth tell what Fancy sees:

The knots of joy, the gems of love,   95
Whose motion makes all graces move,
Whose bought incaved doth yield such sight,
Like cunning painter shadowing white.
The gartering place with child-like sign
Shows easy print in metal fine.   100
    But there again the flesh doth rise
In her brave calves, like crystal skies,
Whose Atlas is a smallest small
More white than whitest bone of whale.
    There oft steals out that round clean foot,   105
This noble cedar's precious root,
In show and scent pale violets,
Whose step on earth all beauty sets.
    But back unto her back, my Muse,
Where Leda's swan his feathers mews,   110
Along whose ridge such bones are met
Like comfits round in marchpane set.
    Her shoulders be like two white doves
Perching within square royal rooves,
Which leaded are with silver skin,   115
Passing the hate-spot ermelin.
    And thence those arms derived are;
The Phoenix's wings are not so rare
For faultless length and stainless hue.
    Ah, woe is me, my woes renew,   120
Now course doth lead me to her hand,
Of my first love the fatal band,
Where whiteness doth for ever sit:
Nature herself enamelled it.
For there, with strange compact, doth lie   125
Warm snow, moist pearl, soft ivory.
There fall those sapphire-coloured brooks
Which conduit-like with curious crooks
Sweet islands make in that sweet land.
As for the fingers of the hand,   130
The bloody shafts of Cupid's war,
With amethysts they headed are.
    Thus hath each part his beauty's part;
But how the Graces do impart
To all her limbs a special grace   135
Becoming every time and place,
Which doth even Beauty beautify,

And most bewitch the wretched eye:
How all this is but a fair inn
Of fairer guests which dwell within,   140
Of whose high praise, and praiseful bliss,
Goodness the pen, heaven paper is,
The ink immortal Fame doth lend.
As I began, so must I end:
    No tongue can her perfections tell   145
    In whose each part all pens may dwell.

21

Epithalamium (Let mother Earth)

Let mother Earth now deck herself in flowers,
To see her offspring seek a good increase,
Where justest love doth vanquish Cupid's powers
And war of thoughts is swallowed up in peace,
    Which never may decrease   5
    But like the turtles fair
    Live one in two, a well united pair,
    Which, that no chance may stain,
    O Hymen long their coupled joys maintain.

O heaven, awake, show forth thy stately face: 10
Let not these slumbering clouds thy beauties hide,
But with thy cheerful presence help to grace
The honest bridegroom and the bashful bride,
    Whose loves may ever bide
    Like to the elm and vine,
    With mutual embracements them to twine: 15
    In which delightful pain,
    O Hymen, long their coupled joys maintain.

Ye Muses all, which chaste affects allow,
And have to Thyrsis showed your secret skill,
To his chaste love your sacred favours bow,   20
And so to him and her your gifts distil
    That they all vice may kill,
    And like to lilies pure
    May please all eyes, and spotless may endure: 25
    Where, that all bliss may reign,
    O Hymen long their coupled joys maintain.

Ye Nymphs, which in the waters empire have,
Since Thyrsis' music oft doth yield you praise,
Grant to the thing which we for Thyrsis crave: 30
Let one time (but long first) close up their days,
   One grave their bodies seize;
   And like two rivers sweet,
  When they, though diverse, do together meet,
   One stream both streams contain: 35
   O Hymen long their coupled joys maintain.

Pan, father Pan, the god of silly sheep,
Whose care is cause that they in number grow,
Have much more care of them that do them keep,
Since from these good the others' good doth flow,   40
   And make their issue show
   In number like the herd
  Of younglings which thyself with love hast reared,
   Or like the drops of rain:
   O Hymen long their coupled joys maintain.   45

Virtue, if not a god, yet God's chief part,
Be thou the knot of this their open vow,
That still he be her head, she be his heart,
He lean to her, she unto him do bow,
   Each other still allow   50
   Like oak and mistletoe,
  Her strength from him, his praise from her do grow:
   In which most lovely train,
   O Hymen long their coupled joys maintain.

But thou, foul Cupid, sire to lawless Lust,   55
Be thou far hence with thy empoisoned dart,
Which, though of glittering gold, shall here take rust,
Where simple love, which chasteness doth impart,
   Avoids thy hurtful art,
   Not needing charming skill   60
  Such minds with sweet affections for to fill:
   Which, being pure and plain,
   O Hymen long their coupled joys maintain.

All churlish words, shrewd answers, crabbed looks,
All privateness, self-seeking, inward spite,   65
All waywardness which nothing kindly brooks,
All strife for toys, and claiming master's right,
   Be hence aye put to flight!

All stirring husband's hate
Gainst neighbours' good for womanish debate   70
Be fled as things most vain:
O Hymen long their coupled joys maintain.

All peacock pride, and fruits of peacock's pride,
Longing to be with loss of substance gay
With recklessness what may thy house betide,   75
So that you may on higher slippers stay,
   For ever hence away:
   Yet let not sluttery,
   The sink of filth, be counted housewifery,
   But keeping wholesome mean: 80
   O Hymen long their coupled joys maintain.

But above all, away vile Jealousy,
The evil of evils, just cause to be unjust:
How can he love, suspecting treachery?
How can she love, where love can not win trust?   85
   Go snake, hide thee in dust,
   Ne dare once show thy face
   Where open hearts do hold so constant place
   That they thy sting restrain:
   O Hymen long their coupled joys maintain.   90

The earth is decked with flowers, the heavens displayed,
Muses grant gifts, nymphs long and joined life,
Pan store of babes, Virtue their thoughts well-stayed,
Cupid's lust gone, and gone is bitter Strife:
   Happy man, happy wife.
   No Pride shall them oppress,   95
   Nor yet shall yield to loathsome Sluttishness,
   And Jealousy is slain;
   For Hymen will their coupled joys maintain.

22

A neighbour mine

A neighbour mine not long ago there was
(But nameless he, for blameless he shall be)
That married had a trick and bonny lass
As in a summer day a man might see;
   But he himself a foul unhandsome groom,   5
   And far unfit to hold so good a room.

Now, whether moved with self-unworthiness,
Or with her beauty, fit to make a prey,
Fell Jealousy did so his brain oppress
That if he absent were but half a day,   10
  He guessed the worst (you wot what is the worst)
  And in himself new doubting causes nursed.

While thus he feared the silly innocent,
Who yet was good because she knew none ill,
Unto his house a jolly shepherd went,   15
To whom our prince did bear a great good will
  Because in wrestling and in pastoral
  He far did pass the rest of shepherds all.

And therefore he a courtier was benamed,
And as a courtier was with cheer received   20
(For they have tongues to make a poor man blamed,
If he to them his duty misconceived):
  And for this courtier should well like his table,
  The goodman bade his wife be serviceable.

And so she was, and all with good intent,   25
But few days passed while she good manner used
But that her husband thought her service bent
To such an end as he might be abused:
  Yet like a coward, fearing stranger's pride,
  He made the simple wench his wrath abide.   30

With chumpish looks, hard words, and secret nips,
Grumbling at her when she his kindness sought,
Asking her how she tasted courtier's lips,
He forced her think that which she never thought:
  In fine, he made her guess there was some sweet   35
  In that which he so feared that she should meet.

When once this entered was in woman's heart,
And that it had inflamed a new desire,
There rested then to play a woman's part,
Fuel to seek, and not to quench the fire: 40
  But, for his jealous eye she well did find,
  She studied cunning how the same to blind.

And thus she did: one day to him she came,
And, though against his will, on him she leaned,
And out gan cry, 'ah, wellaway for shame,   45
If you help not, our wedlock will be stained!'

The goodman, starting, asked what did her move:
She sighed, and said the bad guest sought her love.

He, little looking that she should complain
Of that whereto he feared she was inclined,   50
Bussing her oft, and in his heart full fain,
He did demand what remedy to find:
    How they might get the guest from them to wend,
    And yet the prince, that loved him, not offend.

'Husband', quoth she, 'go to him by and by,   55
And tell him you do find I do him love,
And therefore pray him that of courtesy
He will absent himself, lest he should move
    A young girl's heart to that were shame for both,
    Whereto you know his honest heart were loath.   60

'Thus shall you show that him you do not doubt,
And as for me (sweet husband) I must bear.'
Glad was the man when he had heard her out,
And did the same, although with mickle fear;
    For fear he did, lest he the young man might   65
    In choler put, with whom he would not fight.

The courtly shepherd, much aghast at this,
Not seeing erst such token in the wife,
Though full of scorn, would not his duty miss,
Knowing that evil becomes a household strife,   70
    Did go his way, but sojourned near thereby,
    That yet the ground hereof he might espy.

The wife, thus having settled husband's brain
(Who would have sworn his spouse Diana was),
Watched when she a further point might gain,   75
Which little time did fitly bring to pass:
    For to the court her man was called by name,
    Whither he needs must go for fear of blame.

Three days before that he must sure depart
She written had (but in a hand disguised)   80
A letter such, which might from either part
Seem to proceed, so well it was devised.
    She sealed it first, then she the sealing brake,
    And to her jealous husband did it take.

With weeping eyes (her eyes she taught to weep)   85
She told him that the courtier had it sent:

'Alas,' quoth she, 'thus women's shame doth creep.'
The goodman read on both sides the content:
  It title had: *Unto my only love.*
  Subscription was: *Yours most, if you will prove.*   90

The 'pistle self such kind of words it had:
'My sweetest joy, the comfort of my sprite,
So may thy flocks increase thy dear heart glad,
So may each thing even as thou wishest light,
  As thou wilt deign to read, and gently read,   95
  This mourning ink in which my hearth doth bleed.

'Long have I loved (alas, thou worthy art),
Long have I loved (alas, love craveth love),
Long have I loved thyself: alas, my heart
Doth break, now tongue unto thy name doth move: 100
  And think not that thy answer answer is,
  But that it is my doom of bale or bliss.

'The jealous wretch must now to court be gone;
Ne can he fail, for prince hath for him sent;
Now is the time we may be here alone,   105
And give a long desire a sweet content.
  Thus shall you both reward a lover true,
  And eke revenge his wrong suspecting you.'

And this was all, and this the husband read
With chafe enough, till she him pacified,   110
Desiring that no grief in him he bred
Now that he had her words so truly tried,
  But that he would to him the letter show,
  That with his fault he might her goodness know.

That straight was done, with many a boisterous threat   115
That to the king he would his sin declare;
But now the courtier gan to smell the feat,
And with some words, which showed little care,
  He stayed until the goodman was departed,
  Then gave he him the blow which never smarted.   120

Thus may you see, the jealous wretch was made
The pandar of the thing he most did fear.
Take heed therefore, how you ensue that trade,
Lest that some marks of jealousy you bear:
  For sure, no jealousy can that prevent   125
  Whereto two parties once be full content.

23

Who doth desire

Who doth desire that chaste his wife should be,
First be he true, for truth doth truth deserve:
Then such be he as she his worth may see,
And one man still credit with her preserve.

Not toying kind, nor causelessly unkind,   5
Not stirring thoughts, nor yet denying right,
Not spying faults, nor in plain errors blind,
Never hard hand, nor ever reins too light:

As far from want, as far from vain expense
(The one doth force, the latter doth entice):   10
Allow good company, but keep from thence
All filthy mouths, that glory in their vice.
    This done, thou hast no more, but leave the rest
    To Virtue, Fortune, Time, and woman's breast.

24

As I my little flock

As I my little flock on Ister bank
(A little flock, but well my pipe they couth)
Did piping lead, the Sun already sank
Beyond our world, and ere I got my booth
Each thing with mantle black the Night doth soothe,   5
    Saving the glow-worm, which would courteous be
    Of that small light oft watching shepherds see.

The welkin had full niggardly enclosed
In coffer of dim clouds his silver groats,
Ycleped stars: each thing to rest disposed;   10
The caves were full, the mountains void of goats;
The birds' eye closed, closed their chirping notes;
    As for the nightingale, wood-music's king,
    It August was, he deigned not then to sing.

Amid my sheep, though I saw nought to fear,   15
Yet, for I nothing saw, I feared sore;
Then found I which thing is a charge to bear,
For for my sheep I dreaded mickle more
Than ever for myself since I was bore.

I sate me down, for see to go ne could,   20
And sang unto my sheep lest stray they should.

The song I sang old Languet had me taught,
Languet, the shepherd best swift Ister knew
For clerkly rede, and hating what is nought,
For faithful heart, clean hands and mouth as true: 25
With his sweet skill my skilless youth he drew
   To have a feeling taste of him that sits
   Beyond the heaven, far more beyond your wits.

He said, the music best thilk powers pleased
Was jump concord between our wit and will,   30
Where highest notes to godliness are raised,
And lowest sink not down to jot of ill.
With old true tales he wont mine ears to fill:
   How shepherds did of yore, how now they thrive,
   Spoiling their flock, or while 'twixt them they strive.   35

He liked me, but pitied lustful youth;
His good strong staff my slippery years upbore;
He still hoped well, because I loved truth;
Till, forced to part, with heart and eyes even sore,
To worthy Coriden he gave me o'er.   40
   But thus in oak's true shade recounted he,
   Which now in Night's deep shade sheep heard of me:

Such manner time there was (what time, I not)
When all this Earth, this dam or mould of ours,
Was only woned with such as beasts begot.   45
Unknown as then were they that builden towers;
The cattle wild or tame, in Nature's bowers
   Might freely roam or rest, as seemed them;
   Man was not man, their dwellings in to hem.

The beasts had sure some beastly policy,   50
For nothing can endure where order n'is:
For once the lion by the lamb did lie;
The fearful hind the leopard did kiss;
Hurtless was tiger's paw and serpent's hiss.
   This think I well: the beasts with courage clad   55
   Like senators a harmless empire had.

At which, whether the others did repine
(For Envy harboureth most in feeble hearts)
Or that they all to changing did incline

(As even in beasts their dams leave changing parts)   60
The multitude to Jove a suit imparts,
  With neighing, blaying, braying and barking,
  Roaring and howling, for to have a king.

A king, in language theirs, they said they would
(For then their language was a perfect speech);   65
The birds likewise with chirps and pewing could,
Cackling and chattering, that of Jove beseech.
Only the owl still warned them not to seech
  So hastily that which they would repent:
  But saw they would, and he to deserts went.   70

Jove wisely said (for Wisdom wisely says):
'O beasts, take heed what you of me desire:
Rulers will think all things made them to please,
And soon forget the swink due to their hire.
But since you will, part of my heavenly fire   75
  I will you lend; the rest yourselves must give,
  That it both seen and felt may with you live.'

Full glad they were, and took the naked sprite,
Which straight the Earth yclothed in his clay.
The lion, heart; the ounce gave active might;   80
The horse, good shape; the sparrow, lust to play;
Nightingale, voice, enticing songs to say;
  Elephant gave a perfect memory;
  And parrot, ready tongue that to apply.

The fox gave craft; the dog gave flattery;   85
Ass, patience; the mole, a working thought;
Eagle, high look; wolf, secret cruelty;
Monkey, sweet breath; the cow her fair eyes brought;
The ermine, whitest skin spotted with nought;
  The sheep, mild-seeming face; climbing, the bear;   90
  The stag did give the harm-eschewing fear.

The hare, her sleights; the cat, his melancholy;
Ant, industry; the coney, skill to build;
Cranes, order; storks, to be appearing holy;
Chameleon, ease to change; duck, ease to yield;   95
Crocodile, tears, which might be falsely spilled;
  Ape great thing gave, though he did mowing stand:
  The instrument of instruments, the hand.

Each other beast likewise his present brings;
And (but they drad their prince they oft should want)   100
They all consented were to give him wings.
And aye more awe towards him for to plant,
To their own work this privilege they grant:
   That from thenceforth to all eternity
   No beast should freely speak, but only he.   105

Thus man was made; thus man their lord became;
Who at the first, wanting or hiding pride,
He did to beasts best use his cunning frame,
With water drink, herbs meat, and naked hide,
And fellow-like let his dominion slide,   110
   Not in his sayings say 'I', but 'we',
   As if he meant his lordship common be.

But when his seat so rooted he had found
That they now skilled not how from him to wend,
Then gan in guiltless Earth full many a wound   115
Iron to seek, which 'gainst itself should bend
To tear the bowels that good corn should send.
   But yet the common dam none did bemoan,
   Because, though hurt, they never heard her groan.

Than gan he factions in the beasts to breed,   120
Where helping weaker sort, the nobler beasts,
As tigers, leopards, bears, and lions' seed,
Disdained with this, in deserts sought their rests,
Where famine ravine taught their hungry chests,
   That craftily he forced them to do ill,   125
   Which being done, he afterwards would kill.

For murder done, which never erst was seen,
By those great beasts, as for the weaker's good,
He chose themselves his guarders for to been
'Gainst those of might, of whom in fear they stood,   130
As horse and dog, not great, but gentle blood:
   Blithe were the commons, cattle of the field,
   Tho when they saw their foen of greatness killed.

But they, or spent or made of slender might,
Then quickly did the meaner cattle find;   135
The great beams gone, the house on shoulders light;
For by and by, the horse fair bits did bind;
The dog was in a collar taught his kind;

As for the gentle birds, like case might rue,
When falcon they and goshawk saw in mew.   140

Worst fell to smallest birds and meanest herd,
Who now his own, full like his own he used.
Yet first but wool or feathers off he teared,
And when they were well used to be abused,
For hungry throat their flesh with teeth he bruised;   145
   At length for glutton taste he did them kill;
   At last, for sport their silly lives did spill.

But yet, O man, rage not beyond thy need;
Deem it no gloire to swell in tyranny.
Thou art of blood: joy not to make things bleed;   150
Thou fearest Death: think they are loath to die.
A plaint of guiltless hurt doth pierce the sky:
   And you, poor beasts, in patience bide your hell,
   Or know your strengths, and then you shall do well.

Thus did I sing, and pipe, eight sullen hours   155
To sheep, whom love, not knowledge, made to hear
Now Fancy's fits, now Fortune's baleful stowers.
But then I homeward called my lambkins dear,
For to my dimmed eyes began to appear
   The Night grown old, her black head waxen grey,   160
   Sure shepherd's sign that morn should soon fetch day.

25

O Night, the ease of care

O Night, the ease of care, the pledge of pleasure,
Desire's best mean, harvest of hearts affected,
The seat of Peace, the throne which is erected
Of human life to be the quiet measure:

Be victor still of Phoebus' golden treasure,   5
Who hath our sight with too much sight infected,
Whose light is cause we have our lives neglected,
Turning all Nature's course to self-displeasure.

These stately stars in their now shining faces,
With sinless Sleep, and Silence, Wisdom's mother,   10
Witness his wrong which by thy help is eased:

Thou art therefore of these our desert places
The sure refuge; by thee and by no other
My soul is blest, sense joyed, and fortune raised.

26

Double sestina ('You goat-herd gods')

Strephon Klaius

Strephon. You goat-herd gods, that love the grassy mountains,
   You nymphs, which haunt the springs in pleasant valleys,
   You satyrs, joyed with free and quiet forests:
   Vouchsafe your silent ears to plaining music
   Which to my woes gives still an early morning   5
   And draws the dolour on till weary evening.

Klaius. O Mercury, foregoer to the evening,
   O heavenly huntress of the savage mountains,
   O lovely star, entitled of the morning:
   While that my voice doth fill these woeful valleys,   10
   Vouchsafe your silent ears to plaining music,
   Which oft hath Echo tired in secret forests.

Strephon. I, that was once free burgess of the forests,
   Where shade from Sun, and sports I sought in evening;
   I, that was once esteemed for pleasant music,   15
   Am banished now among the monstrous mountains
   Of huge Despair, and foul Affliction's valleys,
   Am grown a screech-owl to myself each morning.

Klaius. I, that was once delighted every morning,
   Hunting the wild inhabiters of forests,   20
   I, that was once the music of these valleys,
   So darkened am that all my day is evening,
   Heart-broken so, that molehills seem high mountains,
   And fill the vales with cries instead of music.

Strephon. Long since, alas, my deadly swannish music   25
   Hath made itself a crier of the morning,
   And hath with wailing strength climbed highest mountains;
   Long since my thoughts more desert be than forests;
   Long since I see my joys come to their evening,
   And state thrown down to over-trodden valleys.   30

Klaius. Long since the happy dwellers of these valleys
   Have prayed me leave my strange exclaiming music,
   Which troubles their day's work, and joys of evening;

Long since I hate the night, more hate the morning:
Long since my thoughts chase me like beasts in forests   35
And make me wish myself laid under mountains.

Strephon. Me seems I see the high and stately mountains
Transform themselves to low dejected valleys;
Me seems I hear in these ill-changed forests
The nightingales do learn of owls their music;   40
Me seems I feel the comfort of the morning
Turned to the mortal serene of an evening.

Klaius. Me seems I see a filthy cloudy evening
As soon as Sun begins to climb the mountains;
Me seems I feel a noisome scent, the morning,   45
When I do smell the flowers of these valleys;
Me seems I hear, when I do hear sweet music,
The dreadful cries of murdered men in forests.

Strephon. I wish to fire the trees of all these forests;
I give the Sun a last farewell each evening;   50
I curse the fiddling finders out of music;
With envy I do hate the lofty mountains,
And with despite despise the humble valleys;
I do detest night, evening, day and morning.

Klaius. Curse to myself my prayer is, the morning;   55
My fire is more than can be made with forests;
My state more base than are the basest valleys:
I wish no evening more to see, each evening;
Shamed, I hate myself in sight of mountains,
And stop mine ears, lest I grow mad with music.   60

Strephon. For she (whose parts maintained a perfect music,
Whose beauties shined more than the blushing morning,
Who much did pass in state the stately mountains,
In straightness passed the cedars of the forests),
Hath cast me, wretch, into eternal evening,   65
By taking her two suns from these dark valleys.

Klaius. For she (compared with whom the alps are valleys;
She, whose least word brings from the spheres their music;
At whose approach the Sun rose in the evening;
Who, where she went, bare in her forehead morning),   70
Is gone, is gone, from these our spoiled forests,
Turning to deserts our best pastured mountains.

Strephon. These mountains witness shall, so shall these valleys,

Klaius. These forests eke, made wretched by our music:
   Our morning song is this, and song at evening.   75

27

Corona ('I joy in Grief')

Strephon   Klaius

Strephon. I joy in Grief, and do detest all joys;
   Despite delight and, tired with thought of ease,
   I turn my mind to all forms of annoys,
   And with the change of them my fancy please:
   I study that which may me most displease,   5
   And in despite of that displeasure's might
   Embrace that most that most my soul destroys.
   Blinded with beams, fell darkness is my sight;
   Dole on my ruins feeds with sucking smart;
   I think from me, not from my woes, to part.   10

Klaius. I think from me, not from my woes, to part,
   And loathe this time called Life: nay, think that Life
   Nature to me for torment did impart;
   Think my hard haps have blunted Death's sharp knife,
   Not sparing me, in whom his works be rife;   15
   And thinking this, think Nature, Life and Death
   Place Sorrow's triumph on my conquered heart:
   Whereto I yield, and seek no other breath
   But from the scent of some infectious grave;
   Nor of my fortune aught but mischief crave.   20

Strephon. Nor of my fortune aught but mischief crave,
   And seek to nourish that which now contains
   All what I am: if I myself will save,
   Then I must save what in me chiefly reigns,
   Which is the hateful web of Sorrow's pains.   25
   Sorrow, then cherish me, for I am Sorrow:
   No being now but Sorrow I can have:
   Then deck me as thine own; thy help I borrow,
   Since thou my riches art, and that thou hast
   Enough to make a fertile mind lie waste.   30

Klaius. Enough to make a fertile mind lie waste
   Is that huge storm which pours itself on me:

Hailstones of tears, of sighs a monstrous blast,
Thunders of cries; lightnings my wild looks be,
The darkened heaven my soul which nought can see;   35
The flying sprites which trees by roots up tear
Be those despairs which have my hopes quite waste.
The difference is, all folks those storms forbear,
But I cannot; who then myself should fly,
So close unto myself my wracks do lie.   40

Strephon. So close unto myself my wracks do lie:
   Both cause, effect, beginning, and the end
   Are all in me: what help then can I try?
   My ship, myself, whose course to love doth bend,
   Sore beaten doth her mast of Comfort spend;   45
   Her cable, Reason, breaks from anchor, Hope;
   Fancy, her tackling, torn away doth fly;
   Ruin, the wind, hath blown her from her scope;
   Bruised with waves of Care, but broken is
   On rock, Despair, the burial of my bliss.   50

Klaius. On rock, Despair, the burial of my bliss,
   I long do plough with plough of deep Desire;
   The seed Fast-meaning is, no truth to miss;
   I harrow it with Thoughts, which all conspire
   Favour to make my chief and only hire.   55
   But, woe is me, the year is gone about,
   And now I fain would reap, I reap but this,
   Hate fully grown, Absence new sprongen out.
   So that I see, although my sight impair,
   Vain is their pain who labour in Despair.   60

Strephon. Vain is their pain who labour in Despair;
   For so did I when with my angle, Will,
   I sought to catch the fish Torpedo fair.
   Even then Despair did Hope already kill,
   Yet Fancy would perforce employ his skill,   65
   And this hath got: the catcher now is caught,
   Lamed with the angle which itself did bear,
   And unto Death, quite drowned in Dolours, brought
   To Death, as then disguised in her fair face.
   Thus, thus, alas, I had my loss in chase.   70

Klaius. Thus, thus, alas, I had my loss in chase
   When first that crowned Basilisk I knew,
   Whose footsteps I with kisses oft did trace,

Till by such hap as I must ever rue
   Mine eyes did light upon her shining hue,   75
   And hers on me, astonished with that sight.
Since then my heart did lose his wonted place,
   Infected so with her sweet poison's might
   That, leaving me for dead, to her it went:
But ah, her flight hath my dead relics spent.   80

Strephon. But ah, her flight hath my dead relics spent,
   Her flight from me, from me, though dead to me,
   Yet living still in her, while her beams lent
Such vital spark that her mine eyes might see.
   But now those living lights absented be,   85
   Full dead before, I now to dust should fall,
But that eternal pains my soul have hent,
   And keep it still within this body thrall;
   That thus I must, while in this death I dwell,
In earthly fetters feel a lasting hell.   90

Klaius. In earthly fetters feel a lasting hell
   Alas I do; from which to find release
   I would the earth, I would the heavens sell.
But vain it is to think these pains should cease,
   Where Life is Death, and Death cannot breed Peace.   95
   O fair, O only fair, from thee, alas,
These foul, most foul, disasters to me fell;
   Since thou from me (O me) O Sun didst pass.
   There esteeming all good blessings toys,
I joy in Grief, and do detest all joys.   100

Strephon. I joy in Grief, and do detest all joys.
   But now an end, O Klaius, now an end,
   For even the herbs our hateful music stroys,
And from our burning breath the trees do bend.

28

Pastoral elegy (Since that to death)

Since that to death is gone the shepherd high
   Who most the silly shepherd's pipe did prize,
   Your doleful tunes, sweet Muses, now apply.

And you, O trees (if any life there lies
   In trees) now through your porous barks receive   5
   The strange resound of these my causeful cries;

And let my breath upon your branches cleave,
　　My breath, distinguished into words of woe,
　　That so I may signs of my sorrow leave.
But if among yourselves some one tree grow　　　　　10
　　That aptest is to figure misery,
　　Let it embassage bear your griefs to show.
The weeping Myrrh, I think, will not deny
　　Her help to this, this justest cause of plaint.
　　Your doleful tunes, sweet Muses, now apply.　　　15

And thou, poor Earth, whom Fortune doth attaint
　　In Nature's name to suffer such a harm
　　As for to lose thy gem, and such a saint,
Upon thy face let coaly ravens swarm;
　　Let all the sea thy tears accounted be;　　　　　20
　　Thy bowels with all killing metals arm.
Let gold now rust, let diamonds waste in thee;
　　Let pearls be wan with woe their dam doth bear:
　　Thyself henceforth the light do never see.
And you, O flowers, which sometimes princes were,　　25
　　Till these strange alterings you did hap to try,
　　Of prince's loss yourselves for tokens rear.
Lily, in mourning black thy whiteness dye;
　　O Hyacinth, let *Ai* be on thee still.
　　Your doleful tunes, sweet Muses, now apply.　　　30

O Echo, all these woods with roaring fill,
　　And do not only mark the accents last
　　But all, for all reach out my wailful will:
One echo to another echo cast
　　Sound of my griefs, and let it never end　　　　　35
　　Till that it hath all woods and waters passed:
Nay, to the heavens your just complainings send,
　　And stay the stars' inconstant constant race
　　Till that they do unto our dolours bend;
And ask the reason of that special grace　　　　　40
　　That they, which have no lives, should live so long,
　　And virtuous souls so soon should lose their place?
Ask, if in great men, good men do so throng,
　　That he for want of elbow room must die?
　　Or if that they be scant, if this be wrong?　　　45
Did Wisdom this our wretched time espy
　　In one true chest to rob all Virtue's treasure?
　　Your doleful tunes, sweet Muses, now apply.

And if that any counsel you to measure
   Your doleful tunes, to them still plaining say: 50
   To well-felt grief, plaint is the only pleasure.
O light of Sun, which is entitled day,
   O well thou dost that thou no longer bidest;
   For mourning Night her black weeds may display.
O Phoebus, with good cause thy face thou hidest,   55
   Rather than have thy all-beholding eye
   Fouled with this sight, while thou thy chariot guidest.
And well, methinks, becomes this vaulty sky
   A stately tomb to cover him deceased.
   Your doleful tunes, sweet Muses, now apply.   60

O Philomela, with the breast oppressed
   By shame and grief, help, help me to lament
   Such cursed harms as cannot be redressed;
Or, if thy mourning notes be fully spent,
   Then give a quiet ear unto my plaining: 65
   For I to teach the world complaint am bent.
You dimmy clouds, which well employ your staining
   This cheerful air with your obscured cheer,
   Witness your woeful tears with daily raining.
And if, O Sun, thou ever didst appear   70
   In shape which by man's eye might be perceived,
   Virtue is dead, now set thy triumph here.
Now set thy triumph in this world, bereaved
   Of what was good, where now no good doth lie;
   And by thy pomp our loss will be conceived.   75
O notes of mine, yourselves together tie:
   With too much grief methinks you are dissolved.
   Your doleful tunes, sweet Muses, now apply.

Time, ever old and young, is still revolved
   Within itself, and never tasteth end: 80
   But mankind is for aye to nought resolved;
The filthy snake her aged coat can mend
   And, getting youth again, in youth doth flourish:
   But unto man, Age ever Death doth send.
The very trees with grafting we can cherish,   85
   So that we can long time produce their time:
   But man, which helpeth them, helpless must perish.
Thus, thus, the minds which over all do climb,
   When they by years' experience get best graces,
   Must finish them by Death's detested crime.   90

We last short while, and build long-lasting places.
   Ah, let us all against foul Nature cry:
   We Nature's works do help, she us defaces.
For how can Nature unto this reply?
   That she her child, I say, her best child killeth?   95
   Your doleful tunes, sweet Muses, now apply.

Alas, methinks, my weakened voice but spilleth
   The vehement course of this just lamentation:
   Methinks my sound no place with sorrow filleth.
I know not I, but once in detestation   100
   I have myself, and all what life containeth,
   Since Death on Virtue's fort hath made invasion.
One word of woe another after traineth;
   Ne do I care how rude be my invention
   So it be seen what sorrow in me reigneth.   105
O elements, by whose (men say) contention
   Our bodies be in living power maintained,
   Was this man's death the fruit of your dissension?
O Physic's power, which (some say) hath refrained
   Approach of Death, alas, thou helpest meagrely,   110
   When once one is for Atropos distrained.
Great be physicians' brags, but aid is beggarly:
   When rooted moisture fails, or groweth dry,
   They leave off all and say: Death comes too eagerly.
They are but words, therefore, which men do buy   115
   Of any since god Aesculapius ceased.
   Your doleful tunes, sweet Muses, now apply.

Justice, Justice is now, alas, oppressed;
   Bountifulness hath made his last conclusion;
   Goodness for best attire in dust is dressed.   120
Shepherds bewail your uttermost confusion
   And see, by this picture to you presented,
   Death is our home, Life is but a delusion.
For see, alas, who is from you absented.
   Absented? Nay, I say for ever banished   125
   From such as were to die for him contented.
Out of our sight, in turn of hand, is vanished
   Shepherd of shepherds, whose well-settled order
   Private with wealth, public with quiet garnished.
While he did live, far, far, was all disorder;   130
   Example more prevailing than direction,
   Far was home strife, and far was foe from border.
His life a law, his look a full correction,

As in his health we healthful were preserved,
  So in his sickness grew our sure infection,   135
His death our death. But ah, my Muse hath swerved
  From such deep plaint as should such woes descry,
  Which he of us for ever hath deserved.
The style of heavy heart can never fly
  So high, as should make such a pain notorious: 140
  Cease, Muse, therefore; thy dart, O Death, apply:
And farewell prince, whom goodness hath made glorious.

29

Sestina (Farewell, O Sun)

Farewell, O Sun, Arcadia's clearest light;
Farewell, O pearl, the poor man's plenteous treasure;
Farewell, O golden staff, the weak man's might;
Farewell, O Joy, the woeful's only pleasure.
Wisdom, farewell, the skill-less man's direction;   5
Farewell with thee, farewell all our affection.

For what place now is left for our affection,
Now that of purest lamp is quenched the light
Which to our darkened minds was best direction;
Now that the mine is lost of all our treasure,   10
Now Death hath swallowed up our worldly pleasure,
We orphans made, void of all public might?

Orphans indeed, deprived of father's might:
For he our father was in all affection,
In our well-doing placing all his pleasure,   15
Still studying how to us to be a light.
As well he was in peace a safest treasure:
In war his wit and word was our direction.

Whence, whence, alas, shall we seek our direction?
When that we fear our hateful neighbours' might,   20
Who long have gaped to get Arcadians' treasure,
Shall we now find a guide of such affection
Who for our sakes will think all travail light,
And make his pain to keep us safe, his pleasure?

No, no, for ever gone is all our pleasure;   25
For ever wandering from all good direction;
For ever blinded of our clearest light;
For ever lamed of our surest might;

For ever banished from well-placed affection;
For ever robbed of all our royal treasure.   30

Let tears for him therefore be all our treasure,
And in our wailful naming him our pleasure:
Let hating of ourselves be our affection,
And unto death bend still our thoughts' direction.
Let us against ourselves employ our might,   35
And putting out our eyes seek we our light.

Farewell our light, farewell our spoiled treasure;
Farewell our might, farewell our daunted pleasure;
Farewell direction, farewell all affection.

30

Since Nature's works be good

Since Nature's works be good, and Death doth serve
As Nature's work, why should we fear to die?
Since fear is vain, but when it may preserve,
Why should we fear that which we cannot fly?

Fear is more pain than is the pain it fears,   5
Disarming human minds of native might;
While each conceit an ugly figure bears,
Which were not evil well viewed in Reason's light.

Our owly eyes (which dimmed with passions be,
And scarce discern the dawn of coming day),   10
Let them be cleared: and now begin to see,
Our life is but a step in dusty way.
    Then let us hold the bliss of peaceful mind:
    Since this we feel, great loss we cannot find.

From CERTAIN SONNETS

1

To the tune of *Non credo gia piu infelice amante*

The Fire to see my wrongs for anger burneth;
The Air in rain for my affliction weepeth;
The Sea to ebb for grief his flowing turneth;
The Earth with pity dull the centre keepeth;
    Fame is with wonder blazed;   5

Time runs away for sorrow;
Place standeth still, amazed
To see my night of evils which hath no morrow.
  Alas, all only she no pity taketh
  To know my miseries but, chaste and cruel,   10
  My fall her glory maketh:
  Yet still her eyes give to my flames their fuel.

Fire, burn me quite, till sense of burning leave me;
Air, let me draw no more thy breath in anguish;
Sea, drowned in thee, of tedious life bereave me;   15
Earth, take this earth, wherein my spirits languish.
  Fame, say I was not born;
  Time, haste my dying hour;
  Place, see my grave uptorn;
  Fire, Air, Sea, Earth, Fame, Time, Place, show your power. 20
  Alas, from all their help I am exiled,
  For hers am I, and Death fears her displeasure.
  Fie, Death, doth art beguiled:
  Though I be hers, she makes of me no treasure.

2

To the same tune

The nightingale, as soon as April bringeth
Unto her rested sense a perfect waking,
While late-bare Earth, proud of new clothing, springeth,
Sings out her woes, a thorn her song-book making,
  And, mournfully bewailing,   5
  Her throat in tunes expresseth
  What grief her breast oppresseth
  For Tereus' force on her chaste will prevailing.
    O Philomela fair, O take some gladness
    That here is juster cause of plaintful sadness: 10
    Thine earth now springs, mine fadeth;
    Thy thorn without, my thorn my heart invadeth.

Alas, she hath no other cause of anguish
But Tereus' love, on her by strong hand wroken;
Wherein she, suffering all her spirits' languish,   15
Full woman-like complains her will was broken.
  But I who daily craving
  Cannot have to content me,
  Have more cause to lament me,

Since wanting is more woe than too much having. 20
  O Philomela fair, O take some gladness,
  That here is juster cause of plaintful sadness:
  Thine earth now springs, mine fadeth;
  Thy thorn without, my thorn my heart invadeth.

3

To the tune of *Basciami vita mia*

Sleep, baby mine, Desire; nurse Beauty singeth:
Thy cries, O baby, set mine head on aching;
The babe cries: Way, thy love doth keep me waking.

Lully, lully, my babe, Hope cradle bringeth
Unto my children alway good rest taking; 5
The babe cries: Way, thy love doth keep me waking.

Since, baby mine, from me thy watching springeth,
Sleep then a little, pap content is making;
The babe cries: Nay, for that abide I waking.

4

The Seven Wonders of England

Near Wilton sweet, huge heaps of stone are found,
  But so confused that neither any eye
  Can count them just, nor Reason reason try
  What force brought them to so unlikely ground.

To stranger weights my mind's waste soil is bound, 5
  Of Passion's hills, reaching to Reason's sky
  From Fancy's earth passing all number's bound,
  Passing all guess whence into me should fly
    So mazed a mass; or if in me it grows,
    A simple soul should breed so mixed woes. 10

The Breretons have a lake, which when the Sun
  Approaching warms (not else) dead logs up sends
  From hiddenest depth, which tribute, when it ends,
  Sore sign it is the lord's last thread is spun.

My lake is sense, whose still streams never run 15
  But when my Sun her shining twins there bends;
  Then from his depth with force in her begun
  Long drowned hopes to watery eyes it lends:

But when that fails my dead hopes up to take,
Their master is fair warned his will to make.   20

We have a fish, by strangers much admired,
　　Which, caught, to cruel search yields his chief part:
　　With gall cut out, closed up again by art,
　　Yet lives until his life be new required.

A stranger fish myself, not yet expired,   25
　　Though rapt with Beauty's hook, I did impart
　　Myself unto the anatomy desired,
　　Instead of gall, leaving to her my heart:
　　　　Yet live with thoughts closed up, till that she will
　　　　By conquest's right, instead of searching, kill.   30

Peak hath a cave whose narrow entries find
　　Large rooms within, where drops distil amain,
　　Till knit with cold (though there unknown) remain,
　　Deck that poor place with alabaster lined.

Mine eyes the strait, the roomy cave my mind,   35
　　Whose cloudy thoughts let fall an inward rain
　　Of Sorrow's drops, till colder Reason bind
　　Their running fall into a constant vein
　　　　Of Truth, far more than alabaster pure
　　　　Which, though despised, yet still doth Truth endure.   40

A field there is, where, if a stake be pressed
　　Deep in the earth, what hath in earth receipt
　　Is changed to stone, in hardness, cold, and weight:
　　The wood above doth soon consuming rest.

The earth, her ears; the stake is my request: 45
　　Of which, how much may pierce to that sweet seat,
　　To Honour turned, doth dwell in Honour's nest,
　　Keeping that form, though void of wonted heat:
　　　　But all the rest, which fear durst not apply,
　　　　Failing themselves, with withered conscience die.   50

Of ships by shipwreck cast on Albion coast
　　Which, rotting on the rocks, their death do die,
　　From wooden bones and blood of pitch doth fly
　　A bird which gets more life than ship had lost.

My ship, Desire, with wind of Lust long tossed,   55
　　Brake on fair cleeves of constant Chastity
　　Where, plagued for rash attempt, gives up his ghost,

So deep in seas of Virtue beauties lie:
  But of his death flies up a purest love
  Which, seeming less, yet nobler life doth move.   60

These wonders England breeds; the last remains –
  A lady, in despite of nature chaste,
  On whom all love, in whom no love, is placed,
  Where Fairness yields to Wisdom's shortest reins.

An humble pride, a scorn that favour stains;   65
  A woman's mould, but like an angel graced;
  An angel's mind, but in a woman cast:
  A heaven on earth, or earth that heaven contains.
    Now thus this wonder to myself I frame;
    She is the cause that all the rest I am.   70

5

Ring out your bells

Ring out your bells, let mourning shows be spread,
  For Love is dead.
    All love is dead, infected
    With plague of deep disdain:
    Worth as nought worth rejected,   5
    And Faith fair scorn doth gain.
      From so ungrateful fancy,
      From such a female franzy,
      From them that use men thus,
      Good Lord deliver us.   10

Weep, neighbours, weep: do you not hear it said
  That Love is dead?
    His death-bed peacock's folly,
    His winding-sheet is Shame,
    His will False-seeming holy,   15
    His sole executor Blame.
      From so ungrateful fancy,
      From such a female franzy,
      From them that use men thus,
      Good Lord deliver us.   20

Let dirge be sung and trentals rightly read,
  For Love is dead.
    Sir Wrong his tomb ordaineth
    My mistress' marble heart,

Which epitaph containeth: 25
'Her eyes were once his dart.'
   From so ungrateful fancy,
   From such a female franzy,
   From them that use men thus,
   Good Lord deliver us.   30

Alas, I lie! rage hath this error bred.
  Love is not dead:
   Love is not dead, but sleepeth
   In her unmatched mind,
   Where she his counsel keepeth   35
   Till due desert she find.
    Therefore from so vile fancy,
    To call such wit a franzy
    Who Love can temper thus,
    Good Lord deliver us.   40

6

Thou blind man's mark

Thou blind man's mark, thou fool's self-chosen snare
Fond fancy's scum, and dregs of scattered thought,
Band of all evils, cradle of causeless care,
Thou web of will, whose end is never wrought:

Desire, Desire, I have too dearly bought   5
With price of mangled mind thy worthless ware;
Too long, too long asleep thou hast me brought
Who should my mind to higher things prepare.

But yet in vain thou hast my ruin sought,
In vain thou madest me to vain things aspire,   10
In vain thou kindlest all thy smoky fire:

For Virtue hath this better lesson taught,
Within myself to seek my only hire,
Desiring nought but how to kill Desire.

7

Leave me, O Love

Leave me, O Love which reachest but to dust,
And thou, my mind, aspire to higher things:
Grow rich in that which never taketh rust:

What ever fades but fading pleasure brings.

Draw in thy beams, and humble all thy might   5
To that sweet yoke where lasting freedoms be,
Which breaks the clouds, and opens forth the light
That doth both shine and give us sight to see.

O take fast hold: let that light be thy guide
In this small course which birth draws out to death,   10
And think how ill becometh him to slide
Who seeketh heaven, and comes of heavenly breath.
    Then farewell, world, thy uttermost I see;
    Eternal Love, maintain thy life in me.

Splendidis longum valedico nugis

ASTROPHIL AND STELLA

1

Loving in truth, and fain in verse my love to show,
That she (dear she) might take some pleasure of my pain,
Pleasure might cause her read, reading might make her know,
Knowledge might pity win, and pity grace obtain,
    I sought fit words to paint the blackest face of woe,   5
Studying inventions fine her wits to entertain,
Oft turning others' leaves, to see if thence would flow
Some fresh and fruitful showers upon my sunburnt brain.
    But words came halting forth, wanting Invention's stay;
Invention, Nature's child, fled stepdame Study's blows,   10
And others' feet still seemed but strangers in my way.
Thus great with child to speak, and helpless in my throes,
    Biting my truant pen, beating myself for spite,
    'Fool,' said my Muse to me, 'look in thy heart and write.'

2

Not at first sight, nor with a dribbed shot,
    Love gave the wound which while I breathe will bleed:
    But known worth did in mine of time proceed,
Till by degrees it had full conquest got.
I saw and liked, I liked but loved not,   5
    I loved, but straight did not what Love decreed:
    At length to Love's decrees I, forced, agreed,

Yet with repining at so partial lot.
  Now even that footstep of lost liberty
Is gone, and now like slave-born Muscovite   10
I call it praise to suffer tyranny,
And now employ the remnant of my wit
    To make myself believe that all is well,
    While with a feeling skill I paint my hell.

3

Let dainty wits cry on the sisters nine,
That, bravely masked, their fancies may be told:
Or, Pindar's apes, flaunt they in phrases fine,
Enamelling with pied flowers their thoughts of gold:
    Or else let them in statelier glory shine,   5
Ennobling new-found tropes with problems old:
Or with strange similes enrich each line,
Of herbs or beasts, which Ind or Afric hold.
    For me, in sooth, no Muse but one I know:
    Phrases and problems from my reach do grow,   10
And strange things cost too dear for my poor sprites.
    How then? Even thus: in Stella's face I read
    What love and beauty be; then all my deed
But copying is, what in her Nature writes.

4

Virtue, alas, now let me take some rest,
Thou settest a bate between my will and wit:
If vain love have my simple soul oppressed,
Leave what thou likest not, deal not thou with it.
    Thy sceptre use in some old Cato's breast;   5
Churches or schools are for thy seat more fit.
I do confess (pardon a fault confessed)
My mouth too tender is for thy hard bit.
    But if that needs thou wilt usurping be
    The little reason that is left in me,   10
And still the effect of thy persuasions prove,
    I swear, my heart such one shall show to thee
    That shrines in flesh so true a deity,
That, Virtue, thou thy self shalt be in love.

5

It is most true, that eyes are formed to serve
The inward light, and that the heavenly part
Ought to be king, from whose rules who do swerve,
Rebels to Nature, strive for their own smart.
    It is most true, what we call Cupid's dart   5
An image is, which for ourselves we carve,
And, fools, adore in temple of our heart,
Till that good god make Church and churchman starve.
    True, that true Beauty Virtue is indeed,
Whereof this beauty can be but a shade,   10
Which elements with mortal mixture breed;
True, that on earth we are but pilgrims made,
    And should in soul up to our country move:
    True, and yet true that I must Stella love.

6

Some lovers speak, when they their Muses entertain,
Of hopes begot my fear, of wot not what desires,
Of force of heavenly beams, infusing hellish pain,
Of living deaths, dear wounds, fair storms and freezing fires.
    Some one his song in Jove, and Jove's strange tales, attires,   5
Bordered with bulls and swans, powdered with golden rain;
Another, humbler, wit to shepherd's pipe retires,
Yet hiding royal blood full oft in rural vein.
    To some a sweetest plaint a sweetest style affords,
    While tears pour out his ink, and sighs breathe   10
    out his words:
His paper pale despair, and pain his pen doth move.
    I can speak what I feel, and feel as much as they,
    But think that all the map of my state I display,
When trembling voice brings forth that I do Stella love.

7

When Nature made her chief work, Stella's eyes,
In colour black why wrapped she beams so bright?
Would she in beamy black, like painter wise,
Frame daintiest lustre, mixed of shades and light?
    Or did she else that sober hue devise   5
In object best to knit and strength our sight,
Lest, if no veil these brave gleams did disguise,

They, sun-like, should more dazzle than delight?
   Or would she her miraculous power show,
That whereas black seems Beauty's contrary,   10
She even in black doth make all beauties flow?
Both so and thus: she, minding Love should be
   Placed ever there, gave him this mourning weed
   To honour all their deaths who for her bleed.

8

Love, born in Greece, of late fled from his native place,
   Forced by a tedious proof, that Turkish hardened heart
   Is no fit mark to pierce with his fine pointed dart,
And pleased with our soft peace, stayed here his flying race.
But finding these North climes too coldly him embrace,   5
   Not used to frozen clips, he strave to find some part
   Where with most ease and warmth he might employ his art.
At length he perched himself in Stella's joyful face,
   Whose fair skin, beamy eyes, like morning sun on snow,
Deceived the quaking boy, who thought from so pure light   10
Effects of lively heat must needs in nature grow.
But she, most fair, most cold, made him thence take his flight
   To my close heart, where, while some firebrands he did lay,
   He burnt unwares his wings, and cannot fly away.

9

Queen Virtue's court, which some call Stella's face,
   Prepared by Nature's chiefest furniture,
   Hath his front built of alablaster pure;
Gold is the covering of that stately place.
The door, by which sometimes comes forth her grace,   5
   Red porphyr is, which lock of pearl makes sure;
   Whose porches rich (which name of cheeks endure)
Marble, mixed red and white, do interlace.
   The windows now, through which this heavenly guest
Looks over the world and can find nothing such   10
Which dare claim from those lights the name of best,
Of touch they are that without touch doth touch,
   Which Cupid's self from Beauty's mine did draw:
   Of touch they are, and poor I am their straw.

10

Reason, in faith thou art well served, that still
Wouldst brabbling be with Sense and Love in me.
I rather wished thee climb the Muses' hill,
Or reach the fruit of Nature's choicest tree,
  Or seek heaven's course or heaven's inside to see.   5
Why shouldst thou toil our thorny soil to till?
Leave Sense, and those which Sense's objects be:
Deal thou with powers of thoughts, leave Love to Will.
  But thou wouldst needs fight both with Love and Sense,
With sword of Wit giving wounds of dispraise,   10
Till downright blows did foil thy cunning fence:
For, soon as they strake thee with Stella's rays,
  Reason, thou kneeledst, and offeredst straight to prove
  By reason good, good reason her to love.

11

In truth, O Love, with what a boyish kind
  Thou dost proceed in thy most serious ways:
  That when the heaven to thee his best displays,
Yet of that best thou leavest the best behind.
For like a child that some fair book doth find,   5
  With gilded leaves or coloured vellum plays,
  Or at the most on some fine picture stays,
But never heeds the fruit of writer's mind:
  So when thou sawest, in Nature's cabinet,
Stella, thou straight lookest babies in her eyes,   10
In her cheek's pit thou didst thy pitfold set,
And in her breast bo-peep or couching lies,
  Playing and shining in each outward part:
  But, fool, seekest not to get into her heart.

12

Cupid, because thou shinest in Stella's eyes,
  That from her locks, thy day-nets, none scapes free,
  That those lips swell, so full of thee they be,
That her sweet breath makes oft thy flames to rise,
That in her breast thy pap well sugared lies,   5
  That her grace gracious makes thy wrongs, that she,
  What words so e'er she speaks, persuades for thee,
That her clear voice lifts thy fame to the skies:

Thou countest Stella thine, like those whose powers,
Having got up a breach by fighting well,   10
Cry, 'Victory, this fair day all is ours!'
O no, her heart is such a citadel,
   So fortified with wit, stored with disdain,
   That to win it, is all the skill and pain.

13

Phoebus was judge between Jove, Mars, and Love,
   Of those three gods, whose arms the fairest were.
   Jove's golden shield did eagle sables bear,
Whose talons held young Ganymede above:
   But in vert field Mars bare a golden spear   5
      Which through a bleeding heart his point did shove.
      Each had his crest: Mars carried Venus' glove,
Jove on his helm the thunderbolt did rear.
Cupid then smiles, for on his crest there lies
      Stella's fair hair; her face he makes his shield,   10
      Where roses gules are borne in silver field.
Phoebus drew wide the curtains of the skies
   To blaze these last, and sware devoutly then,
   The first, thus matched, were scarcely gentlemen.

14

Alas, have I not pain enough, my friend,
   Upon whose breast a fiercer gripe doth tire
   Than did on him who first stale down the fire,
While Love on me doth all his quiver spend,
But with your rhubarb words you must contend   5
   To grieve me worse, in saying that desire
   Doth plunge my well-formed soul even in the mire
Of sinful thoughts, which do in ruin end?
   If that be sin which doth the manners frame,
Well stayed with truth in word and faith of deed,   10
Ready of wit, and fearing nought but shame:
If that be sin which in fixed hearts doth breed
   A loathing of all loose unchastity,
   Then Love is sin, and let me sinful be.

15

You that do search for every purling spring
   Which from the ribs of old Parnassus flows,

And every flower, not sweet perhaps, which grows
Near thereabouts, into your poesy wring;
You that do dictionary's method bring 5
 Into your rhymes, running in rattling rows;
 You that poor Petrarch's long-deceased woes
With new-born sighs and denizened wit do sing:
 You take wrong ways, those far-fet helps be such
 As do bewray a want of inward touch; 10
And sure at length stolen goods do come to light.
 But if, both for your love and skill, your name
 You seek to nurse at fullest breasts of Fame,
Stella behold, and then begin to indite.

16

In nature apt to like, when I did see
 Beauties which were of many carats fine
 My boiling sprites did thither soon incline,
And, Love, I thought that I was full of thee.
But finding not those restless flames in me 5
 Which others said did make their souls to pine,
 I thought those babes of some pin's hurt did whine,
By my love judging what love's pain might be.
 But while I thus with this young lion played,
Mine eyes (shall I say cursed or blessed?) beheld 10
Stella: now she is named, need more be said?
In her sight I a lesson new have spelled;
 I now have learned Love right, and learned even so
 As who by being poisoned doth poison know.

17

His mother dear Cupid offended late,
 Because that Mars, grown slacker in her love,
 With pricking shot he did not throughly move
To keep the pace of their first loving state.
The boy refused for fear of Mars's hate, 5
 Who threatened stripes if he his wrath did prove.
 But she in chafe him from her lap did shove,
Brake bow, brake shafts, while Cupid weeping sate:
 Till that his grandame Nature, pitying it,
Of Stella's brows made him two better bows, 10
And in her eyes of arrows infinite.
O how for joy he leaps, O how he crows,

And straight therewith, like wags new got to play,
Falls to shrewd turns, and I was in his way.

18

With what sharp checks I in myself am shent
  When into Reason's audit I do go,
  And by just counts myself a bankrupt know
Of all those goods which heaven to me hath lent,
Unable quite to pay even Nature's rent,   5
  Which unto it by birthright I do owe:
  And which is worse, no good excuse can show,
But that my wealth I have most idly spent.
  My youth doth waste, my knowledge brings forth toys,
My wit doth strive those passions to defend   10
Which for reward spoil it with vain annoys.
I see my course to lose myself doth bend:
  I see, and yet no greater sorrow take
  Than that I lose no more for Stella's sake.

19

On Cupid's bow how are my heart-strings bent,
  That see my wrack, and yet embrace the same!
  When most I glory, then I feel most shame;
I willing run, yet while I run, repent.
My best wits still their own disgrace invent;   5
  My very ink turns straight to Stella's name:
  And yet my words, as them my pen doth frame,
Avise themselves that they are vainly spent.
  For though she pass all things, yet what is all
That unto me, who fare like him that both   10
Looks to the skies, and in a ditch doth fall?
O let me prop my mind, yet in his growth,
  And not in nature for best fruits unfit.
  'Scholar,' saith Love, 'bend hitherward your wit.'

20

Fly, fly, my friends, I have my death wound, fly;
See there that boy, that murthering boy I say,
Who like a thief hid in dark bush doth lie,
Till bloody bullet get him wrongful prey.
  So tyrant he no fitter place could spy,   5

Not so fair level in so secret stay
As that sweet black which veils the heavenly eye;
There himself with his shot he close doth lay.
   Poor passenger, pass now thereby I did,
And stayed, pleased with the prospect of the place,   10
While that black hue from me the bad guest hid;
But straight I saw motions of lightning grace,
   And then descried the glistering of his dart:
   But ere I could fly thence, it pierced my heart.

21

Your words, my friend, right healthful caustics, blame
   My young mind marred, whom Love doth windlass so
   That mine own writings, like bad servants, show
My wits, quick in vain thoughts, in virtue lame;
That Plato I read for nought, but if he tame   5
   Such coltish gyres; that to my birth I owe
   Nobler desires, lest else that friendly foe,
Great Expectation, wear a train of shame.
   For since mad March great promise made of me,
If now the May of my years much decline,   10
What can be hoped my harvest time will be?
Sure you say well: your wisdom's golden mine
   Dig deep with learning's spade. Now tell me this
   Hath this world aught so fair as Stella is?

22

In highest way of heaven the Sun did ride,
   Progressing then from fair Twins' golden place,
   Having no scarf of clouds before his face,
But shining forth of heat in his chief pride;
When some fair ladies, by hard promise tied,   5
   On horseback met him in his furious race,
   Yet each prepared, with fan's well-shading grace,
From that foe's wounds their tender skins to hide.
Stella alone with face unarmed marched,
   Either to do like him, which open shone,   10
   Or careless of the wealth because her own.
Yet were the hid and meaner beauties parched,
   Her daintiest bare went free. The cause was this:
   The Sun, which others burned, did her but kiss.

23

The curious wits, seeing dull pensiveness
  Bewray itself in my long settled eyes,
  Whence those same fumes of melancholy rise
With idle pains, and missing aim, do guess.
Some, that know how my spring I did address,   5
  Deem that my Muse some fruit of knowledge plies;
  Others, because the Prince my service tries,
Think that I think state errors to redress.
  But harder judges judge ambition's rage
(Scourge of itself, still climbing slippery place)   10
Holds my young brain captived in golden cage.
O fools, or over-wise! Alas, the race
  Of all my thoughts hath neither stop nor start,
  But only Stella's eyes and Stella's heart.

24

Rich fools there be, whose base and filthy heart
Lies hatching still the goods wherein they flow,
And damning their own selves to Tantal's smart,
Wealth breeding want, more blessed, more wretched grow.
  Yet to those fools heaven such wit doth impart   5
As what their hands do hold, their heads do know,
And knowing, love, and loving, lay apart
As sacred things, far from all danger's show.
  But that rich fool who by blind Fortune's lot
The richest gem of love and life enjoys,   10
And can with foul abuse such beauties blot,
Let him, deprived of sweet but unfelt joys
  (Exiled for aye from those high treasures which
  He knows not) grow in only folly rich.

25

The wisest scholar of the wight most wise
By Phoebus' doom, with sugared sentence says,
That Virtue, if it once met with our eyes,
Strange flames of love it in our souls would raise;
  But, for that man with pain this truth descries,   5
While he each thing in sense's balance weighs,
And so nor will nor can behold those skies
Which inward sun to heroic mind displays,

Virtue of late, with virtuous care to stir
Love of herself, takes Stella's shape, that she   10
To mortal eyes might sweetly shine in her.
It is most true; for since I her did see,
  Virtue's great beauty in that face I prove,
  And find the effect, for I do burn in love.

26

Though dusty wits dare scorn astrology,
And fools can think those lamps of purest light
(Whose numbers, ways, greatness, eternity,
Promising wonders, wonder do invite)
  To have for no cause birthright in the sky,   5
But for to spangle the black weeds of Night;
Or for some brawl, which in that chamber high
They should still dance, to please a gazer's sight:
  For me, I do Nature unidle know,
And know great causes great effects procure,   10
And know those bodies high reign on the low.
And if these rules did fail, proof makes me sure,
  Who oft fore-judge my after-following race
  By only those two stars in Stella's face.

27

Because I oft, in dark abstracted guise,
  Seem most alone in greatest company,
  With dearth of words, or answers quite awry,
To them that would make speech of speech arise,
They deem, and of their doom the rumour flies,   5
  That poison foul of bubbling pride doth lie
  So in my swelling breast that only I
Fawn on myself, and others do despise:
  Yet Pride, I think, doth not my soul possess,
Which looks too oft in his unflattering glass;   10
But one worse fault, Ambition, I confess,
That makes me oft my best friends overpass,
  Unseen, unheard, while thought to highest place
  Bends all his powers, even unto Stella's grace.

28

You that with Allegory's curious frame
  Of others' children changelings use to make,

241

With me those pains, for God's sake, do not take;
I list not dig so deep for brazen fame.
When I say 'Stella', I do mean the same   5
  Princess of Beauty, for whose only sake
  The reins of Love I love, though never slake,
And joy therein, though nations count it shame.
  I beg no subject to use eloquence,
Nor in hid ways to guide Philosophy;   10
Look at my hands for no such quintessence,
But know that I, in pure simplicity,
  Breathe out the flames which burn within my heart,
  Love only reading unto me this art.

29

Like some weak lords, neighboured by mighty kings,
  Too keep themselves and their chief cities free
  Do easily yield, that all their coasts may be
Ready to store their camps of needful things:
So Stella's heart, finding what power Love brings,   5
  To keep itself in life and liberty
  Doth willing grant, that in the frontiers he
Use all to help his other conquerings.
    And thus her heart escapes, but thus her eyes
Serve him with shot, her lips his heralds are,   10
Her breasts his tents, legs his triumphal car,
Her flesh his food, her skin his armour brave;
    And I, but for because my prospect lies
Upon that coast, am given up for a slave.

30

Whether the Turkish new moon minded be
  To fill his horns this year on Christian coast;
  How Poles' right king means, without leave of host,
To warm with ill-made fire cold Muscovy;
If French can yet three parts in one agree;   5
  What now the Dutch in their full diets boast;
  How Holland hearts, now so good towns be lost,
Trust in the shade of pleasing Orange tree;
  How Ulster likes of that same golden bit
Wherewith my father once made it half tame;   10
If in the Scottish court be weltering yet:
These questions busy wits to me do frame.

I, cumbered with good manners, answer do,
But know not how, for still I think of you.

31

With how sad steps, O Moon, thou climbest the skies,
   How silently, and with how wan a face.
   What, may it be that even in heavenly place
That busy archer his sharp arrows tries?
Sure, if that long-with-love acquainted eyes   5
   Can judge of love, thou feelest a lover's case:
   I read it in thy looks; thy languished grace,
To me that feel the like, thy state descries.
   Then even of fellowship, O Moon, tell me,
Is constant love deemed there but want of wit?   10
Are beauties there as proud as here they be?
Do they above love to be loved, and yet
   Those lovers scorn whom that love doth possess?
   Do they call Virtue there ungratefulness?

32

Morpheus, the lively son of deadly Sleep,
   Witness of life to them that living die,
   A prophet oft, and oft an history,
A poet eke, as humours fly or creep:
Since thou in me so sure a power dost keep   5
   That never I with closed-up sense do lie
   But by thy work my Stella I descry
Teaching blind eyes both how to smile and weep,
   Vouchsafe of all acquaintance this to tell:
Whence hast thou ivory, rubies, pearl and gold   10
To show her skin, lips, teeth and head so well?
'Fool,' answers he, 'no Inds such treasures hold,
   But from thy heart, while my sire charmeth thee,
   Sweet Stella's image I do steal to me.'

33

I might – unhappy word – O me, I might,
And then would not, or could not, see my bliss:
Till now, wrapped in a most infernal night,
I find how heavenly day (wretch) I did miss.
   Heart, rend thyself, thou dost thyself but right: 5

No lovely Paris made thy Helen his;
No Force, no Fraud, robbed thee of thy delight,
Nor Fortune of thy fortune author is:
  But to myself myself did give the blow,
While too much wit, forsooth, so troubled me   10
That I respects for both our sakes must show;
And yet could not by rising morn foresee
    How fair a day was near – O punished eyes,
    That I had been more foolish or more wise!

34

Come let me write. 'And to what end?' To ease
  A burdened heart. 'How can words ease, which are
  The glasses of thy daily vexing care?'
Oft cruel fights well pictured forth do please.
'Art not ashamed to publish thy disease?'   5
  Nay, that may breed my fame, it is so rare.
  'But will not wise men think thy words fond ware?'
Then be they close, and so none shall displease.
  'What idler thing than speak and not be heard?'
What harder thing than smart and not to speak?   10
Peace, foolish wit, with wit my wit is marred.
  Thus write I while I doubt to write, and wreak
    My harms on ink's poor loss: perhaps some find
    Stella's great powers, that so confuse my mind.

35

What may words say, or what may words not say,
Where Truth itself must speak like Flattery?
Within what bounds can one his liking stay,
Where Nature doth with infinite agree?
  What Nestor's counsel can my flames allay,   5
Since Reason's self doth blow the coal in me?
And ah what hope that Hope should once see day,
Where Cupid is sworn page to Chastity?
    Honour is honoured that thou dost possess
Him as thy slave; and now long-needy Fame   10
Doth even grow rich, naming my Stella's name.
    Wit learns in thee perfection to express:
Not thou by praise, but praise in thee is raised;
It is a praise to praise, when thou art praised.

36

Stella, whence doth this new assault arise,
A conquered, yelden, ransacked heart to win?
Whereto long since, through my long-battered eyes,
Whole armies of thy beauties entered in,
   And there long since, Love, thy lieutenant, lies,   5
My forces razed, thy banners raised within:
Of conquest do not these effects suffice,
But wilt new war upon thine own begin?
   With so sweet voice, and by sweet Nature so,
In sweetest strength, so sweetly skilled withal   10
In all sweet stratagems sweet Art can show,
That not my soul, which at thy foot did fall
   Long since, forced by thy beams, but stone nor tree,
   By Sense's privilege, can scape from thee.

37

My mouth doth water, and my breast doth swell,
   My tongue doth itch, my thoughts in labour be:
   Listen then, lordings, with good ear to me,
For of my life I must a riddle tell.
Towards Aurora's court a nymph doth dwell,   5
   Rich in all beauties which man's eye can see;
   Beauties so far from reach of words that we
Abase her praise saying she doth excel;
   Rich in the treasure of deserved renown;
Rich in the riches of a royal heart: 10
Rich in those gifts which give the eternal crown;
Who though most rich in these and every part
   Which make the patents of true worldly bliss,
   Hath no misfortune, but that Rich she is.

38

This night, while Sleep begins with heavy wings
   To hatch mine eyes, and that unbitted thought
   Doth fall to stray, and my chief powers are brought
To leave the sceptre of all subject things,
The first that straight my fancy's error brings   5
   Unto my mind is Stella's image, wrought
   By Love's own self, but with so curious draught
That she, methinks, not only shines but sings.

I start, look, hark; but what in closed-up sense
Was held, in opened sense it flies away,   10
Leaving me nought but wailing eloquence.
I, seeing better sights in sight's decay,
 Called it anew, and wooed Sleep again:
 But him, her host; that unkind guest had slain.

39

Come Sleep, O Sleep, the certain knot of peace,
The baiting place of wit, the balm of woe,
The poor man's wealth, the prisoner's release,
The indifferent judge between the high and low;
 With shield of proof shield me from out the prease   5
Of those fierce darts Despair at me doth throw.
O make in me those civil wars to cease:
I will good tribute pay, if thou do so.
 Take thou of me smooth pillows, sweetest bed,
A chamber deaf to noise and blind to light,   10
A rosy garland, and a weary head;
And if these things, as being thine by right,
 Move not thy heavy grace, thou shalt in me,
 Livelier than elsewhere, Stella's image see.

40

As good to write, as for to lie and groan.
 O Stella dear, how much thy power hath wrought,
 That hast my mind, none of the basest, brought
My still kept course, while others sleep, to moan.
Alas, if from the height of Virtue's throne   5
 Thou canst vouchsafe the influence of a thought
 Upon a wretch that long thy grace hath sought,
Weigh then how I by thee am overthrown:
 And then, think thus: although thy beauty be
 Made manifest by such a victory,   10
Yet noblest conquerors do wrecks avoid.
 Since then thou hast so far subdued me,
 That in my heart I offer still to thee:
O do not let thy temple be destroyed.

41

Having this day my horse, my hand, my lance
 Guided so well, that I obtained the prize,

Both by the judgement of the English eyes
And of some sent from that sweet enemy, France,
Horsemen my skill in horsemanship advance,   5
   Town-folks my strength; a daintier judge applies
   His praise to sleight, which from good use doth rise;
Some lucky wits impute it but to chance;
   Others, because of both sides I do take
My blood from them who did excel in this,   10
Think Nature me a man of arms did make.
How far they shoot awry! The true cause is,
   Stella looked on, and from her heavenly face
   Sent forth the beams which made so fair my race.

42

O eyes, which do the spheres of beauty move,
Whose beams be joys, whose joys all virtues be,
Who, while they make Love conquer, conquer Love;
The schools where Venus hath learned chastity:
   O eyes, where humble looks most glorious prove,   5
Only-loved tyrants, just in cruelty,
Do not, O do not, from poor me remove,
Keep still my zenith, ever shine on me.
   For though I never see them but, straightways,
My life forgets to nourish languished sprites,   10
Yet still on me, O eyes, dart down your rays:
And if from majesty of sacred lights,
   Oppressing mortal sense, my death proceed,
   Wracks triumphs be which Love, high set, doth breed.

43

Fair eyes, sweet lips, dear heart, that foolish I
Could hope by Cupid's help on you to prey,
Since to himself he doth your gifts apply
As his main force, choice sport, and easeful stay!
   For when he will see who dare him gainsay,
   Then with those eyes he looks: lo, by and by   5
Each soul doth at Love's feet his weapons lay,
Glad if for her he give them leave to die.
   When he will play, then in her lips he is,
Where, blushing red that Love's self them doth love,   10
With either lip he doth the other kiss:
But when he will for quiet's sake remove

From all the world, her heart is then his room,
Where well he knows no man to him can come.

44

My words I know do well set forth my mind;
  My mind bemoans his sense of inward smart;
  Such smart may pity claim of any heart;
Her heart, sweet heart, is of no tiger's kind,
And yet she hears, and I no pity find,   5
  But more I cry less grace she doth impart.
  Alas, what cause is there so overthwart
That nobleness itself makes thus unkind?
  I much do guess, yet find no truth save this,
That when the breath of my complaints doth touch   10
Those dainty doors unto the court of bliss,
The heavenly nature of that place is such
  That once come there, the sobs of mine annoys
  Are metamorphosed straight to tunes of joys.

45

Stella oft sees the very face of woe
  Painted in my beclouded stormy face,
  But cannot skill to pity my disgrace,
Not though thereof the cause her self she know:
Yet hearing late a fable, which did show   5
  Of lovers never known a grievous case,
  Pity thereof gat in her breast such place
That, from that sea derived, tears' spring did flow.
  Alas, if Fancy, drawn by imaged things,
Though false, yet with free scope more grace doth breed   10
Than servant's wrack, where new doubts honour brings,
Then think, my dear, that you in me do read
  Of lover's ruin some sad tragedy:
  I am not I; pity the tale of me.

46

I cursed thee oft, I pity now thy case,
  Blind-hitting boy, since she, that thee and me
  Rules with a beck, so tyrannizeth thee
That thou must want or food or dwelling-place.
For she protests to banish thee her face.   5

Her face? O Love, a rogue thou then shouldst be,
  If Love learn not alone to love and see
Without desire to feed of further grace.
  Alas, poor wag, that now a scholar art
To such a school-mistress, whose lessons new   10
Thou needs must miss, and so thou needs must smart.
  Yet dear, let me this pardon get of you,
    So long (though he from book mich to desire)
    Till without fuel you can make hot fire.

47

What, have I thus betrayed my liberty?
  Can those black beams such burning marks engrave
  In my free side, or am I born a slave,
Whose neck becomes such yoke of tyranny?
Or want I sense to feel my misery,   5
  Or sprite, disdain of such disdain to have,
  Who for long faith, though daily help I crave,
May get no alms, but scorn of beggary?
  Virtue, awake! beauty but beauty is:
I may, I must, I can, I will, I do   10
Leave following that, which it is gain to miss.
  Let her go. Soft, but here she comes. Go to,
    Unkind, I love you not: O me, that eye
    Doth make my heart give to my tongue the lie.

48

Soul's joy, bend not those morning stars from me,
  Where Virtue is made strong by Beauty's might,
  Where Love is chasteness, Pain doth learn delight,
And Humbleness grows one with Majesty.
Whatever may ensue, O let me be   5
  Co-partner of the riches of that sight;
  Let not mine eyes be hell-driven from that light:
O look, O shine, O let me die, and see.
  For though I oft my self of them bemoan
That through my heart their beamy darts be gone   10
Whose cureless wounds even now most freshly bleed;
  Yet since my death-wound is already got,
    Dear killer, spare not thy sweet cruel shot:
A kind of grace it is to slay with speed.

49

I on my horse, and Love on me, doth try
  Our horsemanships, while by strange work I prove
  A horseman to my horse, a horse to Love,
And now man's wrongs in me, poor beast, descry.
The reins wherewith my rider doth me tie   5
  Are humbled thoughts, which bit of reverence move,
  Curbed in with fear, but with gilt boss above
Of hope, which makes it seem fair to the eye.
  The wand is will; thou, fancy, saddle art,
Girt fast by memory; and while I spur   10
My horse, he spurs with sharp desire my heart.
He sits me fast, however I do stir,
  And now hath made me to his hand so right
  That in the manage myself takes delight.

50

Stella, the fullness of my thoughts of thee
Cannot be stayed within my panting breast,
But they do swell and struggle forth of me,
Till that in words thy figure be expressed.
  And yet, as soon as they so formed be,   5
According to my lord Love's own behest,
With sad eyes I their weak proportion see,
To portrait that which in this world is best.
  So that I cannot choose but write my mind,
And cannot choose but put out what I write,   10
While those poor babes their death in birth do find:
And now my pen these lines had dashed quite,
  But that they stopped his fury from the same,
  Because their forefront bare sweet Stella's name.

51

Pardon mine ears, both I and they do pray,
  So may your tongue still fluently proceed
  To them that do such entertainment need,
So may you still have somewhat new to say.
On silly me do not the burden lay   5
  Of all the grave conceits your brain doth breed,
  But find some Hercules to bear, in steed
Of Atlas tired, your wisdom's heavenly sway.

For me (while you discourse of courtly tides,
Of cunningest fishers in most troubled streams,   10
Of straying ways, when valiant Error guides)
Meanwhile my heart confers with Stella's beams,
   And is even irked that so sweet comedy
   By such unsuited speech should hindered be.

52

A strife is grown between Virtue and Love,
   While each pretends that Stella must be his:
   Her eyes, her lips, her all, saith Love, do this
(Since they do wear his badge) most firmly prove.
But Virtue thus that title doth disprove: 5
   That Stella (O dear name) that Stella is
   That virtuous soul, sure heir of heavenly bliss,
Not this fair outside, which our hearts doth move;
   And therefore, though her beauty and her grace
Be Love's indeed, in Stella's self he may   10
By no pretence claim any manner place.
Well, Love, since this demur our suit doth stay,
   Let Virtue have that Stella's self; yet thus,
   That Virtue but that body grant to us.

53

In martial sports I had my cunning tried,
   And yet to break more staves did me address,
   While with the people's shouts, I must confess,
Youth, luck, and praise even filled my veins with pride;
When Cupid, having me, his slave, descried   5
   In Mars's livery, prancing in the press,
   'What now, sir fool,' said he, 'I would no less:
Look here, I say.' I looked, and Stella spied
   Who, hard by, made a window send forth light.
My heart then quaked, then dazzled were mine eyes,   10
One hand forgot to rule, th'other to fight.
Nor trumpet's sound I heard, nor friendly cries;
   My foe came on, and beat the air for me,
   Till that her blush taught me my shame to see.

54

Because I breathe not love to every one,
   Nor do not use set colours for to wear,

Nor nourish special locks of vowed hair,
Nor give each speech a full point of a groan,
The courtly nymphs, acquainted with the moan   5
  Of them who in their lips Love's standard bear,
'What, he?' say they of me, 'now I dare swear,
He cannot love: no, no, let him alone.'
  And think so still, so Stella know my mind.
Profess indeed I do not Cupid's art: 10
But you, fair maids, at length this true shall find,
That his right badge is but worn in the heart.
  Dumb swans, not chattering pies, do lovers prove:
  They love indeed who quake to say they love.

55

Muses, I oft invoked your holy aid,
  With choicest flowers my speech to engarland so
  That it, despised in true but naked show,
Might win some grace in your sweet skill arrayed;
And oft whole troops of saddest words I stayed,   5
  Striving abroad a-foraging to go,
  Until by your inspiring I might know
How their black banner might be best displayed.
  But now I mean no more your help to try,
Nor other sugaring of my speech to prove,   10
But on her name incessantly to cry:
For let me but name her whom I do love,
  So sweet sounds straight mine ear and heart do hit
  That I well find no eloquence like it.

56

Fie, school of Patience, fie! your lesson is
  Far, far too long to learn it without book:
  What, a whole week without one piece of look,
And think I should not your large precepts miss?
When I might read those letters fair of bliss,   5
  Which in her face teach virtue, I could brook
  Somewhat thy leaden counsels, which I took
As of a friend that meant not much amiss.
  But now that I, alas, do want her sight,
What, dost thou think that I can ever take   10
In thy cold stuff a phlegmatic delight?
No, Patience: if thou wilt my good, then make

Her come and hear with patience my desire:
And then with patience bid me bear my fire.

57

Woe, having made with many fights his own
   Each sense of mine, each gift, each power of mind,
   Grown now his slaves, he forced them out to find
The thoroughest words, fit for Woe's self to groan,
Hoping that when they might find Stella alone,   5
   Before she could prepare to be unkind,
   Her soul, armed but with such a dainty rind,
Should soon be pierced with sharpness of the moan.
   She heard my plaints, and did not only hear,
But them (so sweet is she) most sweetly sing,   10
With that fair breast making woe's darkness clear.
   A pretty case! I hoped her to bring
   To feel my griefs, and she with face and voice
So sweets my pains that my pains me rejoice.

58

Doubt there hath been, when with his golden chain
   The orator so far men's hearts doth bind
   That no pace else their guided steps can find
But as he them more short or slack doth rein,
Whether with words this sovereignty he gain,   5
   Clothed with fine tropes, with strongest reasons lined,
   Or else pronouncing grace, wherewith his mind
Prints his own lively form in rudest brain.
   Now judge by this: in piercing phrases late
   The anatomy of all my woes I wrate;   10
Stella's sweet breath the same to me did read.
   O voice, O face, maugre my speech's might,
   Which wooed woe, most ravishing delight
Even those sad words even in sad me did breed.

59

Dear, why make you more of a dog than me?
   If he do love, I burn, I burn in love;
   If he wait well, I never thence would move;
If he be fair, yet but a dog can be.
Little he is, so little worth is he;   5

He barks; my songs thy own voice oft doth prove.
  Bidden, perhaps he fetcheth thee a glove,
But I unbid fetch even my soul to thee.
  Yet while I languish, him that bosom clips,
That lap doth lap, nay lets, in spite of spite,   10
This sour-breathed mate taste of those sugared lips.
Alas, if you grant only such delight
  To witless things, then love I hope (since wit
  Becomes a clog) will soon ease me of it.

60

When my good angel guides me to the place
  Where all my good I do in Stella see,
  That heaven of joys throws only down on me
Thundered disdains and lightnings of disgrace;
But when the ruggedest step of Fortune's race   5
  Makes me fall from her sight, then sweetly she
  With words, wherein the Muses' treasures be,
Shows love and pity to my absent case.
  Now I, wit-beaten long by hardest fate,
So dull am that I cannot look into   10
The ground of this fierce love and lovely hate:
  Then some good body tell me how I do,
  Whose presence, absence, absence presence is;
  Blessed in my curse, and cursed in my bliss.

61

Oft with true sighs, oft with uncalled tears,
Now with slow words, now with dumb eloquence,
I Stella's eyes assail, invade her ears;
But this at last is her sweet-breathed defence:
  That who indeed infelt affection bears,   5
So captives to his saint both soul and sense
That, wholly hers, all selfness he forbears:
Thence his desires he learns, his life's course thence.
  Now since her chaste mind hates this love in me,
  With chastened mind I straight must show that she   10
Shall quickly me from what she hates remove.
  O Doctor Cupid, thou for me reply,
  Driven else to grant, by angel's sophistry,
That I love not, without I leave to love.

62

Late tired with woe, even ready for to pine
With rage of love, I called my love unkind;
She in whose eyes love, though unfelt, doth shine,
Sweet said that I true love in her should find.
    I joyed, but straight thus watered was my wine,   5
That love she did, but loved a Love not blind,
Which would not let me, whom she loved, decline
From nobler course, fit for my birth and mind:
    And therefore, by her love's authority,
    Willed me these tempests of vain love to fly,   10
And anchor fast myself on Virtue's shore.
    Alas, if this the only metal be
    Of love, new-coined to help my beggary,
Dear, love me not, that you may love me more.

63

O Grammar rules, O now your virtues show,
    So children still read you with awful eyes,
    As my young dove may in your precepts wise
Her grant to me, by her own virtue, know.
For late, with heart most high, with eyes most low,   5
    I craved the thing which ever she denies:
    She, lightning love, displaying Venus' skies,
Lest once should not be heard, twice said, 'No, no.'
    Sing then, my Muse, now *Io Paean* sing;
    Heavens, envy not at my high triumphing,   10
But Grammar's force with sweet success confirm.
    For Grammar says (O this, dear Stella, weigh),
    For Grammar says (to Grammar who says nay?)
That in one speech two negatives affirm.

First song

Doubt you to whom my Muse these songs intendeth,
Which now my breast o'ercharged to music lendeth?
To *you*, to *you*, all song of praise is due,
Only in *you* my song begins and endeth.

Who hath the eyes which marry state with pleasure,   5
Who keeps the key of Nature's chiefest treasure?
To *you*, to *you*, all song of praise is due,
Only for *you* the heaven forgat all measure.

Who hath the lips, where wit in fairness reigneth,
Who womankind at once both decks and staineth? 10
To *you*, to *you*, all song of praise is due,
Only by *you* Cupid his crown maintaineth.

Who hath the feet, whose steps all sweetness planteth,
Who else for whom Fame worthy trumpets wanteth?
To *you*, to *you*, all song of praise is due, 15
Only to *you* her sceptre Venus granteth.

Who hath the breast whose milk doth passions nourish,
Whose grace is such, that when it chides doth cherish?
To *you*, to *you*, all song of praise is due,
Only through *you* the tree of life doth flourish. 20

Who hath the hand which without stroke subdueth,
Who long-dead beauty with increase reneweth?
To *you*, to *you*, all song of praise is due,
Only at *you* all envy hopeless rueth.

Who hath the hair which, loosest, fastest tieth? 25
Who makes a man live, then glad when he dieth?
To *you*, to *you*, all song of praise is due,
Only of *you* the flatterer never lieth.

Who hath the voice which soul from senses sunders?
Whose force but yours the bolt of beauty thunders? 30
To *you*, to *you*, all song of praise is due,
Only with *you* not miracles are wonders.

Doubt you to whom my Muse these notes intendeth,
Which now my breast o'ercharged to music lendeth?
To *you*, to *you*, all song of praise is due, 35
Only in *you* my song begins and endeth.

64

No more, my dear, no more these counsels try,
    O give my passions leave to run their race.
    Let Fortune lay on me her worst disgrace,
Let folk o'ercharged with brain against me cry,
Let clouds bedim my face, break in mine eye, 5
    Let me no steps but of lost labour trace,
    Let all the earth with scorn recount my case,
But do not will me from my love to fly.
    I do not envy Aristotle's wit,

Nor do aspire to Caesar's bleeding fame,　　　　10
Nor aught do care though some above me sit,
Nor hope, nor wish, another course to frame
　　But that which once may win thy cruel heart:
　　Thou art my wit, and thou my virtue art.

65

Love, by sure proof I may call thee unkind
That givest no better ear to my just cries:
Thou whom to me such my good turns should bind
As I may well recount but none can prize.
　　For when, naked boy, thou couldest no harbour find　　5
In this old world, grown now so too too wise,
I lodged thee in my heart; and being blind
By nature born, I gave to thee mine eyes.
　　Mine eyes, my light, my heart, my life: alas,
If so great services may scorned be,　　　　10
Yet let this thought thy tigerish courage pass,
That I perhaps am somewhat kin to thee,
　　Since in thine arms, if learned Fame truth hath spread,
　　Thou bearest the arrow, I the arrow head.

66

And do I see some cause a hope to feed,
Or doth the tedious burden of long woe
In weakened minds quick apprehending breed
Of every image which may comfort show?
　　I cannot brag of word, much less of deed;　　5
Fortune wheels still with me in one sort slow;
My wealth no more, and no whit less my need;
Desire still on the stilts of fear doth go.
　　And yet amid all fears a hope there is
Stolen to my heart, since last fair night, nay day,　　10
Stella's eyes sent to me the beams of bliss,
Looking on me while I looked other way:
　　But when mine eyes back to their heaven did move,
　　They fled with blush which guilty seemed of love.

67

Hope, art thou true, or dost thou flatter me?
　　Doth Stella now begin with piteous eye
　　The ruins of her conquest to espy?

Will she take time, before all wracked be?
Her eyes'-speech is translated thus by thee,   5
   But failest thou not in phrase so heavenly high?
   Look on again, the fair text better try:
What blushing notes dost thou in margin see?
   What sighs stolen out, or killed before full born?
Hast thou found such and such like arguments?   10
Or art thou else to comfort me forsworn?
Well, how so thou interpret the contents,
   I am resolved thy error to maintain,
   Rather than by more truth to get more pain.

68

Stella, the only planet of my light,
   Light of my life, and life of my desire,
   Chief good whereto my hope doth only aspire,
World of my wealth, and heaven of my delight;
Why dost thou spend the treasures of thy sprite   5
   With voice more fit to wed Amphion's lyre,
   Seeking to quench in me the noble fire
Fed by thy worth, and kindled by thy sight?
   And all in vain, for while thy breath most sweet
With choicest words, thy words with reasons rare,   10
Thy reasons firmly set on Virtue's feet,
Labour to kill in me this killing care,
   O think I then, what paradise of joy
   It is, so fair a virtue to enjoy.

69

O joy too high for my low style to show!
   O bliss, fit for a nobler state than me!
   Envy, put out thine eyes, lest thou do see
What oceans of delight in me do flow.
My friend, that oft saw through all masks my woe,   5
   Come, come, and let me pour myself on thee:
   Gone is the winter of my misery,
My spring appears: O see what here doth grow!
   For Stella hath, with words where faith doth shine,
Of her high heart given me the monarchy: 10
I, I, O I may say that she is mine.
And though she give but thus conditionally
   This realm of bliss, while virtuous course I take,
   No kings be crowned but they some covenants make.

70

My Muse may well grudge at my heavenly joy
If still I force her in sad rhymes to creep.
She oft hath drunk my tears, now hopes to enjoy
Nectar of mirth, since I Jove's cup do keep.
   Sonnets be not bound prentice to annoy: 5
Trebles sing high, as well as basses deep;
Grief but love's winter livery is; the boy
Hath cheeks to smile, as well as eyes to weep.
   Come then my Muse, show thou height of delight
In well raised notes; my pen the best it may 10
Shall paint out joy, though but in black and white.
Cease, eager Muse; peace pen, for my sake stay;
   I give you here my hand for truth of this:
   Wise silence is best music unto bliss.

71

Who will in fairest book of Nature know
   How Virtue may best lodged in beauty be,
   Let him but learn of love to read in thee,
Stella, those fair lines which true goodness show.
There shall he find all vices' overthrow, 5
   Not by rude force, but sweetest sovereignty
   Of reason, from whose light those night-birds fly,
That inward sun in thine eyes shineth so.
   And not content to be perfection's heir
Thy self, dost strive all minds that way to move, 10
Who mark in thee what is in thee most fair.
So while thy beauty draws the heart to love,
   As fast thy virtue bends that love to good:
   'But ah,' Desire still cries, 'give me some food.'

72

Desire, though thou my old companion art,
   And oft so clings to my pure love that I
   One from the other scarcely can descry
While each doth blow the fire of my heart,
Now from thy fellowship I needs must part: 5
   Venus is taught with Dian's wings to fly;

I must no more in thy sweet passions lie:
Virtue's gold now must head my Cupid's dart.
   Service and Honour, Wonder with Delight,
Fear to offend, Will worthy to appear,   10
Care shining in mine eyes, Faith in my sprite:
These things are left me by my only dear.
   But thou, Desire, because thou wouldst have all,
   Now banished art – but yet, alas, how shall?

Second song

     Have I caught my heavenly jewel
     Teaching Sleep most fair to be?
     Now will I teach her that she,
     When she wakes, is too too cruel.

     Since sweet Sleep her eyes hath charmed,   5
     The two only darts of Love,
     Now will I with that boy prove
     Some play, while he is disarmed.

     Her tongue waking still refuseth,
     Giving frankly niggard 'no';   10
     Now will I attempt to know
     What 'no' her tongue, sleeping, useth.

     See, the hand which, waking, guardeth,
     Sleeping, grants a free resort;
     Now will I invade the fort: 15
     Cowards Love with loss rewardeth.

     But (O fool) think of the danger
     Of her just and high disdain;
     Now will I, alas, refrain:
     Love fears nothing else but anger.   20

     Yet those lips so sweetly swelling
     Do invite a stealing kiss:
     Now will I but venture this:
     Who will read must first learn spelling.

     O sweet kiss – but ah, she is waking,   25
     Louring beauty chastens me.
     Now will I away hence flee,
     Fool, more fool, for no more taking.

73

Love still a boy, and oft a wanton is,
Schooled only by his mother's tender eye:
What wonder then if he his lesson miss,
When for so soft a rod dear play he try?
    And yet my Star, because a sugared kiss   5
In sport I sucked, while she asleep did lie,
Doth lour, nay chide, nay threat, for only this:
Sweet, it was saucy Love, not humble I.
    But no 'scuse serves; she makes her wrath appear
    In Beauty's throne: see now, who dares come near   10
Those scarlet judges, threatening bloody pain?
    O heavenly fool, thy most kiss-worthy face
    Anger invests with such a lovely grace
That Anger's self I needs must kiss again.

74

I never drank of Aganippe well,
Nor ever did in shade of Tempe sit,
And Muses scorn with vulgar brains to dwell:
Poor layman I, for sacred rites unfit.
    Some do I hear of poets' Fury tell,   5
But (God wot) wot not what they mean by it;
And this I swear, by blackest brook of hell,
I am no pick-purse of another's wit.
    How falls it then, that with so smooth an ease
My thoughts I speak, and what I speak doth flow   10
In verse, and that my verse best wits doth please?
    Guess we the cause: 'What, is it thus?' Fie, no;
    'Or so?' Much less. 'How then?' Sure, thus it is:
My lips are sweet, inspired with Stella's kiss.

75

Of all the kings that ever here did reign,
Edward, named fourth, as first in praise I name:
Not for his fair outside, nor well-lined brain,
Although less gifts imp feathers oft on fame;
    Nor that he could, young-wise, wise-valiant, frame   5
His sire's revenge, joined with a kingdom's gain;
And, gained by Mars, could yet mad Mars so tame
That balance weighed what sword did late obtain;

Nor that he made the flower-de-luce so 'fraid,
Though strongly hedged of bloody lion's paws,   10
That witty Lewis to him a tribute paid:
Nor this, nor that, nor any such small cause;
   But only for this worthy knight durst prove
   To lose his crown, rather than fail his love.

76

She comes, and straight therewith her shining twins do move
   Their rays to me, who in her tedious absence lay
   Benighted in cold woe; but now appears my day,
The only light of joy, the only warmth of love.
She comes with light and warmth which, like Aurora, prove   5
   Of gentle force, so that mine eyes dare gladly play
   With such a rosy morn whose beams, most freshly gay,
Scorch not, but only do dark chilling sprites remove.
   But lo, while I do speak, it groweth noon with me:
Her flamy glistering lights increase with time and place;   10
My heart cries 'ah, it burns'; mine eyes now dazzled be;
No wind, no shade, can cool; what help then in my case,
   But with short breath, long looks, staid feet and walking head,
   Pray that my sun go down with meeker beams to bed?

77

Those looks, whose beams be joy, whose motion is delight;
That face, whose lecture shows what perfect beauty is;
That presence, which doth give dark hearts a living light;
That grace, which Venus weeps that she herself doth miss;
   That hand, which without touch holds more than Atlas might;   5
Those lips, which make death's pay a mean price for a kiss;
That skin, whose pass-praise hue scorns this poor term of 'white';
Those words, which do sublime the quintessence of bliss;
   That voice, which makes the soul plant himself in the ears;
That conversation sweet where such high comforts be   10
As, construed in true speech, the name of heaven it bears,
Makes me in my best thoughts and quietest judgement see
   That in no more but these I might be fully blessed:
   Yet ah, my maiden Muse doth blush to tell the best.

78

O how the pleasant airs of true love be
    Infected by those vapours which arise
    From out that noisome gulf which gaping lies
Between the jaws of hellish Jealousy!
A monster, others' harm, self-misery,   5
    Beauty's plague, Virtue's scourge, succour of lies,
    Who his own joy to his own hurt applies,
And only cherish doth with injury;
    Who since he hath, by Nature's special grace,
    So piercing paws, as spoil when they embrace;   10
So nimble feet, as stir still, though on thorns;
    So many eyes, aye seeking their own woe;
    So ample ears, as never good news know:
Is it not ill that such a devil wants horns?

79

Sweet kiss, thy sweets I fain would sweetly indite
    Which even of sweetness sweetest sweetener art:
    Pleasingest consort, where each sense holds a part,
Which, coupling doves, guides Venus' chariot right;
Best charge, and bravest retreat in Cupid's fight;   5
    A double key which opens to the heart,
    Most rich when most his riches it impart;
Nest of young joys, schoolmaster of delight,
    Teaching the mean at once to take and give;
The friendly fray, where blows both wound and heal;   10
The pretty death, while each in other live;
Poor hope's first wealth, hostage of promised weal,
    Breakfast of Love — but lo, lo, where she is:
    Cease we to praise, now pray we for a kiss.

80

Sweet swelling lip, well mayest thou swell in pride,
    Since best wits think it wit thee to admire:
    Nature's praise, Virtue's stall, Cupid's cold fire,
Whence words not words, but heavenly graces, slide;
The new Parnassus, where the Muses bide;   5
    Sweetener of music, wisdom's beautifier;
    Breather of life, and fastener of desire,
Where Beauty's blush in Honour's grain is dyed.

Thus much my heart compelled my mouth to say,
  But now, spite of my heart, my mouth will stay,   10
Loathing all lies, doubting this flattery is:
  And no spur can his resty race renew
  Without how far this praise is short of you,
Sweet lip, you teach my mouth with one sweet kiss.

81

O kiss, which dost those ruddy gems impart,
Or gems or fruits of new-found paradise,
Breathing all bliss and sweetening to the heart,
Teaching dumb lips a nobler exercise:
  O kiss, which souls, even souls, together ties   5
  By links of love, and only Nature's art,
How fain would I paint thee to all men's eyes,
Or of thy gifts at least shade out some part.
  But she forbids: with blushing words she says
  She builds her fame on higher-seated praise;   10
But my heart burns, I cannot silent be.
  Then since, dear life, you fain would have me peace,
  And I, mad with delight, want wit to cease,
Stop you my mouth with still still kissing me.

82

Nymph of the garden where all beauties be,
  Beauties which do in excellency pass
  His who till death looked in a watery glass,
Or hers whom naked the Trojan boy did see:
Sweet garden nymph which keeps the cherry tree   5
  Whose fruit doth far the Hesperian taste surpass;
  Most sweet-fair, most fair-sweet, do not, alas,
From coming near those cherries banish me.
  For though, full of desire, empty of wit,
  Admitted late by your best-graced grace,   10
I caught at one of them a hungry bit,
Pardon that fault, once more grant me the place,
  And I do swear, even by the same delight,
  I will but kiss, I never more will bite.

83

Good brother Philip, I have borne you long:
  I was content you should in favour creep,

While craftily you seemed your cut to keep,
As though that fair soft hand did you great wrong;
I bare (with envy) yet I bare your song,   5
 When in her neck you did love-ditties peep;
 Nay, more fool I, oft suffered you to sleep
In lilies' nest, where Love's self lies along.
 What, doth high place ambitious thoughts augment?
Is sauciness reward of courtesy?   10
Cannot such grace your silly self content,
But you must needs with those lips billing be
 And through those lips drink nectar from that tongue?
 Leave that, sir Phip, lest off your neck be wrung.

Third song

If Orpheus' voice had force to breathe such music's love
Through pores of senseless trees, as it could make them move;
If stones good measure danced the Theban walls to build
To cadence of the tunes which Amphion's lyre did yield;
 More cause a like effect at leastwise bringeth: 5
 O stones, O trees, learn hearing, Stella singeth.

If love might sweeten so a boy of shepherd brood,
To make a lizard dull to taste love's dainty food;
If eagle fierce could so in Grecian maid delight,
As his light was her eyes, her death his endless night;   10
 Earth gave that love, Heaven (I trow) love refineth:
 O beasts, O birds, look love, lo, Stella shineth.

The birds, beasts, stones, and trees feel this, and feeling love;
And if the trees nor stones stir not the same to prove,
Nor beasts nor birds do come unto this blessed gaze,   15
Know, that small love is quick, and great love doth amaze;
 They are amazed, but you with reason armed:
 O eyes, O ears of men, how are you charmed!

84

Highway, since you my chief Parnassus be,
 And that my Muse, to some ears not unsweet,
 Tempers her words to trampling horse's feet
More oft than to a chamber melody;
Now, blessed you, bear onward blessed me   5
 To her, where I my heart safeliest shall meet.
 My Muse and I must you of duty greet,

With thanks and wishes, wishing thankfully.
  Be you still fair, honoured by public heed,
By no encroachment wronged, nor time forgot,   10
Nor blamed for blood, nor shamed for sinful deed.
And, that you know I envy you no lot
  Of highest wish, I wish you so much bliss,
  Hundreds of years you Stella's feet may kiss.

85

I see the house: my heart, thy self contain!
  Beware full sails drown not thy tottering barge,
  Lest joy, by nature apt sprites to enlarge,
Thee to thy wrack beyond thy limits strain;
Nor do like lords, whose weak confused brain,   5
  Not pointing to fit folks each undercharge,
  While every office themselves will discharge,
With doing all, leave nothing done but pain.
  But give apt servants their due place: let eyes
See Beauty's total sum summed in her face;   10
Let ears hear speech, which wit to wonder ties;
Let breath suck up those sweets; let arms embrace
  The globe of weal; lips Love's indentures make:
  Thou but of all the kingly tribute take.

Fourth song

    Only joy, now here you are,
    Fit to hear and ease my care;
    Let my whispering voice obtain
    Sweet reward for sharpest pain:
    Take me to thee, and thee to me.   5
    'No, no, no, no, my dear, let be.'

    Night hath closed all in her cloak,
    Twinkling stars love-thoughts provoke;
    Danger hence good care doth keep;
    Jealousy itself doth sleep: 10
    Take me to thee, and thee to me.
    'No, no, no, no, my dear, let be.'

    Better place can no man find
    Cupid's yoke to loose or bind;
    These sweet flowers on fine bed too   15
    Us in their best language woo:

Take me to thee, and thee to me.
'*No, no, no, no, my dear, let be.*'

This small light the moon bestows
Serves thy beams but to disclose,
So to raise my hap more high;
Fear not else, none can us spy:
Take me to thee, and thee to me.
'*No, no, no, no, my dear, let be.*'

That you heard was but a mouse;
Dumb Sleep holdeth all the house;
Yet asleep, methinks, they say,
Young folks, take time while you may:
Take me to thee, and thee to me.
'*No, no, no, no, my dear, let be.*'

Niggard Time threats, if we miss
This large offer of our bliss,
Long stay ere he grant the same;
Sweet then, while each thing doth frame:
Take me to thee, and thee to me.
'*No, no, no, no, my dear, let be.*'

Your fair mother is abed,
Candles out, and curtains spread;
She thinks you do letters write;
Write, but first let me indite:
Take me to thee, and thee to me.
'*No, no, no, no, my dear, let be.*'

Sweet, alas, why strive you thus?
Concord better fitteth us;
Leave to Mars the force of hands,
Your power in your beauty stands:
Take me to thee and thee to me.
'*No, no, no, no, my dear, let be.*'

Woe to me, and do you swear
Me to hate, but I forbear?
Cursed be my destinies all,
That brought me so high, to fall;
Soon with my death I will please thee.
'*No, no, no, no, my dear, let be.*'

86

Alas, whence came this change of looks? If I
  Have changed desert, let mine own conscience be
  A still-felt plague, to self condemning me:
Let woe gripe on my heart, shame load mine eye.
But if all faith, like spotless ermine, lie   5
  Safe in my soul, which only doth to thee
  (As his sole object of felicity)
With wings of love in air of wonder fly,
  O ease your hand, treat not so hard your slave;
In justice pains come not till faults do call;   10
Or if I needs (sweet judge) must torments have,
Use something else to chasten me withal
  Than those blessed eyes, where all my hopes do dwell:
  No doom should make one's heaven become his hell.

Fifth song

While favour fed my hope, delight with hope was brought;
Thought waited on delight, and speech did follow thought:
Then grew my tongue and pen records unto thy glory;
I thought all words were lost, that were not spent of thee;
I thought each place was dark but where thy lights would be, 5
And all ears worse than deaf, that heard not out thy story.

I said thou wert most fair, and so indeed thou art;
I said thou wert most sweet, sweet poison to my heart;
I said my soul was thine (O that I then had lied!);
I said thine eyes were stars, thy breasts the milken way, 10
Thy fingers Cupid's shafts, thy voice the angels' lay:
And all I said so well, as no man it denied.

But now that hope is lost, unkindness kills delight;
Yet thought and speech do live, though metamorphosed quite;
For Rage now rules the reins, which guided were by 15
  Pleasure:
I think now of thy faults, who late thought of thy praise;
That speech falls now to blame, which did thy honour raise;
The same key open can, which can lock up a treasure.

Thou then, whom partial heavens conspired in one to frame,
The proof of Beauty's worth, the inheritrix of Fame, 20
The mansion seat of bliss, and just excuse of lovers:
See now those feathers plucked, wherewith thou flewest most
  high:

See what clouds of reproach shall dark thy honour's sky;
Whose own fault casts him down, hardly high seat recovers.

And O my Muse, though oft you lulled her in your lap,   25
And then, a heavenly child, gave her ambrosian pap,
And to that brain of hers your hiddenest gifts infused:
Since she, disdaining me, doth you in me disdain,
Suffer her not to laugh while we both suffer pain;
Princes in subjects wronged must deem themselves abused.   30

Your client poor my self, shall Stella handle so?
Revenge, revenge, my Muse; Defiance' trumpet blow;
Threaten what may be done, yet do more than you threaten.
Ah, my suit granted is: I feel my breast doth swell;
Now child, a lesson new you shall begin to spell: 35
Sweet babes must babies have, but shrewd girls must be beaten.

Think now no more to hear of warm fine-odoured snow,
Nor blushing lilies, nor pearls' ruby-hidden row,
Nor of that golden sea, whose waves in curls are broken:
But of thy soul, so fraught with such ungratefulness,   40
As where thou soon mightest help, most faith doth
     most oppress;
Ungrateful who is called, the worst of evils is spoken.

Yet worse than worst, I say thou art a thief. A thief?
Now God forbid: a thief, and of worst thieves the chief;
Thieves steal for need, and steal but goods, which pain   45
     recovers;
But thou, rich in all joys, dost rob my joys from me,
Which cannot be restored by time nor industry.
Of foes the spoil is evil, far worse of constant lovers.

Yet gentle English thieves do rob, but will not slay;
Thou, English murdering thief, wilt have hearts for thy prey.   50
The name of murderer now on thy fair forehead sitteth,
And even while I do speak my death wounds bleeding be,
Which, I protest, proceed from only cruel thee.
Who may, and will not, save, murder in truth committeth.

But murder, private fault, seems but a toy to thee.   55
I lay then to thy charge unjustest tyranny,
If rule by force without all claim a tyrant showeth:
For those dost lord my heart, who am not born thy slave;
And which is worse, makes me (most guiltless) torments have:
A rightful prince by unright deeds a tyrant groweth.   60

Lo you grow proud with this, for tyrants make folk bow:
Of foul rebellion then I do appreach thee now;
Rebel by Nature's law, rebel by law of Reason:
Thou, sweetest subject, wert born in the realm of Love,
And yet against thy prince thy force dost daily prove; 65
No virtue merits praise, once touched with blot of treason.

But valiant rebels oft in fools' mouths purchase fame:
I now then stain thy white with vagabonding shame,
Both rebel to the son, and vagrant from the mother:
For, wearing Venus' badge in every part of thee, 70
Unto Diana's train thou runaway didst flee:
Who faileth one is false, though trusty to another.

What, is not this enough? Nay, far worse cometh here:
A witch I say thou art, though thou so fair appear.
For, I protest, my sight never thy face enjoyeth 75
But I in me am changed: I am alive and dead;
My feet are turned to roots; my heart becometh lead:
No witchcraft is so evil, as which man's mind destroyeth.

Yet witches may repent; thou art far worse than they:
Alas, that I am forced such evil of thee to say! 80
I say thou art a devil, though clothed in angel's shining,
For thy face tempts my soul to leave the heaven for thee,
And thy words of refuse do pour even hell on me:
Who tempt, and tempted plague, are devils in true defining.

You then, ungrateful thief, you murdering tyrant, you; 85
You rebel runaway, to lord and lady untrue;
You witch, you devil – alas, you still of me beloved:
You see what I can say; mend yet your froward mind,
And such skill in my Muse you, reconciled, shall find
That all these cruel words your praises shall be proved. 90

Sixth song

O you that hear this voice,
O you that see this face,
Say whether of the choice
Deserves the former place:
 Fear not to judge this bate, 5
 For it is void of hate.

This side doth Beauty take,
For that, doth Music speak,

Fit orators to make
The strongest judgements weak: 10
   The bar to plead their right
   Is only true delight.

Thus doth the voice and face,
These gentle lawyers, wage,
Like loving brothers' case,   15
For father's heritage,
   That each, while each contends,
   Itself to other lends.

For Beauty beautifies
With heavenly hue and grace   20
The heavenly harmonies;
And in this faultless face
   The perfect beauties be
   A perfect harmony.

Music more loftily swells   25
In speeches nobly placed,
Beauty as far excels
In action aptly graced,
   A friend each party draws
   To countenance his cause.   30

Love more affected seems
To Beauty's lovely light,
And Wonder more esteems
Of Music's wondrous might:
   But both to both so bent
   As both in both are spent.   35

Music doth witness call
The ear, his truth to try;
Beauty brings to the hall
The judgement of the eye: 40
   Both in their objects such,
   As no exceptions touch.

The Common Sense which might
Be arbiter of this,
To be, forsooth, upright,   45
To both sides partial is:
   He lays on this chief praise,
   Chief praise on that he lays.

Then Reason, princess high,
Whose throne is in the mind,   50
Which music can in sky
And hidden beauties find:
    Say, whether thou wilt crown
    With limitless renown.

Seventh song

Whose senses in so evil consort their stepdame Nature lays,
That ravishing delight in them most sweet tunes do not raise;
Or if they do delight therein, yet are so cloyed with wit,
As with sententious lips to set a title vain on it:
    O let them hear these sacred tunes, and learn in   5
      Wonder's schools,
    To be, in things past bounds of wit, fools, if they be not
      fools.

Who have so leaden eyes as not to see sweet Beauty's show;
Or seeing, have so wooden wits, as not that worth to know;
Or knowing, have so muddy minds, as not to be in love;
Or loving, have so frothy thoughts as easily thence to move: 10
    O, let them see these heavenly beams, and in fair
      letters read
    A. lesson fit, both sight and skill, love and firm love to
      breed.

Hear then, but then with wonder hear; see, but adoring see;
No mortal gifts, no earthly fruits, now here descended be:
See – do you see this face? A face? Nay, image of the skies,   15
Of which the two life-giving lights are figured in her eyes.
    Hear you this soul-invading voice, and call it but a voice,
    The very essence of their tunes, when angels do rejoice.

Eighth song

    In a grove most rich of shade,
    Where birds wanton music made,
    May then young his pied weeds showing,
    New perfumed with flowers fresh growing,

    Astrophil with Stella sweet   5
    Did for mutual comfort meet:
    Both within themselves oppressed,
    But each in the other blessed.

Him great harms had taught much care,
Her fair neck a foul yoke bare: 10
But her sight his cares did banish,
In his sight her yoke did vanish.

Wept they had, alas, the while,
But now tears themselves did smile,
While their eyes, by love directed,   15
Interchangeably reflected.

Sigh they did, but now betwixt
Sighs of woes were glad sighs mixed,
With arms crossed, yet testifying
Restless rest, and living dying.   20

Their ears hungry of each word
Which the dear tongue would afford,
But their tongues restrained from walking
Till their hearts had ended talking.

But when their tongues could not speak   25
Love itself did silence break:
Love did set his lips asunder,
Thus to speak in love and wonder:

'Stella, sovereign of my joy,
Fair triumpher of annoy,   30
Stella, star of heavenly fire,
Stella, lodestar of desire,

Stella, in whose shining eyes
Are the lights of Cupid's skies;
Whose beams, where they once are darted,   35
Love therewith is straight imparted:

Stella, whose voice when it speaks
Senses all asunder breaks,
Stella, whose voice when it singeth
Angels to acquaintance bringeth,   40

Stella, in whose body is
Writ each character of bliss;
Whose face all, all beauty passeth,
Save thy mind, which yet surpasseth:

Grant, O grant – but speech, alas,   45
Fails me, fearing on to pass;

Grant – O me, what am I saying?
But no fault there is in praying:

Grant, O dear, on knees I pray'
(Knees on ground he then did stay)   50
'That not I, but since I love you,
Time and place for me may move you.

Never season was more fit,
Never room more apt for it;
Smiling air allows my reason,   55
These birds sing, "Now use the season."

This small wind which so sweet is,
See how it the leaves doth kiss,
Each tree in his best attiring
Sense of love to love inspiring.   60

Love makes earth the water drink,
Love to earth makes water sink;
And if dumb things be so witty,
Shall a heavenly grace want pity?'

There his hands in their speech fain   65
Would have made tongue's language plain;
But her hands his hands repelling,
Gave repulse all grace excelling.

Then she spake; her speech was such
As not ears, but heart did touch;   70
While such wise she love denied
As yet love she signified:

'Astrophil,' said she, 'my love
Cease in these effects to prove.
Now be still: yet still believe me,   75
Thy grief more than death would grieve me.

If that any thought in me
Can taste comfort but of thee,
Let me, fed with hellish anguish,
Joyless, hopeless, endless languish.   80

If those eyes you praised be
Half so dear as you to me,
Let me home return, stark blinded
Of those eyes, and blinder minded.

If to secret of my heart   85
I do any wish impart
Where thou art not foremost placed,
Be both wish and I defaced.

If more may be said, I say;
All my bliss in thee I lay;   90
If thou love, my love content thee,
For all love, all faith is meant thee.

Trust me, while I thee deny,
In my self the smart I try;
Tyrant Honour thus doth use thee: 95
Stella's self might not refuse thee.

Therefore, dear, this no more move,
Lest, though I leave not thy love,
Which too deep in me is framed,
I should blush when thou art named.'   100

Therewithal away she went,
Leaving him so passion-rent
With what she had done and spoken,
That therewith my song is broken.

Ninth song

Go, my flock, go get you hence,
Seek a better place of feeding,
Where you may have some defence
   From the storms in my breast breeding,
   And showers from mine eyes proceeding.   5

Leave a wretch in whom all woe
Can abide to keep no measure:
Merry flock, such one forego,
   Unto whom mirth is displeasure,
   Only rich in mischief's treasure.   10

Yet alas before you go,
Hear your woeful master's story,
Which to stones I else would show;
   Sorrow only then hath glory,
   When tis excellently sorry: 15

Stella, fiercest shepherdess,
Fiercest, but yet fairest ever,

Stella, whom, O heavens, still bless,
   Though against me she persevere,
   Though I bliss inherit never,   20

Stella hath refused me:
Stella, who more love hath proved
In this caitiff heart to be
   Than can in good ewes be moved
   Toward lambkins best beloved.   25

Stella hath refused me:
Astrophil, that so well served,
In this pleasant spring must see,
   While in pride flowers be preserved,
   Himself only winter-starved.   30

Why, alas, doth she then swear
That she loveth me so dearly,
Seeing me so long to bear
   Coals of love, that burn so clearly,
   And yet leave me helpless merely?   35

Is that love? Forsooth, I trow,
If I saw my good dog grieved,
And a help for him did know,
   My love should not be believed
   But he were by me relieved.   40

No, she hates me, wellaway,
Feigning love somewhat, to please me;
For she knows if she display
   All her hate, death soon would seize me,
   And of hideous torments ease me.   45

Then adieu, dear flock, adieu:
But alas, if in your straying
Heavenly Stella meet with you,
   Tell her, in your piteous blaying,
   Her poor slave's unjust decaying.   50

87

When I was forced from Stella ever dear
(Stella, food of my thoughts, heart of my heart,
Stella, whose eyes make all my tempests clear)
By iron laws of duty to depart,

Alas, I found that she with me did smart: 5
  I saw that tears did in her eyes appear,
I saw that sighs her sweetest lips did part,
And her sad words my sadded sense did hear.
  For me, I wept to see pearls scattered so;
  I sighed her sighs, and wailed for her woe,   10
Yet swam in joy such love in her was seen.
  Thus while the effect most bitter was to me,
  And nothing than the cause more sweet could be,
I had been vexed, if vexed I had not been.

88

Out, traitor Absence: darest thou counsel me
  From my dear captainess to run away,
Because in brave array here marcheth she,
That to win me oft shows a present pay?
  Is faith so weak? Or is such force in thee?   5
When sun is hid, can stars such beams display?
Cannot heaven's food, once felt, keep stomachs free
From base desire on earthly cates to prey?
  Tush, Absence; while thy mists eclipse that light,
  My orphan sense flies to the inward sight,   10
Where memory sets forth the beams of love;
  That where before heart loved and eyes did see,
  In heart both sight and love now coupled be:
United powers make each the stronger prove.

89

Now that of absence the most irksome night
  With darkest shade doth overcome my day,
  Since Stella's eyes, wont to give me my day,
Leaving my hemisphere, leave me in night,
Each day seems long, and longs for long-stayed night;   5
  The night, as tedious, woos the approach of day;
  Tired with the dusty toils of busy day,
Languished with horrors of the silent night,
Suffering the evils both of the day and night,
  While no night is more dark than is my day,   10
Nor no day hath less quiet than my night;
  With such bad mixture of my night and day,
That living thus in blackest winter night,
  I feel the flames of hottest summer day.

90

Stella, think not that I by verse seek fame,
   Who seek, who hope, who love, who live but thee;
   Thine eyes my pride, thy lips my history:
If thou praise not, all other praise is shame.
Nor so ambitious am I as to frame   5
   A nest for my young praise in laurel tree:
   In truth I swear, I wish not there should be
Graved in mine epitaph a poet's name;
   Ne if I would, could I just title make,
That any laud to me thereof should grow,   10
Without my plumes from others' wings I take:
For nothing from my wit or will doth flow,
   Since all my words thy beauty doth indite,
   And love doth hold my hand, and makes me write.

91

Stella, while now, by Honour's cruel might,
   I am from you, light of my life, misled,
   And that fair you, my sun, thus overspread
With Absence' veil, I live in Sorrow's night:
If this dark place yet show, like candle light,   5
   Some beauty's piece, as amber-coloured head,
   Milk hands, rose cheeks, or lips more sweet, more red,
Or seeing jets, black, but in blackness bright:
   They please, I do confess, they please mine eyes;
But why? Because of you they models be,   10
Models such be wood-globes of glistering skies.
Dear, therefore be not jealous over me,
   If you hear that they seem my heart to move:
   Not them, O no, but you in them I love.

92

Be your words made (good sir) of Indian ware,
   That you allow me them by so small rate?
   Or do you cutted Spartans imitate?
Or do you mean my tender ears to spare,
That to my questions you so total are?   5
   When I demand of Phoenix-Stella's state,
   You say, forsooth, you left her well of late.
O God, think you that satisfies my care?

I would know whether she did sit or walk,
How clothed; how waited on; sighed she or smiled;   10
Whereof; with whom; how often did she talk;
With what pastime time's journey she beguiled;
   If her lips deigned to sweeten my poor name?
   Say all, and all well said, still say the same.

Tenth song

   O dear life, when shall it be
   That mine eyes thine eyes may see,
      And in them my mind discover,
   Whether absence have had force
   Thy remembrance to divorce   5
      From the image of thy lover?

   O if I myself find not
   After parting aught forgot,
      Nor debarred from Beauty's treasure,
   Let no tongue aspire to tell   10
   In what high joys I shall dwell:
      Only thought aims at the pleasure.

   Thought therefore I will send thee
   To take up the place for me:
      Long I will not after tarry.   15
   There unseen thou mayest be bold
   Those fair wonders to behold,
      Which in them my hopes do carry.

   Thought, see thou no place forbear;
   Enter bravely everywhere;   20
      Seize on all to her belonging:
   But if thou wouldest guarded be,
   Fearing her beams, take with thee
      Strength of liking, rage of longing.

   Think of that most grateful time   25
   When my leaping heart will climb
      In my lips to have his biding,
   There those roses for to kiss
   Which do breathe a sugared bliss,
      Opening rubies, pearls dividing.   30

   Think of my most princely power,
   When I, blessed, shall devour

With my greedy lickerous senses,
Beauty, music, sweetness, love,
While she doth against me prove   35
   Her strong darts but weak defences.

Think, think, of those dallyings,
When with dove-like murmurings,
   With glad moaning passed anguish,
We change eyes, and heart for heart   40
Each to other do impart,
   Joying till joy make us languish.

O my thoughts, my thoughts, surcease;
Thy delights my woes increase,
   My life melts with too much thinking: 45
Think no more, but die in me,
Till thou shalt revived be
   At her lips my nectar drinking.

93

O fate, O fault, O curse, child of my bliss,
   What sobs can give words grace my grief to show?
   What ink is black enough to paint my woe?
Through me, wretch me, even Stella vexed is.
Yet Truth (if caitiff's breath might call thee) this   5
   Witness with me, that my foul stumbling so
From carelessness did in no manner grow,
But wit, confused with too much care, did miss.
   And do I then myself this vain 'scuse give?
I have (live I, and know this?) harmed thee;   10
Though worlds 'quit me, shall I myself forgive?
Only with pains my pains thus eased be,
   That all thy hurts in my heart's wrack I read:
   I cry thy sighs (my dear) thy tears I bleed.

94

Grief, find the words, for thou hast made my brain
   So dark with misty vapours, which arise
   From out thy heavy mould, that inbent eyes
Can scarce discern the shape of mine own pain.
Do thou then (for thou canst), do thou complain   5
   For my poor soul, which now that sickness tries
   Which even to sense, sense of itself denies,

Though harbingers of Death lodge there his train.
  Or if thy love of plaint yet mine forbears,
As of a caitiff worthy so to die,   10
Yet wail thyself, and wail with causeful tears
That though in wretchedness thy life doth lie,
Yet growest more wretched than thy nature bears,
By being placed in such a wretch as I.

95

Yet sighs, dear sighs, indeed true friends you are,
  That do not leave your least friend at the worst;
  But as you with my breast I oft have nursed,
So grateful now you wait upon my care.
Faint coward Joy no longer tarry dare,   5
  Seeing Hope yield when this woe strake him first;
  Delight protests he is not for the accursed,
Though oft himself my mate-in-arms he sware.
  Nay, Sorrow comes with such main rage, that he
Kills his own children, tears, finding that they   10
By Love were made apt to consort with me.
Only true sighs, you do not go away:
  Thank may you have for such a thankful part,
  Thank-worthiest yet, when you shall break my heart.

96

Thought, with good cause thou likest so well the Night,
  Since kind or chance gives both one livery:
  Both sadly black, both blackly darkened be,
Night barred from sun, thou from thy own sun's light.
Silence in both displays his sullen might,   5
  Slow heaviness in both holds one degree,
  That full of doubts, thou of perplexity;
Thy tears express Night's native moisture right;
  In both a mazefull solitariness;
In Night, of sprites the ghastly powers stir,   10
In thee, or sprites or sprited ghastliness:
But, but (alas) Night's side the odds hath far,
  For that at length yet doth invite some rest:
  Thou, though still tired, yet still dost it detest.

97

Dian, that fain would cheer her friend the Night,
  Shows her oft at the full her fairest face,
  Bringing with her those starry nymphs, whose chase
From heavenly standing hits each mortal wight.
But ah, poor Night, in love with Phoebus' light,   5
  And endlessly despairing of his grace,
  Herself, to show no other joy hath place,
Silent and sad in mourning weeds doth dight:
  Even so (alas) a lady, Dian's peer,
With choice delights and rarest company   10
Would fain drive clouds from out my heavy cheer.
  But woe is me, though Joy itself were she,
  She could not show my blind brain ways of Joy,
While I despair my sun's sight to enjoy.

98

Ah bed, the field where Joy's peace some do see,
  The field where all my thoughts to war be trained,
  How is thy grace by my strange fortune stained!
How thy lee shores by my sighs stormed be!
With sweet soft shades thou oft invitest me   5
  To steal some rest; but, wretch, I am constrained
  (Spurred with Love's spur, though galled and shortly reined
With Care's hard hand) to turn and toss in thee,
  While the black horrors of the silent night
  Paint Woe's black face so lively to my sight   10
That tedious leisure marks each wrinkled line.
  But when Aurora leads out Phoebus' dance
  Mine eyes then only wink, for spite, perchance,
That worms should have their sun, and I want mine.

99

When far spent Night persuades each mortal eye,
  To whom nor Art nor Nature granteth light,
  To lay his then mark-wanting shafts of sight,
Closed with their quivers, in Sleep's armoury,
With windows ope then most my mind doth lie,   5
  Viewing the shape of darkness; and Delight
  Takes in that sad hue, which with the inward night
Of his mazed powers keeps perfect harmony.

But when birds charm, and that sweet air, which is
Morn's messenger, with rose-enamelled skies   10
Calls each wight to salute the flower of bliss:
In tomb of lids then buried are mine eyes,
    Forced by their lord, who is ashamed to find
    Such light in sense, with such a darkened mind.

100

O tears, no tears, but rain from Beauty's skies,
    Making those lilies and those roses grow
    Which, aye most fair, now more than most fair show,
While graceful Pity Beauty beautifies.
O honeyed sighs, which from that breast to rise   5
    Whose pants do make unspilling cream to flow,
    Winged with whose breath so pleasing zephyrs blow
As can refresh the hell where my soul fries:
    O plaints, conserved in such a sugared phrase
    That Eloquence itself envies your praise,   10
While sobbed-out words a perfect music give:
    Such tears, sighs, plaints, no sorrow is, but joy;
    Or if such heavenly signs must prove annoy,
All mirth farewell, let me in sorrow live.

101

Stella is sick, and in that sick-bed lies
Sweetness, that breathes and pants as oft as she;
And Grace, sick too, such fine conclusions tries
That Sickness brags itself best graced to be.
    Beauty is sick, but sick in so fair guise   5
That in that paleness Beauty's white we see;
And Joy, which is inseparate from those eyes,
Stella now learns (strange case!) to weep in thee.
    Love moves thy pain, and like a faithful page,
As thy looks stir, runs up and down, to make   10
All folks prest at thy will thy pain to assuage.
Nature with care sweats for her darling's sake,
    Knowing worlds pass ere she enough can find
    Of such heaven stuff, to clothe so heavenly mind.

102

Where be the roses gone, which sweetened so our eyes?
  Where those red cheeks, which oft with fair increase did
    frame
  The height of Honour in the kindly badge of Shame?
Who hath the crimson weeds stolen from my morning skies?
How doth the colour fade of those vermilion dyes,   5
  Which Nature's self did make, and self engrained the same?
  I would know by what right this paleness overcame
That hue, whose force my heart still unto thraldom ties?
  Galen's adoptive sons, who by a beaten way
  Their judgements hackney on, the fault on Sickness lay;   10
But feeling proof makes me say they mistake it far:
  It is but love, which makes his paper perfect white
  To write therein more fresh the story of delight,
While Beauty's reddest ink Venus for him doth stir.

103

O happy Thames, that didst my Stella bear,
I saw thyself, with many a smiling line
Upon thy cheerful face, Joy's livery wear,
While those fair planets on thy streams did shine.
  The boat for joy could not to dance forbear,   5
While wanton winds, with beauties so divine
Ravished, stayed not, till in her golden hair
They did themselves (O sweetest prison) twine.
  And fain those Aeol's youths there would their stay
Have made, but forced by Nature still to fly,   10
First did with puffing kiss those locks display:
She, so dishevelled, blushed; from window I
  With sight thereof cried out, 'O fair disgrace,
  Let Honour's self to thee grant highest place.'

104

Envious wits, what hath been mine offence,
  That with such poisonous care my looks you mark,
  That to each word, nay sigh, of mine you hark,
As grudging me my sorrow's eloquence?
Ah, is it not enough that I am thence,   5
  Thence, so far thence, that scarcely any spark
  Of comfort dare come to this dungeon dark,

Where rigorous exile locks up all my sense?
  But if I by a happy window pass,
If I but stars upon my armour bear,   10
Sick, thirsty, glad (though but of empty glass)
Your moral notes straight my hid meaning tear
  From out my ribs, and puffing prove that I
  Do Stella love. Fools, who doth it deny?

Eleventh song

'Who is it that this dark night
Underneath my window plaineth?'
It is one who from thy sight
Being (ah) exiled, disdaineth
Every other vulgar light.   5

'Why, alas, and are you he?
Be not yet those fancies changed?'
Dear, when you find change in me,
Though from me you be estranged,
Let my change to ruin be.   10

'Well, in absence this will die;
Leave to see, and leave to wonder.'
Absence sure will help, if I
Can learn how myself to sunder
From what in my heart doth lie.   15

'But time will these thoughts remove;
Time doth work what no man knoweth.'
Time doth as the subject prove;
With time still the affection groweth
In the faithful turtle dove.   20

'What if you new beauties see,
Will they not stir new affection?'
I will think they pictures be,
Image-like, of saints' perfection,
Poorly counterfeiting thee.   25

'But your reason's purest light
Bids you leave such minds to nourish.'
Dear, do reason no such spite;
Never doth thy beauty flourish
More than in my reason's sight.   30

'But the wrongs love bears will make
Love at length leave undertaking.'
No, the more fools it do shake
In a ground of so firm making
Deeper still they drive the stake.   35

'Peace, I think that some give ear;
Come no more, lest I get anger.'
Bliss, I will my bliss forbear,
Fearing, sweet, you to endanger,
But my soul shall harbour there.   40

'Well, be gone, be gone I say,
Lest that Argus' eyes perceive you.'
O, unjust is Fortune's sway,
Which can make me thus to leave you,
And from louts to run away.   45

105

Unhappy sight, and hath she vanished by,
    So near, in so good time, so free a place?
    Dead glass, dost thou thy object so embrace
As what my heart still sees thou canst not spy?
I swear by her I love and lack, that I   5
    Was not in fault, who bent thy dazzling race
    Only unto the heaven of Stella's face,
Counting but dust what in the way did lie.
    But cease, mine eyes, your tears do witness well
That you, guiltless thereof, your nectar missed.   10
Cursed be the page from whom the bad torch fell,
Cursed be the night which did your strife resist,
    Cursed be the coachman, which did drive so fast,
    With no worse curse than absence makes me taste.

106

O absent presence! Stella is not here:
    False flattering Hope, that with so fair a face
    Bare me in hand, that in this orphan place
Stella, I say my Stella, should appear.
What sayest thou now? Where is that dainty cheer   5
    Thou toldest mine eyes should help their famished case?
    But thou art gone, now that self-felt disgrace
Doth make me most to wish thy comfort near.

But here I do store of fair ladies meet
  Who may, with charm of conversation sweet,   10
Make in my heavy mould new thoughts to grow:
  Sure they prevail as much with me, as he
  That bade his friend, but then new maimed, to be
Merry with him, and not think of his woe.

107

Stella, since thou so right a princess art
  Of all the powers which life bestows on me,
  That ere by them aught undertaken be
They first resort unto that sovereign part:
Sweet, for a while give respite to my heart,   5
  Which pants as though it still should leap to thee,
  And on my thoughts give thy lieutenancy
To this great cause, which needs both use and art;
  And as a queen, who from her presence sends
Whom she employs, dismiss from thee my wit,   10
Till it have wrought what thy own will attends.
On servants' shame oft master's blame doth sit:
  O let not fools in me thy works reprove,
  And scorning say, 'See, what it is to love!'

108

When Sorrow, using mine own fire's might,
  Melts down his lead into my boiling breast,
  Through that dark furnace to my heart oppressed
There shines a joy from thee, my only light:
But soon as thought of thee breeds my delight,   5
  And my young soul flutters to thee, his nest,
  Most rude Despair, my daily unbidden guest,
Clips straight my wings, straight wraps me me in his night,
  And makes me then bow down my head and say:
'Ah, what doth Phoebus' gold that wretch avail   10
Whom iron doors do keep from use of day?'
So strangely (alas) thy works in me prevail,
  That in my woes for thee thou art my joy,
  And in my joys for thee my only annoy.

MARY SIDNEY (HERBERT), COUNTESS OF PEMBROKE

MARY SIDNEY (HERBERT),
COUNTESS OF PEMBROKE

Dates: 1561–1621. Born 27 October 1561 at Ticknall Place, Bewdley, Worcestershire, sister to Philip (and Robert); her godfather was William, Earl of Pembroke. Childhood spent between Penshurst and Ludlow Castle. Educated at home in French, Italian, music and (probably) Latin and Greek. Joined her mother at court 1575 (?), where she met and (22 April 1577) married Henry Herbert, 2nd Earl of Pembroke. Moved to the Pembroke home Wilton House, Wiltshire, which she and her brother Philip set about establishing as an 'academy' of arts and letters on the continental humanist model. Her circle included Spenser, Shakespeare, Donne, Drayton, Samuel Daniel, Fulke Greville, Nicholas Breton, Abraham Fraunce and Ben Jonson. She bore four children between 1580 and 1584; 1586 saw the deaths not only of her beloved Philip but of her father and mother as well. Subsequently, as patron and writer, she dedicated herself to Philip's memory, translating his friend Philippe du Plessis Mornay's *Discours de la vie et de la Mort*, Petrarch's *Trionfo della Morte* (early 1590s) and undertaking the completion of the *Psalms* project. In addition she edited her brother's *Arcadia* (1593) and *Defence of Poesie* (1595), and the collected works, which included the corrected *Astrophil and Stella* (1598). Her husband died 18 January 1601 and her subsequent life seems to have been largely private and is relatively undocumented. She died in London 25 September 1621 and was buried in Salisbury Cathedral.

1

*The Triumph of Death, translated out of Italian by the
Countess of Pembroke: the first chapter*

That gallant lady, gloriously bright,
  The stately pillar once of worthiness
  And now a little dust, a naked sprite,
'Turned from her wars a joyful conqueress:
  Her wars, where she had foiled the mighty foe   5
  Whose wily stratagems the world distress,
And foiled him, not with sword, with spear or bow,
  But with chaste heart, fair visage, upright thought,
  Wise speech, which did with honour linked go:
And Love's new plight to see strange wonders wrought 10
  With shivered bow, chaste arrows, quenched flame,
  While here some slain, and there lay others caught.
She, and the rest (who in the glorious fame
  Of the exploit, her chosen mates, did share)
  All in one squadronet close ranged came: 15
A few, for Nature makes true glory rare,
  But each alone (so each alone did shine)
  Claimed whole historian's, whole poet's, care.
Borne in green field a snowy ermelin,
  Coloured with topazes, set in fine gold,   20
  Was this fair company's unfoiled sign.
No earthly march but heavenly did they hold:
  Their speeches holy were, and happy those
  Whose so are born to be with them enrolled.
Clear stars they seemed which did a sun unclose 25
  Who, hiding none, yet all did beautify
  With coronets decked with violet and rose;
And as gained honour filled with jollity
  Each gentle heart, so made they merry cheer.
  When lo, an ensign sad I might descry: 30
Black and in black a woman did appear,
  Fury with her such as I scarcely know
  If like at Phlegra with the giants were.
'Thou dame (quoth she) that doth so proudly go,
  Standing upon thy youth and beauty's state, 35
  And of thy life the limits dost not know,
Lo, I am she, so fierce, importunate,
  And deaf and blind entitled oft by you:
  You, whom with Night ere evening I await.

I to their end the Greekish nation drew: 40
    The Trojan first, the Roman afterward
    With edge and point of this my blade I slew,
And no barbarian my blow could ward
    Who, stealing on with unexpected wound,
    Of idle thoughts have many thousand marred.   45
And now no less to you-ward am I bound,
    While life is dearest, ere to cause you moan,
    Fortune some bitter with your sweets compound'.
'To this thou right or interest hast none,
    Little to me, but only to this spoil',   50
    Replied the she who in the world was one:
'This charge of woe on others will recoil,
    I know, whose safety on my life depends;
    For me, I thank who shall me hence assoil'.
As one whose eyes some novelty attend   55
    And, what it marked not first it spied at last,
    New wonders with itself, now comprehends:
So fared the cruel, deeply overcast
    With doubt awhile, then spake: 'I know them now;
    I now remember when my teeth they passed'.   60
Then with less frowning, and less darkened, brow:
    'But thou that leadest this goodly company
    Didst never yet unto my sceptre bow;
But on my counsel if thou wilt rely
    (Who may enforce thee), better is by far   65
    From age, and age's loathsomeness, to fly:
More honoured by me than others are
    Thou shalt thee find, and neither fear nor pain
    The passage shall of thy departure bar'.
'As likes that Lord who in the heaven doth reign   70
    And thence this All doth moderately guide;
    As others do, I shall thee entertain':
So answered she; and I withal descried
    Of dead appear a never-numbered sum,
    Pestering the plain from one to the other side.   75
From India, Spain, Cathay, Morocco come,
    So many ages did together fall,
    That worlds were filled, and yet they wanted room.
There saw I (whom their times did happy call)
    Popes, emperors, and kings: but strangely grown,   80
    All naked now, all needy, beggars all.
Where is that wealth? Where are those honours gone,

Sceptres, and crowns, and robes, and purple dye,
    And costly mitres set with pearl and stone?
O wretch who dost in mortal things affy: 85
    Yet who but doth (and if in the end they die
    Themselves beguiled) they find but right, say I.
What means this toil? O blind, O more than blind:
    You all return to your great mother old,
    And hardly leave your very names behind.   90
Bring me (who doth your studies well behold,
    And of your cares not manifestly vain)
    One: let him tell me (when he all hath told)
So many lands to win, what boots the pain?
    And on strange lands, tributes to impose   95
    (With hearts still greedy their own loss to gain)?
After all these, wherein you winning lose
    Treasures and territories dear bought with blood,
    Water and bread hath a far sweeter close,
And gold and gem gives place to glass and wood.   100
    But lest I should too long digression make,
    To turn to my first task I think it good.
Now that short glorious life her leave to take
    Did near unto the utmost instant go,
    And doubtful step, at which the world doth quake.   105
Another number then themselves did show
    Of ladies such as bodies yet did lade:
    If Death could piteous be, they fain would know;
And deep they did in contemplation wade
    Of that cold end, presented there to view,   110
    Which must be once, and must but once, be made.
All friends and neighbours were this care-full crew,
    But Death with ruthless hand one golden hair,
    Chosen from out those amber tresses, drew:
So cropped the flower of all this world most fair,   115
    To show upon the excellentest thing
    Her supreme force, and for no hate she bare.
How many drops did flow from briny spring
    In who there saw those sightful fountains dry
    For whom this heart so long did burn and sing!   120
For her, in midst of moan and misery,
    Now reaping once what Virtue's life did sow,
    With joy she sat retired silently.
'In peace (cried they), right mortal goddess, go!'
    And so she was, but that in no degree   125

293

Could Death entreat, her coming to forslow.
What confidence for others if that she
    Could fry and freeze in few nights' changing cheer?
    O human hopes, how fond and false you be!
And for this gentle Soul if many a tear   130
    By pity shed did bathe the ground and grass,
    Who saw doth know: think thou that dost but hear.
The sixth of April, one o'clock it was
    That tied me once, and did me now untie:
    Changing her copy, thus doth Fortune pass!   135
None so his thrall, as I my liberty;
    None so his death, as I my life do rue,
    Staying with me who fain from it would fly:
Due to the world, and to my years was due,
    That I (as first I came) should first be gone –   140
    Not her leaf quailed, as yet but freshly new.
Now, for my woe: guess not by it what is shown,
    For I dare scarce once cast a thought thereto
    So far I am off, in words, to make it known:
'Virtue is dead, and dead is Beauty, too;   145
    And dead is Courtesy,' in mournful plight
    The ladies said; 'And now what shall we do?
Never again such grace shall bless our sight;
    Never like wit shall we from woman hear;
    And voice, replete with angelic delight'.   150
The soul, now pressed to leave that bosom dear
    (Her virtues all uniting now in one)
    There, where it passed, did make the heavens clear;
And of the enemies, so hardly none
    That once before her showed his face obscure,   155
    With her assault till Death had thorough gone.
Past plaint and fear, when first they could endure
    To hold their eyes on that fair visage bent,
    And that despair had made them now secure:
Not as great fires violently spent,   160
    But in themselves consuming: so her flight
    Took that sweet sprite, and passed in peace content;
Right like unto some lamp of clearest light
    Little and little wanting nutriture
    Holding to end a never-changing plight.   165
Pale? no, but whitely; and more whitely pure
    Than snow on windless hill that flaking falls;
    As one whom labour did to rest allure.

And when that heavenly guest those mortal walls
   Had left, it nought but sweetly sleeping was   170
   In her fair eyes what folly 'dying' calls:
Death fair did seem to be in her fair face.

The second chapter of the Triumph of Death

That night which did the dreadful hap ensue
   That quite eclipsed (nay, rather, did replace)
   The Sun in skies and me bereave of view,
Did sweetly sprinkle through the airy space
   The summer's frost (which-with Tithon's bride   5
   Cleareth of dream the dark confused face)
When lo, a lady, like unto the tide
   With orient jewels crowned, from thousands more
   Crowned as she to me I coming spied;
And first her hand, sometime desired so,   10
   Reaching to me, at once she sighed and spake
   (Whence endless joys yet in my heart do grow):
'And knowest thou her, who made thee first forsake
   The vulgar path and ordinary trade,
   While her their mark thy youthful thoughts did make?'15
Then down she sat, and me sit down she made:
   Thought, wisdom, meekness in one Grace did strive
   On pleasing bank in bay and beech's shade.
'My goddess, who me did and doth revive,
   Can I but know? (I sobbing answered)   20
   But art thou dead (ah, speak!) or yet alive?'
'Alive am I, and thou as yet art dead;
   And as thou art shalt so continue still
   Till, by thy ending hour, thou hence be led.
Short is our time to live and long our will: 25
   Then let with heed thy deeds and speeches go
   Ere that approaching term his course fulfil'.
Quoth I, 'When this our light to end doth grow
   Which we call life (for thou by proof hast tried)
   Is it such pain to die? That, make me know'.   30
'While thou (quoth she) the vulgar make thy guide,
   And on their judgements, all obscurely blind,
   Dost yet rely, no bliss can thee betide:
Of loathsome prison to each gentle mind
   Death is the end; and only who employ   35
   Their cares on mud therein displeasure find.

Even this my death, which yields thee such annoy
    Would make in thee far greater gladness rise
    Couldest thou but taste least portion of my joy'.
So spake she with devoutly-fixed eyes   40
    Upon the heavens; then did in silence fold
    Those rosy lips, attending there replies:
'Torments invented by the tyrants old,
    Diseases which each part torment and toss,
    Causes that death we most bitter hold'.   45
'I not deny (quoth she) but that the cross
    Preceding death extremely martyreth,
    And more, the fear of that eternal loss.
But when the panting soul in God takes breath,
    And weary heart affecteth heavenly rest,   50
    An unrepented sigh, not else, is death.
With body, but with spirit ready pressed,
    Now at the furthest of my living ways,
    There sadly-uttered sounds my ear possessed:
"O hapless he who, counting times and days,   55
    Thinks each a thousand years, and lives in vain,
    No more to meet her while on earth he stays;
And on the water now, now on the main,
    Only on her doth think, doth speak, doth write,
    And in all times one manner still retain".   60
Herewith I thither cast my failing sight,
    And soon espied, presented to my view
    Who oft did, thee restraining, me incite:
Well I her face and well her voice I knew
    (Which often did my heart reconsolate),   65
    Now wisely grave, then beautifully true.
And sure, when I was in my fairest state,
    My years most green, myself to thee most dear
    (Whence many much did think and much debate),
That life's best joy was all most bitter cheer   70
    Compared to that death most mildly sweet
    Which comes to men, but comes not everywhere.
For I that journey passed with gladder feet
    Than he from hard exile that homeward goes
    (But only ruth of thee) without regret'.   75
'For that faith's sake time once enough did show,
    Yet now to thee more manifestly plain,
    In face of Him who all doth see and know:
Say, lady, did you ever entertain

Motion or thought more lovingly to me   80
(Not loving Honour's height) my tedious pain?
For those sweet wraths, those sweet disdains in you,
    In those sweet peaces written in your eye,
    Diversely many years my fancies drew'.
Scarce had I spoken but, in lightning wise   85
    Beaming, I saw that gentle smile appear,
    Sometimes the Sun of my woe-darkened skies.
Then, sighing, thus she answered: 'Never were
    Our hearts but one, nor ever two shall be:
    Only thy flame I tempered with my cheer;   90
This only way could save both thee and me.
    Our tender fame did this support require:
    The mother hath a rod, yet kind is she.
How oft this said my thoughts: "In love, nay fire,
    Is he; now to provide must I begin,   95
    And ill providers are fear and desire."
Thou sawest what was without, not what within.
    And as the brake the wanton steed doth tame,
    So did this thee from thy disorders win.
A thousand times wrath in my face did flame: 100
    My heart meanwhile with love did inly burn,
    But never will my reason overcame;
For if, woe-vanquished, once I saw thee mourn,
    Thy life or honour jointly to preserve
    Mine eyes to thee sweetly did I turn.   105
But if thy passion did from reason swerve,
    Fear in my words and sorrow in my face
    Did then to thee for salvation serve.
These arts I used with thee. Thou rannest this race
    With kind acceptance. Now sharp disdain   110
    Thou knowest, and hast it sung in many a place.
Sometimes thine eyes pregnant with teary rain
    I saw, and at the sight: "Behold, he dies:
    But if I help (said I), the signs are plain".
Virtue for aid did then with love advise;   115
    If spurred by love, thou tookest some running toy:
    "So soft a bit (quoth I) will not suffice".
Thus glad and sad, in pleasure and annoy,
    What red, cold, pale: thus far I have thee brought,
    Weary but safe, to my no little joy'.   120
Then I with tears and trembling: 'What it sought
    My faith hath found, whose more than equal meed

Were this; if this, for truth could pass my thought'.
'Of little faith (quoth she) should this proceed
    If false it were, or if unknown from me   125
    [The flames withal seemed in her face to breed]:
If liking in mine eyes the world did see
    I say not now; of this right fain I am,
    Those chains that tied my heart well liked me;
And well me likes – if true it be – my fame,   130
    Which far and near by thee related goes;
    Nor in thy love could aught but measure blame:
That only failed; and while in acted woes
    Thou needs wouldest show, what I could not but see,
    Thou didst thy heart to all the world disclose.   135
Hence sprang my zeal, which yet distempereth thee
    (Our concord such in everything beside
    As when united Love and Virtue be).
In equal flames our loving hearts were tried
    (At least when once thy love had notice got):   140
    But one to show, the other sought to hide;
Thou didst for mercy call with weary throat:
    In fear and shame I did in silence go
    (So much desire became of little note).
But not the less becomes concealed woe,   145
    Nor greater grows it uttered, than before:
    Through fiction, Truth will neither ebb nor flow.
But cleared I not the darkest mists of yore
    When I thy words alone did entertain,
    Singing for thee *My love dares speak no more?*   150
With thee my heart; to me I did restrain
    Mine eyes; and thou thy share canst hardly brook,
    Leesing (by me) the less, the more to gain,
Not thinking if a thousand times I took
    Mine eyes from thee, I many thousands cast   155
    Mine eyes on thee, and still with pitying look:
Whose shine no cloud had ever overcast
    Had I not feared in thee those coals to fires
    I thought would burn too dangerously fast,
But to content thee more ere I retire,   160
    For end of this I something wilt thee tell
    Perchance agreeable to thy desire:
In all things fully blessed and pleased well,
    Only in this I did myself displease:
    Born in too base a town for me to dwell;   165

And much I grieved that, for thy greater ease
  At least, it stood not near thy flowery nest
  (Else far enough from whence I did thee please):
So might the heart on which I only rest,
  Not knowing me, have fit itself elsewhere,   170
  And I less name, less notice, have possessed'.
'Oh no (quoth I): for me the heavens' third sphere,
  To so high love advanced by special grace,
  Changeless to me, though changed thy dwelling were.
Be as it will, yet my great honour was'.   175
  'And is as yet (she said); but thy delight
  Makes thee not mark how fast the hours do pass:
See from her golden bed Aurora bright
  To mortal eyes returning sun and day
  Breast-high above the ocean bare to sight.   180
She (to my sorrow) calls me hence away,
  Therefore thy words in Time's short limits bind,
  And say in brief if more thou have to say'.
'Lady (quoth I), your words most sweetly kind
  Have easy made whatever erst I bare,   185
  But what is left of you to live behind.
Therefore to know this my only care,
  If slow or swift shall come our meeting day?'
  She (parting) said, 'As my conjectures are,
Thou without me long time on earth shalt stay'.   190

2

from *The Psalms of David . . . begun by the noble and
learned gent. Sir Philip Sidney, knight, and finished by the
Right Honourable the Countess of Pembroke his sister*

(1)

Dedicatory poem: To the angel spirit of the most excellent Sir Philip Sidney

To thee, pure sprite, to thee alone's addressed
  This coupled work, by double interest thine:
  First raised by thy blessed hand, and what is mine
Inspired by thee, thy secret power impressed.
  So dared my Muse with thine itself combine,   5
  As mortal stuff with that which is divine:
Thy lightning beams give lustre to the rest

That heaven's King may deign his own transformed
    In substance, no, but superficial tire
    By thee put on: to praise, not to aspire   10
To those high tones, so in themselves adorned,
    Which angels sing in their celestial choir;
    And all of tongues with soul and voice admire
These sacred hymns by kingly prophet formed.

Oh, had that soul, which Honour brought to rest,   15
    Too soon not left and reft the world of all
    What man could show (which we Perfection call),
This half-maimed piece had sorted with the best.
    Deep wounds enlarged, long festered in their gall,
    Fresh-bleeding smart: not eye but heart tears fall: 20
Ah, memory, what needs this new arrest?

Yet here behold (oh wert thou to behold!)
    This finished now thy matchless Muse begun –
    The rest but pieced, as left by thee undone.
Pardon, O blessed soul, presumption too, too bold: 25
    If love and zeal such error ill become,
    'Tis zealous love, love which hath never done,
Nor can enough in world of words unfold.

And sith it hath no further scope to go,
    Nor other purpose but to honour thee,   30
    Thee in thy works where all the graces be
(As little streams with all their all do flow
    To their great sea, due tribute's grateful fee)
    So press my thoughts, my burthened thoughts, in me
To pay the debt of infinites I owe   35

To thy great worth: exceeding Nature's store,
    Wonder of men, sole-born Perfection's kind,
    Phoenix thou wert; so rare thy fairest mind
Heavenly-adorned, Earth justly might adore,
    Where truthful praise in highest glory shined: 40
    For there alone was praise to truth confined,
And where but there to live for evermore?

Oh! when to this accompt, this cast-up sum,
    This reckoning made, this audit of my woe,
    I call my thoughts, whence so strange passions flow,   45
How works my heart, my senses stricken dumb,
    That would thee more than ever heart could show!

And all too short: who knew thee best doth know
There lives no wit that may thy praise become.

Truth I invoke (who scorn elsewhere to move,   50
    Or here in aught my blood should partialise),
    Truth, sacred Truth, thee sole to solemnise
Those precious rites well known best minds approve;
    And who but doth hath Wisdom's open eyes
    (Not owly blind the fairest light still flies)   55
Confirm no less? At least 'tis sealed above,

Where thou art fixed among thy fellow lights:
    My day put out, my life in darkness cast,
    Thy angel's soul with highest angels placed
There blessed sings, enjoying heaven-delights,   60
    Thy Maker's praise; as far from earthly taste
    As here thy works, so worthily embraced
By all of worth, where never Envy bites.

As goodly buildings to some glorious end,
    Cut off by Fate before the Graces had   65
    Each wondrous part in all their beauties clad
(Yet so much done as art could not amend):
    So thy rare works (to which no wit can add)
    In all men's eyes which are not blindly mad
Beyond compare above all praise extend.   70

Immortal monuments of thy fair fame
    (Though not complete, nor in the reach of thought),
    How on that passing piece Time would have wrought
Had heaven so spared the life of life to frame
    The rest? But ah! such loss hath this world aught   75
    Can equal it? or which like grievance brought?
Yet there will live thy ever-praised name,

To which these dearest offerings of my heart
    (Dissolved to ink, while pen's impressions move
    The bleeding veins of never-dying love)   80
I render here: these wounding lines of smart,
    Sad characters indeed of simple love
    (Not art nor skill which abler wits do prove)
Of my full soul receive the meanest part.

Receive these hymns, these obsequies receive.   85
    If any mark of thy sweet sprite appear
    Well are they born, no title else shall bear.

I can no more. Dear soul, I take my leave:
   Sorrow still strives, would mount thy highest sphere
   Presuming so just cause might meet thee there.   90
Oh happy change, could I so take my leave!

        By the sister of that
        incomparable Sidney

(2)

Psalm 88 Domine Deus

My God, my Lord, my help, my health:
    To thee my cry
    Doth restless fly,
  Both when of Sun the day
  The treasures doth display,   5
And Night locks up his golden wealth.

Admit to presence what I crave:
    O bow thine ear
    My cry to hear,
  Whose soul with ills and woes   10
  So flows, so overflows,
That now my life draws nigh the grave.

With them that fall into the pit
    I stand esteemed,
    Quite forceless deemed,   15
  As one who, free from strife
  And stir of mortal life,
Among the dead at rest doth sit;

Right like unto the murdered sort
    Who in the grave   20
    Their biding have
  Whom now thou dost no more
  Remember as before,
Quite, quite cut off from thy support.

Thrown down into the grave of graves   25
    In darkness deep
    Thou dost me keep,
  Where lightning of thy wrath
  Upon me lighted hath,
All overwhelmed with all thy waves.   30

Who did know me, whom I did know,
    Removed by thee
    Are gone from me.
    Are gone? that is the best:
    They all me so detest   35
That now abroad I blush to go.

My wasted eye doth melt away,
    Fleeting amain
    In streams of pain
    While I my prayers send,   40
    While I my hands extend,
To thee, my God, and fail no day.

Alas, my Lord, will then be time,
    When men are dead,
    Thy truth to spread?   45
    Shall they, whom Death hath slain,
    To praise thee live again,
And from their lowly lodgings climb?

Shall buried mouths thy mercies tell?
    Dust and decay   50
    Thy truth display?
    And shall thy works of mark
    Shine in the dreadful dark?
Thy justice where oblivions dwell?

Good reason then, I cry to thee   55
    And, ere the light,
    Salute thy sight,
    My plaint to thee direct.
    Lord, why dost thou reject
My soul, and hide thy face from me?   60

Ay me, alas, I faint, I die,
    So still, so still
    Thou dost me fill
    (And hast from youngest years)
    With terrifying fears   65
That I, in trance, amazed do lie.

All over me thy furies passed;
    Thy fears my mind
    Do fettering bind,
    Flowing about me so   70

  As flocking waters flow:
No day can overrun their haste.

Who erst to me were near and dear
  Far now – O far –
  Disjoined are.   75
  And when I would them see
  Who my acquaintance be,
As darkness they to me appear.

(3)

Psalm 130 De profundis

From depth of grief
  Where drowned I lie,
Lord, for relief
  To thee I cry:
My earnest, vehement, crying, praying,   5
Grant quick, attentive, hearing, weighing.

  O Lord, if thou
    Offences mark,
  Who shall not bow
    To bear the cark?   10
But with thy justice mercy dwelleth,
Whereby thy worship more excelleth.

  On thee my soul,
    On thee (O Lord)
  Dependeth whole;   15
    And on thy word,
Though sore with blot of sin defaced,
Yet surest hope hath firmly placed.

  Who longest watch,
    Who soonest rise,   20
  Can nothing match
    The early eyes,
The greedy eyes my soul erecteth
While God's true promise it expecteth.

  Then Israel   25
    On God attend:
  Attend him well
    Who, still thy friend,

In kindness hath thee dear esteemed
And often, often, erst redeemed.   30

    Now, as before,
      Unchanged he
    Will thee restore,
      Thy state will free,
All wickedness from Jacob driving,   35
Forgetting follies, faults forgiving.

(4)

Psalm 148 Laudate Dominum

Inhabitants of heavenly land
    As loving subjects praise your king:
You that among them highest stand,
    In highest notes 'Jehovah' sing;
    Sing angels all, on care-full wing   5
      You that his heralds fly;
    And you whom he doth soldiers bring
      In field his force to try.

O praise him, Sun, the sea of light,
    O praise him, Moon, the light of sea;   10
You pretty Stars, in robe of Night
    As spangles twinkling, do as they.
    Thou Sphere, within whose bosom play
      The rest that earth emball;
    You waters banked with starry bay: 15
      O praise, O praise him all.

All these, I say, advance that name
    That doth eternal being show:
Who bidding, into form and frame
    (Not being yet) they all did grow;   20
    All formed, framed, founded so,
      Till ages' utmost date
    They place retain, they order know,
      They keep their first estate.

When Heaven hath praised, praise Earth anew: 25
    You dragons first (her deepest guests);
Then soundless deeps, and what in you
    Residing low or moves, or rests;
    You flames, affrighting mortal breasts;

You stones that clouds do cast;   30
You feathery snows from Winter's nests;
    You vapours, Sun's appast;

You boisterous winds, whose breath fulfils
    What in his word his will sets down;
Ambitious mountains, courteous hills;   35
    You trees that hills and mountains crown
    (Both you that, proud of native gown,
        Stand fresh and tall to see,
    And you that have your more renown
        By what you bear, than be);   40

You beasts in woods untamed that range;
    You that with men familiar go;
You that your place by creeping change,
    Or airy streams with feathers row;
    You stately kings; you subjects low;   45
        You lords and judges all;
    You others whose distinctions show
        How sex or age may fall:

All these, I say, advance that name
    More high than skies, more low than ground.   50
And since, advanced by the same,
    You Jacob's sons stand chiefly bound,
    You Jacob's sons be chief to sound
        Your God, Jehovah's, praise:
    So fits them well on whom is found   55
        Such bliss he on you lays.

3

.A dialogue between two shepherds, Thenot and Piers, in
praise of ASTRÆA, made by that excellent lady, the
Lady Mary, Countess of Pembroke, at the Queen's
Majesty's being at her house at   anno 15

Thenot I sing divine Astræa's praise:
        O Muses, help my wits to raise,
        And heave my verses higher.
Piers   Thou needest the truth but plainly tell,
        Which much I doubt thou canst not well,   5
        Thou art so oft a liar.

Then. If in my song no more I show
    Than heaven, and earth, and sea do know,
      Then truly I have spoken.
Piers Sufficeth not no more to name,   10
    But being no less, the like, the same,
      Else laws of truth be broken.

Then. Then say: she is so good, so fair,
    With all the earth she may compare,
      Not Momus' self denying.   15
Piers Compare may think where likeness holds;
    Nought like to her the earth enfolds:
      I looked to find you lying.

Then. Astræa sees with Wisdom's sight;
    Astræa works by Virtue's might;   20
      And jointly both do stay in her.
Piers Nay, take from them her hand, her mind,
    The one is lame, the other blind:
      Shall still your lying stain her?

Then. Soon as Astræa shows her face   25
    Straight every ill avoids the place,
      And every good aboundeth.
Piers Nay, long before her face doth show,
    The last doth come, the first doth go:
      How loud this lie resoundeth!   30

Then. Astræa is our chiefest joy,
    Our chiefest guard against annoy,
      Our chiefest wealth, our treasure.
Piers Where chiefest are, there others be:
    To us none else but only she: 35
      When wilt thou speak in measure?

Then. Astræa may be justly said,
    A field in flowery robe arrayed
      In season freshly springing.
Piers That spring endures but shortest time,   40
    This never leaves Astræa's clime:
      Thou liest instead of singing.

Then. As heavenly light that guides the day
    Right so doth shine each lovely ray
      That from Astræa flyeth.   45
Piers Nay, darkness oft that light enclouds:

Astræa's beams no darkness shrouds:
　How loudly Thenot lieth!

Then.　Astræa rightly term I may
　　A manly palm, a maiden bay,　　　　　　50
　　　Her verdure never dying.
Piers　Palm oft is crooked, bay is low:
　　She still upright, still high doth grow:
　　　Good Thenot, leave thy lying.

Then.　Then, Piers, of friendship, tell me why,　　55
　　My meaning true, my words should lie
　　　And strive in vain to raise her?
Piers　Words from conceit do only rise:
　　Above conceit her honour flies:
　　　But silence, nought can praise her.　　　60

MICHAEL DRAYTON

MICHAEL DRAYTON

Dates: 1563–1631. Born at Hartshill, Warwickshire, son of William; became a page in the household of Henry Goodere of Polesworth (who was knighted in 1586). Upon his death in 1595 Goodere 'bequeathed' (Drayton's own word) the poet to the service of Lucy, Countess of Bedford, and from 1597–1602 he was playwright for Philip Henslowe at the Rose and Fortune Theatres. In 1603 he was the 'Esquire' of Sir Walter Aston upon his installation as a Knight of the Bath and subsequently dedicated several works to him. 1608 saw an unsuccessful attempt, with others, to manage the Whitefriars Playhouse and the Children of the King's Revels. In 1612 he dedicated the first part of his topographical epic *Poly-Olbion* to Prince Henry; he became acquainted with William Drummond in 1618; and he died in 1631 and was buried in Westminster Abbey. His many works after *Endymion and Phoebe* include: *Mortimeriados* (1596); *England's Heroical Epistles* (1597); *The Owl* (1604); *Poems Lyric and Pastoral* and *Odes* (1606); *Poly-Olbion* (1612; 1622); and *The Muses' Elysium* (1630).

ENDYMION AND PHOEBE. IDEA'S LATMUS

Phoebus erit nostri princeps, et carminis Author.

Dedication: To the excellent and most accomplished
Lady, Lucy, Countess of Bedford.

Great Lady, essence of my chiefest good,
　Of the most pure and finest tempered spirit,
　Adorned with gifts, ennobled by thy blood,
　Which by descent true virtue dost inherit:
That virtue which no fortune can deprive,　　　　　　　5
　Which thou by birth takest from thy gracious mother
　(Whose royal minds with equal motion strive
　Which most in honour shall excel the other):
Unto thy fame my Muse herself shall task,
　Which rainest upon me thy sweet golden showers;　　10
　And but thyself no subject will I ask,
　Upon whose praise my soul shall spend her powers.
Sweet Lady, then, grace this poor Muse of mine,
Whose faith, whose zeal, whose life, whose all, is thine.

　　　　　　　　Your Honour's humbly
　　　　　　　　devoted,
　　　　　　　　　Michael Drayton.

ENDYMION AND PHOEBE

In Ionia, whence sprang old poets' fame,
From whom that sea did first derive her name,
The blessed bed whereon the Muses lay,
Beauty of Greece, the pride of Asia,
Whence Archelaus (whom times historify)   5
First unto Athens brought philosophy:
In this fair region, on a goodly plain
Stretching her bounds unto the bordering main,
The mountain Latmus overlooks the sea,
Smiling to see the ocean billows play: 10
Latmus, where young Endymion used to keep
His fairest flock of silver-fleeced sheep;
To whom Sylvanus often would resort,
At barley-break, to see the satyrs sport;
And when rude Pan his tabouret list to sound,   15
To see the fair nymphs foot it in a round,
Under the trees which on this mountain grew
As yet the like Arabia never knew:
For all the pleasures Nature could devise
Within this plot she did imparadise;   20
And great Diana, of her special grace,
With vestal rites had hallowed all the place.
Upon this mount there stood a stately grove
(Whose reaching arms to clip the welkin strove)
Of tufted cedars and the branching pine,   25
Whose bushy tops themselves do so entwine
As seemed, when Nature first this work begun,
She then conspired against the piercing Sun,
Under whose covert (thus divinely made)
Phœbus' green laurel flourished in the shade.   30
Fair Venus' myrtle, Mars his warlike fir,
Minerva's olive, and the weeping myrrh,
The patient palm which thrives in spite of hate,
The poplar to Alcides consecrate;
Which Nature in such order had disposed,   35
And therewithal these goodly walks enclosed,
As served for hangings and rich tapestry
To beautify this stately gallery.
Embroidering these in curious trails along
The clustered grapes, the golden citrons hung: 40
More glorious than the precious fruit were these

313

Kept by the dragon in Hesperides,
Or gorgeous arras in rich colours wrought
With silk from Afric or from India brought.
Out of this soil sweet bubbling fountains crept,   45
As though for joy the senseless stones had wept,
With straying channels dancing sundry ways,
With often turns, like to a curious maze;
Which, breaking forth, the tender grass bedewed,
Whose silver sand with orient pearl was strewed,   50
Shadowed with roses and sweet eglantine,
Dipping their sprays into this crystalline;
From which the birds the purple berries pruned
And to their loves their small recorders tuned.
The nightingale (woods' herald of the spring),   55
The whistling ouzel, mavis carolling,
Tuning their trebles to the waters' fall
(Which made the music more angelical)
Whilst gentle Zephyr, murmuring among,
Kept time and bore the burden to the song.   60
About whose brims, refreshed with dainty showers,
Grew amaranthus and sweet gilliflowers,
The marigold (Phœbus' beloved friend),
The moly (which from sorcery doth defend),
Violet, carnation, balm and cassia,   65
Idea's primrose, coronet of May.
Above this grove a gentle fair ascent,
Which by degrees of milk-white marble went.
Upon the top a paradise was found,
With which Nature this miracle had crowned,   70
Impaled with rocks of rarest precious stone
Which like the flames of Aetna brightly shone
And served as lanterns furnished with light
To guide the wandering passengers by night;
For which fair Phœbe, sliding from her sphere,   75
Used oft-times to come and sport her there,
And from the azure starry-painted sky
Embalmed the banks with precious lunary;
That now her Menalus she quite forsook
And unto Latmus wholly her betook,   80
And in this place her pleasure used to take,
And all was for her sweet Endymion's sake:
Endymion, the lovely shepherd boy,
Endymion, great Phœbe's only joy,

Endymion, in whose pure-shining eyes   85
The naked fairies danced the hay-de-guys.
The shag-haired satyrs, mountain-climbing race,
Have been made tame by gazing in his face.
For this boy's love the water nymphs have wept,
Stealing oft-times to kiss him whilst he slept   90
And, tasting once the nectar of his breath,
Surfeit with sweet and languish unto death;
And Jove oft-times bent to lascivious sport,
And coming where Endymion did resort,
Hath courted him, inflamed with desire,   95
Thinking some nymph was clothed in boy's attire.
And often-times the simple rural swains,
Beholding him in crossing o'er the plains,
Imagined Apollo from above
Put on this shape to win some maiden's love.   100
This shepherd Phœbe ever did behold,
Whose love already had her thoughts controlled:
From Latmus top, her stately throne, she rose,
And to Endymion down beneath she goes.
Her brother's beams now had she laid aside,   105
Her horned crescent, and her full-faced pride
(For had she come adorned with her light
No mortal eye could have endured the sight):
But like a nymph, crowned with a flowery twine,
And not like Phœbe, as herself, divine.   110
An azured mantle purfled with a veil,
Which in the air puffed like a swelling sail,
Embossed rainbows did appear in silk,
With wavy streams as white as morning's milk;
Which ever as the gentle air did blow,   115
Still with the motion seemed to ebb and flow.
About her neck a chain twice twenty fold,
Of rubies set in lozenges of gold,
Trussed up in trammels and in curious pleats,
With sphery circles falling on her teats.   120
A dainty smock of cypress, fine and thin,
O'er cast with curls next to her lily skin:
Through which the pureness of the same did show
Like damask roses strewed with flakes of snow,
Discovering all her stomach to the waist,   125
With branches of sweet circling veins enchased.
A coronet she wore of myrtle boughs

Which gave a shadow to her ivory brows.
No smoother beauty mask did beauty smother:
'Great lights dim less yet burn not one another',   130
Nature abhors to borrow from the mart,
'Simples fit beauty, fie on drugs and art'.
  Thus came she where her love Endymion lay,
Who with sweet carols sang the night away;
And as it is the shepherd's usual trade,   135
Oft on his pipe a roundelay he played.
As meek he was as any lamb might be,
Nor never lived a fairer youth than he:
His dainty hand the snow itself did stain,
Or her to whom Jove showered in golden rain: 140
From whose sweet palm the liquid pearl did swell,
Pure as the drops of Aganippe's well,
Clear as the liquor which fair Hebe spilt.
His sheephook silver, damasked all with gilt,
The staff itself of snowy ivory,   145
Studded with coral, tipped with ebony;
His tresses, of the raven's shining black,
Straggling in curls along his manly back;
The balls which Nature in his eyes had set,
Like diamonds enclosing globes of jet,   150
Which sparkled from their milky lids outright,
Like fair Orion's heaven-adorning light
  (The stars, on which her heavenly eyes were bent
And fixed still with lovely blandishment)
For whom so oft disguised she was seen   155
As she celestial Phœbe had not been.
Her dainty buskins laced unto the knee,
Her pleated frock tucked up accordingly,
A nymph-like huntress, armed with bow and dart,
About the woods she scours the long-lived hart;   160
She climbs the mountains with the light-foot fauns
And with the satyrs scuds it o'er the lawns;
In music's sweet delight she shows her skill,
Quavering the cittern nimbly with her quill;
Upon each tree she carves Endymion's name   165
In Gordian knots, with Phœbe to the same.
To kill him venison now she pitched her toils,
And to this lovely ranger brings the spoils;
And thus whilst she by chaste desire is led
Unto the downs where he his fair flocks fed,   170

Near to a grove she had Endymion spied
Where he was fishing by a river side
Under a poplar, shadowed from the Sun,
Where merrily to court him she begun:
'Sweet boy (quoth she) take what thy heart can wish: 175
When thou dost angle, would I were a fish:
When thou art sporting by the silver brooks,
Put in thy hand, thou needest no other hooks.
Hard-hearted boy, Endymion look on me:
Nothing on earth I hold too dear for thee.   180
I am a nymph, and not of human blood,
Begot by Pan on Isis' sacred flood.
When I was born, upon that very day
Phœbus was seen the reveller to play:
In Jove's high house the gods assembled all,   185
And Juno held her sumptuous festival:
Oceanus that hour was dancing spied,
And Tithon seen to frolic with his bride;
The halcyons that season sweetly sang,
And all the shores with shouting sea-nymphs rang.   190
And on that day, my birth to memorise,
The shepherds hold a solemn sacrifice.
The chaste Diana nursed me in her lap,
And I sucked nectar from her down-soft pap.
The well wherein this body bathed first,   195
Who drinks thereof shall never after thirst:
The water hath the lunacy appeased,
And by the virtue cureth all diseased.
The place wherein my bare feet touch the mould,
Made up in balls, for pomander is sold.   200
See, see, these hands have robbed the snow of white;
These dainty fingers, organs of delight;
Behold these lips, the lodestones of desire,
Whose words enchant, like Amphion's well-tuned lyre;
This foot, art's just proportion doth reveal,   205
Signing the earth with heaven's own manual seal.
Go, play the wanton, I will tend thy flock,
And wait the hours as duly as a clock;
I'll deck thy ram with bells and wreaths of bay,
And gild his horns upon the shearing day,   210
And with a garland crown thee shepherds' king,
And thou shalt lead the gay girls in a ring;
Birds with their wings shall fan thee in the Sun,

And all the fountains with pure wine shall run;
I have a choir of dainty turtle doves,   215
And they shall sit and sweetly sing our loves.
I'll lay thee on the swans' soft downy plume,
And all the wind shall gently breath perfume;
I'll plait thy locks with many a curious plait,
And chafe thy temples with a sacred heat.   220
The Muses still shall keep thee company,
And lull thee with enchanting harmony:
If not all these, yet let my virtues move thee,
A chaster nymph, Endymion, cannot love thee.'
   But he imagined she some nymph had been   225
Because she was apparelled in green;
Or happily, some of fair Flora's train,
Which oft did use to sport upon the plain.
He tells her, he was Phœbe's servant sworn,
And oft in hunting had her quiver born,   230
And that to her virginity he vowed,
Which in no hand by Venus was allowed;
Then unto her a catalogue recites
Of Phœbe's statutes and her hallowed rites,
And of the grievous penalty inflicted   235
On such as her chaste laws had interdicted.
Now he requests that she would stand aside
Because the fish her shadow had espied;
Then he entreats her that she would be gone,
And at this time to let him be alone;   240
Then turns him from her in an angry sort,
And frowns and chafes that she had spoiled his sport;
And then he threatens her, if she did stay,
And told her, great Diana came this way.
But for all this, this nymph would not forbear,   245
But now she smoothes his crispy-curled hair
And when he (rudely) willed her to refrain,
Yet scarcely ended, she begins again:
'Thy ewes (quoth she) with milk shall daily spring
And to thy profit yearly twins shall bring,   250
And thy fair flock (a wonder to behold)
Shall have their fleeces turned to burnished gold;
Thy bateful pasture to thy wanton thews
Shall be refreshed with nectar-dropping dews;
The oak's smooth leaves, syrupped with honey-fall,   255
Trickle down drops to quench thy thirst withall;

The cruel tiger will I tame for thee,
And gently lay his head upon thy knee;
And by my spells the wolves' jaws will I lock
And (as good shepherds) make them guard thy flock.   260
I'll mount thee bravely on a lion's back
To drive the foamy-tusked boar to wrack;
The brazen-hoofed yelling bulls I'll yoke,
And with my herbs the scaly dragon choke:
Thou in great Phœbe's ivory coach shalt ride   265
Which, drawn by eagles, in the air shall glide.
I'll stay the time, it shall not steal away,
And twenty moons as seeming but one day.
Behold (fond boy) this rosin-weeping pine,
This mournful larix, dropping turpentine,   270
This mounting keda, thus with tempests torn,
With inky tears continually to mourn.
Look on this tree which blubbereth amber gum,
Which seems to speak to thee, though it be dumb,
Which being senseless blocks, as thou dost see,   275
Weeps at my woes, that thou mightest pity me.
O thou art young and fit for love's profession,
Like wax which warmed quickly takes impression.
Sorrow in time with floods those eyes shall wear
Whence pity now cannot extort a tear.   280
Fond boy, with words thou mightest be overcome,
"But love surprised the heart, the tongue is dumb";
But as I can, I'll strive to conquer thee,
Yet tears and sighs my weapons needs must be:
My sighs move trees, rocks melting with my tears,   285
But thou art blind and, cruel, stoppest thine ears.
Look in this well (if beauty men allow)
Though thou be fair, yet I as fair as thou:
I am a vestal and a spotless maid,
Although by love to thee I am betrayed;   290
But sith (unkind) thou dost my love disdain,
To rocks and hills my self I will complain'.

   Thus with a sigh her speeches off she broke,
The whilst her eyes to him in silence spoke;
And from the place this wanton nymph arose,   295
And up to Latmus all in haste she goes:
Like to a nymph on shady Cytheron,
The swift Ismænos, or Thirmodoon,
Gliding like Thetis on the fleet waves borne,

Or she which trips upon the ears of corn;   300
Like swallows when in open air they strive,
Or like the fowl which towering falcons drive.
But whilst the wanton thus pursued his sport,
Deceitful Love had undermined the fort,
And by a breach (in spite of all deniance)   305
Entered the fort which lately made defiance,
And with strong siege had now begirt about
The maiden sconce which held the soldier out.
'Love wants his eyes, yet shoots he passing right',
His shafts our thoughts, his bow he makes our sight; 310
His deadly piles are tempered by such art
As still directs the arrow to the heart.
He cannot love, and yet forsooth he will;
He sees her not, and yet he sees her still;
He goes unto the place she stood upon,   315
And asks the poor soil whither she was gone.
Fain would he follow her, yet makes delay;
Fain would he go, and yet fain would he stay.
He kissed the flowers depressed with her feet,
And swears from her they borrowed all their sweet. 320
Fain would he cast aside this troublous thought,
But still, like poison, more and more it wrought;
And to himself thus often would he say:
'Here my love sat, in this place did she play;
Here in this fountain hath my goddess been,   325
And with her presence hath she graced this green.'
    Now black-browed Night, placed in her chair of jet,
Sat wrapped in clouds within her cabinet,
And with her dusky mantle overspread
The path the sunny palfreys used to tread;   330
And Cynthia, sitting in her crystal chair
In all her pomp, now rid along her sphere.
The honeyed dew, descended in soft showers,
Drizzled in pearl upon the tender flowers;
And Zephyr hushed, and with a whispering gale 335
Seemed to harken to the nightingale,
Which in the thorny brakes with her sweet song
Unto the silent Night bewrayed her wrong.
    Now fast by Latmus, near unto a grove
Which by the mount was shadowed from above,   340
Upon a bank Endymion sat by night,
To whom fair Phœbe lent her friendly light.

And sith his flocks were laid them down to rest,
Thus gives his sorrows passage from his breast:
'Sweet leaves (quoth he) which with the air do   345
    tremble
Oh how your motions do my thoughts resemble:
With that mild breath, by which you only move,
Whisper my words in silence to my love;
Convey my sighs, sweet civet-breathing air,
In doleful accents to my heavenly fair;   350
You murmuring springs, like doleful instruments
Upon your gravel sound my sad laments,
And in your silent bubbling as you go
Consort yourselves like music to my woe.'
And lifting now his sad and heavy eyes   355
Up, towards the beauty of the burnished skies,
'Bright lamps (quoth he) the glorious welkin bears,
Which clip about the planets' wandering spheres
And in your circled maze do ever roll,
Dancing about the never-moving pole;   360
Sweet nymph, which in fair Elice dost shine,
Whom thy surpassing beauty made divine,
Now in the arctic constellation,
Smile, sweet Callisto, on Endymion;
And thou, brave Perseus, in the northern air,   365
Holding Medusa by the snaky hair,
Jove's shower-begotten son, whose valour tried,
In seventeen glorious lights are stellified;
Which wonnest thy love, left as a monster's prey;
And thou, the lovely fair Andromeda,   370
Born of the famous Ethiopian line,
Darting these rays from thy transpiercing eyne,
To thee the bright Cassiopey, with these
Whose beauty strove with the Nereides,
With all the troop of the celestial band,   375
Which on Olympus in your glory stand;
And you, great wandering lights, if from your spheres
You have regard unto a shepherd's tears,
Or (as men say) if over earthly things
You only rule as potentates and kings,   380
Unto my love's event sweet stars direct
Your kindest revolution and aspect,
And bend your clear eyes from your thrones above
Upon Endymion, pining thus in love.'
    Now, ere the purple dawning yet did spring   385

The constellations near the pole arctic

The joyful lark began to stretch her wing,
And now the cock, the morning's trumpeter,
Played hunt's-up for the day star to appear:
Down slideth Phœbe from her crystal chair
'Sdayning to lend her light unto the air,   390
But unto Latmus all in haste is gone,
Longing to see her sweet Endymion;
At whose departure all the planets gazed,
As at some seld-seen accident amazed
Till, reasoning of the same, they fell at odds   395
So that a question grew amongst the gods,
Whether, without a general consent,
She might depart their sacred parliament?
But what they could do was but all in vain,
Of liberty they could her not restrain;   400
For of the seven sith she the lowest was,
Unto the earth she might the easiest pass.
Sith only by her moisty influence
Of earthly things she hath pre-eminence,
And under her man's mutable estate,   405
As with her changes, doth participate;
And from the working of her waning source
The uncertain waters held a certain course,
Throughout her kingdom she might walk at large
Whereof as Empress she had care and charge;   410
And as the Sun unto the day gives light,
So is she only mistress of the night;
Which whilst she in her oblique course doth guide,
The glittering stars appear in all their pride,
Which to her light their friendly lamps do lend   415
And on her train as handmaids do attend.
And thirteen times she through her sphere doth run
Ere Phœbus full his yearly course have done;
And unto her of women is assigned,
Predominance of body and of mind,   420
That as of planets she most variable,
So of all creatures they most mutable.
But her sweet Latmus, which she loves so much,
No sooner once her dainty foot doth touch
But that the mountain with her brightness shone   425
And gave a light to all the horizon
(Even as the Sun, which darkness long did shroud,
Breaks suddenly from underneath a cloud),

So that the nymphs which on her still attended
Knew certainly great Phœbe was descended;⁣   430
And all approached to this sacred hill,
There to await their sovereign goddess' will.
And now the little birds, whom Nature taught
To honour great Diana as they ought
(Because she is the goddess of the woods,   435
And sole preserver of their hallowed floods)
Set to their consort in their lower springs,
That with the music all the mountain rings;
So that it seemed the birds of every grove
Which should excel and pass each other strove,   440
That in the higher woods and hollow grounds
The murmuring Echo everywhere resounds.
The trembling brooks their sliding courses stayed
The whilst the waves one with another played,
And all the flocks in this rejoicing mood   445
As though enchanted do forbear their food.
The herds of deer down from the mountains flew,
As loath to come within Diana's view,
Whose piercing arrows from her ivory bow
Had often taught her powerful hand to know.   450
And now from Latmus looking towards the plains,
Casting her eyes upon the shepherd swains,
Perceived her dear Endymion's flock were strayed
And he himself upon the ground was laid
Who, late recalled from melancholy deep,   455
The chanting birds had lulled now asleep
For why the music in this humble kind
As it first found, so doth it leave, the mind;
And melancholy, from the spleen begun,
By passion moved, into the veins doth run;   460
Which, when this humour as a swelling flood
By vigour is infused in the blood,   *The effect of*
                                                     Melancholy
The vital spirits doth mightily appall,
And weakeneth so the parts organical;
And when the senses are disturbed and tired   465
With what the heart incessantly desired,
Like travellers with labour long oppressed
Finding release, eftsoons they fall to rest.
   And coming now to her Endymion
(Whom heavy sleep had lately ceased upon)   470
Kneeling her down him in her arms she clips,

And with sweet kisses sealeth up his lips;
Whilst from her eyes, tears streaming down in showers
Fell on his cheek like dew upon the flowers
In globy circles, like pure drops of milk   475
Sprinkled on roses or fine crimson silk.
Touching his brow, 'This is the seat (quoth she)
Where Beauty sits in all her majesty'.
She calls his eyelids 'those pure crystal covers
Which do include the looking glass of lovers';   480
She calls his lips 'the sweet delicious folds
Which rare perfume and precious incense holds';
She calls his soft smooth alabaster skin,
'The lawn which angels are attired in';
'Sweet face (quoth she), but wanting words I spare   485
     thee:
Except to heaven alone I should compare thee'.
And whilst her words she wasteth thus in vain,
Sporting herself the time to entertain,
The frolic nymphs, with music's sacred sound,
Enter the meadows dancing in a round   490
And unto Phœbe straight their course direct,
Which now their joyful coming did expect,
Before whose feet their flowery spoil they lay,
And with sweet balm his body do embay.
And on the laurels growing there along   495
Their wreathed garlands all about they hung,
And all the ground within the compass load
With sweetest flowers whereon they lightly trod.
With nectar then his temples they bedew,
And kneeling softly kiss him all arew.   500
Then in brave galliards they themselves advance
And in the Thyas' Bacchus' stately dance;
Then, following on fair Flora's gilded train,
Into the groves they thus depart again.
And now to show her powerful deity   505
(Her sweet Endymion more to beautify)
Into his soul the goddess doth infuse
The fiery nature of a heavenly Muse,
Which in the spirit labouring by the mind
The   Partaketh of celestial things by kind: 510
excellency of   For why the soul being divine alone,
the soul   Exempt from vile and gross corruption,
Of heavenly secrets comprehensible
(Of which the dull flesh is not sensible)

And by one only powerful faculty   515
Yet governeth a multiplicity,
Being essential, uniform, in all,
Not to be severed nor dividual;
But in her function holdeth her estate
By powers divine in her ingenerate,   520
And so by inspiration conceiveth
What heaven to her by divination breatheth.
But they no sooner to the shades were gone,
Leaving their goddess by Endymion,
But by the hand the lovely boy she takes   525
And from his sweet sleep softly him awakes,
Who, being struck into a sudden fear
Beholding thus his glorious goddess there,
His head transpierced with this sudden glance,
Became as one late cast into a trance: 530
Wiping his eyes not yet of perfect sight,
Scarcely awaked, amazed at the light,
His cheeks now pale then lovely blushing red
(Which oft increased, and quickly vanished)
And as on him her fixed eyes were bent,   535
So to and fro his colour came and went:
Like to a crystal near the fire set,
Against the brightness rightly opposite,   *The causes*
Now doth retain the colour of the flame   *of the*
And, lightly moved, again reflects the same;   540   *external sign*
For our affection, quickened by her heat,   *of passion*
Allayed and strengthened by a strong conceit,
The mind disturbed forthwith doth convert
To an internal passion of the heart
By motion of that sudden joy or fear   545
Which we receive either by the eye or ear.
For by retraction of the spirit and blood,
From those exterior parts where first they stood,
Into the centre of the body sent,
Returns again more strong and vehement;   550
And in the like extremity made cold,
About the same, themselves do closely hold;
And though the cause be like in this respect,
Works by this means a contrary effect.
    Thus whilst this passion hotly held his course,   555
Ebbing and flowing from his springing source,
With the strong fit of this sweet fever moved

At sight of her which he entirely loved
(Not knowing yet great Phœbe this should be,
His sovereign goddess, queen of chastity),   560
Now like a man whom Love had learned art,
Resolved at once his secrets to impart;
But first repeats the torments he had passed,
The woes endured since time he saw her last;
Now he reports, he noted whilst she spake   565
The bustling winds their murmur often brake
And, being silent, seemed to pause and stay
To listen to her what she meant to say.
'Be kind (quoth he) sweet nymph unto thy lover,
My soul's sole essence and my senses' mover,   570
Life of my life, pure image of my heart,
Impressure of conceit, invention, art: ·
My vital spirit receives his spirit from thee;
Thou art that all which ruleth all in me;
Thou art the sap and life whereby I live,   575
Which powerful vigour dost receive and give;
Thou nourished the flame wherein I burn,
The north whereto my heart's true touch doth turn.
Pity my poor flock, see their woeful plight,
Their master perished living from thy sight,   580
Their fleeces rent, my tresses all forlorn:
I pine, whilst they their pasture have forborn.
Behold (quoth he) this little flower below
Which here within this fountain brim doth grow'.
With that, a solemn tale begins to tell   585
Of this fair flower and of this holy well,
A goodly legend many winters old,
Learned by the shepherds sitting by their fold,
How once this fountain was a youthful swain,
A frolic boy, and kept upon the plain.   590
'Unfortunate it happed to him (quoth he)
To love a fair nymph as I now love thee:
To her his love and sorrow he imparts,
Which might dissolve a rock of flinty hearts;
To her he sues, to her he makes his moan,   595
But she more deaf and hard than steel or stone.
And thus one day, with grief of mind oppressed,
As in this place he laid him down to rest,
The gods at length upon his sorrows look,
Transforming him into this purling brook,   600

Whose murmuring bubbles softly as they creep,
Falling in drops, the channel seems to weep.
But she, thus careless of his misery,
Still spends her days in mirth and jollity,
And coming one day to the riverside,   605
Laughing for joy when she the same espied,
This wanton nymph in that unhappy hour
Was here transformed into this purple flower,
Which towards the water turns itself again
To pity him by her unkindness slain'.   610
 She, as it seemed, who all this time attended,
Longing to hear that once his tale were ended,
Now like a jealous woman she repeats
Men's subtleties and natural deceits;
And by example strives to verify   615
Their fickleness and vain inconstancy,
Their hard obdurate hearts and wilful blindness,
Telling a story wholly of unkindness.
But he, who well perceived her intent,
And to remove her from this argument,   620
Now by the sacred fount he vows, and swears
By lovers' sighs and by her hallowed tears.
By holy Latmus now he takes his oath,
That all he spake was in good faith and troth;
And for no frail uncertain doubt should move her, 625
Vows secrecy, the crown of a true lover.
 She, hearing this, thought time that she revealed
That kind affection which she long concealed,
Determineth to make her true love known
Which she had borne unto Endymion: 630
'I am no huntress nor no nymph (quoth she),
As thou perhaps imaginest me to be.
I am great Phœbe, Latmus' sacred queen,
Who from the skies have hither passed unseen;
And by thy chaste love hither was I led,   635
Where full three years thy fair flock have I fed
Upon these mountains and these fertile plains,
And crowned thee king of all the shepherd swains.
Nor wanton nor lascivious is my love,
Nor never lust my chaste thoughts once could move; 640
But sith thou thus hast offered at my shrine,
And of the gods hast held me most divine,
Mine altars thou with sacrifice hast stored,

And in my temples hast my name adored,
And of all other most hast honoured me,   645
Great Phoebe's glory thou alone shalt see.'
  This spake, she putteth on her brave attire,
As being burnished in her brother's fire,
Purer than that celestial shining flame
Wherein great Jove unto his leman came,   650
Which quickly had his pale cheeks overspread
And tincted with a lovely blushing red.
Which whilst her brother Titan for a space
Withdrew himself to give his sister place,
She now is darkened to all creatures' eyes   655
Whilst in the shadow of the earth she lies
(For that the earth of nature cold and dry,
A very chaos of obscurity,
Whose globe exceeds her compass by degrees,
Fixed upon her superficies,   660
When in his shadow she doth hap to fall
Doth cause her darkness to be general).
  Thus whilst he laid his head upon her lap
She in a fiery mantle doth him wrap,
And carries him up from this lumpish mould   665
Into the skies, whereas he might behold
The earth in perfect roundness of a ball
(Exceeding globes most artificial)
Which in a fixed point Nature disposed,
And with the sundry elements enclosed,   670
Which as the centre permanent doth stay
When as the skies in their diurnal sway
Strongly maintain the ever-turning course,
Forced alone by their First Mover source,
Where he beholds the airy regions,   675
Whereas the clouds and strange impressions,
Maintained by coldness, often do appear
And by the highest region of the air
Unto the clearest element of fire,
Which to her silver foot-stool doth aspire.   680
Then doth she mount him up into her sphere,
Imparting heavenly secrets to him there,
Where, lightened by her shining beams, he sees
The powerful planets, all in their degrees;
Their sundry revolutions in the skies,   685
And by their working how they sympathise,

All in their circles severally prefixed
And in due distance each with other mixed;
The mansions which they hold in their estate,
Of which by nature they participate;   690
And how those signs their several places take
Within the compass of the zodiac,
And in their several triplicities consent   *The signs in*
Unto the nature of an element,   *their triplicities*
To which the planets do themselves disperse,   695 *participate with the*
Having the guidance of this universe,   *elements*
And do from thence extend their several powers
Unto this little fleshly world of ours
(Wherein her Maker's workmanship is found
As in contriving of this mighty round   700
In such strange manner and such fashion wrought
As doth exceed man's dull and feeble thought)
Guiding us still by their directions;
And that our fleshly frail complexions
Of elemental natures grounded be   705
With which our dispositions most agree:
Some of the fire and air participate
And some of water and of earthy state,
As hot and moist with chilly cold and dry,
And unto these the other contrary;   710
And by their influence powerful on the earth,
Predominant in man's frail mortal birth,
And that our lives' effects and fortunes are
As is that happy (or unlucky) star
Which, reigning in our frail nativity,   715
Seals up the secrets of our destiny
With friendly planets in conjunction set,
Or else with other merely opposite.
And now to him her greatest power she lent
To lift him to the starry firmament,   720
Where he beheld that milky stained place
By which the Twins and heavenly Archer trace
The Dog which doth the furious Lion beat
(Whose flaming breath increaseth Titan's heat)
The tear-distilling mournful Pleiades   725
Which on the earth the storms and tempests raise,
And all the course the constellations run
When in conjunction with the Moon or Sun,
When towards the fixed arctic they arise,

When towards the antarctic, falling from our eyes.   730
And having imped the wings of his desire
And kindled him with this celestial fire,
She sets him down and, vanishing his sight,
Leaves him enwrapped in this true delight.
Now wheresoever he his fair flock fed   735
The Muses still Endymion followed;
His sheep as white as swans or driven snow,
Which beautified the soil with such a show
As where he folded in the darkest night
There never needed any other light.   740
If that he hungered and desired meat
The bees would bring him honey for to eat,
Yet from his lips would not depart away
Till they were loaden with ambrosia.
And, if he thirsted, often there was seen   745
A bubbling fountain spring out of the green
With crystal liquor filled unto the brim,
Which did present her liquid store to him.
If he would hunt, the fair nymphs at his will
With bow and quivers would attend him still,   750
And whatsoever he desired to have,
That he obtained if he the same would crave.
   And now at length the joyful time drew on
She meant to honour her Endymion,
And glorify him on that stately mount   755
Whereof the goddess made so great account.
She sends Jove's winged herald to the woods,
The neighbour fountains, and the bordering floods,
Charging the nymphs which did inhabit there
Upon a day appointed to appear   760
And to attend her sacred majesty
In all their pomp and great solemnity.
Having obtained great Phœbus' free consent
To further her divine and chaste intent
(Which thus imposed as a thing of weight),   765
In stately troop appear before her straight
The fauns and satyrs from the tufted brakes,
Their bristly arms wreathed all about with snakes,
Their sturdy loins with ropes of ivy bound,
Their horned heads with woodbine chaplets crowned, 770
With cypress javelins, and about their thighs
The flaggy hair disordered loosely flies.

The Oreads, like to the Spartan maid,
In murrey sendal gorgeously arrayed
With gallant green scarves girded in the waist,　　775
Their flaxen hair with silken fillets laced,
Woven with flowers in sweet lascivious wreaths,
Moving like feathers as the light air breathes,
With crowns of myrtle, glorious to behold,
Whose leaves are painted with pure drops of gold;　　780
With trains of fine bisse chequered all with frets
Of dainty pinks and precious violets,
In branched buskins of fine cordwain,
With spangled garters down unto the shin
Fringed with fine silk of many a sundry kind,　　785
Which like to pennons waved with the wind.
The hamadryads, from their shady bowers,
Decked up in garlands of the rarest flowers
Upon the backs of milk-white bulls were set,
With horn and hoof as black as any jet,　　790
Whose collars were great massy golden rings,
Led by their swains in twisted silken strings.
Then did the lovely dryades appear
On dappled stags which bravely mounted were,
Whose velvet palms with nosegays rarely dight,　　795
To all the rest bred wonderful delight.
And in this sort, accompanied with these,
In triumph rid the watery Naiades
Upon sea-horses trapped with shining fins,
Armed with their maily impenetrable skins,　　800
Whose scaly crests like rainbows bended high
Seemed to control proud Iris in the sky.
Upon a chariot was Endymion laid,
In snowy tissue gorgeously arrayed
Of precious ivory covered o'er with lawn,　　805
Which by four stately unicorns was drawn;
Of ropes of orient pearl their traces were,
Pure as the path which doth in heaven appear;
With rarest flowers enchased and overspread
Which served as curtains to this glorious bed,　　810
Whose seat of crystal in the sunbeams shone
Like thunder-breathing Jove's celestial throne.
Upon his head a coronet installed
Of one entire and mighty emerald,
With richest bracelets on his lily wrists　　815

Of helitropium, linked with golden twists;
A bevy of fair swans which, flying over,
With their large wings him from the Sun do cover,
And easily wafting as he went along,
Do lull him still with their enchanting song,   820
Whilst all the nymphs on solemn instruments
Sound dainty music to their sweet laments.
   And now great Phœbe in her triumph came,
With all the titles of her glorious name:
Diana, Delia, Luna, Cynthia,   825
Virago, Hecate, and Elythia,
Prothyria, Dictynna, Proserpine,
Latona, and Lucina, most divine;
And in her pomp began now to approach
Mounted aloft upon her crystal coach,   830
Drawn o'er the plains by four pure milk-white hinds
Whose nimble feet seemed winged with the winds.
Her rarest beauty being now begun
(But newly borrowed from the golden Sun)
Her lovely crescent with a decent space   835
By due proportion beautified her face,
Till having fully filled her circled side
Her glorious fulness now appeared in pride;
Which long her changing brow could not retain
But, fully waxed, began again to wane.   840
Upon her brow (like meteors in the air)
Twenty and eight great gorgeous lamps she bare;
Some, as the welkin, shining passing bright,
Some not so sumptuous, others lesser light,
Some burn, some other, let their fair lights fall,   845
Composed in order geometrical.
And, to adorn her with a greater grace
And add more beauty to her lovely face,
Her richest globe she gloriously displays
Now that the Sun had hid his golden rays   850
(Lest that his radiance should her suppress
And so might make her beauty seem the less);
Her stately train laid out in azured bars,
Powdered all thick with troops of silver stars;
Her airy vesture yet so rare and strange   855
As every hour the colour seemed to change,
Yet still the former beauty doth retain
And ever came unto the same again.

Then fair Astræa of the Titans' line,
Whom equity and justice made divine,   860
Was seated here upon the silver beam
And with the reins guides on this goodly team,
To whom the Charites led on the way,
Aglaia, Thalia, and Euphrosyne:
With princely crowns they in the triumph came,   865
Embellished with Phœbe's glorious name.
These forth before the mighty goddess went
As princes' heralds in a parliament,
And in their true consorted symphony
Record sweet songs of Phœbe's chastity.   870
Then followed on the Muses, sacred nine,
With the first number equally divine,
In virgins' white, whose lovely maiden brows
Were crowned with triumphant laurel boughs;
And on their garments, painted out in glory,   875
Their offices and functions in a story,
Emblazoning the fury and conceit
Which on their sacred company await.
    For none but these were suffered to approach
Or once come near to this celestial coach   880
But these two of the numbers, nine and three,
Which, being odd, include an unity,
Into which number all things fitly fall
And therefore named theological.
And first composing of this number nine   885
(Which of all numbers is the most divine)
From orders of the angels doth arise,
Which be contained in three hierarchies,
And each of these three hierarchies in three,
The perfect form of true triplicity;   890
And of the hierarchies I spake of erst,
The glorious Epiphania is the first,
In which the high celestial orders been
Of Thrones, Cherub, and the Seraphim;
The second holds the mighty Principates,   895
The Dominations and the Potestates;
The Ephionia, the third hierarchy,
Which Virtues, Angels and Archangels be:
And thus by threes we aptly do define
And do compose this sacred number nine.   900
Yet each of these nine orders grounded be

Upon some one particularity.
Then as a poet I might so infer
Another order when I spake of her:
From these the Muses only are derived,   905
Which of the angels were in nine contrived;
These heaven-inspired babes of Memory
Which, by a like attracting sympathy,
Apollo's prophets in their furies wrought,
And in their spirit enchanting numbers taught   910
To teach such as at poesy repine
That it is only heavenly and divine,
And manifest her intellectual parts,
Sucking the purest of the purest arts.
And unto these as by a sweet consent   915
The sphery circles are equivalent,
From the first mover, and the starry heaven,
To glorious Phœbe, lowest of the seven,
Which Jove in tuneful diapasons framed
Of heavenly music, of the Muses named;   920
To which the soul in her divinity
(By her creator made of harmony)
Whilst she in frail and mortal flesh doth live,
To her nine sundry offices do give,
Which offices united are in three,   925
Which like the orders of the angels be,
Prefiguring thus by the number nine
The soul, like to the angels, is divine.
And from these nines those conquerors renowned
(Which with the wreaths of triumph oft were   930
   crowned
Which by their virtues gained the Worthies' name
First had this number added to their fame
(Not that the worthiest men were only nine,
But that the number of itself divine,
And as a perfect pattern of the rest,   935
Which by this holy number are expressed).
Nor chivalry this title only gained
But might as well by wisdom be obtained;
Nor in this number men alone included,
But unto women well might be alluded   940
Could wit, could worlds, could times, could ages find
This number of Eliza's heavenly kind.
And those rare men, which learning highly prized,
By whom the constellations were devised,

And by their favours learning highly graced,   945
For Orpheus' harp nine stars in heaven placed,
This sacred number to declare thereby
Her sweet consent and solid harmony,
And man's heroic voice, which doth impart
The thought conceived in the inward heart;   950
Her sweetness on nine instruments doth ground,
Else doth she fail in true and perfect sound.
Now of this three in order to dispose,
Whose trinary doth justly nine compose:
First in the form of this triplicity   955
Is shadowed that mighty Trinity
Which still in steadfast unity remain
And yet of three one Godhead do contain
From this eternal living Deity.
As by a heaven-inspired prophecy   960
Divinest poets first derived these,
The fairest Graces, Jove-born Charites;
And in this number music first began,
The Lydian, Dorian, and the Phrygian
Which, ravishing in their soul-pleasing vein,   965
They made up seven in a higher strain.
And all those signs which Phœbus doth ascend
Before he bring his yearly course to end,
Their several natures mutually agree,
And do concur in this triplicity;   970
And those interior senses with the rest,
Which properly pertain to man and beast,
Nature herself in working so devised
That in this number they should be comprised.

But to my tale I must return again: 975
Phœbe to Latmus thus conveyed her swain
Under a bushy laurel's pleasing shade,
Amongst whose boughs the birds sweet music made,
Whose fragrant branch-embossed canopy
Was never pierced with Phœbus' burning eye;   980
Yet never could this paradise want light,
Illumined still with Phœbe's glorious sight.
She laid Endymion on a grassy bed,
With summer's arras richly overspread,
Where from her sacred mansion next above   985
She might descend and sport her with her love,
Which thirty years the shepherd safely kept,

Who in her bōsom soft and soundly slept;
Yet as a dream he thought the time not long,
Remaining ever beautiful and young: 990
And what in vision there to him befell
My weary Muse some other time shall tell.

   Dear Colin, let my Muse excused be,
Which rudely thus presumes to sing by thee,
Although her strains be harsh, untuned, and ill,   995
Nor can attain to thy divinest skill.
   And thou, the sweet Musaeus of these times,
Pardon my rugged and unfiled rhymes,
Whose scarce invention is too mean and base
When Delia's glorious Muse doth come in place.   1000
   And thou, my Goldey, which in summer days
Hast feasted us with merry roundelays,
And when my Muse scarce able was to fly
Didst imp her wings with thy sweet poesy.
   And you, the heirs of ever-living fame,   1005
The worthy titles of a poet's name,
Whose skill and rarest excellence is such
As spiteful Envy never yet durst touch,
To your protection I this Poem send,
Which from proud Momus may my lines defend.   1010
   And if, sweet maid, thou deignest to read this story,
Wherein thine eyes may view thy virtues' glory,
Thou purest spark of Vesta's kindled fire,
Sweet nymph of Ankor, crown of my desire,
The plot which for their pleasure heaven devised,   1015
Where all the Muses be imparadised:
Where thou do live, there let all graces be
(Which want their grace if only wanting thee);
Let stormy winter never touch the clime,
But let it flourish as in April's prime;   1020
Let sullen Night that soil ne'er overcloud,
But in thy presence let the earth be proud.
If ever Nature of her work might boast,
Of thy perfection she may glory most,
To whom fair Phœbe hath her bow resigned,   1025
Whose excellence doth live in thee refined
And, that thy praise Time never should impair,
Hath made my heart thy never-moving sphere.
Then, if my Muse give life unto thy fame,

Thy virtues be the causers of the same;   1030
And from thy tomb some oracle shall rise,
To whom all pens shall yearly sacrifice.

FINIS.

SIR JOHN DAVIES

SIR JOHN DAVIES

Dates: 1569–1626. Born at Tisbury, Wiltshire, in 1569, son of Mary, and of John (who died the following year). Sent to school at Winchester (1580); entered the Queen's College, Oxford, 1584, thence proceeding (perhaps without graduating) to read law at the Middle Temple (1587). His mother died in 1590, and 1592 saw him travelling on the continent. He was called to the Bar in 1595, the year in which his *Epigrams* were published. *Orchestra* (written early 1594) was published in 1596, but his quarrel with its original dedicatee, Richard Martin, led to his expulsion from the Middle Temple and disbarment soon followed (1597; he was readmitted in 1601). Publication of the long philosophical poem on the nature of the soul, *Nosce Teipsum* (1599) preceded publication of the *Hymns of Astraea* the same year. Other literary works include: *Gulling Sonnets* (1597), *Ten Sonnets to Philomel* (1602), *Yet Another Twelve Wonders of the World*, *A Lottery*, and *A Contention betwixt a Wife, a Widow and a Maid* (1608). Davies was elected MP for Corfe Castle, Dorset, in 1601; appointed Solicitor-General for Ireland and knighted (1603); appointed Attorney-General for Ireland (1606); elected MP for Fermanagh in 1612 and Speaker of the Irish Parliament's Lower House in 1613. Back in England from 1619, he was a circuit judge and MP for Newcastle-under-Lyme (1621) before being appointed Lord Chief Justice a month before he died in December, 1626.

HYMNS OF ASTRÆA IN ACROSTIC VERSE

HYMN 1
Of Astræa

E arly before the day doth spring
L et us awake, my Muse, and sing,
I t is no time to slumber:
S o many joys this time doth bring
A s Time will fail to number.   5

B ut whereto shall we bend our lays?
E ven up to heaven, again to raise
T he maid which, thence descended,
H ath brought again the golden days
A nd all the world amended.   10

R udenesse it self she doth refine,
E ven like an alchemist divine,
G ross times of iron turning
I nto the purest form of gold,
N ot to corrupt till heaven wax old,   15
A nd be refined with burning.

HYMN 2
To Astræa

E ternal virgin, goddess true,
L et me presume to sing to you:
I ove, even great Jove, hath leisure
S ometimes to hear the vulgar crew,
A nd hears them oft with pleasure.   5

B lessed Astræa, I in part
E njoy the blessings you impart,
T he peace, the milk and honey,
H umanity, and civil art,
A richer dower than money.   10

R ight glad am I that now I live
E ven in these days whereto you give
G reat happiness and glory:
I f after you I should be born
N o doubt I should my birth day scorn,   15
A dmiring your sweet story.

HYMN 3
To the Spring

E arth now is green and heaven is blue:
L ively Spring, which makes all new,
I olly Spring doth enter;
S weet young sunbeams do subdue
A ngry, aged Winter.   5

B lasts are mild and seas are calm,
E very meadow flows with balm,
T he Earth wears all her riches:
H armonious birds sing such a psalm
A s ear and heart bewitches.   10

R eserve (sweet Spring) this nymph of ours
E ternal garlands of thy flowers,
G reen garlands never wasting:
I n her shall last our state's fair spring,
N ow and for ever flourishing,   15
A s long as heaven is lasting.

HYMN 4
To the Month of May

E ach day of thine, sweet month of May,
L ove makes a solemn holy-day.
I will perform like duty
S ince thou resemblest every way
A stræa, queen of Beauty.   5

B oth you fresh beauties do partake,
E ither's aspect doth Summer make:
T houghts of young Love awaking
H earts you both do cause to ache
A nd yet be pleased with aching.   10

R ight dear art thou and so is she,
E ven like attractive sympathy
G ains unto both like deareness:
I ween this made antiquity
N ame thee, sweet May, of Majesty,   15
A s being both like in clearness.

HYMN 5
To the Lark

E arly, cheerful, mounting Lark,
L ight's gentle usher, morning's clerk,
I n merry notes delighting:
S tint awhile thy song, and hark
A nd learn my new inditing   5

B ear up this hymn, to heaven it bear,
E ven up to heaven, and sing it there:
T o heaven each morning bear it;
H ave it set to some sweet sphere,
A nd let the angels hear it.   10

R enowned Astræa, that great name,
E xceeding great in worth and fame,
G reat worth hath so renowned it,
I t is Astræa's name I praise:
N ow then, sweet Lark, do thou it raise,   15
A nd in high heaven resound it.

HYMN 6
To the Nightingale

E very night, from even till morn,
L ove's chorister, amid the thorn,
I s now so sweet a singer,
S o sweet as for her song I scorn
A pollo's voice and finger.   5

B ut, nightingale, since you delight
E ver to watch the starry night,
T ell all the stars of heaven,
H eaven never had a star so bright
A s now to Earth is given.   10

R oyal Astræa makes our day
E ternal with her beams, nor may
G ross darkness overcome her;
I now perceive why some do write:
N o country hath so short a night   15
A s England hath in summer.

HYMN 7
To the Rose

E ye of the garden; queen of flowers;
L ove's cup wherein he nectar pours,
I ngendered first of nectar;
S weet nurse-child of the Spring's young Hours
A nd Beauty's fair character;   5

B est jewel that the Earth doth wear
E ven when the brave young Sun draws near
T o her hot love pretending;
H imself likewise like form doth bear
A t rising and descending.   10

R ose, of the queen of love beloved:
E ngland's great kings, divinely moved,
G ave roses in their banner:
I t showed that Beauty's rose indeed
N ow in this age should them succeed   15
A nd reign in more sweet manner.

HYMN 8
To all the Princes of Europe

E urope, the Earth's sweet paradise,
L et all thy kings that would be wise
I n politic devotion
S ail hither to observe her eyes
A nd mark her heavenly motion.   5

B rave princes of this civil age,
E nter into this pilgrimage:
T his saint's tongue is an oracle,
H er eye hath made a prince a page,
A nd works each day a miracle.   10

R aise but your looks to her, and see
E ven the true beams of Majesty;
G reat princes, mark her duly:
I f all the world you do survey,
N o forehead spreads so bright a ray,   15
A nd notes a prince so truly.

HYMN 9
To Flora

E mpress of flowers, tell where a way
L ies your sweet court this merry May
I n Greenwich garden alleys,
S ince there the heavenly powers do play,
A nd haunt no other valleys.   5

B eauty, Virtue, Majesty,
E loquent Muses, three times three,
T he new fresh Hours and Graces,
H ave pleasure in this place to be
A bove all other places.   10

R oses and lilies did them draw
E re they divine Astræa saw;
G ay flowers they sought for pleasure:
I nstead of gathering crowns of flowers
N ow gather thy Astræa's dowers   15
A nd bear to heaven that treasure.

HYMN 10
The Month of September

E ach month hath praise in some degree:
L et May to others seem to be
In sense the sweetest season;
S eptember thou art best to me
A nd best dost please my Reason.   5

B ut neither for thy corn nor wine
E xtol I those mild days of thine,
T hough corn and wine might praise thee:
H eaven gives thee honour more divine,
A nd higher fortunes raise thee.   10

R enowned art thou, sweet month, for this:
E mong thy days her birthday is.
G race, Plenty, Peace and Honour
I n one fair hour with her were born:
N ow since they still her crown adorn,   15
A nd still attend upon her.

345

HYMN II
To the Sun

E ye of the world, fountain of light,
L ife of day, and death of night,
I humbly seek thy kindness:
S weet, dazzle not my feeble sight,
A nd strike me not with blindness.   5

B ehold me mildly from that face,
E ven where thou now dost run thy race,
T he sphere where now thou turnest;
H aving, like Phaethon, changed thy place,
A nd yet hearts only burnest.   10

R ed in her right cheek thou dost rise:
E xalted after in her eyes,
G reat glory there thou showest.
I n the other cheek when thou descendest
N ew redness unto it thou lendest,   15
A nd so thy round thou goest.

HYMN I2
To her Picture

E xtreme was his audacity,
L ittle his skill that finished thee:
I am ashamed and sorry
S o dull her counterfeit should be,
A nd she so full of glory.   5

B ut here are colours red and white,
E ach line and each proportion right;
T hese lines, this red, and whiteness
H ave wanting yet a life and light,
A majesty and brightness.   10

R ude counterfeit, I then did err;
E ven now, when I would needs infer
G reat boldness in thy maker:
I did mistake, he was not bold,
N or durst his eyes her eyes behold,   15
A nd this made him mistake her.

HYMN 13
Of her Mind

E arth now adieu: my ravished thought,
L ifted to heaven, sets thee at nought.
I nfinite is my longing
S ecrets of angels to be taught,
A nd things to heaven belonging.   5

B rought down from heaven, of angels' kind,
E ven now do I admire her mind:
T his is my contemplation,
H er clear sweet spirit which is refined
A bove human creation.   10

R ich sunbeam of the eternal light,
E xcellent soul, how shall I write:
G ood angels make me able;
I cannot see but by your eye,
N or, but by your tongue, signify   15
A thing so admirable.

HYMN 14
Of the Sunbeams of her Mind

E xceeding glorious is this star:
L et us behold her beams afar
I n a side line reflected;
S ight bears them not when near they are
A nd in right lines directed.   5

B ehold her in her virtues' beams
E xtending Sun-like to all realms –
T he Sun none views too nearly.
H er well of goodness in these streams
A ppears right well and clearly.   10

R adiant virtues, if your light
E nfeeble the best judgements' sight,
G reat splendour above measure
I s in the mind from whence you flow:
N o wit may have access to know   15
A nd view so bright a treasure.

HYMN 15
Of her Wit

E ye of that mind most quick and clear,
L ike heaven's eye, which from his sphere
I nto all things pryeth,
S ees through all things everywhere,
A nd all their natures tryeth.   5

B right image of an angel's wit,
E xceeding sharp and swift like it,
T hings instantly discerning;
H aving a nature infinite
A nd yet increased by learning.   10

R ebound upon thy self thy light,
E njoy thine own sweet precious sight;
G ive us but some reflection:
I t is enough for us if we,
N ow in her speech, now policy,   15
A dmire thine high perfection.

HYMN 16
Of her Will

E ver well affected Will,
L oving goodness, loathing ill,
I nestimable treasure:
S ince such a power hath power to spill,
A nd save us at her pleasure,   5

B e thou our law, sweet Will, and say
E ven what thou wilt, we will obey
T his law, if I could read it:
H erein would I spend night and day,
A nd study still to plead it.   10

R oyal Freewill, and only free,
E ach other will is slave to thee:
G lad is each will to serve thee:
I n thee such princely power is seen
N o spirit but takes thee for her queen   15
A nd thinks she must observe thee.

HYMN 17
Of her Memory

E xcellent jewels would you see,
L ovely Ladies? come with me:
I will (for love I owe you)
S how you as rich a treasury,
A s east or west can show you.   5

B ehold (if you can judge of it)
E ven that great storehouse of her wit,
T hat beautiful large table:
H er Memory, wherein is writ
A ll knowledge admirable.   10

R ead this fair book and you shall learn
E xquisite skill if you discern:
G ain heaven by this discerning;
I n such a Memory divine,
N ature did form the Muses nine,   15
A nd Pallas, queen of learning.

HYMN 18
Of her Phantasy

E xquisite curiosity,
L ook on thy self with judging eye;
I f ought be faulty leave it:
S o delicate a Phantasy
A s this will straight perceive it.   5

B ecause her temper is so fine,
E ndued with harmonies divine,
T herefore if discord strike it
H er true proportions do repine
A nd sadly do mislike it.   10

R ight otherwise a pleasure sweet
E ver she takes in actions meet,
G racing with smiles such meetness.
I n her fair forehead beams appear:
N o summer's day is half so clear,   15
A dorned with half that sweetness.

HYMN 19
Of the Organs of her Mind

E clipsed she is, and her bright rays
L ie under veils, yet many ways
I s her fair form revealed:
S he diversely herself conveys
A nd cannot be concealed.   5

B y instruments her powers appear
E xceedingly well-tuned and clear:
T his lute is still in measure,
H olds still in tune, even like a sphere,
A nd yields the world sweet pleasure.   10

R esolve me, Muse, how this thing is:
E ver a body like to this
G ave heaven to earthly creature?
I am but fond this doubt to make:
N o doubt the angels bodies take   15
   A bove our common nature.

HYMN 20
Of the Passions of her Heart

E xamine not the inscrutable Heart,
L ight Muse, of her, though she in part
I mpart it to the subject:
S earch not, although from heaven thou art,   5
A nd this an heavenly object.

B ut since she hath a heart, we know
E ver some passions thence do flow,
T hough ever ruled with Honour:
H er judgement reigns, they wait below,   10
A nd fix their eyes upon her.

R ectified so, they in their kind
E ncrease each virtue of her mind,
G overned with mild tranquillity:
I n all the regions under heaven   15
N o state doth bear itself so even
A nd with so sweet facility.

HYMN 21
Of the Innumerable Virtues of her Mind

E re thou proceed in this sweet pains,
L earn, Muse, how many drops it rains
I n cold and moist December;
S um up May flowers and August's grains
A nd grapes of mild September.   5

B ear the seas' sands in memory,
E arth's grasses and the stars in sky,
T he little motes which, mounted,
H ang in the beams of Phoebus' eye
A nd never can be counted.   10

R ecount these numbers numberless
E re thou her virtue canst express:
G reat wits this count will cumber;
I nstruct thy self in numbering schools:
N ow courtiers use to beg for fools   15
A ll such as cannot number.

HYMN 22
Of her Wisdom

E agle-eyed Wisdom, life's lodestar,
L ooking near on things afar;
I ove' best beloved daughter
S hows to her spirit all things that are
A s Jove himself hath taught her.   5

B y this straight rule she rectifies
E ach thought that in her heart doth rise:
T his is her clear true mirror,
H er looking glass wherein she spies
A ll forms of Truth and Error.   10

R ight princely Virtue, fit to reign,
E nthronized in her spirit remain,
G uiding our fortunes ever;
I f we this star once cease to see,
N o doubt our state will shipwrecked be,   15
A nd torn and sunk for ever.

HYMN 23
Of her Justice

E xiled Astræa is come again:
L o here she doth all things maintain
I n number, weight, and measure:
S he rules us with delightful pain
A nd we obey with pleasure.   5

B y love she rules more than by law:
E ven her great mercy breedeth awe:
T his is her sword and sceptre;
H erewith she hearts did ever draw,
A nd this guard ever kept her.   10

R eward doth sit in her right hand;
E ach Virtue thence takes her garland
G athered in Honour's garden:
I n her left hand (wherein should be
N ought but the sword) sits Clemency,
A nd conquers Vice with pardon.   15

HYMN 24
Of her Magnanimity

E ven as her state, so is her Mind
L ifted above the vulgar kind:
I t treads proud Fortune under;
S unlike it sits above the wind,
A bove the storms and thunder.   5

B rave Spirit, large Heart, admiring nought,
E steeming each thing as it ought,
T hat swelleth not, nor shrinketh:
H onour is always in her thought,
A nd of great things she thinketh.   10

R ocks, pillars, and heavens' axle-tree
E xemplify her constancy:
G reat changes never change her;
I n her sex fears are wont to rise:
N ature permits, Virtue denies,
A nd scorns the face of danger.   15

HYMN 25
Of her Moderation

E mpress of kingdoms though she be,
L arger is her sovereignty
I f she her self do govern:
S ubject unto her self is she
A nd of her self true sovereign.   5

B eauty's crown though she do wear,
E xalted into Fortune's chair,
T hroned like the queen of pleasure:
H er Virtues still possess her ear
A nd counsel her to Measure.   10

R eason, if she incarnate were,
E ven Reason's self could never bear
G reatness with Moderation:
I n her one temper still is seen:
N o liberty claims she as queen   15
A nd shows no alteration.

HYMN 26
To Envy

E nvy, go weep: my Muse and I
L augh thee to scorn: thy feeble eye
I s dazzled with the glory
S hining in this gay poesy
A nd litle golden story.   5

B ehold how my proud quill doth shed
E ternal nectar on her head:
T he pomp of coronation
H ath not such power her fame to spread
A s this my admiration.   10

R espect my pen as free and frank,
E xpecting not reward nor thank:
G reat wonder only moves it;
I never made it mercenary;
N or should my Muse this burden carry   15
A s hired, but that she loves it.

FINIS.

Orchestra, or, a Poem of Dancing. Judicially proving the true observation of time and measure in the authentical and laudable use of Dancing. Ovid, *Art. aman.* lib. 1. *Si vox est, canta: si mollia brachia, salta: Et quacunque potes dote placere, place.* (1596 title)

Orchestra, or, a Poem expressing the Antiquity and Excellency of Dancing. In a dialogue between Penelope, and one of her wooers. Not finished. (1622 title)

Dedication (1596)

To his very friend, Ma. Rich: Martin

To whom shall I this dancing poem send,
This sudden, rash, half-capriole of my wit?
To you, first mover and sole cause of it,
Mine-own-self's better half, my dearest friend.
Oh would you yet my Muse some honey lend   5
From your mellifluous tongue, whereon doth sit
Suada in majesty, that I may fit
These harsh beginnings with a sweeter end!
You know the modest sun full fifteen times
Blushing did rise, and blushing did descend,   10
While I in making of these ill-made rhymes
My golden hours unthriftily did spend:
Yet, if in friendship you these numbers praise,
I will mispend another fifteen days.

Dedication (1622)

To the Prince

Sir, whatsoever you are pleased to do
It is your special praise that you are bent
And sadly set your princely mind thereto:
Which makes you in each thing so excellent.
Hence is it that you came so soon to be   5
A man-at-arms in every point aright;
The fairest flower of noble chivalry;
And of Saint George his band the bravest knight.
And hence it is that all your youthful train
In activeness and grace you do excel   10
When you do courtly dancings entertain:
Then Dancing's praise may be presented well

354

To you, whose action adds more praise thereto
Than all the Muses with their pens can do.

ORCHESTRA

1

Where lives the man that never yet did hear
Of chaste Penelope, Ulysses' queen?
Who kept her faith unspotted twenty year
Till he returned, that far away had been
And many men and many towns had seen: 5
    Ten year at siege of Troy he lingering lay,
    And ten year in the Midland Sea did stray.

2

Homer (to whom the Muses did carouse)
A great deep cup with heavenly nectar filled,
The greatest deepest cup in Jove's great house   10
(For Jove himself had so expressly willed)
He drank off all, ne let one drop be spilled:
    Since when his brain, that had before been dry,
    Became the wellspring of all poetry.

3

Homer doth tell in his abundant verse   15
The long laborious travels of the man;
And of his lady too he doth rehearse
How she illudes with all the art she can
The ungrateful love which other lords began:
    For of her lord false Fame long since had sworn   20
    That Neptune's monsters had his carcass torn.

4

All this he tells, but one thing he forgot,
One thing most worthy his eternal song:
But he was old and blind and saw it not,
Or else he thought he should Ulysses wrong   25
To mingle it his tragic acts among;
    Yet was there not, in all the world of things,
    A sweeter burden for his Muse's wings.

5

The courtly love Antinous did make
(Antinous, that fresh and jolly knight   30
Which of the gallants that did undertake
To win the widow had most wealth and might,
Wit to persuade, and beauty to delight) –
    The courtly love he made unto the queen
    Homer forgot, as if it had not been.   35

6

Sing then, Terpischore, my light Muse, sing
His gentle art and cunning courtesy:
You, lady, can remember everything,
For you are daughter of Queen Memory.
But sing a plain and easy melody,   40
    For the soft mean that warbleth but the ground
    To my rude ear doth yield the sweetest sound.

7

One only night's discourse I can report:
When the great torchbearer of heaven was gone
Down in a mask unto the Ocean's court   45
To revel it with Tethys all alone,
Antinous, disguised and unknown,
    Like to the Spring in gaudy ornament
    Unto the castle of the princess went.

8

The sovereign castle of the rocky isle   50
Wherein Penelope the princess lay
Shone with a thousand lamps, which did exile
The shadows dark and turned the night to day:
Not Jove's blue tent, what time the sunny ray
    Behind the bulwark of the earth retires,   55
    Is seen to sparkle with more twinkling fires.

9

That night the queen came forth from far within
And in the presence of her court was seen,
For the sweet singer Phaemius did begin

To praise the worthies that at Troy had been,   60
Somewhat of her Ulysses she did ween
    In his grave hymn the heavenly man would sing,
    Or of his wars, or of his wandering.

10

Pallas that hour, with her sweet breath divine,
Inspired immortal beauty in her eyes   65
That with celestial glory she did shine
Brighter than Venus when she doth arise
Out of the waters to adorn the skies:
   The wooers all amazed do admire,
   And check their own presumptuous desire.   70

11

Only Antinous, when at first he viewed
Her star-bright eyes that with new honour shined,
Was not dismayed, but therewithal renewed
The noblesse and the splendour of his mind;
And as he did fit circumstances find,   75
    Unto the throne he boldly gan advance,
    And with fair manners wooed the queen to dance:

12

'Goddess of women, sith your heavenliness
Hath now vouchsafed itself to represent
To our dim eyes (which, though they see the less,   80
Yet are they blest in their astonishment),
Imitate heaven, whose beauties excellent
   Are in continual motion day and night,
   And move thereby more wonder and delight.

13

'Let me the mover be, to turn about   85
Those glorious ornaments that youth and love
Have fixed in you, every part throughout;
Which, if you will in timely measure move,
Not all those precious gems in heaven above
    Shall yield a sight more pleasing to behold   90
    With all their turns and tracings manifold.'

14

With this the modest princess blushed and smiled,
Like to a clear and rosy eventide,
And softly did return this answer mild:
'Fair sir, you needs must fairly be denied   95
Where your demand cannot be satisfied:
    My feet, which only Nature taught to go,
    Did never yet the art of footing know.

15

'But why persuade you me to this new rage?
For all disorder and misrule is new;   100
For such misgovernment in former age
Our old divine forefathers never knew
Who, if they lived, and did the follies view
    Which their fond nephews make their chief affairs,
    Would hate themselves that had begot such   105
    heirs.'

16

'Sole heir of Virtue and of Beauty both,
Whence cometh it (Antinous replies)
That your imperious virtue is so loth
To grant your beauty her chief exercise?
Or from what spring doth your opinion rise   110
    That dancing is a frenzy and a rage,
    First known and used in this new-fangled age?

17

The
antiquity of
dancing

'Dancing (bright lady) then began to be
When the first seeds whereof the world did spring,
The Fire, Air, Earth, and Water, did agree,   115
By Love's persuasion (Nature's mighty king)
To leave their first disordered combating
    And in a dance such measure to observe
    As all the world their motion should preserve.

18

'Since when they still are carried in a round,   120
And changing come one in another's place:
Yet do they neither mingle nor confound,

But every one doth keep the bounded space
Wherein the dance doth bid it turn or trace:
    This wondrous miracle did Love devise,   125
    For dancing is love's proper exercise.

19

'Like this he framed the gods' eternal bower,
And of a shapeless and confused mass
By his through-piercing and digesting power
The turning vault of heaven formed was,   130
Whose starry wheels he hath so made to pass,
    As that their movings do a music frame,
    And they themselves still dance unto the same.

20

'Or if this All, which round about we see
(As idle Morpheus some sick brains hath taught)   135
Of undivided motes compacted be,
How was this goodly architecture wrought?
Or by what means were they together brought?
    They err that say they did concur by chance:
    Love made them meet in a well-ordered dance: 140

21

'As when Amphion with his charming lyre
Begot so sweet a siren of the air
That with her rhetoric made the stones conspire
The ruins of a city to repair
(A work of Wit and Reason's wise affair):   145
    So Love's smooth tongue the motes such measure
      taught
    That they joined hands, and so the world was
      wrought.

22

'How justly then is dancing termed new
Which with the world in point of time begun?
Yea, Time itself (whose birth Jove never knew   150
And which indeed is elder than the Sun)
Had not one moment of his age outrun
    When out leaped Dancing from the heap of things

And lightly rode upon his nimble wings.

23

'Reason hath both their pictures in her treasure,   155
Where Time the measure of all moving is
And Dancing is a moving all in measure.
Now, if you do resemble that to this
And think both one, I think you think amiss:
    But if you judge them twins, together got,   160
    And Time first born, your judgment erreth not.

24

'Thus doth it equal age with Age enjoy,
And yet in lusty youth forever flowers,
Like Love his sire, whom painters make a boy,
Yet is he eldest of the heavenly powers;   165
Or like his brother Time, whose winged Hours,
    Going and coming, will not let him die,
    But still preserve him in his infancy.'

25

This said, the queen with her sweet lips divine
Gently began to move the subtle air,   170
Which, gladly yielding, did itself incline
To take a shape between those rubies fair,
And, being formed, softly did repair
    With twenty doublings in the empty way
    Unto Antinous' ears, and thus did say: 175

26

'What eye doth see the heaven but doth admire
When it the movings of the heavens doth see?
Myself, if I to heaven may once aspire,
If that be dancing, will a dancer be;
But as for this your frantic jollity,   180
    How it began or whence you did it learn
    I never could with Reason's eye discern.'

27

Antinous answered: 'Jewel of the earth,
Worthy you are that heavenly dance to lead;

But for you think our Dancing base of birth   185
And newly born but of a brain-sick head,
I will forthwith his antique gentry read,
    And, for I love him, will his herald be,
    And blaze his arms, and draw his pedigree.

28

'When Love had shaped this world (this great fair
    wight   *The original*
                                        190 *of dancing*
That all wights else in this wide womb contains)
And had instructed it to dance aright
A thousand measures with a thousand strains
Which it should practise with delightful pains
    Until that fatal instant should revolve   195
    When all to nothing should again resolve,

29

'The comely order and proportion fair
On every side did please his wandering eye
Till, glancing through the thin transparent air,
A rude disordered rout he did espy   200
Of men and women that, most spitefully,
    Did one another throng and crowd so sore
    That his kind eye in pity wept therefore.

30

'And swifter than the lightning down he came,
Another shapeless Chaos to digest: 205
He will begin another world to frame,
For Love, till all be well, will never rest.
Then with such words as cannot be expressed
    He cuts the troops, that all asunder fling,
    And ere they wist he casts them in a ring.   210

31

'Then did he rarefy the element
And in the centre of the ring appear.
The beams that from his forehead spreading went
Begot a horror and religious fear
In all the souls that round about him were,   215
    Which in their ears attentiveness procures,
    While he with suchlike sounds their minds allures:

32

*The speech
of Love
persuading
men to learn
dancing*

‘ "How doth Confusion's mother, headlong Chance,
Put Reason's noble squadron to the rout?
Or how should you have the governance   220
Of Nature's children, heaven and earth throughout,
Prescribe them rules, and live yourselves without?
  Why should your fellowship a trouble be,
  Since man's chief pleasure is society?

33

‘ "If sense hath not yet taught you, learn of me   225
A comely moderation and discreet,
That your assemblies may well ordered be
When my uniting power shall make you meet:
With heavenly tunes it shall be tempered sweet
  And be the model of the world's great frame,   230
  And you, Earth's children, Dancing shall it name.

34

‘ "Behold the world how it is whirled round:
And for it is so whirled, is named so;
In whose large volume many rules are found
Of this new art, which it doth fairly show: 235
For your quick eyes, in wandering to and fro
  From east to west, on no one thing can glance
  But, if you mark it well, it seems to dance.

35

*By the
orderly
motion of
the fixed
stars*

‘ "First you see fixed in this huge mirror blue
Of trembling lights a number numberless: 240
Fixed they are named, but with a name untrue,
For they all move, and in a dance express
The great long year that doth contain no less
  Than threescore hundreds of those years in all
  Which the Sun makes with his course natural.   245

36

‘ "What if to you these sparks disordered seem,
As if by Chance they had been scattered there?
The gods a solemn measure do it deem
And see a just proportion everywhere,

And know the points whence first their movings 250
    were,
    To which first points when all return again,
    The axle-tree of heaven shall break in twain.

37

' "Under that spangled sky five wandering flames
(Besides the king of day and queen of night)
Are wheeled around, all in their sundry frames, 255
And all in sundry measures do delight:
Yet altogether keep no measure right,
    For by itself each doth itself advance,
    And by itself each doth a galliard dance.

38

' "Venus, the mother of that bastard Love 260
Which doth usurp the world's great marshal's name,
Just with the Sun her dainty feet doth move,
And unto him doth all her gestures frame:
Now after, now afore, the flattering dame
    With divers cunning passages doth err, 265
    Still him respecting that respects not her.

39

' "For that brave Sun, the father of the day,
Doth love this Earth, the mother of the night,
And like a reveller in rich array
Doth dance his galliard in his leman's sight, 270
Both back, and forth, and sideways, passing light:
    His princely grace doth so the gods amaze
    That all stand still and at his beauty gaze.

40

' "But see the Earth when he approacheth near,
How she for joy doth spring and sweetly smile; 275
But see again her sad and heavy cheer
When changing places he retires awhile.
But those black clouds he shortly will exile,
    And make them all before his presence fly
    As mists consumed before his cheerful eye. 280

41

' "Who doth not see measures of the Moon
Which thirteen times she danceth every year?
And ends her pavan thirteen times as soon
As doth her brother, of whose golden hair
She borroweth part and proudly doth it wear.   285
  Then doth she coyly turn her face aside,
  That half her cheek is scarce sometimes descried.

42

Of the Fire ' "Next her, the pure, subtle, and cleansing Fire
Is swiftly carried in a circle even,
Though Vulcan be pronounced by many a liar   290
(The only halting god that dwells in heaven):
But that foul name may be more fitly given
  To your false fire, that far from heaven is fall,
  And doth consume, waste, spoil, disorder all.

43

Of the Air ' "And now behold your tender nurse, the Air,   295
And common neighbour that aye runs around:
How many pictures and impressions fair
Within her empty regions are there found
Which to your senses dancing do propound?
  For what are breath, speech, echoes, music,   300
   winds,
  But dancings of the Air in sundry kinds?

44

' "For when you breathe the Air in order moves,
Now in, now out, in time and measure true;
And when you speak, so well she dancing loves
That doubling oft, and oft redoubling new,   305
With thousand forms she doth herself endue;
  For all the words that from your lips repair
  Are nought but tricks and turnings of the air.

45

' "Hence is her prattling daughter, Echo, born,
That dances to all voices she can hear: 310
There is no sound so harsh that she doth scorn,
Not any time wherein she will forbear

The airy pavement with her feet to wear;
    And yet her hearing sense is nothing quick,
    For after time she endeth every trick.   315

46

' "And thou, sweet Music, Dancing's only life,
The ear's sole happiness, the Air's best speech,
Lodestone of fellowship, charming rod of strife,
The soft mind's paradise, the sick mind's leech,
With thine own tongue thou trees and stones canst   320
    teach,
    That when the Air doth dance her finest measure
    Then art thou born, the gods' and men's sweet
    pleasure.

47

' "Lastly, where keep the Winds their revelry,
Their violent turnings and wild whirling hays,
But in the Air's tralucent gallery,
Where she herself is turned a hundred ways   325
While with those maskers wantonly she plays?
    Yet in this misrule they such rule embrace
    As two at once encumber not the place.

48

' "If then Fire, Air, wandering and fixed lights   330
In every province of the imperial sky,
Yield perfect forms of Dancing to your sights,
In vain I teach the ear that which the eye
With certain view already doth descry;
    But for your eyes perceive not all they see,   335
    In this I will your senses' master be:

49

' "For lo, the sea that fleets about the land   *Of the sea*
And like a girdle clips her solid waist
Music and measure both doth understand,
For his great crystal eye is always cast   340
Up to the Moon and on her fixed fast;
    And as she danceth in her pallid sphere,
    So danceth he about the centre here.

50

' "Sometimes his proud green waves in order set
One after other flow unto the shore,   345
Which, when they have with many kisses wet,
They ebb away in order, as before;
And to make known his courtly love the more
     He oft doth lay aside his three-forked mace
     And with his arms the timorous Earth embrace.   350

51

' "Only the Earth doth stand forever still:
He rocks remove not, nor her mountains meet
(Although some wits enriched with learning's skill
Say heaven stands firm and that the earth doth fleet
And swiftly turneth underneath their feet);   355
     Yet, though the Earth is ever steadfast seen,
     On her broad breast hath Dancing ever been.

52

Of the rivers ' "For those blue veins that through her body spread,
Those sapphire streams which from great hills do spring
(The Earth's great dugs; for every wight is fed   360
With sweet fresh moisture from them issuing)
Observe a dance in their wild wandering;
     And still their dance begets a murmur sweet,
     And still the murmur with the dance doth meet.

53

' "Of all their ways I love Meander's path   365
Which, to the tunes of dying swans, doth dance
Such winding sleights: such turns and tricks he hath,
Such creeks, such wrenches, and such dalliance
That (whether it be hap or heedless chance)
     In this indented course and wriggling play   370
     He seems to dance a perfect cunning hay.

54

' "But wherefore do these streams forever run?
To keep themselves forever sweet and clear;
For let their everlasting course be done
They straight corrupt and foul with mud appear.   375

O ye sweet nymphs that beauty's loss do fear,
 Contemn the drugs that physic doth devise
 And learn of Love this dainty exercise.

55

' "See how those flowers, that have sweet beauty too
(The only jewels that the earth doth wear),   380
When the young Sun in bravery her doth woo,
As oft as they the whistling wind do hear
Do wave their tender bodies here and there;
 And though their dance no perfect measure is,
 Yet oftentimes their music makes them kiss.   385

*Of other
things upon
the earth*

56

' "What makes the vine about the elm to dance
With turnings, windings, and embracements round?
What makes the lodestone to the north advance
His subtle point, as if from thence he found
His chief attractive virtue to redound?   390
 Kind Nature first doth cause all things to love:
 Love makes them dance and in just order move.

57

' "Hark how the birds do sing, and mark then how,
Jump with the modulation of their lays,
They lightly leap and skip from bough to bough.   395
Yet do the cranes deserve a greater praise
Which keep such measure in their airy ways
 As when they all in order ranked are
 They make a perfect form triangular:

58

' "In the chief angle flies the watchful guide,   400
And all the followers their heads do lay
On their foregoers' backs, on either side;
But for the captain hath no rest to stay
His head, forwearied with the windy way
 He back retires; and then the next behind,   405
 As his lieutenant, leads them through the wind.

59

' "But why relate I every singular,
Since all the world's great fortunes and affairs
Forward and backward raped and whirled are
According to the music of the spheres,   410
And Chance herself her nimble feet upbears
    On a round slippery wheel that rolleth aye,
    And turns all states with her imperious sway?

60

' "Learn then to dance, you that are princes born
And lawful lords of earthly creatures all: 415
Imitate them, and thereof take no scorn
(For this new art to them is natural)
And imitate the stars celestial;
    For when pale Death your vital twist shall sever,
    Your better parts must dance with them forever." 420

61

'Thus Love persuades, and all the crown of men
That stands around doth make a murmuring,
As when the wind, loosed from his hollow den,
Among the trees a gentle bass doth sing,
Or as a brook through pebbles wandering: 425
    But in their looks they uttered this plain speech,
    That they would learn to dance if Love would teach.

62

How Love taught men to dance. Rounds, or country dances.

'Then first of all he doth demonstrate plain
The motions seven that are in nature found:
Upward and downward, forth and back again,   430
To this side and to that, and turning round:
Whereof a thousand brawls he doth compound,
    Which he doth teach unto the multitude,
    And ever with a turn they must conclude.

63

'As when a nymph, arising from the land,   435
Leadeth a dance with her long watery train
Down to the sea: she wries to every hand

And every way doth cross the fertile plain;
But when at last she falls into the main,
    Then all her traverses concluded are   440
    And with the sea her course is circular.

64

'Thus when at first Love had them marshalled
(As erst he did the shapeless mass of things)
He taught them rounds and winding hays to tread,
And about trees to cast themselves in rings: 445
As the two Bears, whom the first mover flings
    With a short turn about heaven's axle-tree,
    In a round dance for ever wheeling be.

65

'But after these, as men more civil grew,   *Measures*
He did more grave and solemn measures frame
With such fair order and proportion true,   450
And correspondence every way the same,
That no fault-finding eye did ever blame:
    For every eye was moved at the sight
    With sober wondering and with sweet delight.   455

66

'Not those young students of the heavenly book,
Atlas the great, Prometheus the wise,
Which on the stars did all their lifetime look,
Could ever find such measures in the skies,
So full of change and rare varieties;   460
    Yet all the feet whereon these measures go
    Are only spondees, solemn, grave, and slow.

67

'But for more divers and more pleasing show,   *Galliards*
A swift and wandering dance he did invent,
With passages uncertain, to and fro,
Yet with a certain answer and consent   465
To the quick music of the instrument:
    Five was the number of the music's feet,
    Which still the dance did with five paces meet.

68

'A gallant dance, that lively doth bewray 470
A spirit and a virtue masculine:
Impatient that her house on earth should stay
(Since she herself is fiery and divine),
Oft doth she make her body upward flyne
　　With lofty turns and caprioles in the air, 475
　　Which with the lusty tunes accordeth fair.

69

Corrantos 'What shall I name those current traverses,
That on a triple dactyl foot do run,
Close by the ground, with sliding passages
(Wherein that dancer greatest praise hath won 480
Which with best order can all orders shun;
　　For everywhere he wantonly must range,
　　And turn, and wind, with unexpected change)?

70

Lavoltas 'Yet is there one, the most delightful kind,
A lofty jumping, or a leaping round, 485
Where arm in arm two dancers are entwined
And whirl themselves with strict embracements bound,
And still their feet an anapaest do sound:
　　An anapaest is all their music's song,
　　Whose first two feet are short and third is long: 490

71

'As the victorious twins of Leda and Jove
(That taught the Spartans dancing on the sands
Of swift Eurotas) dance in heaven above,
Knit and united with eternal bands:
Among the stars their double image stands, 495
　　Where both are carried with an equal pace,
　　Together jumping in their turning race.

72

'This is the net wherein the Sun's bright eye
Venus and Mars entangled did behold,
For in this dance their arms they so imply 500

As each doth seem the other to enfold.
What if lewd wits another tale have told,
 Of jealous Vulcan, and of iron chains?
 Yet this true sense that forged lie contains.

73

'These various forms of Dancing Love did frame, 505
And besides these a hundred million mo;
And as he did invent he taught the same
With goodly gesture and with comely show,
Now keeping state, now humbly honouring low:
 And ever for the persons and the place 510 *Grace in*
 He taught most fit and best according grace.   *Dancing*

74

'For Love within his fertile working brain
Did then conceive those gracious virgins three
Whose civil moderation doth maintain
All decent order and conveniency 515
And fair respect and seemly modesty:
 And then he thought it fit they should be born,
 That their sweet presence Dancing might adorn.

75

'Hence is it that these Graces painted are
With hand in hand, dancing an endless round; 520
And with regarding eyes, that still beware
That there be no disgrace amongst them found:
With equal foot they beat the flowery ground,
 Laughing or singing as their passions will;
 Yet nothing that they do becomes them ill. 525

76

'Thus Love taught men, and men thus learned of Love
Sweet music's sound with feet to counterfeit:
Which was long time before high-thundering Jove
Was lifted up to heaven's imperial seat;
For though by birth he were the prince of Crete, 530
 Nor Crete nor heaven should the young prince
  have seen
 If dancers with their timbrels had not been.

371

77

The use and forms of Dancing in sundry affairs of man's life 'Since when all ceremonious mysteries,
All sacred orgies and religious rites,
All pomps and triumphs and solemnities,   535
All funerals, nuptials, and like public sights,
All parliaments of peace, and warlike fights,
  All learned arts, and every great affair
  A lively shape of dancing seems to bear.

78

'For what did he, who with his ten-tongued lute   540
Gave beasts and blocks an understanding ear;
Or rather into bestial minds and brute
Shed and infused the beams of Reason clear?
Doubtless for men that rude and savage were
  A civil form of dancing he devised,   545
  Wherewith unto their gods they sacrificed.

79

'So did Musaeus, so Amphion did,
And Linus with his sweet enchanting song,
And he whose hand the Earth of monsters rid
And had men's ears fast chained to his tongue,   550
And Theseus too, his wood-born slaves among,
  Used Dancing as the finest policy
  To plant religion and society.

80

'And therefore now the Thracian Orpheus' lyre
And Hercules himself are stellified,   555
And in high heaven, amidst the starry choir,
Dancing their parts, continually do slide;
So, on the zodiac, Ganymede doth ride,
  And so is Hebe, with the Muses nine,
  For pleasing Jove with dancing, made divine.   560

81

'Wherefore was Proteus said himself to change
Into a stream, a lion, and a tree,
And many other forms fantastic strange,

As in his fickle thought he wished to be,
But that he danced with such facility   565
    As, like a lion, he could pace with pride,
    Ply like a plant, and like a river slide?

82

'And how was Caeneus made at first a man,
And then a woman, then a man again,
But in a dance? which, when he first began,   570
He the man's part in measure did sustain,
But when he changed into a second strain
    He danced the woman's part another space,
    And then returned into his former place.

83

'Hence sprang the fable of Tiresias   575
That he the pleasure of both sexes tried:
For in a dance he man and woman was,
By often change of place from side to side.
But, for the woman easily did slide
    And smoothly swim with cunning hidden art,   580
    He took more pleasure in a woman's part.

84

'So to a fish Venus herself did change,
And swimming through the soft and yielding wave
With gentle motions did so smoothly range
As none might see where she the water drave: 585
But this plain truth that falsed fable gave,
    That she did dance with sliding easiness,
    Pliant and quick in wandering passages.

85

'And merry Bacchus practised dancing, too,
And to the Lydian numbers rounds did make.   590
The like he did in the Eastern India do,
And taught them all, when Phoebus did awake
And when at night he did his coach forsake,
    To honour heaven and heaven's great rolling eye
    With turning dances and with melody.   595

373

86

'Thus they who first did found a commonweal,
And they who first religion did ordain,
By Dancing first the peoples' hearts did steal;
Of whom we now a thousand tales do feign:
Yet do we now their perfect rules retain   600
  And use them still in such devices new
  As in the world, long since their withering, grew.

87

'For, after towns and kingdoms founded were,
Between great states arose well-ordered war;
Wherein most perfect measure doth appear,   605
Whether their well-set ranks respected are
In quadrant forms or semi-circular,
  Or else the march, when all the troops advance
  And to the drum in gallant order dance.

88

'And after wars, when white-winged Victory   610
Is with a glorious triumph beautified,
And everyone doth *Io Io* cry,
Whiles all in gold the conqueror doth ride,
The solemn pomp that fills the city wide
  Observes such rank and measure everywhere   615
  As if they all together dancing were.

89

'The like just order mourners do observe
(But with unlike affection and attire)
When some great man that nobly did deserve,
And whom his friends impatiently desire,   620
Is brought with honour to his latest fire:
  The dead corpse, too, in that sad dance is moved,
  As if both dead and living Dancing loved.

90

'A diverse cause, but like solemnity,
Unto the temple leads the bashful bride,   625
Which blusheth like the Indian ivory

374

Which is with tip of Tyrian purple dyed:
A golden troop doth pass on every side
  Of flourishing young men and virgins gay
  Which keep fair measure all the flowery way. 630

91

'And not alone the general multitude,
But those choice Nestors, which in council grave
Of cities and of kingdoms do conclude,
Most comely order in their sessions have:
Wherefore the wise Thessalians ever gave 635
  The name of "Leader of their Country's Dance"
  To him that had their country's governance.

92

'And those great masters of the Liberal Arts
In all their several schools do Dancing teach:
For humble Grammar first doth set the parts 640
Of congruent and well-according speech;
Which Rhetoric, whose state the clouds doth reach,
  And heavenly Poetry, do forward lead,
  And diverse measures diversely do tread.

93

'For Rhetoric, clothing Speech in rich array, 645
In looser numbers teacheth her to range
With twenty tropes, and turnings every way,
And várious figures, and licentious change;
But Poetry, with rule and order strange,
  So curiously doth move each single pace 650
  As all is marred if she one foot misplace.

94

'These arts of Speech the guides and marshals are:
The Logic leadeth Reason in a dance
(Reason, the Cynosure and bright lodestar
In this world's sea to avoid the rock of Chance), 655
For with close following and continuance
  One reason doth another so ensue
  As in conclusion still the dance is true.

375

95

'So Music to her own sweet tunes doth trip
With tricks of 3, 5, 8, 15, and more: 660
So doth the art of numbering seem to skip
From even to odd in her proportioned score:
So do those skills whose quick eyes do explore
    The just dimension both of earth and heaven
    In all their rules observe a measure even.   665

96

'Lo, this is Dancing's true nobility,
Dancing, the child of Music and of Love;
Dancing itself, both love and harmony,
Where all agree and all in order move;
Dancing, the art that all arts do approve: 670
    The fair character of the world's consent,
    The heaven's true figure, and the Earth's ornament.'

97

The queen (whose dainty ears had borne too long
The tedious praise of that she did despise),
Adding once more the music of the tongue   675
To the sweet speech of her alluring eyes,
Began to answer in such winning wise
    As that forthwith Antinous' tongue was tied,
    His eyes fast fixed, his ears were open wide.

98

'Forsooth (quoth she) great glory you have won   680
To your trim minion, Dancing, all this while,
By blazing him Love's first begotten son,
Of every ill the hateful father vile,
That doth the world with sorceries beguile,
    Cunningly mad, religiously profane,   685
    Wit's monster, reason's canker, sense's bane.

99

'Love taught the mother that unkind desire
To wash her hands in her own infant's blood;
Love taught the daughter to betray her sire

Into most base unworthy servitude;   690
Love taught the brother to prepare such food
    To feast his brother that the all-seeing Sun,
    Wrapped in a cloud, the wicked sight did shun.

100

'And even this self-same Love hath dancing taught:
An art that shows the idea of his mind   695
With vainness, frenzy, and misorder fraught,
Sometimes with blood and cruelties unkind:
For in a dance Tereus' mad wife did find
    Fit time and place, by murder of her son,
    To avenge the wrong his traitorous sire had   700
    done.

101

'What mean the mermaids when they dance and sing
But certain death unto the mariner?
What tidings do the dancing dolphins bring
But that some dangerous storm approacheth near?
Then sith both Love and Dancing liveries bear   705
    Of such ill hap, unhappy may I prove
    If, sitting free, I either dance or love!'

102

Yet once again Antinous did reply: *True Love*
'Great queen, condemn not Love the innocent   *inventor of*
For this mischievous Lust, which traitorously   710 *Dancing*
Usurps his name and steals his ornament;
For that true Love, which Dancing did invent,
    Is he that tuned the world's whole harmony
    And linked all men in sweet society.

103

'He first extracted from the earth-mingled mind   715
That heavenly fire or quintessence divine
Which doth such sympathy in Beauty find
As is between the elm and fruitful vine
And so to Beauty ever doth incline:
    Life's life it is, and cordial to the heart,   720
    And of our better part the better part.

104

'This is true Love, by that true Cupid got,
Which danceth galliards in your amorous eyes,
But to your frozen heart approacheth not:
Only your heart he dares not enterprise.   725
And yet through every other part he flies,
    And everywhere he nimbly danceth now,
      Though in yourself yourself perceive not how.

105

'For your sweet beauty, daintily transfused
With due proportion throughout every part,   730
What is it but a dance where Love hath used
His finer cunning and more curious art
Where all the elements themselves impart,
    And turn, and wind, and mingle with such measure,
      That the eye that sees it surfeits with the   735
        pleasure?

106

'Love in the twinkling of your eyelids danceth,
Love danceth in your pulses and your veins,
Love, when you sew, your needle's point advanceth,
And makes it dance a thousand curious strains
Of winding rounds, whereof the form remains,   740
    To show that your fair hands can dance the hay,
      Which your fine feet would learn as well as they.

107

'And when your ivory fingers touch the strings
Of any silver-sounding instrument,
Love makes them dance to those sweet murmurings   745
With busy skill and cunning excellent:
O that your feet those tunes would represent
    With artificial motions to and fro,
      That Love this art in every part might show.

108

'Yet your fair soul, which came from heaven above   750
To rule this house, another heaven below,
With divers powers in harmony doth move;

And all the virtues that from her do flow
In a round measure hand in hand do go.
    Could I now see, as I conceive, this dance,   755
    Wonder and love would cast me in a trance.

109

'The richest jewel in all the heavenly treasure
That ever yet unto the Earth was shown
Is perfect Concord, the only perfect pleasure   *Concord.*
That wretched Earth-born men have ever known;   760
For many hearts it doth compound in one,
    That whatso one doth will, or speak, or do,
    With one consent they all agree thereto.

110

'Concord's true picture shineth in this art,
Where divers men and women ranked be,   765
And every one doth dance a several part,
Yet all as one in measure do agree,
Observing perfect uniformity:
    All turn together, all together trace,
    And all together honour and embrace.   770

111

'If they, whom sacred Love hath linked in one,
Do as they dance in all their course of life,
Never shall burning grief nor bitter moan
Nor factious difference nor unkind strife
Arise betwixt the husband and the wife: 775
    For whether forth, or back, or round he go,
    As the man doth so must the woman do.

112

'What if, by often interchange of place,
Sometime the woman gets the upper hand?
That is but done for more delightful grace,   780
For on that part she doth not ever stand,
But as the measure's law doth her command
    She wheels about and, ere the dance doth end,
    Into her former place she doth transcend.

113

'But not alone this correspondence meet 785
And uniform consent doth Dancing praise,
Comeliness. For Comeliness, the child of Order sweet,
Enamels it with her eye-pleasing rays:
Fair Comeliness ten hundred thousand ways
　　Through dancing sheds itself and makes its shine 790
　　With glorious beauty and with grace divine.

114

'For Comeliness is a disposing fair
Of things and actions in fit time and place,
Which doth in Dancing show itself most clear
When troops confused, which here and there do trace 795
Without distinguishment or bounded space,
　　By Dancing's rule into such ranks are brought
　　As glads the eye and ravisheth the thought.

115

'Then why should Reason judge that reasonless
Which is Wit's offspring and the work of Art, 880
Image of Concord and of Comeliness?
Who sees a clock moving in every part,
A sailing pinnace, or a wheeling cart,
　　But thinks that Reason, ere it came to pass,
　　The first impulsive cause and mover was? 805

116

'Who sees an army all in rank advance
But deems a wise commander is in place
Which leadeth on that brave victorious dance?
Much more in Dancing's art, in Dancing's grace,
Blindness itself may Reason's footstep trace: 810
　　For of Love's maze it is the curious plot,
　　And of man's fellowship the true-love knot.

117

'But if these eyes of yours (lodestars of love,
Showing the world's great dance to your mind's eye)
Cannot with all their demonstrations move 815

Kind apprehension in your fantasy
Of Dancing's virtue and nobility,
    How can my barbarous tongue win you thereto,
    Which heaven and Earth's fair speech could never
      do?

118

'O Love my king: if all my wit and power   820
Have done you all the service that they can,
O be you present in this present hour,
And help your servant and your true liegeman:
End that persuasion which I erst began.
    For who in praise of Dancing can persuade   825
    With such sweet force as Love, which
      Dancing made?'

119

Love heard his prayer and, swifter than the wind,   *A passage to*
Like to a page in habit, face, and speech,   *the*
He came, and stood Antinous behind,   *description*
And many secrets to his thoughts did teach.   *of Dancing*
At last a crystal mirror he did reach   830 *in this age.*
    Unto his hands, that he with one rash view
    All forms therein by Love's revealing knew.

120

And, humbly honouring, gave it to the queen
With this fair speech: 'See, fairest queen (quoth he), 835
The fairest sight that ever shall be seen,
And the only wonder of posterity,
The richest work in Nature's treasury;
    Which she disdains to show on this world's stage,
    And thinks it far too good for our rude age.   840

121

'But in another world divided far,
In the great fortunate triangled isle
Thrice twelve degrees removed from the north star,
She will this glorious workmanship compile
Which she hath been conceiving all this while   845
    Since the world's birth, and will bring forth at last

When six and twenty hundred years are past.'

122

Penelope the queen, when she had viewed
The strange eye-dazzling admirable sight,
Fain would have praised the state and pulchritude;   850
But she was stroken dumb with wonder quite.
Yet her sweet mind retained her thinking might:
  Her ravished mind in heavenly thoughts did dwell,
  But what she thought no mortal tongue can tell.

123

You, lady Muse, whom Jove the counsellor   855
Begot of Memory, Wisdom's treasuress,
To your divining tongue is given a power
Of uttering secrets large and limitless:
You can Penelope's strange thoughts express
  Which she conceived, and then would fain have   860
   told,
  When she the wondrous crystal did behold.

124

Her winged thoughts bore up her mind so high
As that she weened she saw the glorious throne
Where the bright Moon doth sit in majesty:
A thousand sparkling stars about her shone,   865
But she herself did sparkle more alone
  Than all those thousand beauties would have done
  If they had been confounded all in one.

125

And yet she thought those stars moved in such measure
To do their sovereign honour and delight   870
As soothed her mind with sweet enchanting pleasure,
Although the various change amazed her sight
And her weak judgment did entangle quite.
  Beside, their moving made them shine more clear,
  As diamonds moved more sparkling do appear.   875

126

This was the picture of her wondrous thought;
But who can wonder that her thought was so,

Sith Vulcan, king of Fire, that mirror wrought
(Who things to come, present, and past doth know)
And there did represent in lively show   880
    Our glorious English court's divine image,
    As it should be in this our golden age.

127

Away, Terpsichore, light Muse, away,
And come, Urania, prophetess divine:
Come, Muse of heaven, my burning thirst allay: 885
Even now for want of sacred drink I tine.
In heavenly moisture dip this pen of mine,
    And let my mouth with nectar overflow,
    For I must more than mortal glory show.

128

O that I had Homer's abundant vein   890
I would hereof another *Ilias* make;
Or else the man of Mantua's charmed brain,
In whose large throat great Jove the Thunderer spake.
O that I could old Geoffrey's Muse awake,
    Or borrow Colin's fair heroic style,   895
    Or smooth my rhymes with Delia's servant's file;

129

O could I, sweet companion, sing like you,
Which of a shadow under a shadow sing;
Or like fair Salice's sad lover true,
Or like the bee, the marigold's darling,   900
Whose sudden verse Love covers with his wing:
    O that your brains were mingled all with mine.
    To enlarge my wit for this great work divine.

130

Yet Astrophel might one for all suffice,
Whose supple Muse chameleon-like doth change   905
Into all forms of excellent device:
So might the swallow, whose swift Muse doth range
Through rare ideas and inventions strange,
    And ever doth enjoy her joyful spring,
    And sweeter than the nightingale doth sing.   910

131

O that I might that singing swallow hear,
To whom I owe my service and my love:
His sugared tunes would so enchant mine ear
And in my mind such sacred fury move
As I should knock at heaven's great gate above   915
    With my proud rhymes, while of this heavenly state
    I do aspire the shadow to relate.

FINIS.

[In 1622 Davies cancelled stanzas 127–31 and supplied the
following statement and stanzas]

Here are wanting some stanzas describing Queen
Elizabeth. Then follow these.

(127a)

Her brighter dazzling beams of majesty
Were laid aside, for she vouchsafed awhile
With gracious, cheerful, and familiar eye
Upon the revels of her court to smile:
For so Time's journeys she doth oft beguile,
    Like sight no mortal eye might elsewhere see,
    So full of state, art, and variety.

(128a)

For of her barons brave and ladies fair
(Who had they been elsewhere most fair had been)
Many an incomparable lovely pair
With hand in hand were interlinked seen,
Making fair honour to their sovereign Queen:
    Forward they paced and did their pace apply
    To a most sweet and solemn melody.

(129a)

So subtle and curious was the measure,
With such unlooked for change in every strain,
As that Penelope, rapt with sweet pleasure,
Weened she beheld the true proportion plain
Of her own web, weaved and unweaved again:

But that her art was somewhat less, she thought,
And on a mere ignoble subject wrought

(130a)

For here, like to the silkworm's industry,
Beauty itself out of itself did weave
So rare a work and of such subtlety
As did all eyes entangle and deceive
And in all minds a strange impression leave:
    In this sweet labyrinth did Cupid stray,
    And never had the power to pass away.

(131a)

As when the Indians, neighbours of the morning,
In honour of the cheerful rising Sun,
With pearl and painted plumes themselves adorning
A solemn stately measure have begun,
The god, well-pleased with that fair honour done,
    Sheds forth his beams and doth their faces kiss
    With that immortal glorious face of his,

(132a)

So &c. &c.

ABBREVIATIONS

Agrippa (1651): H. C. AGRIPPA, *Three Books of Occult Philosophy*, tr. J.F. (London, 1651).

Alciati (1551): ANDREA ALCIATI, *Emblemata* (Lyons, 1551).

Allen (1970): D. C. ALLEN, *Mysteriously Meant: The Rediscovery of Pagan Symbolism and Allegorical Interpretation in the Renaissance* (1970).

Allen (1963): R. H. ALLEN, *Star Names: Their Lore and Meaning* (1963 edn).

Ansell Robin (1932): P. ANSELL ROBIN, *Animal Lore in English Literature* (1932).

Brooks-Davies (1977): DOUGLAS BROOKS-DAVIES, *Spenser's 'Faerie Queene': A Critical Commentary on Books I and II* (1977).

Brooks-Davies (1983): DOUGLAS BROOKS-DAVIES, *The Mercurian Monarch: Magical Politics from Spenser to Pope* (1983).

Burrow (1986): J. A. BURROW, *The Ages of Man* (1986).

Chew (1962): S. C. CHEW, *The Pilgrimage of Life* (1962).

Comes (1567): NATALIS COMES, *Mythologiae* (Venice, 1567).

Curtius (1967): E. R. CURTIUS, *European Literature and the Latin Middle Ages*, tr. W. R. Trask (1967).

D'Ancona (1983): MIRELLA LEVI D'ANCONA, *Botticelli's 'Primavera': A Botanical Interpretation, Including Astrology, Alchemy and the Medici* (1983).

DNB: Dictionary of National Biography.

Fowler (1975): A. D. S. FOWLER, *Conceitful Thought: The Interpretation of English Renaissance Poems* (1975).

Fraunce (1592): ABRAHAM FRAUNCE, *The Third Part of the Countesse of Pembrokes Yvychurch* (London, 1592).

Harrier (1975): R. E. HARRIER, *The Canon of Sir Thomas Wyatt's Poetry* (1975).

Heninger (1977): S. K. HENINGER, JR, *The Cosmographical Glass: Renaissance Diagrams of the Universe* (1977).

Henkel and Schöne (1967): ARTHUR HENKEL AND ALBRECHT SCHÖNE, *Emblemata* (1967).

Hutton (1984): JAMES HUTTON, *Themes of Peace in Renaissance Poetry*, ed. Rita Guerlac (1984).

Kantorowicz (1958): E. H. KANTOROWICZ, *Laudes Regiae: A Study in Liturgical Acclamations and Mediaeval Ruler Worship* (1958).

Klibansky, Saxl, Panofsky (1964): RAYMOND KLIBANSKY, FRITZ SAXL, ERWIN PANOFSKY, *Saturn and Melancholy* (1964).

Linche (1599): RICHARD LINCHE, *The Fountaine of Ancient Fiction* (London, 1599).

Mason (1959): H. A. MASON, *Humanism and Poetry in the Early Tudor Period* (1959).

Ovid, *Met.*: OVID, *Metamorphoses*, tr. Arthur Golding (1567), ed. J. F. Nims (1961). *Note*: all line refs are to this edition unless otherwise stated.

Panofsky (1955): ERWIN PANOFSKY, *Meaning in the Visual Arts* (1955 edn).

Panofsky (1962): ERWIN PANOFSKY, *Studies in Iconology: Humanistic Themes in the Art of the Renaissance* (1962 edn).

Peacham (1612): HENRY PEACHAM, *Minerva Britanna* (London, 1612).

Petrarch, tr. Morley (1971): *Lord Morley's 'Triumphs of Fraunces Petrarcke': The First English Translation of the 'Trionfi'*, ed. D. D. Carnicelli (1971).

Ripa (1603): CESARE RIPA, *Iconologia* (Rome, 1603).

Sessions (1986): W. A. SESSIONS, *Henry Howard, Earl of Surrey* (1986).

Seznec (1961): JEAN SEZNEC, *The Survival of the Pagan Gods: The Mythological Tradition and Its Place in Renaissance Humanism and Art*, tr. B. F. Sessions (1961 edn).

Sidney, *Misc. Prose* (1973): *Miscellaneous Prose of Sir Philip Sidney*, ed. Kathleen Duncan-Jones and Jan van Dorsten (1973).

Spenser, *FQ*: EDMUND SPENSER, *The Faerie Queene* (1596).

Stevens (1961): JOHN STEVENS, *Music and Poetry in the Early Tudor Court* (1961).

Strong (1987): ROY STRONG, *The Cult of Elizabeth* (1987 edn).

Taylor (1969): *Thomas Taylor the Platonist: Selected Writings*, ed. Kathleen Raine and G. M. Harper (1969).

Tervarent (1958): GUY DE TERVARENT, *Attributs et Symboles dans l'Art Profane 1450–1600* (1958).

Thomson (1964): PATRICIA THOMSON, *Sir Thomas Wyatt and His Background* (1964).

Tilley: M. P. TILLEY, *A Dictionary of Proverbs in England in the Sixteenth and Seventeenth Centuries* (1950).

Tillyard (1929): E. M. W. TILLYARD, *The Poetry of Sir Thomas Wyatt: A Selection and a Study* (1929).

Tuve (1966): ROSEMOND TUVE, *Allegorical Imagery: Some Mediaeval Books and Their Posterity* (1966).

Valeriano (1602): PIERIO VALERIANO, *Hieroglyphica* (Lyons, 1602).

Warner (1985): MARINA WARNER, *Monuments and Maidens: The Allegory of the Female Form* (1985).

Whiting (1968): B. J. WHITING, *Proverbs, Sentences and Proverbial Phrases from English Writings Mainly before 1500* (Leyden, 1968).

Whitney (1586): GEOFFREY WHITNEY, *A Choice of Emblemes* (1586).

Wilkins (1969): EITHNE WILKINS, *The Rose-Garden Game: The Symbolic Background to the European Prayer-Beads* (1969).

Wilson (1939): E. C. WILSON, *England's Eliza* (1939).

Wind (1967): EDGAR WIND, *Pagan Mysteries in the Renaissance* (1967 edn).

Yates (1975a): FRANCES YATES, *Astraea: The Imperial Theme in the Sixteenth Century* (1975).

Yates (1975b): FRANCES YATES, *The Rosicrucian Enlightenment* (1975 edn).

Yates (1978): *Giordano Bruno and the Hermetic Tradition* (1978).

NOTES

SIR THOMAS WYATT

The Wyatt canon and the question of textual authority

Several manuscript and printed sources exist for W's poems, the most important of which are: Egerton MS 2711 (abbrev. E); Devonshire MS Add 17492 (abbrev. D); the Arundel Harington MS (A); the Blage MS (B) and (the primary printed source) *Songes and Sonettes, written by the ryght honorable Lorde Henry Howard late Earle of Surrey, and other* (1557), otherwise known by its printer's name as *Tottel's Miscellany* (T). E contains fair copies of many of W's poems and some poems and corrections in W's own hand. Many of its poems are explicitly ascribed to W. D, like the other MSS, is a miscellany of poems by W and others without the authority of the poet's own handwriting. It contains poems not in E and ascribed to W, but those poems that it does share with E seem to be earlier versions than those in E. A appears to derive from E with clear evidence of editorial modification; while B is another miscellany which was early on in the possession of W's friend Sir George Blage but which is now generally agreed to have little textual authority. T prints a large block of poems by W for some of which there is no other source. Although based on accurate sources, its texts are the product of considerable editorial tampering, however: the result of Tottel's refusal to accept W's metrical 'roughnesses'. Editors generally accept as W's those attributed to him by contemporary or near-contemporary sources. There are, though, many anonymous poems which 'sound' like W but could well be the work of any other talented courtier. I have printed some of these doubtful attributions while for the most part printing poems known to be by W. In all cases I have indicated authenticity and the primary MS (or printed) source upon which my text is based. I have included a few textual notes.

Order

There is some feeling that the order preserved in E might be chronological. In deference to this I have adopted the following strategy: I have tried to give the modern reader a set of bearings by following the lead of the Penguin editor, Rebholz, by subdividing the poems generically into sonnets, epigrams, etc. Within each group I have printed poems from E first and in the order in which they appear in E. Other than that, the order is my own, often thematic, one.

Metre

Modernisation has several disadvantages, a main one being, in the case of W, the obscuring of metrical intention (e.g. no. 72 with its refrain 'What means this?' which, in the original spelling 'What meyns thys' immediately gains an extra syllable). In addition to these local problems there is the larger scale question, how far were W's longer lines attempting to become (and falling short of) the iambic pentameter paradigm? T clearly thought W's ear inexpert and modified accordingly. Modern thinking inclines (allowing for scribal error and other imponderables) to trust the poems: to detect the heavy thump of the mediaeval alliterative line where relevant; to be aware of the strong possibility of romance (esp. French) pronunciations and accentuations, etc.: to approach each poem, in other words, with as few metrical preconceptions as possible.

Modern editions

The Works of Henry Howard, Earl of Surrey, and of Sir Thomas Wyatt, the Elder, ed. G. F. Nott, 2 vols (London, 1815–16; repr. 1965).

The Poems of Sir Thomas Wiat, ed. A. K. Foxwell, 2 vols (London: Univ. of London Press, 1913).

The Poetry of Sir Thomas Wyatt: A Selection and a Study, ed. E. M. W. Tillyard (London: Scholartis Press, 1929).

The Collected Poems of Sir Thomas Wyatt, ed. Kenneth Muir (London: Routledge and Kegan Paul, 1949).

Sir Thomas Wyatt and his Circle: Unpublished Poems, ed. Kenneth Muir (Liverpool: Liverpool University Press, 1961).

Collected Poems of Sir Thomas Wyatt, ed. Kenneth Muir and Patricia Thomson (Liverpool: Liverpool University Press, 1969).

Sir Thomas Wyatt: Collected Poems, ed. Joost Daalder (London: Oxford University Press, 1975).

Sir Thomas Wyatt: The Complete Poems, ed. R. A. Rebholz (Harmondsworth: Penguin, 1978).

Sir Thomas Wyatt, a Literary Portrait: Selected Poems, with Full Notes, Commentaries and a Critical Introduction, ed. H. A. Mason (Bristol: Bristol Classical Press, 1986).

Note also:

Tottel's Miscellany (1557–87), ed. H. E. Rollins, 2 vols (Cambridge, Mass.: Harvard University Press, 1928; rev. edn 1965).

The Arundel Harington Manuscript of Tudor Poetry, ed. Ruth Hughey, 2
    vols (Columbus, Ohio: Ohio State University Press, 1960).
Songes and Sonnettes (Tottel's Miscellany) 1557 (Menston, Yorks.:
    Scolar Press, 1967).

On textual and canonical problems the following are essential
reading:

RAYMOND SOUTHALL, *The Courtly Maker: An Essay on the Poetry of
    Wyatt and his Contemporaries* (Oxford: Basil Blackwell, 1964).
H. A. MASON, *Editing Wyatt* (Cambridge: Cambridge Quarterly
    Publications, 1972).
R. C. HARRIER, *The Canon of Sir Thomas Wyatt's Poetry* (Cambridge,
    Mass.: Harvard U.P., 1975).

FURTHER READING

CALDWELL, E. C. 'Recent Studies in Sir Thomas Wyatt (1970–87)',
    English Literary Renaissance, 19 (1989).
CHAMBERS, E. K. *Sir Thomas Wyatt and Some Collected Studies* (1933).
DAALDER, JOOST. 'Editing Wyatt', *Essays in Criticism*, 23 (1973).
ESTRIN, B. L. 'Becoming the Other/the Other Becoming in Wyatt's
    Poetry', *ELH: A Journal of English Literary History*, 51 (1984).
FERRY, ANNE. *The 'Inward' Language: Sonnets of Wyatt, Sidney,
    Shakespeare, Donne* (1983).
FISHMAN, BURTON. 'Recent Studies in Wyatt and Surrey', *English
    Literary Renaissance*, 1 (1971).
FOLEY, S. M. *Sir Thomas Wyatt* (1990).
FOXWELL, A. K. *A Study of Sir Thomas Wyatt's Poems* (1911).
HANGEN, E. C. *A Concordance to the Complete Poetical Works of Sir
    Thomas Wyatt* (1941).
HARDING, D. W. 'The Rhythmical Intention in Wyatt's Poetry', *Scrutiny*,
    14 (1946).
JENTOFT, C. W. *Sir Thomas Wyatt and Henry Howard, Earl of Surrey: A
    Reference Guide* (1980).
MASON, H. A. *Humanism and Poetry in the Early Tudor Period* (1959).
MUIR, KENNETH. *Life and Letters of Sir Thomas Wyatt* (1963).
PETERSON, D. L. *The English Lyric from Wyatt to Donne* (1967).
ROSS, D. M. *Self-Revelation and Self-Protection in Wyatt's Lyric Poetry*
    (1988).
SPEARING, A. C. *Medieval to Renaissance in English Poetry* (1985).
STEVENS, JOHN. *Music and Poetry in the Early Tudor Court* (1961).
THOMSON, PATRICIA. 'Wyatt and the Petrarchan Commentators',
    Review of Engish Studies, 10 (1959).
THOMSON, PATRICIA. *Sir Thomas Wyatt and his Background* (1964).
THOMSON, PATRICIA. *Wyatt: The Critical Heritage* (1974).

Note: the abbrevn MT denotes the Muir-Thomson edn of 1969.
Number in bold at the beginning of each note denotes number given to
each poem in this edition.

SONNETS: note the indebtedness to Petrarch.

1 E; T attribs to W; transln of Petrarch, *rime*, 102. 1–4: Julius Caesar
wept crocodile tears when sent Pompey's head by Ptolemy (Lucan, *Civil
War*, 9. 1035–41); 5–8: mentioned, e.g., by Petrarch in one of his letters
(MT, 264).

2 E attribs to W; imitn of Petrarch, *rime* 190 (or of imitns of Petrarch):
may refer to W's relnship with Anne Boleyn when Henry VIII claimed
her (MT, 267); 6 *deer*: punning on *dear*; 8 *net . . . wind*: proverbial
(Tilley W 416); 11 *diamonds*: chastity, good faith, fortitude (Tervarent
(1958), cols 147–8); 13 *Noli . . . am*: 'Touch me not' (Christ to Mary
Magdalene in John 20:17); Matt. 22:21 ('Render therefore unto Caesar
the things which are Caesar's'). But as a Latin motto it was inscribed on
the collars of Caesar's deer. Caesar here = presumably Henry VIII.

3 E attribs to W; transln of *rime*, 82. 1 *Was I never*: I have never
been. . . ; 6 *yfixed*: Chaucerian archaism (= fixed).

4 E attribs to W; transln of *rime*, 224. 2 *lovely*: loving (Petr. has *cortese*);
4 *error*: wandering; 6 *sparkling*: dispersing, scattering (Petr's *interotte*:
halting).

5 E attribs to W; no source. For the iconography of Love (Cupid) see
Sidney, *Arcadia* poems 2n below. 3 *Seneca*: stoic philosopher (d. AD 65.)
who advised detachment from worldliness; *Plato* directed that mundane
love was insignificant in comparison with the contemplation of Good-
ness, Truth and Beauty; 8 *liever*: i.e. liefer (preferable).

6 E attribs to W; transl. from 2 consecutive *strambotti* by Serafino
d'Aquilano (d. 1500): MT, 279–80. 14: proverbial (Tilley S87 and
S184).

7 E attribs to W; no source. 1–3 *file* = (i) polish/polishing (ii) rascal
(*OED File* sb 4) (iii) defile; 4 *frame*: shape; 8 *guiled*: beguiled, deceived.

8 E attribs to W; transln of *rime*, 134. 4 *seize on*: E reads *seson*,
modernised by Daalder as 'season', citing *OED Season* v. 5, 'to seize
upon'; 5 *That*: Love; 13 *Death, Life* D: lyffe and deth E.

9 E attribs to W; transln of *rime*, 189. The ship allegory is a common-
place: e.g. Wyatt nos **67** and **80** below and Sidney, *Certain Sonnets*, **4**
below. 3 *rock and rock*: Petr. has Scylla and Charybdis, tradnlly assoc.
with lust and greed (Allen (1970), 150); *enemy*: Cupid; 6 *light*: trivial;
case: (i) circumstance, (ii) body; 12 *stars*: the lady's eyes (as in Sidney, *AS*
26, etc.).

10 E attribs to W; transln of *rime*, 173. 1 *Advising*: gazing at; 2 *he*:
Cupid; 6 *he . . . he*: Cupid . . . the mind; 5 *sweet bitter*: Petr's *dolce . . .
amar* (l.5) invites W to recall the Ital. *amare/amaro* pun (love/bitter): cf.
Wind (1967), 92, and 161–2 on its Sapphic origins, and Fraunce (1592),

46; 8 *fire*: the lover's desire; *ice*: the lady's frigidity; 14 *root . . . fruit*: looks back to l.5 (*worldly paradise*) and hints at Venus's assocn with the apples of love (Wind, 84–5 and Sidney *Arcadia* poems 20 below).

11 E attribs to W; transln of *rime*, 21. 3 *do not use*: are not accustomed; 5 *other*: i.e. woman; 12 *natural kind*: the heart's natural function is (i) to pump the blood of life (ii) to love.

12 E attribs to W; transl. from a sonnet attrib. to Jacopo Sannazaro (d. 1530): MT, 295. 6 *tire*: tear (from falconry); 13 *the restless* (MT): that restlesse E and A; but see Daalder, 29n.

13 E; in W sects of A and T. In tradn of Petrarchan (and other mediaeval) dream poems. 6 *mew*: den, prison (i.e. bed); 7: i.e. made me wake up (*sprite* = breath (*spiritus*), soul); 9 *body dead*: i.e. in sleep (hence *unaware of pain*) the dreamer's mind roams free and has its *delight*.

14 E attribs to W. There are a few echoes of Chaucer. 2 *lust*: pleasure; 3 *sluggardy*: Chaucer, *Knight's Tale* (1 (A) 1042): 'May wole have no slogardie a-nyght' and (for 4, *Arise . . . observance*), 1045: 'And seith "Arys, and do thyn observaunce' (also *Troilus and Criseyde*, 2.111–12), referring to 1st May celebrns (Ovid, *Fasti*, 5.185–6); 6–7: W had been imprisoned twice in May, in 1534 and 1536; 10 *ruler . . . May*: presumably Venus, whose main zodiacal sign Taurus rules the first three weeks of May (see 67.3n below); 9 *Sephame* (E): Sephances (A); Stephan (T): identif. as Edward Sephame, known to have cast a horoscope for Edward VI (Daalder, 83n).

15 E attribs to W. 1 *waker Care*: i.e., Care who prevents sleep; 3 *cheer*: face (*OED Cheer* sb 1); *distain*: colour (with blushing and pallor); 7 *refrain*: avoid; 8 *Brunet*: probably Anne Boleyn (the line is W's revision; original E read 'her that did set our country in a rore', which makes the identificn even clearer); 9 *Phyllis*: Elizabeth Darrell, the mistress of W's later years? (Chambers in MT, 335).

16 D. 1–2 *proverb*: Daalder cites Whiting (1968) A8: 'To him that abides shall betide well'.

17 A; T attribs to W. Imitn of Petrarch, *rime*, 269. T sees it as a love poem, entitling it 'The lover laments the death of his love', but it is more likely to be about the execn of W's patron Thomas Cromwell (28 July 1540). 1 *pillar*; emblem of constancy and magnificence as a moral virtue; 14 *ease* (T): cause (A): Daalder and Rebholz both amend to *cease*.

EPIGRAMS

Generically, witty brief poems with a pointed conclusion. Classical in origin; but W was inspired by the *strambotti* of Serafino d'Aquilano and the epigrams of Clément Marot (d. 1544).

18 E attribs to W.

19 E attribs to W. 6–8: allude to the neo-Platonic *mors osculi* (death of the kiss) tradn which signifies the union of mortal and immortal: Wind (1967), 154–7 ('Amor as a God of Death'): cf. Sidney, *AS* 81.5–6n below.

20 E attribs to W. Possibly (like **18**) infl. by John Skelton, *Philip Sparrow*, 210–29; 5 *blind master*: Cupid.

21 E attribs to W. W accompanied Henry VIII and Anne Boleyn to France in Oct. 1532 and here records, perhaps, his changed feelings towards her (cf. **2** and **15**). 8 *briers*: difficulties (with hints of obstacles to passion where the lady is the rose).

22 E attribs to W. 1 *The enemy*: Death; *all kind*: all living things; 5 *Despair*: cf. Sidney, *AS* 39n. below, and (more precisely) the exchange of arrows between Love and Death in Alciati (1551), 167 (*De Morte, & Amore*).

23 E attribs to W; transln from Serafino (MT, 317) but ll. 1, 3 and 8 are proverbial (Tilley R179, P457, W188): Daalder, 65.

24 E attribs to W; transln of anon. Ital. *strambotto* (MT, 319–20). For the story of the Mary who killed and devoured her infant at the siege of Jerusalem (AD 70), see Josephus, *Jewish War*, 6.2.4; W modifies his Italian source in the mother's favour. I have capitalised Pity and Famine to emphasise the element of psychomachia: for the personifications, see Ripa (1603), 401–3 and 63.

25 E attribs to W and entitles it 'In Spain', which W left in June 1539. 1 *Tagus*: Spanish and Portuguese river, the gravel of which was frequently compared to gold dust; 4 *gainward*: against (i.e. eastward); 5–6: London is like a crescent moon snuggling within the curves of the Thames. But *moon* is esp. appropriate since Brutus, legendary founder and namer of Britain, travelled here when instructed to do so in a dream by the moon goddess Diana (Geoffrey of Monmouth, *History of the Kings of Britain*, 1.11). He also founded Troynovant (London).

26 E; written in W's hand. On Cupid see **5**n above.

27 D; in W section. 7 *Tantalus*: see Sidney, *AS* 24n below.

28 A; in W section. The answer, it has been suggested, is either a kiss or the lady's virginity.

29 B.

30 D; in W section; transl. from Serafino (MT, 421).

31 A; in T's W section; transln of Seneca, *Thyestes*, 391–403. 1 *slipper*: slippery.

32 B; T attribs to W. Acrostic addressed to Lady Anne Stanhope, wife of Henry VIII's Master of the Horse, Sir Michael.

33 T attribs to W.

34 T attribs to W. Prob. written during W's imprisonment in early 1541. 1 *Lux* (T): Hill MS reads Luckes; probably the actual name of a bird and punning on *luck*; but the Latin spelling *Lux* (= Light) seems more appropriately to contrast with the darkness of prison.

35 B; transl. from a contemp. Latin epigram which masqueraded as being by Ausonius (MT, 397). Dido, queen and founder of Carthage, killed herself out of loyalty to her dead husband when pressed by neighbouring Iarbas to marry him; Virgil, *Aeneid* 4, narrates that she killed herself because betrayed by Aeneas (the 'lies' of l.8): see Ralegh, **27** below ('I am that Dido').

SATIRES

36 Written after one of W's periods of imprisonment in the Tower (1536 or 1541). Imitn of Alamanni's *Satire* 10 (in *Works*, 1532–3): MT, 347–9. The *terza rima* comes from Alamanni. For textual variants see MT, Daalder, Rebholz, A (ed Hughey), T (ed Rollins). 1 *John Poyntz*: one of Henry VIII's courtiers; 9 *stroke*: of whipping or execution (Anne Boleyn had been exec. in 1536); 10–13: it has always been my habit (*meant*) to esteem the great less than 'the common sort' do, who judge by externals...; 15–16: I am not one to attack Honour while desiring it; 18: I can no more readily become a liar than one can dye black another colour; 23 *Venus and Bacchus*: the goddess of love burgeons under the influence of the wine god. In the original Italian, and recalling the traditional assocn of the two (Chaucer, *Plt. of Fowls*, 260–75; Ovid, *Heroides*, 17.75–88, etc.); 27 *wolves... lambs*: not in original: W recalls Matt. 10:16; 32 *for*: instead of; 37 *state*: rule; 38 *damn*: sentence, condemn; 37–42: Livy, *History*, summaries 114 tells how Cato of Utica, after losing against Julius Caesar at the battle of Thapsus in 46 BC, committed suicide rather than fall into Caesar's hands; 45 *lion ... coward*: heraldic allusion (*OED Coward* adj. B 2): the *lion coward* is depicted with tail between legs; 48 *Alexander*: Alexander the Great (d. 323 BC), warrior and world conqueror; 48–9 *Pan ... Apollo*: alludes to the contest between Pan (the goat-man god of nature) on his reed pipes and Apollo (god of music and poetry) on his lyre: doltish Midas adjudged Pan the victor and was given the ears of an ass by Apollo in recompense (Ovid, *Met.* (1567) 11. 171–201); 50–1: *Sir Thopas* is Chaucer's parodic (and incomplete) chivalric tale (*CT* B^2 1902ff.); *The Knight's Tale* (I (A) 859ff.) is the genuine article; 67 *Favel*: personification of cunning and duplicity (*OED Favel* sb B 3); 84 *lusty leas*: pleasant fields; 86 *clog*; any impediment (e.g. the king's prohibition); proverbial (MT, 354); 100 *Kent and Christendom*: witty (and deeply felt, in view of W's birth place) reversal of the proverb 'in Kent or Christendom' (Tilley K 16 and Spenser, *Shep. Cal.*, 'Sept.', 153 and E.K.'s gloss (Kent remained unconverted under King Ethelbert and so 'was counted no part of Christendome')).

37 In W sections of A and T. Aesop's fable of the country and town mice was available in many versions to W: see Thomson (1964), 259–67. 3 *livelood*: livelihood; 9 *meat*: food (i.e. scarcely any food); 10 *dight*: put in order; 15 *wellaway*: alas; 45 *rood*: cross (of Christ); 53 *steaming*: shining, glaring; 60 *wondrous*: MSS and T read *wonders*; I agree with Rebholz in not treating it as a verb and modernising accordingly; 61 *tho*: then; 64 *silly*: unfortunate; 78 *sergeant*: guard; 81 *lust*: desire, will; 86 *grapes ... briers*: proverbial (Tilley G411: Daalder); 88 *hay*: net for catching rabbits (*conies*); 108–9 *Virtue*: for Virtue as a female (in contrast to the embraced *lusts* or harlots), sun bright and holding a spear to combat Vice, see (e.g.) Ripa (1603), 510–11.

38 E; in W sections of A and T. T's title: 'How to use the court and himself therein, written to Sir Francis Brian' (Brian = diplomat and confidant of Henry VIII; he was also a poet and apparently attracted to proverbs). Possibly written 1541; more likely mid 1530s. 1–4: cf. Tilley S738 and S885; 16 *nappy . . . nonce*: with a good head for the occasion; 18 *groins*: grunts; 19 *chaw*: chew; *moulded*: mildewed (mouldy); 20 *pearls*: Matt. 7:6; 21 *ass*: cf. Midas's punishment for not appreciating Apollo's lyre (36.48–9n above); 22 *sacks of dirt*: monks; 44: the assumption is that dogs don't like cheese and will let you have it back – with interest!; 45 *cant*: portion; 47 *Kitson*: not identified, but may be the wealthy upstart merchant Sir Thomas Kitson: Raymond Southall, 'Wyatt and Kitson', *Notes and Queries*, 219(1974), 403–4; 60 *deburse*: disburse; 65 *mule*: cf. W's rondeau 'Ye old mule' (MT no 35): in part a corruption of Latin *mulier* (woman); *bite . . . bridle*: proverbial (Tilley B670); 75 *Pandar*: who helped Troilus seduce Criseyde (Chaucer, *Tr. and Cris.*, Bk 3); 91 *water . . . sieve*: Tilley W111.

RONDEAUX

Introd. by W (give or take a few other examples) from French models (structural characteristics = 15 lines; a repeated refrain that circles back to the opening words; strictly limited rhyme sounds).

39 E attribs to W. Possibly imit. an unknown French rondeau with Petr., *rime*, 121 as source. 10 *hold*: gripped tight (imprisoned).
40 E attribs to W.
41 E attribs to W. 5 *appair*: impair; 12 *Iwis*: truly, certainly.
42 E attribs to W. Possible imitn of unknown French rondeau with Petr., *rime*, 153 as source.
43 E attribs to W.

CANZONI

A *canzone* is a stanzaic poem of some length with a complex rhyme scheme. Although W produced other poems that are arguably *canzoni* (see Rebholz, 383), I limit my labelling to 2 translns of Petrarchan *canzoni*.

44 A attribs to W, as does T; transln of *rime*, 360 (a *canzone*): MT, 267–71. 1 *enemy*: Cupid; *froward*: perverse; 2 *Queen*: Reason; *accited*: summoned; 8 *left foot*: appetite (MT citing commentator on Petr.): one's weaker (sinister) self; 18 *deceivable*: deceitful; 19 *prest*: lively, ready; 26 *araced*: araised (uplifted); 45 *strait pressions*: tight pressures (MT); 76 *sells*: betrays; *clattering*: chattering, talking idly; 81 *frame*: state; 84 *dastard*: dullard; 85 *Atrides*: son of Atreus (Agamemnon): for him and Achilles (87) see Homer's *Iliad*; 88 *Scipion*: Cornelius Scipio Africanus major, who defeated Carthaginian *Hannibal* (86) in 202 BC; 94 *under the moon*: i.e. on earth (the sublunary region in Ptolemaic astronomy): the

Notes

moon is also assoc. with earthly honour (Valeriano (1602), 44, *s.v.*
Nobilitas (p. 474); 100 *frame*: form; 101 *Gentleness*: Courtesy (as in
amour courtois); 111–12 *serpent . . . sting*: proverbial; 118 *Doubting*:
fearing; 124 *bit*: reverses the emblem of the bridle and bit of temperance
and restraint (Wind (1967), plate 41); 128–33: neo-Platonic (love as the
means to the divine): cf. Spenser, *Four Hymns*; 140: is the *price* Henry
VIII and the *she* Anne Boleyn?

45 In E in W's hand; title W's. W = ambassador to Spain between
June 1537 and June 1539. Transln of Petr's *canzone, rime* 37 (MT, 335–
7). Metre: poulter's measure. 4 *spindle*: belonging to the 3 classical Fates
who spin and cut the thread of human life; 6 *weal*: happiness; 12 *wrap*
(A): Daalder and Rebholz prefer D's *rape* (= seize): E has *wrape*: either
modernisation suits the sense; 15 *bend*: suggesting the movement of the
sun across the 2 hemispheres and *bend* = constrain (*OED Bend* v 2): W
as a prisoner of time; 24 *dear . . . face*: poss. Elizabeth Darrell (sonnet 15
above); 37 *mete*: measure out; 38 *them entermete*: place themselves
between; 40 *Phoebus*: Phoebus Apollo, the sun god; 42 *record*: memory;
bate: abate, diminish; 50 *bewray*: reveal; 51 *accumbered*: oppressed; 59
assay: try; 60 *fraughted*: freighted; 64 *case*: skin (cf. carcase); 69 *crisped*:
tightly curled; *pride*: exalted position; glory (i.e. the blazing midday sun),
but here referring to the beloved's hair (so that the *stars* are eyes); 78
train: draw; 87 *fro*: from; 88 *other will*: Henry VIII wished W to remain
at the Spanish Imperial court at the beginning of 1539 despite his anxiety
to return.

LYRICS (or songs): the largest body of W's output.

46 E attribs to W.
47 E attribs to W. 2 *reflection*: echo; 21 *meed*: reward.
48 E attribs to W. 1 *wot not*: this is the MS reading. T has 'I wot not
what to say'; Daalder and Rebholz print Maxwell's emendn (followed by
Mason (1972), 108) 'I not well' (where *not* = an ellipsis of *ne wot*); 5
joyous: trisyllable.
49 E attribs to W. E's first example of the concatenated form that was a
favourite with W (linking by repetn of last and succeeding first lines of
stanzas and overall circular structure). 18 *raked*: racked, tortured (as in
modern *racked with pain*); 30 *so hawks*: i.e. by deprivation.
50 E attribs to W. 2 *stalking*: walking softly, with hints of pursuing
game; 7 *Busily*: eagerly; 16 *gentleness*: confirms the poem's preoccupn
with the courtly love code; 17 *forsaking*: not necessarily abandonment:
maybe *refusal* of the lover's advances (*strange* = distant, cold in manner):
Fowler (1975), 14; 19 *newfangleness*: fickleness (and search for novelty);
20 *kindly*: ironic, or: according to her (cruel) nature.
51 E attribs to W.
52 E attribs to W. 4 *Forbear*: restrain.

397

53 E; A and D attrib to W. 1 *Fancy*: imagination, fantasy, also love (*OED Fancy* sb 8 b): cf. Spenser, *FQ*, III. xii. 7 (Fancy like a winged boy accompanied by Desire).

54 E attribs to W. 7 *mo*: more; 15 *overthwart*: perverse, contrary.

55 E attribs to W. Possibly based on pop. song, with echoes of a courtly love May game involving Robin Hood: Stevens (1961), 186–7. 1 *Robin*: affectionate and common name (not necess. Robin Hood); 2 *Jolly*: amorous; 3 *leman*: sweetheart; 12 *Le plaintif*: the one who complains (legal); with hints of lament (Fr. *plaintif*): cf. l. 24.

56 E attribs to W. 23 *mischief*: distress; 31 *ball*: Fortune tradnlly stands on a ball or wheel to suggest her inconstancy: Alciati (1551), 133; 33 *rede*: counsel, advice (bec. Despair always advises suicide).

57 E; A and D attrib. to W. 3 *Lust*: pleasure; *refused*: left; 8–9: maybe 'How did I fix my thought so steadfastly (on my beloved's constancy) without (realising that it would lead to) wretchedness (*dis-pleasure*)': *steadfastly* is undermined by fickle Fortune (l.10); 11 *revolted*: turned (revolved): see 56.31n; 31 *burden*: weight; (musical) refrain and bass line.

58 E attribs to W. 3 *list*: desired; 27 *redress*: compensation and remedy; 28 *hire*: reward.

59 E attribs to W. 1 *Lute*: specif. assoc. with love and lust (Peacham (1612), 127) and love melancholy; 7 *lead . . . stone*: lead is much too soft to chisel on (engrave) a marble (tomb) stone; and the implicit identificn of the lover's song with lead makes him a love-melancholic (under the patronage of dull and heavy Saturn, to whom the metal is dedicated: Agrippa (1651), 1.25); 19–20: Cupid will make the lady still feel the pains of love (note the equation of Cupid's drawn bow and the lover's strung lute with its curved belly); 28 *moon*: identif. with virginity.

60 E attribs to W. 1–2 *Chance*: in effect, Fortune (which the mind would like to dominate); 14: *for liberty*: because of its lack.

61 E attribs to W. 7–8: on Cupid see Sidney, *Arcadia* poems 2 and n below; 21 *Fancy*: 53.1n above; 22 *goodman . . . cow*: proverbial (Tilley M103): *goodman* = master (respectful form of address); 24 *reck*: care, trouble oneself about.

62 D; E attribs to W. 1 *swan*: tradnl (see Sidney, *AS* 54.13 and n below).

63 D attribs to W; also in E, partly torn. 1 *In eternum*: forever; *determed*: determined; 9 *trace*: follow, participate in; *put . . . press*: exerted myself; 18 *feeble . . . ground*: Tilley F619, but more likely the biblical origin, Matt. 7:26–7 (house built on sand), where the sand was assoc. with fickle (female) Fortune: Chew (1962), 66–7. The rock is identified with God (the Christian meaning of the phrase *in eternum*).

64 E attribs to W. The echo effect of the final line of each stanza may derive from Serafino or Filosseno (MT, 315–6). 6 *Forbear*: refrain.

65 E attribs to W. 5 *waste*: waste away; 10–11: speaking offers no remedy; 18 *reck*; 61.24n.

66 E attribs to W. 2 *degree*: in mediaeval thought, the successive stage of intensity of the elementary quality of a body (*OED Degree* sb 6c): i.e.

heat, dryness, moisture, cold; 6 *heat and cold*: elemental qualities and Petrarchan (sonnet 8 above).

67 E; A and T attrib to W. Based on the concept of Venus as goddess of sea and islands (bec. born from the sea and worshipped on Gk island of Cytherea, after which she was often named). The poem also addresses her as planetary Venus. 3 *chief house*: strictly speaking, *house* refers to the division of the celestial sphere into 12 astrologically significant sections, while the zodiac (the narrow band through which the planets appear to move) is divided into 12 *signs* or *mansions*. If W is speaking loosely, Venus has two zodiacal *houses*, Taurus and Libra, both of which are fertile (Ptolemy, *Tetrabiblos*, 1.17), though Taurus (the spring sign) is *chief* since Venus is partic. strong in this sign. If W is speaking precisely, then he alludes to the astrol. *houses*, numbers 6, 8 and 12 of which were esp. unpropitious. The seventh concerned wives, and maybe W implies that Venus is in this house (or even the first, which concerned life). I think he refers to Taurus. 4 *joy and delight*: attribs of Venus; 5 *carefully*: i.e. full of care; 7 *en voguant la galère*: while rowing the galley (but *et vogue la galère* = come what may: MT, 318): the connection of Venus with boats is commonplace (cf. Botticelli's *Birth of Venus* with its shell-boat, and Cleopatra on her barge in Sh's *Ant. and Cleop.*, 2.2.190ff.); 8 *doubt*: fear; 10 *fleeteth*: floats; 16 *reducing*: bringing again (Latin *re-duco*): note the pun on *grace*, since the 3 Graces are the handmaids of Venus (see Sidney, *Arcadia* poems 20.134n below).

68 E attribs to W. For the water-stone as an image for the wearing away of the beloved's hard heart, see Petrarch, *rime*, 265; also Serafino (MT, 321–3). It is, of course, proverbial (Tilley D618). 10 *froward*: perverse; *out of frame*: disordered (referring to structure of body, etc.); 15 *tiger*: for the female as tiger see Virgil, *Aeneid*, 11.577 (Amazonian Camilla, protected by virgin moon deity, dressed in tiger skin) and Sh., *3 Henry VI*, 1.4 (cf. 103.11–12 below).

69 E; attribs to W. 10 *in Him did* (Mason (1972), 74; see MT, 323–4): in hid (E and A); MT amend to *in heaven did*.

70 E attribs to W. Part imitn of Petr., *rime*, 199 (MT, 325). 8 *Departed*: separated; 10 *goodly begone*: 'exquisitely fashioned' (Tillyard (1929), 167): see *OED Bego* v 6. But Rebholz, 433 sees a contrast with *alone* in l.11 and suggests another meaning of *bego* (*OED* sense 5), i.e. *surround*: the lady's hand is *goodly* when enclosed by the lover's hand; *alone* it is cruelly rejecting; 18 *repair*: adorn.

71 E attribs to W. 3 *fro*: from (i.e., wherever it is, it comes from there into my breast); 6 *receipt*: receptacle.

72 D attribs to W. Poss. imit. Ovid, *Amores*, 1.2.1–4. 1 *means* (Rebholz): menythe D. But 32 reads *menys* in D, and as Rebholz, 414 remarks, such a poem must begin and end with the same word. Apart from this instance, my text discriminates between D's *menys* and *menythe*.

73 T attribs to W. 12 *no . . . go*: to move not at all; 20 *fancy*: 53.1n (here, probably love).

74 D attribs to W.

75 D attribs to W. 1 *knot*: symbol of love; *strain*: bind tightly.

76 T attribs to W.

77 D; T attribs to W. Free imitn of *rime*, 206 (MT, 406–7), a *canzone*; though I prefer to include it among the lyrics. 8 *straiter*: make tighter; 13–14: i.e., report of me may always. . . ; 42 *hire*: 58.28n above; 45–6 *Rachel . . . Leah*: Jacob serves Laban 7 years for his daughter Rachel; but on the wedding night Laban substitutes the elder daughter Leah. Jacob is promised Rachel also if he serves another 7 years (Gen. 29).

78 T attribs to W. 3 *point*: important matter; 4 *convert*: change your attitude.

79 D attribs to W. On the musical background, see Stevens (1961), 135. 1 *lute*: 59.1n above; 2 *liketh*: pleases; 18 *wreak*: vent wrath, take revenge.

80 D attribs to W (but Harrier (1975), 38–45 argues that it is not W's). 1 *Mirth . . . ship*: laughter is assoc. with the benefits of Venus (Hesiod, *Theogony*, 989), as is the ship (67 above); 3 *bote*: bit (in displeasure: MT, 414): *OED Bite* v. (D spells it *boate*, which harks back to *ship* with haunting illogicality); 5 *book*: commonplace book; 31 *reck*: care.

81 D attribs to W. 7 *Besprent*: besprinckled; 13 *overthwart affects*: opposing passions.

82 D. 1 *Deem as ye list*: judge as you wish; 13 *At that*: i.e., at what; 19 *none* (Nott): no D; 22 *Unto*: until.

83 B. 1 *heavy*: *hartye* original B; 12 *sickerness*: certainty; 24 *Nor*: *But* original B; *steering doth*: *that my death* original B: but see Rebholz, 512 who detects from the MS mess 'that steering it doth'.

84 D attribs to W. 4 *grame*: sorrow; 9 *wealth*: well-being.

85 T attribs to W. 3 *fee*: reward; 13 *mean*: lament (*OED Mean* sb 1).

86 D attribs to W. 2 *debate*: contention; 17 *it*: i.e., the true nature; 29 *leave*: permission.

87 B. 1 *Quondam*: once; 3 *trace*: path, way (*OED Trace* sb¹ 1); 8 *dissever*: separate; 14 *mo*: many.

88 D. 2 *set so light*: regard as trivial; 3 *bond*: bound (i.e., he = her *bondman* or slave); 9 *well*: i.e., not besotted with a lover; *hold*: restrain.

89 D. 9 *assays*: trials; 11 *denays*: denials.

90 D and B. 3 *bond*: 88.3n; 10: *refrain*: avoid; 11 *mean*: the middle way (assoc. with Virtue: Aristotle, *Nicomachean Ethics* 1106B); 13 *Diverse*: Men B; 17 *do thus decay*: take that way B; 26 *for envy and spite*: by outward sight B; 29 *Praying you*: I pray ye B; 31 *weed*: literally, clothing (i.e., outward appearance); 32 *however*: howsoever B; 36 *whatever*: whatsoever B; 38 *you all*: all them B; 39 *may*: do B; 40 *be*: dy B.

91 D. 15 *Thought* (Nott): Though D; 18 *One so unkind* (Nott): blank in MS; 23 *But that you* (Nott): But you D.

92 B. 17 *brakes*: bracken, undergrowth; 31 *cote* (my reading): cost B; coast Daalder: but *turtles* (turtle doves, emblems of love and fidelity) are more likely to be in a loft or cote; 46 *please me* (MT): please B; 67 *storms*: conj. MT; blank in B; 71 *desert* (Rebholz): desprat B.

93 B. Probably W's, with *Viat* (l.3 of inscription) punning on his name, which is thus flanked by Innocence, Truth and Faith. The first two lines do not make grammatical sense in Latin. The last line echoes Ps. 17:9 ('[Keep me] . . . from my deadly enemies, who compass me about'). W was doubtless in the Tower, from which on 19 May 1536 he could well have seen Anne Boleyn's execution. 1–10 transl. Seneca, *Phaedra*, 1123–40, with the refrain *circa Regna tonat* coming from l. 1140 (MT, 415): he [Jove] thunders around thrones (or kingdoms). 4: i.e., you leave court only when ejected by the disdain of others; 9 *Health*: well-being; *debate*: variance; 14 *revert*: fall back again; 24: note the ship metaphor (*low* = humbly).

94 Parker MS (T attribs to W). Probably about a lover. 2 *unsparred*: unbolted; 4 *Whether*: which; 5 *Certes*: truly.

95 D. 3 *in hold*: in its possession; 14 *that other*: i.e., what others.

96 T attribs to W. 1 *will*: i.e., the moral faculty (enabling him to escape from love); 4 *wanhope*: despair; 7 *swelting*: swooning; 9 *ay*: ever; 11 *starve*: die; 22 *incontinent*: straight away.

97 D (first ascr. to W, with reservations, by Foxwell). 2 *again*: in return; 5 *Whereas*: where; 6–23: description of love melancholy (*wearish* (8) = shrivelled): cf. Chaucer, *Knight's Tale*, 1 (A), 1355–79; 18 *visions fantastical*: i.e., produced by the imagination (or *cellula fantastica*, where the imagination was believed to be housed in the brain): see the Chaucer passage; 24 *Record of*: witness; *Terence*: Publius Terentius Afer (d. 159 BC), Roman comic playwright; 28 *mort*: dead, inanimate; 31 *Lucrece*: raped by Sextus Tarquinius and killed herself to affirm her honour: Ovid, *Fasti*, 2.685–852; *her lord*: Foxwell and MT: our lord D (maybe suggesting that Lucretia is an anticipation of the virgin martyrs); 36 *guerdon*: requital; 49 *cordial*: of the heart; 50 *revulsed*: drawn out by medical skill (*art*).

98 D. Note the refrain pattern. 2 *plain*: lament: 7 *weenest*: think; 9 *overthwart*: 54.15n; 13 *peevish*: perverse; 31: the (courteous) refusal to reveal her name is tradnl.

99 D; A and T attrib. to W. 2 *hold*: 95.3n; 3 *sufferance*: suffering; 6 *iwis*: indeed, certainly; 21 *Fantasy*: (also *Fancy*, 30): see 53.1n and 97.18n above.

100 D. 8 *mischieved*: harmed; 12 *bestad*: situated.

101 D attribs to W. 1 *unwarely*: unexpectedly; 5–6 *eye . . . heart*: cf. (again) Chaucer, *Knight's Tale*, 1 (A), 1096–7; 7 *glide* (T): slide D; 8 *face* (T): place D; 11 *upon* (T): on D.

102 T attribs to W. 1 *Sufficed not*: did it not suffice.

103 B; T attribs to W. 4 *reverse*: send back; 9–12: tradnl (Nott cites Virgil, *Aeneid*, 4. 366–7); and see 68.15n above; 17–24: cf. **68** above.

104 D; T attribs to W. Note the concatenation (49n above). 3 *privy*: secretly or to a secret place; 9 *kit*: cut (the thread is derived from the Fates (45.4n above)); 10 *case*: situation; also body.

105 D. 1 *welfare*: well-being; 2: = I have lost my virtue; 3 *cark*: fret; 4 *lullay-by-by*: the lady has been left pregnant or with a child (Nott suggested the latter); 6 *shift*: expedient; 9 *pretence*: purpose; 23 *falsed* (Nott): falsehood D.

106 T attribs to W. Adaptn of 3 passages from Boethius, *Of the Consolation of Philosophy*: Book 3, metre 5 (st. 1); metre 6 (st. 2); metre 3 (st. 3). 2 *will*: sexual appetite; 5 *Thulee*: T's spelling (= furthest north; Thule and India are in Boethius); 17 *Indian stones*: pearls (the best of which reputedly came from India): Boethius has 'pearls from the Indian shore'.

107 B. MT introd. it into the W canon but suggest it 'may well be earlier than the sixteenth century'. 12 *setteth ... right nought*: completely ignores (undervalues).

108 B. 15 *not revert*: i.e., won't cease loving.

109 B. 3 *droppy*: dripping; 6 *marvellously*: exciting wonder; 8–28: the 'murdered man' appears in a dream as an image of the lover's own despair, offering the tradnl suicide by dagger, etc.; 14 *More* (Rebholz): Soo B.

110 E, in W's hand. Unfinished; W may have been working on it when he died, therefore I place it last. D. Scott, *TLS*, 13 September 1963, 696 argues for a 1539 date and gives as source for W's information about the planetary orbits Joannes de Sacrobosco's well-known *De sphaera* in the edns with commentary by J. Faber Stapulensis (Paris, 1527, 1534, 1538). W describes the Ptolemaic system: for diagrams see Heninger (1977), and cf. Sir John Davies, *Orchestra*, below. 1 *Dido ... knight*: when Dido entertains Aeneas at Carthage in north Africa, Iopas sings of the order of the universe about which he has learned from Atlas (*Aeneid*, 1.723–47); 2 *Juno*: queen of heaven and Aeneas's enemy; 3 *Atlas*: Sidney, *Arcadia* poems 20.103n and *AS*, 51.7–8n below; 6 *frame*: structure; 7 *heavenly powers*: the 8 spheres enclosed by the 9th (the *primum mobile*, l.11); 8 *repugnant kinds*: the 4 (mutually antagonistic) elements which envelop the earth in the ascending order: water; air; fire; 10 *Without the which*: around which (i.e., the earth); 12 *firmament*: sphere of fixed stars; *containing* the planetary spheres in that it is, counting from earth, beyond (therefore enveloping) them; 15 *source*: the act of rising (*OED Source* sb, 2 a,b); 17 *case*: container; 18 *two points*: the poles (23); 23–4 *stars ... Arctic*: the pole star is in Ursa minor (Gk *arktos* = bear); 24 *hight*: called; 25–31: on the confusions introd. by W's revisions, see Rebholz, 492 (i.e. the failure to distinguish clearly between the axis of the *primum mobile* (and earth) and the axes of the other spheres: but see 75–7 below); 31 *erring seven*: the wandering (unfixed) planets (Gk *planein* = to wander); so called bec., in comparison with the 'fixed' stars, their positions in relation to each other were noticeably variable. The 7, counting outward from earth, were: moon; Mercury; Venus; Sun; Mars; Jupiter; Saturn; 32 *repugnant*: opposite (they move eastward, the *primum mobile* westward); 33 *smaller byways*: the straying of the 7 planets from their fundamental eastward movement (cf. ll.67–8); 36 *space*: time; 39–40: W abandons the 9-sphere theory to consider the frequently-mooted possibility that there was a *secundum mobile*; 41–6: *seventh*: sphere of Saturn,

whose revolutionary period was, roundly, 30 years (but Faber's precise figure is 29 years 16 days); Saturn, slowest of the planets, is assoc. with cold, dryness, old age, etc. (Ptolemy, *Tetrabiblos*, 1.4); 47–50: Jupiter, *younger* bec. mythologically Saturn's son, and astrologically *benign* (Ptolemy, *ibid.*), returns to his fixed point in approx. 12 years; 51–2: Mars, the warrior and red planet, has a revolutionary period of 2 years (Faber's figure, correcting Sacrobosco, is 1 year 322 days); 53–4: Sacrobosco's and Faber's figure (365 days 6 hours); the sun = the *day's eye*; 55–7: Venus, whose actual revolutionary period is 348 days; 58–9: Mercury's figure is 339 days; 60 *calcars*: calculators (of horoscopes); 70: i.e., I have called the sphere of the fixed stars the eighth.

HENRY HOWARD, EARL OF SURREY

Text

There is no holograph of S's poems and no obviously superior source. Tottel (T) printed most of the poems and, since S was far less metrically 'irregular' than Wyatt, T seems to have meddled less with his texts. I have therefore used T as copy text wherever possible, emending where necessary from the Arundel Harington MS (AH, ed Hughey) and BL MS Add 36529. The *Aeneid* extracts (S translated Books 2 and 4) are from Tottel's *Certaine Bokes of Virgiles Æneis turned into English meter* (1557).

For reasons of space I have regretfully, as with Wyatt, been severe on the biblical paraphrases, though I have included one (Psalm 88). Otherwise (and apart from the need to select from the *Aeneid* transln, again for reasons of space) this selection is virtually complete.

Order

Only some of S's poems can be dated; hence I have preferred generic groupings and, within those groups, a broadly thematic organisation.

Modern editions

See under Wyatt modern editions: Nott, Tottel, and *Arundel Harington MS*, ed Hughey. In addition:

The Poems of Henry Howard, Earl of Surrey, ed. F. M. Padelford (Seattle: Univ. of Washington Press, 1920). Rev edn 1928, repr. 1966.

Surrey's Fourth Boke of Virgill, ed. and introd. Herbert Hartman (London and New York: Oxford U.P., 1933).

The 'Aeneid' of Henry Howard, Earl of Surrey, ed. F. H. Ridley (Berkeley and Los Angeles: Univ. of California Press, 1963).

Henry Howard, Earl of Surrey: Poems, ed. Emrys Jones (Oxford: Clarendon Press, 1964).

Henry Howard, Earl of Surrey: Selected Poems, ed. Dennis Keene (Manchester: Carcanet, 1985).

FURTHER READING

BAPST, EDMOND. *Deux gentilshommes-poètes de la cour d'Henry VIII* (1891).

CALDWELL, E. C. 'Recent Studies in Henry Howard, Earl of Surrey (1970–89)', *English Literary Renaissance*, 19 (1989).

CASADY, EDWIN. *Henry Howard, Earl of Surrey* (1938).

CHAPMAN, H. W. *Two Tudor Portraits: Henry Howard, Earl of Surrey and Lady Katherine Grey* (1960).

DAVIS, W. R. 'Contexts in Surrey's Poetry', *English Literary Renaissance*, 4 (1974).

FISHMAN, BURTON. 'Recent Studies in Wyatt and Surrey', *English Literary Renaissance*, 1 (1971).

HARDISON, O. B. 'Tudor Humanism and Surrey's Translation of the *Aeneid*', *Studies in Philology*, 83 (1986).

JENTOFT, C. W. 'Surrey's Five Elegies: Rhetoric, Structure, and the Poetry of Praise', *PMLA (Publications of the Modern Language Association of America)*, 91 (1976).

JENTOFT, C. W. *Sir Thomas Wyatt and Henry Howard, Earl of Surrey: A Reference Guide* (1980).

LITTLEFIELD, T. H. *Of Ancient Liberty: A Study of Surrey's Translation of Books II and IV of the 'Aeneid'*, unpub. Ph.D. (Columbia), 1963.

MUMFORD, I. L. 'Musical Settings to the Poems of Henry Howard, Earl Surrey', *English Miscellany*, 8 (1957).

PADELFORD, F. M. 'The MS Poems of Henry Howard, Earl of Surrey', *Anglia*, 29 (1906).

PHILBIN, J. H. *A Metrical Analysis of the Blank Verse of Henry Howard, Earl of Surrey*, unpub. Ph.D. (Yale), 1963.

RICHARDSON, D. A. 'Humanistic Intent in Surrey's *Aeneid*', *English Literary Renaissance*, 6 (1976).

RIDLEY, FLORENCE. 'Surrey's Debt to Gavin Douglas', *PMLA*, 76 (1961).

SESSIONS, W. A. *Henry Howard, Earl of Surrey* (1986).

ZITNER, S. P. 'Truth and Mourning in a Sonnet by Surrey', *ELH: A Journal of English Literary History*, 50 (1983).

SONNETS

1 Inspired by Petrarch, *rime*, 310, but note the conscious mediaevalisms. 1 *soote*: sweet; 3–4 *nightingale*: S suppresses the mythol. implications of Petr's *Philomel* (see Sidney, *Arcadia* poems 28.61n below) and replaces his *Procne* (swallow) with the *turtle* dove, emblem of fidelity (Sidney, *ibid.*, 21.6n and Wyatt, 92.31n above). The nightingale also = a tradnl figure for the poet; the dove often sings of loss; 6 *pale*: fence; 8 *fleet*: float, swim; also fade (in allusion to Pisces, the Fish, last of the winter zodiacal signs: (Fowler (1975), 23–4); 9 *adder . . . slough*: emblem of renewal (cf. S's transln of *Aen.* 2.608–12) and of the yearly cycle (Tervarent (1958), col. 349); 11 *mings*: remembers (also *mengs*, mixes): the bee is a Platonic emblem of the poet; 12 *bale*: harm.

2 Source: Ariosto, *Orlando Furioso*, 1. 78–9 (2 fountains, of lust and indifference). 1 *Cyprus . . . Venus*: the island was the ancient seat of Venus (Linche (1599), s.v. Venus), and see also Wyatt, 67n above.

3 Inspired by *rime*, 164 and Virgil, *Aen.* 4.702–15 (S's transln). 4: it is the *stars* that do the bringing. For *Night's chair* (chariot) see Ripa (1603), 59.

4 Text: MS Add 36529. Transl. *rime*, 140: cf. W's 'The long love' (MT, 4). 1 *doth reign and live* (MS): liveth, and reigneth (T); *within* (MS): in (T); 2 *And* (MS): That (T); 5 *But she* (MS): She (T); *taught me love* (MS): me taught to love (T); 7 *look* (MS): cloak (T); 10 *where he doth lurk and plain* (MS): whereas he lurkes, and plains (T); 12 *pain* (MS): pains (T); 14 *the* (MS): his (T); *takes his* (MS): taketh (T).

5 Text: MS Add 36529. Transl. *rime*, 145 (and Horace, *Odes*, 1.22). 2 *may* (MS): do (T); 4 T reads: In presence prest of people madde or wise; 5 T reads: . . . hye, or yet in lowe; 6 *the long* (MS): longest (T); 7 *clear weather* (MS): clearest day (T); *mists* (MS): clowdes (T); 8 *be* (MS): are (T); 9 T reads: . . . in heaven, in earth, or els in hell; 10 *in dale* (MS): or dale (T); 12 *ill fame, or good* (MS): evyll fame, or good (T); 13 *with that only* (MS): onely with this; 14 T reads: Content my selfe, although my chaunce be nought.

6 Thomas Nashe's *Unfortunate Traveller* (1594) is an elaborate fictional reading of S's own literary fiction about his relnship with 'Geraldine'. She is, historically, Lady Elizabeth Fitzgerald, daughter of the 9th Earl of Kildare, Gerald Fitzgerald, born around 1528 in Ireland and brought to England in 1533, where she entered the service of Princess Elizabeth in 1539 and of Queen Catherine Howard (1540). The poem's courtly love mode has caused critical problems, as has the ref. to Windsor, where S was confined in 1537 (see sonnet 11): if the poem was written then, Geraldine would have been an unacceptable 9; but if it was written when S visited Windsor in May 1541 for the Feast of the Garter she would have been 13, a suitable age to receive the addresses of a courtly lover. Simply, we do not know when the poem was written, nor do we know anything about the relationship it enshrines. 1 *Tuscan*: variant form of *Tuscany*; 2: the Fitzgeralds (Geraldines) were supposedly descended from the Florentine Giraldi; 3 *isle*: Ireland; 6 *dame*: Lady Elizabeth Grey, 4th daughter of Thomas, Marquis of Dorset, grand-daughter of Edward IV's queen Elizabeth Woodville, and a first cousin of Henry VIII (*DNB*); 8 *ghostly food*: spiritual nourishment or Holy Communion (Sessions (1986), 64); 13 *Beauty* (MS Add 36529): Her beauty (T).

7 6 *lively dooms*: quick judgements.

8 Text: MS Add 36529. Transl. *rime*, 11. 1 *you, madame* (MS): my Ladye (T); 2 *Your* (MS): Her (T); *cornet*: head-dress with veil (hence the point of l. 14); 3 T reads: . . . *she knew my griefe was growen* . . .; 4 *chased clean* (MS): driveth (T); 5 *Whiles* . . . *did* (MS): That . . . do (T); 6 T reads: *The which unwares* . . .; 7 T reads: *But on her face mine eyes mought never rest*; 8 *But* . . . *ye* . . . *you* (MS): Yet .·. she . . . her (T); 9 *Your* . . . *tress was* (MS): Her . . . tresses (T); 10: om. in MS. T reads: *Her smilyng lokes that hid thus evermore*. I print Padelford's conjecture; 11 T reads: *And that restraines which I desire so sore*; 14 T reads: *Whereby the light of her faire lokes I lost*.

9 S was commander of Boulogne from Sept. 1545 to March 1546; his headquarters were in the Lower Town. 10 *guide*: i.e. Cupid.

10 6 *peason*: peas; 8 *geason*: niggardly, barren.

11 Text: MS Add 36529. S was ordered to be confined at Windsor for striking Sir Edward Seymour at Hampton Court: Seymour had repeated the rumour that S was in sympathy with the Pilgrimage of Grace rebellion (1536). For the attitude of chin on hand, cf. Dürer's *Melancholia*. S utilises the tradnl contrast between Melancholy and youthful Venerean pleasure (Klibansky, Panofsky, Saxl (1964), *passim*). 3 *Each* (MS): The (T); 4 *Ver*: Spring (Chaucerian); 5 *wedded birds*: this tradnlly occurred on St Valentine's Day (cf. Chaucer, *Plt of Fowls*, 309–10 and S's poem 21.20); 7 *hateless . . . debate*: brief mock battle or skirmish.

12 Text: MS Add 36529. The *king* is Sardanapalus, last ruler of the Assyrian empire initiated by Ninus and Semiramis; reputedly lustful, slothful, and a transvestite. He revealed his martial character when challenged by rebels, but was besieged by them in Nineveh and eventually killed his wives, concubines, and himself. S's poem probably glances at Henry VIII. 1 *Assyrians'* (MS): Assyrian (T); 3 *afire* (MS): on fire (T); 4 *Vanquished did yield* (MS): Did yeld, vanquisht (T); 8 *charge*: weight.

13 Text: MS Add 36529. Cf. 33: an epitaph for W, who died 11 October 1542 (I have excluded S's third tribute, 'In the rude age', because of the impossible state of its text). 2 *Some*: i.e. Edmund Bonner and Simon Heynes, as a result of whose accusations of treason W was sent to the Tower in 1541; 3 *sown* (MS): swolne (T); 4 *Yield . . . head*: cf. W's sonnet 1 and n above; 14 *Pyramus*: Ovid, *Met.*, 4.67–201 and Chaucer, *Legend of Good Women*, legend 2 (the serious implicns of this tale to S's meaning should not be underestimated).

14 1 *great Macedon*: Alexander, who after defeating the Persian Darius, placed his copy of Homer in a rich chest (*ark*), one of the spoils of victory; 4 *gests*: tales of deeds performed (Latin *gesta*); 6: for W's psalm paraphrases see M T, 98–125; 12 *Uriah*: David killed Uriah after committing adultery with his wife (2 Sam. 11–12): a clear allusion to the Davidic King Henry VIII.

15 Not in T. Text: William Camden, *Remaines of a Greater Worke, concerning Britaine* (1605). S's life had been saved by his friend Thomas Clere on 19 September 1544 during the English siege of Montreuil; Clere died of wounds received there on 14 April 1545 and was buried in the Howard Chapel at Lambeth parish church. 1: modifies the epitaph Virgil was reputed by Donatus to have written for himself (*Mantua gave birth to me . . . Parthenope now holds me*); Clere was born at Ormesby in Norfolk; 2 *hight*: high (Camden); 3 *Ormonde's race*: alludes to the Boleyns, since Clere's uncle Thomas Boleyn, Earl of Wiltshire and of Ormonde, was Anne Boleyn's father by Elizabeth Howard, daughter of S's grandfather, Thomas Howard, Earl of Surrey and 2nd Duke of Norfolk; 4 *cousin*: i.e. Anne Boleyn; 5 *Shelton*: Clere's mistress Mary Shelton, another cousin of Anne Boleyn (*chase* = chose); 7–9: *Kelsall* was burned during the English expedition to Scotland in October 1542; S and Clere took part in the siege of *Landrecy* in the Netherlands in October 1543; *Bullen* = Boulogne (punning on Boleyn), which Henry VIII captured in September 1544; *Muttrell* = Montreuil; 12 *four*: emended

from Camden's *seven* (for the number symbolism, see Fowler (1975)), 32–7); 14 *timely*; *soon* and *aptly* (because of the signif. of 28 as the number of years in the perfect life).

SONGS AND ELEGIES

16 11–12: i.e. *Iphigeneia*; 19 *repair*: gathering (of people); 28 *draweth in ure*: comes into being (literally, into operation).

17 Maybe one of S's first poems. 8 *Penelope*: Odysseus's chaste and faithful wife; 14: utilises the mediaeval complaint of Nature tradn.

18 7–12 *Boreas*: north wind (i.e. S is in Scotland: see 15.7–9n above); and note the Petrarchism in l. 12 (as in st. 1 as a whole); *freeze*: i.e. froze; 13 *sun*: S is now (from October 1543) in the Netherlands and France.

19 Note the adoption of a female voice (as in the complaints of women to their betraying and/or lost lovers in Ovid's *Heroides*), maybe, as also in no 20, that of his wife. S is presumably in France. 8–10: cf. W's sonnet 9n above; 26–35: note the Dido motif (*Aen.*, 4. 780ff. in S's translsn): Dido utters *Heroides* 7.

20 Text: T, variants from AH. Another complaint on the model of **19**. 2 *step in your foot*: join in the dance/chorus; 4 *skills them not*: is of no importance to them; 11 AH reads: *That I was wontt for to embrace contentid myndes*; 13 *There . . . safely me him* (AH): Where . . . sone him home me (T); 20 *That . . . lie* (AH): That my dere Lorde (ay me alas) me thinkes I se him die (T); 22 *T . . . son*: S's eldest son, Thomas, born 10 March 1536, and the likely addressee of no. **35**; 24 *Now welcome home* (AH): welcome my lord (T); 27 *saluteth*: greets (with a kiss); 34 T reads: *Sum hidden place, wherein to slake the gnawing of my mind*; *steal*: to conceal quietly; 36 *some* (AH): good (T); 41 *conjure* = T's reading: MS reads (implausibly) *convart*; 43 *such* (AH): this (T).

21 Along with no. **22**, built on the figure of the lamenting Troilus. See esp. Chaucer's *Troilus*, 1. 155 ff. 19 *Ver*: see 11.4n and *Troilus*, 1.156–7: 'when clothed is the mede/With newe grene, of lusty Ver the pryme'; 20: cf. **11**.5n above; 23 *feres*: mates; 34 *Unwittingly*: Unwillingly (T); *to malice thy pretence*: impugn your claim to authority (Jones); 35 *beck*: nod; 45–8: cf. Chaucer's *Troilus*, 1.232–8 (S's *mirror* (47) = Chaucer's *ensample* (l. 232)).

22 A pastoral complaint: cf. Spenser, *Shep. Cal*, 'January'. 1 *Boreas*: **18**.7–12n above; 6 *palm*: used of the willow, emblem of melancholy (sitting under a tree = also a melancholic posture, as in the frontispiece to Burton's *Anat. of Melancholy*); 8 *attaint*: infect; 15 *pen*: i.e. quill pen; 26–32: the lover manifests an extreme form of love melancholy verging on despair (the landscape is iconographically appropriate to both: see Spenser, *FQ*, I. ix); 27 *rashly*: impetuously; 52 *Priam* = king of Troy (cf. S's translsn of *Aen*. 2); 78: note the ref. to Ch's poem; 80 *blue*: constancy (*Troilus*, 3.885 (Jones)), truth, and hope for the after life (since it is the colour of the heavens): Brooks-Davies (1977), 95.

23 19 *in thy respect*: compared to you.

24 4 *weal*: well-being; 5–8: cf. *rime*, 22, also used in S's no. 27.21–30 (Jones); 30 *leech*: physician; 34 *cheer*: face; 37 *riveth*: shatters; 48 *Good Hope*: a common personificn in courtly love allegories; 44 *knot*: Sidney, *Arcadia* poems 21.47 and n below; 49 *to serve . . . patiently*: the refrain of W's no. 76 above; 59 *refared*: i.e. referred (= entrusted, restored); 60: cf. Chaucer's *Knight's Tale*, 1 (A) 2768–70.

25 1 *careless*: i.e. put on without care because the lover is so preoccupied with his melancholy (cf. *As You Like It* (New Arden), 3.2. 363–74).

26 Reply to 25, attrib. to S only in 2nd edn of T. Text: AH.Cf. the female impersonations of 19 and 20; 22 *Susan*: the story of Susannah and the elders appeared in Daniel 13 (Vulgate/Douay) but was relegated to the OT apocrypha by the Protestant reformers; *fraughted*: filled with; 28 *Childe*: young nobleman.

27 Text: T (variants from MS Add 36529). *Terza rima.* 21–30: echoing *rime*, 22.1–6 (cf. 24.5–8n above); 32–4; *rime*, 35.1–4; *haunted* = frequented; 33 *cheer*: 24.34n above; 36 *lace*: snare and (love) knot; 40–5: see W's sonnet 9n above.

28 Text: T (variants from MS Add 36529). 1–14: Ariosto, *Orl. Fur.* 2.1; 4 *froward*: adverse; 5–6: cf. Sidney, *AS* 65 and 72nn below; 7 *easy*: slight; 15-end: cf. Petr., *Triumph of Love*, 3.151–87 (tr. Morley (1971), 99); 15 *Lo, by these rules* (MS): So by this meanes (T); *can* (MS): may (T); 17 *convert my will* (MS): content my self (T); 19 *dissembled* (MS): dissembling (T); 22 *cheek* (MS): cheekes (T); 23: proverbial; 24 *hammer*: see 33.6; *know* (MS): wote (T); 25 *can*: know; 28 *can* (MS): doth (T); 37 *spleen*: seat of melancholy (hence forced, mirthless, laughter); 38 *clean*: completely; 39 *withouten* (MS): with others (T); 40 *lion . . . whelp*: a lion brought up with a dog will become tractable after seeing the dog beaten (Rollins, *Tottel*, 2. 133 citing Topsell, *Hist. of four-footed Beasts* (1607)). As Jones notes, the lion was a heraldic beast of the Howards (see 29.30n); 48 *may . . . will* (MS): will . . . may (T); 49 *those* (MS): the (T); 50 *That . . . that* (MS): The . . . the (T).

29 Text: T (variants from AH). The lady is tradnlly identif. as Anne Seymour (cf. 11n above), wife of Sir Edward Seymour, Earl of Hertford, an enemy of S's. The wolf is the emblem of her family, the Stanhopes, as the lion was of the Howards (28.40n above). 1 *fere*: companion; 2 *eke*: also; *cheer*: countenance; 4 *port*: bearing; 5 *gentle*: noble; 7 *make*: peer, companion; 11 *fierce* (AH): coy (T); *froward*: 28.4n; 12 *Toward* (AH): Unto (T); 13 *beck*: 21.35n; 14 *unmeet*: unworthy; 16 *trow*: believe; 19–20 *beforn . . . forlorn* (AH): before . . . forlore (T); 21 *weet*: know; 23 *Forthwith* (AH): With that (T); 30 *king*: James IV of Scotland, vanquished by S's grandfather, Thomas Howard, 2nd Duke of Norfolk, at Flodden Field in September 1513. In recognition of the victory he was granted 'an addition to his coat of arms – on a bend in his shield a demilion, gules, pierced in the mouth with an arrow' (*DNB*); 35–40 refer to Lord Thomas Howard, half brother to S's father, Thomas, 3rd Duke of Norfolk. His secret marriage to Lady Margaret Douglas, daughter of Henry VIII's sister Margaret, led to his being imprisoned in the Tower for treason in July 1536, since she was heir to the throne after Parliament had declared the Princesses Mary and Elizabeth illegitimate. He died in October 1537; 37 *both* (AH): om. T; 41 *Other*: maybe *others*, or may refer in the singular to Lady Margaret, who was also confined to the Tower; *life, to* (AH): lives, doe (T); 42 T reads: *willes . . . are* (*right* omitted); 49 *fed . . . flee* (AH): fled . . . slay (T); 53 *wist*: know; 54 *trained . . . by* (AH): trapt . . . with (T); 55 *bow* (AH): love (T); 56 *to . . . a . . . fawn* (AH): to . . . of . . . sort (T); 60 *stale*: decoy bird; *that for no* (AH): nor for no (T); 64 *Thus* (AH): This (T); 65 *In . . . whereof* (AH): And for . . . therof (T); 67 *hap* (AH): luck (T); 69 *too low* (AH): and bow (T); 76 *boots*: avails.

30 23 *plage*: a form of *pledge* and *plague*, and punning on both; 26–8: cf. 24.59–60.

31 Based on Horace, *Satires*, 1.1 (opening) and *Ars Poetica*, 156ff. (on the ages of man: on which see also J. A. Burrow (1986) *passim*); 1 *study*: deep thought; 15–28: the narrator becomes his own death's head (cf. Hamlet with Yorick's skull), his bed an image of the tomb; 17 *chaps*: jaws; 20 *true belief*: scripture.

32 Text: T, variants from MS Add 36529. For the Windsor setting, see S's sonnet 11n above. 3 *king's son*: literally: Henry Fitzroy, Duke of Richmond, illegitimate son of Henry VIII, who married S's sister, Lady Mary Howard; *childish*: with the overtones of *childe* as in 26.28n (Jones); *Priam*: cf. 22.52n; 7 *maidens' tower*: where the ladies of the court dwelled (Nott); 9 *sales* (= rooms) (MS): seates (T); 13 *palm play*: form of tennis in which the ball was struck with the palm of the hand; 16 *bait*: attract; *leads*: roof leads (i.e., they are watching from the battlements); 17 *helm*: helmet (with a lady's favour tied to it); 19 *the . . . overwhelm* (MS): one should another whelme (T); 21 *meads* (MS): meade (T); 27 *soft* (MS): ofte (T); 29 *holts*: copses; 32 *a* (MS): of (T) ('*Chasse à forcer* is the old hunting term for that game which is run down, in opposition to the *chasse à tirer*, that which is shot' (Nott)); 33 *void walls* (MS): wide vales (T): cf. S's translm of *Aen.* 4.104, Dido alone, mourning 'within her palace void'; 34 *revive within* (MS): reviveth in (T); 40 *nights* (MS): night (T); 41 *my* (MS): the (T); 45: cf. Troilus addressing Criseyde's house (*Troilus*, 5.550); 47 *didst* (MS): doest (T); 48 *lief*: dear; 49 *Echo*: see Sidney, *Arcadia* poems 7n below (MS reads 'Eache alas'; 1574 Tottel reads 'Eche stone, alas'); 53 *greater*: Richmond's death (in 1536, of consumption, aged 17), which upset S deeply.

33 Cf. S's sonnet 13 above. This epitaph was first publ. in *An excellent Epitaffe of syr Thomas Wyat, with two other compendious dytties* (1542). 1: Hudson (*Modern Language Notes*, 45 (1930), 541–3) notes that this translates the epitaph of the Italian warrior Jacopo Trivulzio (here, dead, rests once for all the man who, alive, never rested); 5 *Wisdom*: one of the *heavenly gifts* (of the Holy Ghost), the other 6 of which follow: *scientia* (which bestows temperance) st. 3; *intellectus* (st. 4); *pietas* (st. 5); *consilium* (st. 6); *timor domini* (dread of the Lord), st. 7;

fortitudo (force), st. 8 (Fowler (1975), 26ff.); 7 *stithe*: anvil; 15 *for*: i.e., for lack of, or because of Time (who killed him so soon); 29 *corse*: body; 35: alludes to W's paraphrase of the 7 *Penitential Psalms* (M T, 98–125), which were numerologically connected with the 7 *heavenly gifts* (Tuve (1966), 113).

ETHICAL AND RELIGIOUS POEMS

34 1 *Ratclif*: Thomas Ratcliffe, 3rd Earl of Sussex (d. 1583), a relative of S's; 5: cf. Ecclesiasticus 27:25 (Jones); 6: cf. Wyatt's epigram, probably written during his last imprisonment, which concludes 'Sure I am, Brian, this wound shall heal again,/But yet, alas, the scar shall still remain'.
35 Transl. Horace, *Odes*, 2.10. 1 *Thomas*: see 20.22n; *compass*: measure, due proportion; 4 *freat*: destroy; 5 *halseth*: invokes; *golden mean*: the mid-point of virtue, maintained between extremes (excess and defect) of vice (Aristotle, *Nicomachean Ethics*, 1106B); for the nautical metaphor exemplifying these extremes, see Francis Quarles, *Emblemes* (1639), 3.15, citing St Augustine (Give us grace to hold a middle course betwixt Scylla and Charybdis), and cf. Allen (1970), 150; 8 *glome*: i.e. gloom (= scowl); 15–16: Phoebus Apollo will cease to be Apollo the destroyer with his bow and arrows (named from Gk *apollumi* = destroy) and will take up his other role of god of poetry with his harp/lyre.
36 Text: T, variants from MS Add 36529. Transln of Martial, *Epigrams*, 10.47. 1 *for to* (MS): that do (T); 5 *nor strife* (MS): no strife (T); 8 *continuance*: antiquity; 10 T reads: *Trew wisdom joyned with simplenesse*; 12 *may bear no sovereignty* (MS): the wit may not oppresse (T); 13 *debate*: argumentativeness; *The . . . wise* (MS): The faithful wife (T); 16 *Neither with . . . nor* (MS): Ne wish for . . . ne (T).
37 Text: AH. *Terza rima*. 'On 1 April 1543 S was charged before the privy council with having eaten flesh in Lent, and with having broken at night the windows of citizens' houses and of churches in the city of London by shooting small pebbles at them with a stone-bow. . . On the first charge he pleaded a license; he admitted his guilt on the second accusation' (*DNB*). Thomas Clere and Thomas Wyatt, the poet's son, were, among others, also implicated in the events. S was committed to the Tower for some 4 weeks and produced the following poem on the matter. How serious it is has been hotly debated: Mason (1959), 243–5 argues that it is a serious expression of Protestant sentiments; others argue that S's familial Catholicism make him temperamentally opposed to Protestantism. Neither the poem's wit not its revisionary and apocalyptic rigour should be underestimated. 7 *convert*: transform; 14 *secret sin*: cf. Ps. 90:8 (Thou hast set our iniquities before thee, and our secret sinnes in the light of thy countenance: Geneva Bible); 16–17: cf. the guilty king's sleeplessness in Shakespeare's 2 *Henry IV*, 3.1; 18 *night*: the time of judgement (2 Kings 19:35; Daniel 5.30); 20–22: for the bow as a weapon against the type of earthly sin, Babel, see Jer. 50:14, 29; but S specifies *stones*, and his *bow* was more of a catapult, so he probably also identif.

himself as a Davidic victor over a sinful Goliath (1 Samuel 17). For the *scourge*, see esp. Is. 10:5–6 and 26, and for the *rap*, cf. the knock at the door of Rev. 3:20; 28–41: list of the 7 deadly sins in preparn for the mention of the *Whore* of line 51 (i.e., the Antichrist Whore of Babylon of Rev. 17), since the Whore rides on a 7-headed beast (Rev. 17:3), the heads of which were identif. with the sins (Tuve (1966), 102–3). There was no fixed order for the sins; but S adopts a familiar scheme that recalls the one followed by Chaucer's *Parson's Tale*. This makes *sloth* central (4th out of 7) to stress its figurative significance to sleeping, and consequently sinful, London (its inhabitants are *sluggards* at line 20), for *sloth* is 'nurse' of all the vices (Chaucer, opening to *Second Nun's Prologue*) and kin to despair. Since the scheme S uses is that followed by moralists and iconographers pairing the gifts of the Holy Ghost with their opposite vices, there is a suggestion that Davidic S exemplifies *fortitude* (the gift that displaces sloth) in waking the sluggard citizens: compare S's use of the gifts in no. 33; 53 *Babylon*: city of sin (Jer. 50, Is. 47) identif. by Protestant reformers with Catholic corruption; 56ff.: various apocalyptic echoes, but esp. Ezek. 5, 6, Rev. 18.

38 Text: MS Add 36529, where it is prologue to Ps. 88. Probably written while S was awaiting execution. 5 *Denny*: Sir Anthony Denny, who may well have affixed the royal seal to S's death warrant; 7 *David*: sinner, penitent, type of Christological virtue but also, in reformation monarchical politics, an increasingly complex figure (Kantorowicz (1958)).

39 Text: MS Add 36529. See headnote to 38. S, who also paraphrased the first 4 chapters of Ecclesiastes and Psalms 8, 55 and 73, chose texts relevant to his imprisonment and imminent death. Like W, S followed the Latin paraphrases made by Joannes Campensis (1532): Mason (1959), 241–8, M T, 356ff. His biblical text was, of course, the Latin Vulgate. 8 *bruit*: report, reputation; 16 *bain*: bathe; *appair*: weaken; 22 *elect*: probably with Protestant overtones; 25 *endured*: hardened.

40 Prologue to S's paraphrase of Ps. 73. Cf. headnote to 39. For the ship metaphor cf. 35. 11 *Blage*: Sir George Blage, an extreme Protestant, with whom S had quarrelled shortly before his committal for treason; 12 *David*: ref. to the psalm translns.

41 S's last poem, according to his son. Text: T. Line 8 = missing. 13 *glass*: mirror (actual, or imagined as 'a mirror of the mind'). The *wretch* of line 16 may (as Keene suggests) be S himself about to be beheaded; or it may be another (untraced, but possibly Sir Richard Southwell, S's accuser, whom S had offered to duel with).

TRANSLATION FROM THE *AENEID*

Written late 1530s, publ. 1554 (Book 4) and 1557 (Books 2 and 4). The first blank verse poems in English (a brilliant attempt to emulate the effect of Virgil's own unrhyming hexameters) and influenced by Gavin Douglas's *Aeneid* translln (1513 and circulated in MS; publ. 1553). Text: Tottel. For the textual problems resulting from the existence of 3 separate versions of Book 4, see G. D. Willcock, *Modern Language Review*, 14 (1919), 163–72; 15 (1920), 113–23; and 17 (1922), 131–49.

Notes

BOOK 2

1 *whisted*: were silent; 11: i.e., a mercenary soldier of Ulysses; 22 *Minerva*: Athenian goddess of wisdom but also the guardian deity of Troy; 35 *fet*: reached; 36 *dole*: grief; 40 *Pyrrhus*: warrior son of Achilles (see 2.681ff. below); *Achilles*: one of the main Greek antagonists against Troy; *pight*: pitched (camp); 42 *scatheful*: harmful; 343: the *cheer* (face) is Hector's (Priam's eldest son and chief Trojan hero); 346 *bowlen*: swollen; 347 *strait*: tight; 352 *crisped*: curled; 355 *frankly*: freely; 358 *lets*: obstacles; 371 *that*: i.e., what (has been done); 375 *privy*: private (i.e., household); 379 *Vesta*: goddess of the hearth whose symbol was fire: Aeneas brought her eternal flame from Troy to Italy; 380 *fillets*: headbands (emblems of chastity); 392 *silly*: simple; 395 *Deiphobus*: another of Priam's sons; 396 *flash*: sudden burst of flame; 397 *Ucalegon*: one of the Trojan elders; 402 *feres*: companions; 403 *brent*: burned; 406 *Panthus*: another Trojan elder; 421 *Sinon*: the man left behind by the Greeks who persuaded the Trojans to take the horse into their city; 712 *Pelide*: i.e., Achilles, son of Peleus by Thetis; 714 *Neoptolem*: Neoptolemus (= young warrior), the usual name for Pyrrhus; *swerved . . . kind*: deviated from his (inherited) nature; 721 *fine*: end; 727 *stock*: tree trunk, but also (via family tree) the progenitor of a race; 735 *Creusa*: daughter of Priam, and Aeneas's wife; 737 *Iulus*: alternative name for Ascanius, son of Creusa and Aeneas (cf. 786); 741 *lopen*: leapt; 742 *irked*: wearied; 745 *Helen*: wife of Menelaus and abducted by Paris to Troy: hence the Trojan war; 750 *wreaks*: injuries; 751 *make*: husband; 770 *wroke*: revenged; 772 *cinder*: ashes; 774 *blessed mother*: Venus; 788 *cure*: care (Latin *cura*); 800 *Neptunus*: Latin name for Poseidon, god of the sea, who, in conjunction with Apollo, built the walls of Troy for Laomedon; 803 *Juno*: queen of heaven and Aeneas's enemy; 805 *wood*; mad; 808 *Pallas*: Athene, virgin and armed deity of wisdom whose shield bore the head of snaky-locked Medusa the Gorgon (synonymous with *Minerva*: l. 22n above); 821 *gledes*: embers; 971 *sheen*: shining; 1002 *ugsome*: loathsome; 1021 *clepes*: cries, shouts; 1037 *Hesperian*: i.e., western (Italy); 1054 *accoll*: embrace; 1059 *mates*: companions; 1064 *Lucifer*: light-bringer (the morning star); 1065 *lusty*: pleasant; but possibly a copyist's error for *lofty* (Virgil's *summae . . . Idae*; *Ida* = a mountain near Troy).

BOOK 4

2 *playe*: wound (Hargrave MS reads *plage* = plague, etc.); 10 *dank* (T): darke (1554 text); but *dank* translates V's *umentemque . . . umbram*; 15 *cheer*: countenance; 18: i.e., Cowardice denotes a heart that has deviated from its true nature; 24 *genial brands*: nuptial torches (dedicated to Hymen, god of marriage); 27 *brother*: Sychaeus was murdered by his brother-in-law, Dido's brother Pygmalion; 32 *lord*: Jupiter; 34 *Shame-fastness*: modesty (but here denoting rather 'sense of decorum'); 37 *surprised*: translating V's *lacrimis . . . obortis* (welling tears);38

bained: bathed; 42 *Cinders* (T): Doth dust (1554 text); 43 *dole*: grief, mourning; 56 *Why shall*: Why should; 58 *purveyance*: Providence; 67 *Orion*: the evening appearance of the constellation in November marks the onset of winter storms (see Geneva gloss on Job 38:31: 'which starre bringeth in winter'); 706 *whist*: *Aen.* 2.1n above; 708 *thicks*: thickets; 718 *assay*: try, test the worth of; 728 *woe-begone*: translating V's *perdita* (*ruined* or *desperate* one); 864 *wards*: apartments; 868 *weed*: clothing; 869 *study*: perplexity (cf. 31.1n above); 879 *unwroken*: unavenged; 887 *besprent*: besprinkled; 889 *bruit*: report; 926 *Iris*: Juno's messenger; 927 *throwing*: struggling (V's *luctantem*); 932 *Proserpine*: queen of the underworld; 938 *Pluto*: king of the underworld; 943 *resolve*: melt away (V's *dilapsus*).

SIR WALTER RALEGH

Text and canon

Apart from the holograph MS which contains four poems (Hatfield House, Cecil papers, 144), there are no authorised texts. Most of the printed texts were published posthumously. Although there are good quality MS anthologies (esp. Bodleian MS Rawlinson Poetry 85, and British Library MS Harley 7392 and 6910), the number of MSS containing some at least of the poems attributed to R is so large that the total of textual variants creates severe editorial difficulties. Despite the labours of John Hannah and Agnes Latham, we still need a full modern edn of R's poetry which will, among other things, ponder again the problems of attribution; for what Agnes Latham calls 'Ralegh's jealously preserved anonymity' means that most attributions are traditional rather than proved (or, indeed, provable). And this means in turn that even such a favourite as 'The passionate man's pilgrimage' (no. 24) can have its authorship competently questioned.

My aim in this edn, therefore, given its scope, has been to provide readable conservative texts. There is nothing here that will surprise a reader of Latham's edns. I print the poems in the chronological order established by Latham; and I include all the poems currently attributed to R with the exceptions of Latham (1951) nos 2 (Sweet are the thoughts), 3 (Lady farewell), 19 (Now Serena), 27 (The word of denial), 32 (What tears, dear Prince), 33 (Here lies Hobinall), 34 (Next Caesar's birth), 39 (My broken pipes), and some of the verse translns from *The History of the World*.

Modern editions

The Courtly Poets from Raleigh to Montrose, ed. John Hannah (London, 1870).

The Poems of Sir Walter Ralegh, ed. A. M. C. Latham (London: Constable, 1929).

The Phoenix Nest (1593), ed. H. E. Rollins (Cambridge, Mass.: Harvard U.P., 1931; repr. 1969). Contains several poems by R.

The Poems of Sir Walter Ralegh, ed. A. M. C. Latham (London: Routledge and Kegan Paul, 1951).

Walter Oakeshott, *The Queen and the Poet* (London: Faber and Faber, 1960). Part 2 is a tendentious edn of the poems to Cynthia.

Sir Walter Ralegh: Selected Prose and Poetry, ed. A. M. C. Latham (London: Athlone Press, 1965).

A Choice of Sir Walter Ralegh's Verse, ed. Robert Nye (London: Faber and Faber, 1972).

Sir Walter Ralegh: Selected Writings, ed. Gerald Hammond (Manchester: Carcanet, 1984; repr. Penguin Books, 1986).

FURTHER READING

ADAMSON, J. H. AND H. F. FOLLAND *The Shepherd of the Ocean: An Account of Sir Walter Ralegh and his Times* (1969).

BRADBROOK, M. C. *The School of Night: A Study in the Literary Relationships of Sir Walter Ralegh* (1936; 1965).

EDWARDS, PHILIP. *Sir Walter Ralegh* (1953; 1976).

GREENBLATT, S. J. *Sir Walter Ralegh: The Renaissance Man and his Roles* (1973).

LEFRANC, PIERRE. *Sir Walter Ralegh, Écrivain: l'oeuvre et les idées* (1968).

MAY, S. W. 'Companion Poems in the Ralegh Canon', *English Literary Renaissance*, 13 (1983).

MILLS, J. L. 'Recent Studies in Ralegh', *English Literary Renaissance*, 15 (1985).

MILLS, J. L. *Sir Walter Ralegh: A Reference Guide* (1986).

RUDICK, MICHAEL. *The Poems of Sir Walter Ralegh: An Edition* (unpub. Ph.D. diss., Chicago, 1970).

TONKIN, HUMPHREY. 'Sir Walter Ralegh, 1900–1968', *Elizabethan Bibliographic Supplements*, 17 (1971).

WALLACE, W. M. *Sir Walter Ralegh* (1959).

WILSON, JEAN. *Entertainments for Elizabeth I* (1980).

YATES, F. A. *The Occult Philosophy in the Elizabethan Age* (1979).

VARIOUS POEMS

1 Text: George Gascoigne, *The Steel Glass* (1576). R's poem commends G's satire, a 'mirror' held up to the age. 4 *percase*: perhaps; 8 *pain*: care taken; 18 *hardly*: with difficulty.

2 Text: *The Phoenix Nest* (1593). 5–8: puzzling, but perhaps: 'yet those who are rich in zeal, etc. – all those, now you are dead, would write elegies for you; and, indeed, your death has doubled their number'; 11 *seeled*: with eyes closed (from falconry); 12 *timeless*: premature, untimely; 17 *king . . . name*: S's godfather was Philip II of Spain; 20 *sort*: consort, but also 'be classified with' (*OED* Sort vb 10); 21 *Kent*: S's birthplace was Penshurst in Kent; he went to Christ Church, Oxford, in 1567; 23 *prime*: early manhood (prime of youth: *OED Prime* sb II.8); 26 *treat . . . kings*: in 1577 S was chosen by Eliz. to be her ambassador to the new German emperor Rudolf II; 32 *her*: Elizabeth's; 39 *Castilian*: Philip II; 43 *dure*: last; 55 *Envy*: for Envy bitten by a snake see Ripa (1603), 241–2; 57–8 *Hannibal*: Count Hannibal Gonzago died at the battle of Zutphen; *Scipio* = Scipio Africanus (see Wyatt, no. 44) who reputedly died in the same year (183 BC) as the Carthaginian general *Hannibal*, whose enmity towards Rome is charted by R in his *Hist. of the World*, Book 5 (see 5.6.2 for the deaths of Scipio and Hannibal); *Scipio* was celebrated for his statemanship and military prowess (but was accused of treachery towards the end of his life); *Cicero* for his eloquence, moral

wisdom and statesmanship; *Petrarch* as poet, lover and humanist.

3 Text: sts 1–4, William Byrd, *Psalms, Sonnets and Songs of Sadness and Piety* (1588); st. 5, Bodl. MS Rawlinson Poetry 85. 1 *false Love*: cf. Sidney, *Arcadia* poem 2 above and Panofsky (1962), ch. 4. R describes sensual passion as opposed to the spiritual love of the Platonic tradn, and utilises a series of commonplaces (the Petrarchan sea of sorrows; Love as angler, as in Donne's 'The Bait'; the maze of love, etc.); 7–8: the shift of gender (cf. l.19) suggests either that R is thinking momentarily of his beloved, or of Venus (in which case *serpent* links with Eve, often identif. as the cause of carnal concupiscence in Adam); or that he was familiar with the tradn of Love as a woman (Panofsky, figs 83–4); l.7 also recalls the proverbial, originally Virgilian, *anguis in herba* (snake in the grass: *Ecl.*, 3.93) modified to accommodate the tradn of the diabolic Cupid crowned with flowers (Panofsky, fig. 88); 25 *sith*: since; *trains*: deceits (*OED* Train sb²); 27 *bewrayed*: revealed; 28 *kind*: (my) nature; 29 *Desire*: personified in *FQ*, III. xii. 9.

4 George Puttenham, *Art of English Poesy* (1589), 3.19, pp. 165, 167 printed st. 3 and the opening couplet of st. 6, identifying them as R's. The complete poem, addressed to Queen Eliz., was discovered in 1958 in what was then Phillips MS 3602, and transcribed in Oakeshott (1960), 154, minus sts 1, 2: for the MS see his plate 8. L. G. Black, 'A Lost Poem by Queen Elizabeth', *Times Lit. Supp.*, 23 May 1968, p. 535 printed another version from Archbishop Marsh's Library, Dublin (MS 2.3.5.21), together with the queen's verse reply. 2 *life's soul* (Marsh MS): limb's joy (Phillips); 4 *fancy*: imagination; 10 *smoke* (Phillips): smokes (Puttenham): means *incense*; 14 *worldlings' band*: the fetters of worldly demands; 21: Fortune is tradnlly blindfold (Ripa (1603), 169) and (the witty point of l.24) emblematic of female fickleness.

5 Text: *The Phoenix Nest*. Puttenham, *op. cit.*, p. 168 quotes the last 2 lines as an example of '*Ploche*, or the Doubler': i.e., 'a speedy reiteration of one word, but with some little intermission by inserting one or two words between'.

6 Text: *ibid*. A celebrn of Eliz. as the moon goddess, Diana, who is also goddess of the woods and of the hunt (R uses an alternative name, Cynthia, in 19). 1 *harmless*: bec. it does not burn like the sun's; 2 *dews*: thought, like pearls, to be offspring of the moon; 3 *glory*: halo (Gloriana = Sp's name for Eliz. in *FQ*); 6 *knights*: cf. Sp's knights of the Order of Maidenhead (*FQ*, II. iii. 42, etc.); 7: Eliz. is mistress of the ocean as moon goddess of the tides: she also holds sway over her favourite Sir 'Water' (see no. 19, *passim*); 10 *In . . . pure*: She Mistress-like makes all things to be pure (*England's Helicon* (1600)); *In aye*: forever; *mistresslike*: through her power as sovereign; 11: the repetns of the moon's cycle make her an emblem of eternity (cf. Sp's *Mutability Cantos*, vi. 8 (Cynthia reigns in everlasting glory. . . . Cynthia did sit, that never still did stand)); R wittily reverses the tradn that the moon's rapid orbit makes her an emblem of fickle Fortune; 13: she guides Time's chariot by virtue of the fact that she is, along with the sun, the main planet by which we measure time; 14

Mortality: in the Ptolemaic system everything below the moon's sphere (sublunary) is subject to decay: but Eliz's personal motto is *semper eadem* (always the same): see 20n; 15: astral influences reach earth only by passing through her sphere; 16 *Virtue*: often depicted as an armed maiden of the Diana type (Ripa (1603), 508–9), though more frequently assoc. with the sun (*ibid.*, 510–12): another witty reversal, continued in l.18: *Circe*, daughter of the Sun, is the witch who tempts men to unreason and transforms them into beasts in *Odyssey*, 10.

7 Text: *ibid.* Transln of Book 2, sonnet 8 of Philippe Desportes' *Diane* (1573): Latham (1951), 105–8. R departs from his original in ll. 13–4 by admitting Despair and Death rather than having the hermit-lover praying 'to a painting of Love and that of my mistresses' that he has 'always before [his] eyes'. 3 *recure*: remedy; 10 *stay*: rest: hope as the lover's staff is proverbial (Proteus in Sh's 2 *Gent. of Verona*, 3.1: 'Hope is a lover's staff; walk with that,/And manage it against despairing thoughts').

8 Text: *ibid.* Title from (anon), *Le Prince d'Amour* (1660). For the refrain see no. 19, 120–4 and *Hist. of the World*, 1. 2. 5 (of the 7th age of man, dedicated to sorrowful Saturn: 'wherein our days are sad and overcast, and in which we find by dear and lamentable experience . . . that all our vain passions and affections past, the sorrow only abideth'). 2 *dandled*: pampered.

9 Text: Edmund Spenser, *Faerie Queene* (1590). Along with 10, R's two commendatory sonnets to Sp on his epic. Sp's *Letter of the Author's* expounding the 'continued allegory, or dark conceit' of his poem was addressed to R. *Conceit*, as in R's title, = both *concept* and *construct of images*. 1 *Laura*: Petrarch's beloved, the subject of the *rime*: since his love for her was a matter of poetic address only, she remained (to him) virgin, hence *vestal* (l. 2): *Vesta* = virginal Roman goddess of the domestic fire; 6 *Faery Queen*: Eliz., the dedicatee and subject of the poem; 10 *Oblivion* . . . *Laura*: a neat paradox since Ital. *lauro* = laurel, an evergreen symbolising immortality. But note also the *laurel* = emblematic of virginity bec. of Daphne (Ovid, *Met.* 1. 665–700) and, bec. it was also used to crown victors (*ibid.*), it = emblem of heroic poetry (hence Sp displaces Homer, ll. 13–14).

10 2 *Philomena*: Philomel (*Met.*, 6. 544 ff.), emblem of poetry; see also Sidney, *Arcadia* poems 28.61n; 5 *Beauty*: Eliz's beauty is praised throughout *FQ*, but esp. in Book III (e.g., proem); 7 *Chastity*: the subject of *FQ* III; *Temperance*: the subject of Book II.

11 Text: *Le Prince d'Amour*. The 2 MS versions name the addressee as Eliz's maid of honour, Anne Vavasor. The imagery is that of courtly love as derived from the *Roman de la Rose*, etc: the lady as castle whose virtue is a flower.

12(a) Text: *England's Helicon* (1600). R's poem is one of several replies to Marlowe's, though only one other appears in *Eng. Hel. 9 beds of roses*: the flowers of Venus but also of mutability, as R's reply, ll. 13–15, typically notices (cf. *FQ*, II. xii. 75,77); 10 *posies*: the original spelling *poesies* brings out the commonplace pun: flowers *and* poems; 12 *myrtle*:

dedic. to Venus; 17 *ivy*: emblem of female deities: also emblem of wine god Bacchus who = companion to Venus; 18 *coral*: precious, and from Venus's element, the sea; *amber*: again precious, and believed to bestow fertility on women; 22 *May morning*: when the rites of the fertility and flower goddess Flora were celebrated (Ovid, *Fasti*, 5. 185–6).

12(b) Text: *ibid.* 7 *Philomel*: 10.2n above.

13 Text: Francis Davison, *A Poetical Rhapsody* (1602). The circular structure (opening rhyme of last st. picking up concluding rhyme of st. 1) is apt for a poem that is a *posy* or circular garland: see 12(a), 10n. 1 *Conceit*: a whim (and see 9 above): belonging to Imagination, it is opposed to Reason (l. 4); 19: *Desire* accompanies *Fancy* (18) in Sp's *FQ*, III. xii. 27–8: his blindness derives from Cupid's; 25: common Petrarchan image; 27–8: in the 16th cent. *fly* often means *moth*, and the moth attracted to and destroyed by a flame = a familiar emblem of the lover's fate.

14 Text: BL MS Add 22602. I assume that the whole poem is by R (see Latham (1951), 115–7), though there are arguments that ll. 7 ff. are by Robert Ayton (e.g. C. B. Gullans in *Studies in Bibliography*, 13 (1960), 191–8). 7 *Empress*: punning on *impresa* and *impress* (she = an emblem inscribed on his heart); 3.27n above.

15 Text: BL MS Harleian 6917. Cf. R's reply to Marlowe, 12(b); comprises a *blason* and *contrablason* (see Sidney, *Arcadia* poems 20). The fabrication of a love-object is a favourite Elizabethan theme: cf. *FQ*, I. i. 45, III, viii. 5–9; 22 *doth* (BL MS Add. 25707): doe (MS Harl.); 26 *discovers*: removes the cover of (to reveal the skeleton): 2 MSS read *discolours*; 31–6: in 1618 R will rewrite this stanza as no. 30.

16 Text: Bodl. MS Rawl. Poet. 85. Draws on ballads on the subject of pilgrimages to the shrine of Our Lady at Walsingham in Norfolk (cf. *Hamlet*, 4. 5. 22). 9–10: Latham (1965), 212 suggests that these lines distinguish Eliz's auburn hair from blonde and brown; 29–32: cf. Cupid in 3 above; 33 *dureless*: unenduring, transient; 40 *conceits*: fantasies.

17 Text: Hatfield MS (Cecil papers, 144), in R's own hand: on the queen's having no use for his verses.

18 Text: *ibid.* Critical tradn has the sonnet refer to R's imprisonment in the Tower in 1592 bec. of Eliz's anger at his marriage to Eliz. Throckmorton. 4 *her*: Eliz. I (and Envy).

THE OCEAN TO CYNTHIA

19 Text: *ibid.* I have not followed Latham and others in printing *Cynthia* with stanza divisions bec. (it is thought) they make this puzzling text easier for the modern reader. The original is undivided except at: ll. 56–7; 119–20; 200–1; 212–13; 220–1; 286–7; 294–5; 318–19; 404–5; 473–4. For the suggestion that 'the end of a sheet may possibly, in the writer's mind, stand sometimes for a division' see Latham (1951), 126.

Title The subject of a longstanding debate. Latham reads the numerals as 11 (Latham (1951), 122), others, including Philip Edwards, *Sir Walter*

Ralegh (London: Longmans, Green and Co, 1953), 96n, as 21 (following Hannah). I read vi: see D. and M. Brooks-Davies, 'The Numbering of Sir Walter Ralegh's 'Ocean to Cynthia': A Problem Solved', *Notes and Queries*, 236 (1991); but compare S. M. Clanton in *Studies in Philology*, 82 (1985).

Occasion Unknown, but probably the product of his imprisonment in the Tower after the Throckmorton marriage. It is clearly a complaint by R at the way the moon queen Eliz. has treated him. Stephen Greenblatt, *Sir Walter Ralegh* (New Haven and London: Yale U.P., 1973), rightly emphasises the poem's private nature and, I think again rightly, questions whether it was ever intended to be a long poem: the book numbers are gestures rather than signs of work completed or seriously intended. Sp in his dedic. sonnet to R in the *FQ* refers to 'thy fair Cynthia's praise'; and in *FQ*, III proem 4 he refers to 'that sweet verse . . . In which a gracious servant pictures/His Cynthia, his heaven's fairest light'. But in *Colin Clout's Come Home Again* (1591; publ. 1595) and dedic. to R after R's visit to him in Ireland, Sp notes of R: 'His song was all a lamentable lay,/ Of great unkindness, and of usage hard,/Of Cynthia, the Lady of the sea,/Which from her presence faultless him debarred' (ll. 164–7). 3 *died*: i.e., died to me; 22–4 *broken ears . . . flowers*: R's characteristic imagery seems here to recall the tradnl iconography of Eliz. as Astræa with her ear of corn and as Flora with her flowers: see Davies, *H Astræa*, headnote and hymns 4 and 9; 25 *Sun*: emblem of monarchical power: see 97n below; 28 *nor Philomen*: an ill omen indeed, since Philomel (see 10.2n) sang of her barbarous rape by Tereus, and of how he also cut out her tongue; 29 *flocks*, etc.: the pastoral motif picked up by Sp in *Colin Clout*; 37 *invention*: inspiration; 40 *transpiercant*: piercing through; 41 *adamant*: source of attraction (identif. with loadstone): also identif. at this period with diamond, emblem of invincibility and faith (and see Wyatt, no. 2.11n above); 42 *conceit*: image; 49 *sithes*; sighs; 58 *conceit*: belief, opinion; 61: planned voyages, perhaps even that of 1595; 69: the account of Eliz's fickleness culminates at this point in the celebrated Petrarchan image (*rime*, 224); 96 *sithing*: sighing and, in this poem, punning on Time's and Death's ravaging scythe (and cf. l. 49; bec. of its shape the scythe is also emblematic of the crescent moon); 97 *Phoebus*: the sun (as monarch, 106): brotherly counterpart to Phoebe, another name for the moon (cf. l. 271); 116: the memory of her acted as a balm (cf. 24.7n); 120: R first attracted Eliz's attention in 1582; 123: textual self-reminiscence: see 8n above; 125 *sorrowful success*: the sorrow that ensues; 177 *prime*: youth (that is Love's ground . . .); 189 *vestal*: see 9.2n; 192 *vade*: fade (the spelling may retain R's Devonshire burr): but *vade* itself means *depart* (see 20.4n); 201 *want . . . want*: need . . . lack; 203 *woman . . . fashion*: a woman in mere outward show (*OED Fashion* sb 7); 205: in Ptolemaic astronomy an envelope of elements enshrouded the earth in the ascending order water, air, fire: water is thus the immediate protector of earth from fire (the phrasing may recall Genesis 1:7); 21; *fantasy*: mood (with the sense of *impression* or *image*); 211

kind: i.e., women, tradnlly fickle; 250 *reaves*: forcibly deprives (the sun =
here the image of the Petrarchan mistress's power and of monarchical
absolutism): Cynthia does, of course, borrow her light from the sun; 263
tokens: jewelled emblematic pendants; 271 *Belphoebe*: the beautiful
moon (*bellaPhoebe*), a *persona* for Eliz. invented by Sp for *FQ* (1590),
where she represents the queen's private self as 'a most virtuous and
beautiful lady' (*Letter of the Author's*, addressed to R). As such she
appears in II. iii and is a major figure in Book III, the book in which the sea
features most prominently. In III. v Sp records R's love for Eliz, and in the
1596 *FQ*, R's banishment is recorded in IV. vii and viii where Timias (=
R) grieves for the loss of his 'liefest love' Belphoebe; 278 *foiled*: trampled
down; 280 *wonted*: accustomed; 296 *dureless*: unlasting; 308 *incarnate*:
deep pink or red; 309 *fields*: punning on the heraldic sense (surface of an
escutcheon); 327 *Queen . . . Belphoebe*: cf. 271n. R here makes clear the
distinction between the queen's two roles (or 'bodies') also made by Sp in
his *Letter*: that of the public self as the embodiment of the state, and that
of the private, human self; 328: the lion of the royal coat of arms,
symbolising wrath as well as magnanimity, displaces the *dove* of Venus
and concord. A dove is the successful messenger of reconciliation
between forlorn Timias and Belphoebe in *FQ*, IV. viii. 3ff.: 342: R
alludes to the quartering of a corpse after execution; 374 *affecteth*: is
inclined to; *depraving*: defamation; 391 *assays*: assails, assaults (also:
puts to the test); 392 *pearl*: lunar stone, thus dedic. to Cynthia: but C. S.
Lewis argued from R's spelling, *perrellike*, that the word is *perrie-like*
(*perrie* = collection of gems): Oakeshott (1960), 196; 396: *intentive*:
devoting earnest attention; 404: the dots and ruled line appear in the MS;
410 *The*: That; 413 *But that*: Nevertheless; 419: Oakeshott (1960), 198
compares *FQ*, III. v. 50 (Belphoebe and Timias); 429 *it*: i.e., the mind,
with its image of Eliz; 432: 308n above; 440: *take . . . kind*: assume an
immortal nature; 450–54: a commonplace; 460 *fretting*: destroying
(also: eating a pattern into); 471 *worren*: worn; 478 *Arabian*: desert; but
partic. appropr. bec. *Arabia felix* (fortunate Arabia) was the reputed
home of the Phoenix, emblem of Eliz's uniqueness (Yates (1975a), 58,
65–6; Sidney, *Arcadia* poems, 9.102n); 487–8: Leander's love for Hero
had been most recently the subject of Marlowe's poem (completed by
George Chapman, 1598): Leander drowns one night while swimming
across the Hellespont to visit Hero in Sestos after a storm has put out the
guiding light. When Hero sees his corpse, she throws herself into the sea.
Book 22. The basis for no. 28.

LATER POEMS

20 Text: see Oakeshott (1960), 205–9 and plate 5; first printed by
George Seddon in *Illustrated London News*, 28 February 1953. In R's
own hand in flyleaf of notebook of maps and other material for *Hist. of
the World*; prob. written 1602 or earlier. Poss. an epilogue to an
entertainment for Eliz.; or poss. a 'retrospect' featuring the Elizabethan

iconography familiar from Davies' *H Astr.*, etc. 2–3: 3 names for the moon are linked with the goddess of flowers (Davies, *H Astr.*, 4 and 9) and Aurora, dawn goddess; 4 *Beauty*: cf. *H Astr.*, 4; *vade*: depart; 8 *darling*: favourite (of Nature and the nation); 9–10: cf. Sp's expression of wonder, *FQ*, II proem 2: the *summer* also signifies gold, which R connects with Peru in vast quantities in his *The Discovery of the large, rich, and beautiful Empire of Guiana* (London, 1596), 93; 11–12: perhaps there should be a comma after *conquering* (Eliz. conquers time, she masters all . . .): in any case, both lines allude to her personal motto *semper eadem* (always the same); 13 *elemental fire*: see Davies, *Orchestra*, 378–84n; 18 *quintessential*: made of the 5th (purest) element, of which the heavenly bodies were composed; also alchemically identif. with the elixir of life (drinkable gold, which bestowed immortality); 20 *ever . . . the same*: translates *semper eadem*; 23–4: spelled *Princes . . . Or* in MS, which could yield the alternative reading: 'Princes of world's affection,/Or praises, but deceive her'; 25–6 *quill . . . angel's wing*: a self-quotation (see 10.12, with the same rhyme).

21 Text: Francis Davison, *A Poetical Rhapsody* (1608; 1611). A popular poem to which several 'answers' were composed (Latham (1951), 128–38). 16 *faction*: Latham adopts and defends the reading *affection*, found in 3 MSS; 25 *brave*: swagger; dress extravagantly; 26 *beg . . . more*: i.e., from the monarch's favour; 28 *Seek* (various MSS): Like (Davison); 31 *Zeal*: fervent enthusiasm; *wants*: lacks; 33 *metes*: measures; 43 *wrangles*: debates; 44 *tickle*: dubious, difficult to deal with: *niceness*: subtlety; 50 *prevention*: 'the action of forestalling, or securing an advantage over another person by previous action, or of baffling or stopping another person in the execution of his designs' (*OED*, sense 4a); 75 *Although*: all texts except Davison, who reads *But*.

22 Text: Bodl. MS Malone 19. Title from John Donne (the younger), *Poems of Lord Pembroke and Sir Benjamin Ruddier* (1660). 5 *crosses*: afflictions: also (possibly) coins (*OED Cross* sb 20); 10 *trump*: in the card-game sense and punning on trumpet of Day of Judgement (1 Cor. 15:52); 11 *Dead bones*: dice; 15 *strange* (MS Rawl.): strong (Malone); 15–17 *Herald . . . horn*: i.e., a cockerel (which marked the end of the Christmas Saturnalia when it crew on 12th Night, 6 January): for the feast, see Enid Welsford, *The Fool: His Social and Literary History* (Garden City, N.Y.: Doubleday, 1961 edn), ch. 9.

23 Text: BL MS Add 23229. Title from MS Malone 19.

24 Text: *Daiphantus, or The Passions of Love . . . by An. Sc. . . . Whereunto is added The Passionate Man's Pilgrimage* (1604). Latham (1951), 142–3 lists some of the many textual variants. A few MSS suggest in their subtitle to the poem that it was written shortly before his (reprieved) execution in November–early December 1603. There is also a strong feeling that it may not be R's at all: e.g., Philip Edwards, 'Who Wrote "The Passionate Man's Pilgrimage"?', *English Literary Renaissance*, 4 (1974), 83–97. 1 *scallop-shell*: pilgrim's emblem: originally a sign that a pilgrim had visited the shrine of St James of Compostella (also

shape of baptismal vessel for holy water); 3 *scrip*: small satchel or wallet carried by pilgrim; 5 *gage*: pledge (Colossians 1:27: '. . . which is Christ in you, the hope of glory'); 7 *Blood*: Christ's redemptive blood, which *embalms* the body in the sense of (i) preventing it from decaying by bestowing immortality (1 Cor. 15:52–4) and (ii) anointing fragrantly, because pilgrims were anointed before setting off on their journeys; 9 *white*: colour of purity and innocence (Daniel 12:10: 'Many shall be purified and made white'; also Rev. 7:14: 'white in the blood of the Lamb', where it is the colour of the robes of 'them that were slain for the word of God' (Rev. 6: 9, 11)); *palmer*: pilgrim, evidence of whose journey to the Holy Land was a palm leaf, emblem of righteousness and eternal life (Jean Daniélou, S.J., *Primitive Christian Symbols*, tr. Donald Attwater (London: Burns and Oates, (1964), ch. 1); 25 *suckets*: sweet-meats (candied, or in syrup): in connection with ll. 12 and 16, note the promised land flowing with milk and honey in e.g. Joshua 5:6 and Rev. 20:24; 32–4: recalling the iconography of the Heavenly Jerusalem (Rev. 21) with (*inter alia*) its *saphire* and *pearl*. *Diamonds* symbolise faith; *rubies* signify love and suffering (the *blood* of l. 7), and *coral*, because of its colour, was also associated with blood (and see 12(a), 18n above); 42 *angels*: punning on the gold coin known as *angel*; 43 *twelve million*: apocalyptic symbolism again, since the Heavenly Jerusalem is proportioned by 12s (e.g., Rev. 7:4, 14:1, 21: 12, 17, etc.); 49 *movest*: propose as a motion; 50: note the neatness of the pun in relation to l. 9 and n and 57; 54 *noon*: lunchtime but also symbolic of judgement (Panofsky (1955), 262); 55 *stroke*: of bell, of axe; 56: alluding to the 'crown of glory' (1 Peter 5:4) and to Christ as the head of the church (Ephes. 5:23, 1 Cor. 11:3).

25 Text: Orlando Gibbons, *The First Set of Madrigals or Motets* (1612). Only 5 of many MSS attribute it to R. There are numerous textual variants. For a radically different text see Michael Rudick in *Studies in Philology*, 83 (1986), 76–87. 2 *division*: a form of variation in which long notes are split up into shorter decorative ones; 3 *tiring houses*: dressing rooms; 7 *sun*: emblem of judgement (cf. *judicious* in l. 5): 24.54n.

26 Text: prefatory sonnet to Sir Arthur Gorges, *Lucan's Pharsalia* (1614). G was a first cousin of R's and accompanied him on his expedition to the Azores (1597). 13 *translate*: (i) render into English and (ii) reincarnate, as Hammond (1984), 285n points out (the notion of such reincarnations is common in the period: see esp. *FQ*, IV. ii. 32–4).

VERSE TRANSLATIONS FROM *THE HISTORY OF THE WORLD*

27 Text: R's *The History of the World* (1614). I include here 16 of the most substantial of the many verse translations with which R illustrates his argument in the *History*. (3) Juvenal, *Sat.* 15: *Egyptians*: on the Renaissance interest in Egypt, see Erik Iversen, *The Myth of Egypt and its*

Hieroglyphics in European Tradition (Copenhagen: G. E. C. Gad, 1961);
(4) *Orpheus to Musaeus*: see Davies, *Orchestra*, 637n; Justin argues for
Orpheus as one of the *prisci theologii* who had enjoyed revelation from
Moses; (8) Ovid, *Amores: Tantalus*: see Sidney, *AS* 24.3n; (10) Horace,
Odes: Danaë: for another version of the myth, see *FQ*, III. xi. 31: her
father was Acrisius; (12) Virgil, *Aeneid*, 3. 104–12: *Cybel's rites*: Cybele
= the mountain in Phrygia which was the seat of the worship of the great
mother goddess of the same name, whose followers adored her with the
noise of cymbals, etc.; (15) Ausonius, *Epigrams*: included in Ren. edns of
Ausonius, but actually spurious. See Wyatt, no. 35 above; text in MT,
Wyatt, p. 397.

LAST POEMS

28 Text: BL MS Add 27407. Latham (1951), 149–50 sees it as
'intermediate' between *Cynthia* Book 22 and the 'Petition' (no. 29) since
it begins with the opening two stanzas of *Cynthia*, 22 and concludes with
a version of the 'Petition'. 43–4 *first . . . Britons*: the accession of Scottish
James I/VI in 1603 on Eliz's death made the title particularly appropriate.
29 Text: MS Drummond (Edinburgh). Despite Drummond's dating of
1618, Latham (1951), 151 suggests that the *Empress* reference, and the
ref. to 'this widow land' in draft 1 (no. 28), together with other details,
make a date of 1603 'not out of place'. 14 *descrived*: described (in
writing); 28–30: more applicable to the charge that R conspired with
Spain in 1603 than that he helped provoke war with Spain in 1618
(Latham, *ibid.*); 35 *her we had*: Eliz. I, who died on 24 March 1603.
30 Text: *Cinq Cents de Colbert*, 467 (Bibl. Nat., Paris); transcr. in *TLS*
13 October 1932, p. 734, by H. Bibas. There are many versions of this
poem, a number of which support the assertion made in the title. It is a
recasting of the final stanza of no. 15.
31 Text: *Remains of Sir Walter Ralegh* (1651). Title: *snuff*: 'that portion
of a wick . . . which is partly consumed in the cause of burning to give
light, and in the case of a candle requires to be removed at intervals'
(*OED Snuff* sb 1.1).

SIR PHILIP SIDNEY

Poems from the Arcadia

S's massive pastoral prose romance was written for his sister Mary, Countess of Pembroke, and published in 3 books in 1590 (*The Countesse of Pembrokes Arcadia, written by Sir Philippe Sidnei*). Its text breaks off in mid-sentence. 1593 saw a 5-book version *Now since the first edition augmented and ended*. In fact, it comprised a virtual reprint of the 1590 text together with an ending to Book 3 and the addition of two more books. From various references we know that contemporaries were aware of an earlier version, MSS of which were identified only in the early years of this century. Now known as the *Old Arcadia (OA)*, it was first published in 1926 by A. Feuillerat, and is available in an authoritative edn by Jean Robertson (1973). Her edn enables us to see that the ending to Book 3 and Books 4 and 5 are in essentials the last 3 books of the original *OA*, whereas its first 2 books are considerably different from the 1590 and 1593 texts (the 1590 text is known now as the *New Arcadia (NA)* and available in a definitive edn by Victor Skretkowicz (1987)). The 5-book (or -act) *Arcadia* seems to have been written between mid-1577 and spring 1581, according to Robertson; the unfinished *NA* exists in a MS dated 1584.

The *Arcadia* in both versions is interspersed with poems, with each book or act, except the last, ending in a group of eclogues. These poems predate *Certain Sonnets* and *Astrophil and Stella*.

Copy text

1590 for the poems in Books 1 to 3 and 1593 for those in the remainder of Book 3 and Books 4 and 5 (abbrev. to 90 and 93 respectively). I have compared my texts with those in Robertson and Skretkowicz and in Ringler's edn of the *Poems*. Occasionally I have adopted a reading from the 1598 edn (*The Countess of Pembrokes Arcadia . . . Now the Third Time published*; abbrev. 98).

Order of poems

As in *OA*.

Titles

There are none in the original texts. I have introduced them where they seem helpful, and I identify each poem with an *incipit*.

Modern editions

The Prose Works of Sir Philip Sidney, ed. Albert Feuillerat, 4 vols (Cambridge: Cambridge U.P., 1912–26; repr. 1962).

The Poems of Sir Philip Sidney, edn. W. A. Ringler, Jr (Oxford: Clarendon Press, 1962).

Philip Sidney: Selected Poetry and Prose, ed. David Kalstone (New York: New American Library, 1970).

Sir Philip Sidney: Selected Poems, ed. Katherine Duncan-Jones (Oxford: Clarendon Press, 1973).

The Countess of Pembroke's Arcadia (the 'Old Arcadia'), ed. Jean Robertson (Oxford: Clarendon Press, 1973).

The Countess of Pembroke's Arcadia, ed. Maurice Evans (Harmondsworth: Penguin, 1977).

Sir Philip Sidney: Selected Prose and Poetry, ed. Robert Kimbrough (Madison: Univ. of Wisconsin Press, 1983).

Sir Philip Sidney: the Old Arcadia, ed. Katherine Duncan-Jones (Oxford and New York: Oxford University Press, 1985).

The Countess of Pembroke's Arcadia (the 'New Arcadia'), ed. Victor Skretkowicz (Oxford: Clarendon Press, 1987).

Sir Philip Sidney: Selected Writings, ed. Richard Dutton (Manchester: Carcanet, 1987).

Sir Philip Sidney, ed. Katherine Duncan-Jones. Oxford Authors (Oxford and New York: Oxford U.P., 1989).

FURTHER READING

ALWES, D. B. AND W. L. GODSHALK, 'Recent Studies in Sidney (1978–86)', *English Literary Renaissance*, 18 (1988).

BUXTON, JOHN. *Sir Philip Sidney and the English Renaissance* (1954).

BUXTON, JOHN. *Elizabethan Taste* (1966).

COLAIANNE, A. J. AND W. L. GODSHALK, 'Recent Studies in Sidney (1970–77)', *English Literary Renaissance*, 8 (1978).

CONNELL, DOROTHY. *Sir Philip Sidney: The Maker's Mind* (1977).

COOPER, S. M. *The Sonnets of Astrophel and Stella: A Stylistic Study* (1968).

DONOW, H. S. (ed.) *A Concordance to the Poems of Sir Philip Sidney* (1975).

English Literary Renaissance, 2:1 (1972) special issue *The Achievement of Sir Philip Sidney*.

FOWLER, ALASTAIR. *Triumphal Forms: Structural Patterns in Elizabethan Poetry* (1970).

FOWLER, ALASTAIR. *Conceitful Thought: The Interpretation of English Renaissance Poems* (1975).

GALM, J. A. *Sidney's Arcadian Poems* (1973).

GODSHALK, W. L. 'Recent Studies in Sidney (1940–69)', *English Literary Renaissance*, 2 (1972).

HAMILTON, A. C. *Sir Philip Sidney: A Study of his Life and Works* (1977).

HENINGER, S. K. *Sidney and Spenser: The Poet as Maker* (1989).

HOWELL, ROGER. *Sir Philip Sidney: The Shepherd Knight* (1968).

KALSTONE, DAVID. *Sidney's Poetry: Contexts and Interpretations* (1965).

KIMBROUGH, ROBERT. *Sir Philip Sidney* (1971).

KINNEY, A. F. (ed.) *Essential Articles for the Study of Sir Philip Sidney* (1986).

KINNEY, A. F. (ed.) *Sidney in Retrospect: Selections from 'English Literary Renaissance'* (1988).

LEVER, J. W. *The Elizabethan Love Sonnet* (1956).

MCCOY, R. C. *Sir Philip Sidney: Rebellion in Arcadia* (1979).

MOORE, DENNIS. *The Politics of Spenser's Complaints and Sidney's Philisides Poems* (1982).

MYRICK, K. O. *Sir Philip Sidney as a Literary Craftsman* (1935).

NICHOLS, J. G. *The Poetry of Sir Philip Sidney: An Interpretation in the Context of his Life and Times* (1974).

OSBORN, J. M. *Young Philip Sidney, 1572–1577* (1972).

RAITIERE, M. N. *Faire Bitts: Sir Philip Sidney and Renaissance Political Theory* (1984).

RUDENSTINE, N. L. *Sidney's Poetic Development* (1967).

Sidney Newsletter (1980–).

STILLMAN, R. E. *Sidney's Poetic Justice: 'The Old Arcadia', Its Eclogues and Renaissance Pastoral Traditions* (1986).

WALLER, GARY AND M. D. MOORE (EDS) *Sir Philip Sidney: The Interpretation of Renaissance Culture* (1984).

WASHINGTON, M. A. *Sir Philip Sidney: An Annotated Bibliography of Modern Criticism, 1941–1970* (1972).

WEINDER, A. D. *Sir Philip Sidney and the Poetics of Protestantism: A Study of Contexts* (1978).

WILSON, MONA. *Sir Philip Sidney* (1931).

YOUNG, R. B. *Three Studies in the Renaissance: Sidney, Jonson, Milton* (1958).

1 From Book 1, first eclogues. Lalus challenges Dorus to a virtuoso 'expressing of his passions'. The pastoral song contest originates with Theocritus, *Idylls*, 5–9 and Virgil, *Eclogues*, 3, 7. 1 *Lalus*: renamed Thyrsis in 93; 7 *pie*: magpie; 24 *Her*: Pamela; 25 *Pan*: nature- and shepherd god, half goat, half man, who plays reed pipes; 26 *Kala*: Beautiful (Gk); her marriage to L is celebrated in 21; 31 *coney*: rabbit; 35 *nice to touch*: reserved about being touched; *peized*: weighed; 55 *glasseth*: reflects; 60 *inure*: accustom; 61 *harnished*: harnessed; 85–96: at the end of *OA* Bk 1 Pamela swooned after being chased by a bear which Dorus killed. She recovers to find him kissing her and rejects him with disdain; 100–105: the language of magic; 108 *one* (98); *that (90)*; 124 *weed*: garb; 126 *gins*: traps; 128 *myrtle*: dedicated to Venus; 130 *pelf*: wealth; 138 *way-menting*: lamentation; 151 *mould*: body, punning on *mould* as

Philip Sidney

earth in which one is buried (*OED Mould* sb¹ 2, sb³ 10b); 165 *eyne*: eyes.
2 First eclogues; spoken by shepherd Dicus in *OA*, transferred to 2.14 in
NA. 90 does not have stanza divns. Dicus revises the tradnl iconography
of Cupid (see notes to *AS* 62, 65 and 72 below) to produce an attack on
sensual love. 4 *gloses*: false appearances; 10 *Phoebus*: loved Daphne
(*Met.*, 1. 545ff.); 12 *third*: S's invention (horn for cuckolds); 14–17:
Met., 1. 727ff.: Juno, jealous of Jupiter's love for the cow Io, set 100-eyed
Argus to watch her; Mercury killed him. But this pedigree is S's invention.
3 Book 2; sung by Cleophila (the disguised Pyrocles) about Philoclea.
4 Book 2; sung by Basilius about Cleophila.
5 Book 2; sung by Dorus (really prince Musidorus) to Pamela. 5
Wanhope: Despair.
6 Book 2; written by Philoclea on a stone in a copse.
7 Book 2; Cleophila (Pyrocles) inscribes this with a willow stick (for
grief) on sand (= mutability). 1–6 recall myth of Narcissus
who fell in love with his own face reflected in water having rejected the
nymph Echo (*Met.*, 3. 431ff.).
8 End of Book 2, birthday hymn to Phoebus Apollo sung by Basilius,
Gynecia, Pamela and Philoclea. 3 *shines* (Rob., Ring.): shine (90); 5–6:
the sun god slew the dragon Python, poisonous symbol of evil (*Met.*, 1.
525–42); 7: *Latona*, impregnated by Jupiter, gave birth to Phoebe/Diana
on the isle of Delos after being chased over the earth by Juno, then gave
birth to Phoebus Apollo; 10 *brickle*: brittle.
9 Second eclogues *OA*; printed in 2.12 by 90, which omits ll. 1–4 and
185–90. Histor (narrator of events past) repeats the pastoral lament sung
by Plangus (Lament) to Boulon (Counsel) about the imprisonment and
imminent death of his beloved Erona. 90 has Basilius reply to Plangus. 4
refrain: check, restrain; 17: a commonplace: cf. *King Lear*, 4.1; 25: cf.
Ecclesiastes 1:18; 26 *book*: for the symbolism see Curtius (1967), ch. 16;
29–31: the four elements, represented in the body by the four humours
(blood, phlegm, black and yellow bile), fight each other for supremacy:
balance and 'repose' belonged only to prelapsarian Adam: Klibansky,
Saxl, Panofsky (1964), 99n, 103; 33 *whipping top*: *Aeneid*, 7. 383; 34
beast, tree: alludes to man's possession of the sensitive soul which he
shares with beasts and to the vegetative soul which he shares with plants:
e.g., engraving from Bouelle in Heninger (1977), 163; 35 *stone*:
touchstone; 40 *haps*: events; 66 *causeful* (Rob. and Ring.): irefull (90);
71–82: commonplaces of Christian Stoic consolation encouraging
'patience'. For God's *scourge* see Prov. 3:11–12; 102 *Phoenix*: fabulous
Arabian bird, only one of which existed at one time; assoc. with sun god
Osiris as emblem of renewal; also symbol of uniqueness and perfection;
106 *dam*: Clymene, Phaëthon's mother by Apollo. For the rivalry
between him and his father and the consequent threatened destruction of
the earth, see *Met.*, 2. 1ff.; 107–14 *Vulcan's spite*: fire. Vulcan,
blacksmith of the gods, designed Apollo's palace and was also Venus's
husband; for Mars's adultery with Venus, see *AS* 13n; 111 *flames* (Rob.
and Ring.): flame (90); *witold*: cuckold; 139 *wink*; close eyes (be blind

428

to); 143 *grammar*: discipline; 157 *this* (Rob. and Ring.): thy (90); 175 *spilled*: spoiled; 184 *ass*: Aesop, *Fables*, 275, ed. Chambry (1967).

10 Second eclogues; sung by Philisides (persona for S himself) in *OA* and 93, but attrib. to a 'young melancholy shepherd' in 90. An experiment in hexameters, it belongs to the Renaissance genre of echo songs that has its origin in the myth of Narcissus (7n above). Here, the shepherd frames 'his voice in those deserte places, as to what words he would have the *Echo* replie . . . and so kindly framed a disputation betwixt himselfe and it'. Copy text 93. 2 *What bars me*: Who debars me (90); 3 *have met*: doo meete (90); 4 *then*: and (90); 17 *thy*: the (90); 18 *thy*; th' (90); 21 *leans*: leades (90); 33 *such news, but*: such bad newes: how (90); *Orts*: 90 etc spell *Oughts* as do Rob. and Ring. I have followed Duncan-Jones (1973): her printing of *Orts* (= scraps, fragments) is clearly right; 36 *among*: above (90); *of virtue the most. Most*: a title. A tittle (90); 42 *like*: very (90); 44 *Whence*: How (90); 49–50: 90 reads: Tell yet againe, how name ye the goodly made evill? A devill. /Devill? in hell where such Devill is, to that hell I doo goe. Goe.

11 Second eclogues. In *OA* and 93, not in 90, as all hereafter unless noted otherwise: text 93. Dorus sings 'these verses, called asclepiadics'.
11 *Science*: Knowledge; 18 *Envy*: tradnlly depicted with a snake: Whitney (1586), 94; Ripa (1603), 241–2; 20 *humorist*: someone under the extreme influence of a particular bodily humour (9.29–31n above); *puddled*: muddied; 33 *stains*: outdoes.

12 Book 3; written by Basilius to Cleophila. 10 *prove*: undergo; 11 *title*: claim.

13 Book 3; Cleophila leaves Basilius and sings this at the entrance to a cave. 2 *by* (98): of (93); 7 *windows . . . light*: the five senses.

14–15 Book 3. Led by singing from within the cave, Cleophila finds 'upon a stone a little waxe light set, and under it a piece of paper with these verses verie lately . . . written in it' by Basilius's wife Gynecia.

16 Book 3; Dorus tells of seeing Dametas with the shepherdess Charita and of hearing her sing this song to him.

17 Book 3; Dametas's reply to Charita. 14 *sleekstone*: stone used for polishing or smoothing; 18 *gage*: pledge.

18 Book 3; Musidorus to Pamela as a lullaby: note that for hypnotic effect there are only two rhyme sounds: cf. 13 and *AS* 89.

19 Book 3; Basilius to Cleophila by moonlight. For the 2 suns motif, used earlier by Basilius, see *FQ*, V.iii. 19;14 *brother's*: Apollo and Diana were twins (8.7n above).

20 Book 3, printed in 2.11 in 90. Text 90. Sung by Pyrocles (remembering it as sung by Philisides) to Philoclea; technically a *blason*, or catalogue of the beloved's beauties. 10 *lines* (Rob. and Ring.): line (90); 24 *Aurora*: dawn goddess; 25 *queen-apple*: early variety of apple (apples = emblems of love); 27 *ivory*: cf. *Song of Solomon* 7:4 (also, ivory = emblematic of Venus); 39 *rubies . . . roses*: emblems of love and fruitfulness; *rubies* also = wisdom (Prov. 3:15); *pearl* = wisdom (Mat. 7:6) and virginity; 49 *towers*: neck as tower in *Song of Sol.* 4:4 and 7:4; 53 *lovely* (Rob. and

Ring.): livelie (90); 54 *babe*: Cupid; 55 *pommels*: balls, bosses (deriv. from and punning on *pomme* = apple); 56 *azure*: i.e. heavenly; 57 *porphyry*: red/purple stone; 60 *Milky*: the Milky Way, so named, according to one tradn, from the milk spilt from Juno's breast when she awoke to find that Mercury had placed the infant Hercules to suckle at it and pushed the baby away. The *lilies* of l. 62 also recall this milk, some of which was fabled to have fallen to earth and given lilies their whiteness (Jonson, note to *Hymenaei*, l. 199; ed. Orgel (1969)); 62 *lilies*: in love poetry = virginity as well as purity and whiteness (Song of Sol. 2:1,2,16; 5:13, etc.); 88 *Her*: omitted 90; *Ovid's song*: a general ref.; but see *Amores*, 1.5.22; 97 *bought*: curve; 103 *Atlas*: the ankle holding up the 'skies' of her calves (*Atlas* = giant son of the Titans Iapetus and Asia who holds the skies on his shoulders); 104 *whale*: the bone is white (hence pure); but whales tradnlly deceived by trapping the unwary with their scented breath (cf. 107); 105 *There oft* (Rob. and Ring.): Thereout (90); 106 *cedar*: sacred, noble, immortal and constant (the more it is shaken, the more stable it becomes: Webster, *Duchess of Malfi*, 1.1); 107 *violets*: emblematic of Venus (purple), of virginity (white); 110 *Leda's swan*: Jupiter metamorphosed himself into a swan in order to rape Leda (*Met.*, 6. 134); *mews*: moults, changes; 112 *marchpane*: marzipan; 113 *doves*: Venus's birds (and cf. Song of Sol. 2:14, 5:2, etc.); 116 *ermelin*: the ermine signifies purity and chastity (see *AS* 86) bec. it would rather die than get its coat soiled; *spot* (Rob. and Ring.): sport (90); 118 *Phoenix*: see 9.102n above; 134 *Graces*: Aglaia, Thalia, Euphrosyne, handmaids of Venus and symbols of love and its attributes (beauty, kindness, pleasure): Wind (1967), 50–1; 146 *pens* (Rob. and Ring.): tongues (90).

21 Third eclogues. Text 93. Epithalamium (marriage poem) sung by Dicus to celebrate the marriage of Kala and Thyrsis (changed from Lalus in *OA*). 3 *Cupid*: lust, as opposed to the temperate sexual appetite required in marriage: cf. 55ff.; 6 *turtles*: doves, emblems of conjugal felicity (and cf. 20.113n); 9 *Hymen*: god of marriage; 15–16 *elm and vine*: emblems of faith in love (Whitney (1586), 62), the elm symbolising supposed masculine strength, the vine female dependence; 28 *Nymphs*: their element is tradnlly water; 30 grant to: assent to; 33 hinting at the tradn of river marriages (e.g. *FQ*, IV. xi); 47 *knot*: emblem of marital union; 51 *oak, mistletoe*: continuing the idea of male superiority (15–16n above): the oak = strength, the mistletoe, dependence. But Druidically the two together symbolise felicity and prosperity: Pliny, *Natural History*, 16.95 and Brooks-Davies (1983), 173; 82: cf. *AS* 78n; 86 *snake*: treachery.

22 Third eclogues. Nico replies to 21 with this fable. 3 *trick*: neat; 31 *chumpish*: sullen; 51 *Bussing*: kissing; 74 *Diana*: goddess of virginity; 102 *bale*: woe; 117 *feat*: trick.

23 Third eclogues. Pas replies to Nico's 22.

24 Third eclogues, *OA* and 93. Sung by Philisides. Text 90, where it is transferred to first eclogues and sung by an anon. shepherd. 1 *Ister*: Danube (S was instructed by the Huguenot statesman Hubert Languet – see ll. 22–3 – in Vienna about history, politics, etc); *couth*: knew; 24

rede: learning; 29 *thilk*: those; 30 *jump*: precise; 38 *I*: he (90); 43–54: a tradnl conflation of the classical golden age (*Met.*, 1.103ff.) with Isaiah 11; 44 *mould*: pattern (see also 1.151n above); 45 *woned*: inhabited; 50 *policy*: polity, government; 63 *king*: combines Aesop's fable of King Log (ed. Chambry, 66) with I Samuel 8 on the Jews choosing a king; 74 *swink*: labour; 75ff.: *fire*, etc.: myth of Prometheus as maker of man (Apollodorus, 1.7.1); the following lines (man and the animals) also recall the Hermetic account of man's creation as popularised by Pico della Mirandola in his *Oration: on the Dignity of Man* (1486); 80 *ounce*: lynx; 89 *ermine*:20.116n above (the animals are all given their usual attributes); 93 *coney*: 1.31n; 97 *mowing*: grimacing; 115ff.: Ovid on the iron age (*Met.* 1. 143ff.); 134 *Tho*: then; 140 *mew*: cage; 145 *throat* (Rob. and Ring.): teeth (90); 148–54: S reputedly disliked hunting intensely; 157 *stowers*: tumults.

25 Book 4. Text 93. Basilius.

26 Fourth eclogues *OA*, second eclogues 93, Book 1 in 90. Text 90. A double sestina (the sestina, developed by the troubadour Arnaut Daniel, comprises 6 × 6 line stanzas and a 3-line conclusion, each stanza ringing precisely-predetermined changes on the same rhyme words). 7 *Mercury*: the evening star (Brooks-Davies (1983), 115n) also shepherd god, inventor of music, and guide of the souls of the dead (psychopomp); 8 *huntress*: the moon goddess Diana is a hunter and wood deity; 9 *star*: Venus, the morning star; 12 *Echo*: see 7n above; 13 *burgess*: free man; 18 *screech-owl*: bird of ill omen (Isaiah 34:14, etc.); 25 *swannish*: the swan was believed to sing only once in its life, at the moment of death; 42 *serene*: dew or light evening rain, thought to be poisonous; 61 *she*: Urania, whose name means 'heavenly one', with whom both Strephon and Klaius are in love and whose departure from Arcadia the poem laments. She is not the Muse of that name but rather Venus Urania, Heavenly Love and Beauty.

27 Fourth eclogues *OA*, second eclogues 90 and 93. Text 90. Str. and Kl. continue their lament, Str. beginning 'this Dizaine' and Kl. 'answer[ing] in that kinde of verse, which is called the Crown' (i.e. a structure in which the last line of each stanza becomes the first line of the succeeding stanza and the final line of the poem repeats the first). 9 *Dole . . . feeds*: 90. A textual crux: Rob. and Ring. prefer *OA*'s 'Dwell in my ruines, feede': but cf. *Dolours* at l. 68; 17 *heart* (Rob. and Ring.): brest (90); 41ff.: a common allegory (e.g. *FQ*, II. xii. 1–42); 46 *anchor*: Hebr. 6:19; 49 *Care* (Rob. and Ring.): Cares (90); 63 *Torpedo*: electric ray (the numbness of Despair): Henkel and Schöne (1967), 693–4; 72 *Basilisk*: fabulous beast so named from crown marking on head (Gk *basileus* = king), it could kill with a glance; 87 *have* (Rob. and Ring.): should (90); 93 *sell* (Rob. and Ring.): fell (90).

28 fourth eclogues *OA* and 93, where it is a lament for Basilius's death; Book 3 90, where it is sung for the death of Amphialus. An early English instance of the formal pastoral elegy as originated by Theocritus, *Idyll* 1 and Virgil, *Eclogue* 5: cf. *Shep. Cal.*, 'November', though S's direct model is eclogue 11 of Sannazaro's *Arcadia*. 2 *Who (93)*: Whom (90); 7 *cleave (93)*: leave (90); 13 *Myrrh*: Myrrha was changed into a gum-weeping tree after her incestuous affair with her father (*Met.*, 10. 327ff.); 16 *attaint*: condemn (also sully); 29 *Hyacinth*: *Met.*, 10. 168ff. tell of Hyacinthus, loved and accidentally killed by Apollo. He was turned into the flower that bears his name 'in shape a Lillye' (cf. l. 28), its petals inscribed with the Greek cry of lament *ai* ('in a new made flowre thou shalt with letters represent/Our syghings': *Met.*, 10. 217–18). The original spelling *Hiacinthe* preserves not just the sound but also the letters (*ia/ai*); 31 *Echo*: 7n; 61 *Philomela*: raped by Tereus, she had her tongue ripped out and was eventually turned into a nightingale (*Met.*, 6. 544ff.); 79–95: a common sentiment in all pastoral elegy (e.g. *Shep. Cal.*, 'November', 83–92); 79–80 *Time . . . end*: alluding to Time's connection with the never-ending (circular) snake *ouroboros*: Panofsky (1962), 72–3 and fig. 36; 82–3 *snake*: emblem of (solar) renewal because it sloughs its skin: Whitney (1586), 212; Macrobius, *Saturnalia*, 1.20; 97 *spilleth*: spoils; 106–7: cf. 9.29–31n; 111 *Atropos*: the third of the three fates who control the thread of destiny, she is the one who causes death by cutting the filament of each individual life; *distrained*: seized as payment; 116 *Aesculapius*: god of medicine who, for reviving Hippolytus from the dead, was flung by Jupiter into Hades.

29 fourth eclogues *OA* and 93. A sestina (see 26n), it is sung immediately after no. 28. Text 93. 3 *golden staff*: sceptre; 4 *woeful's* (Rob. and Ring.): joyfulls (93); 14 *he*: Basilius.

30 Book 5 *OA* and 93, sung by Musidorus in prison. Text 93.

CERTAIN SONNETS

32 miscellaneous poems, probably 1578–81, publ. at end of 1598 *Arcadia* as *Certaine Sonets written by Sir Philip Sidney: Never before printed*. Text 98 in all cases.

1 Also used in *NA* (90), 3.15. 4 *centre*: the earth was at the centre of the Ptolemaic universe, immediately surrounded by, in order, envelopes of water, air and fire; 9 *all only she (90)*: a lovely she (98).

2 1–9 Philomela and Tereus: 28.61n.

3 The only poem of S's to survive in his own hand. For the underlying image see *AS* 71.14.

4 Title as printed in the original. 1–4 *Wilton*: home of S's sister the Countess of Pembroke, it is 8 miles or so from Stonehenge; 6 *Passion's* (Ring.): passion (98); 11–14 *Brereton*, Chesire = the eponymous home of the Brereton family: the story had wide currency; 13 *hiddenest* (Ring.): hideous (98); 21–4 *fish*: pike; 41–4: story found in William Harrison, *Description of Britain* in Ralph Holinshed, *First and Second Volumes of Chronicles* (1587 edn), 130 (Ring's note); 51–4 *Albion*: original name of Britain; *bird*: barnacle goose, believed to hatch from viscous substance exuded from hulks (Ansell Robin (1932), 32–6).

5 8 *franzy*: frenzy; 13 *peacock's folly*: Pride; 21 *trentals*: set of 30 requiem masses.

7 6 *sweet yoke*: Matt. 11:29–30 (my yoke is easy); *Splendidis . . . nugis*: I say a long farewell to gaudy trifles (source untraced).

ASTROPHIL AND STELLA

As well as the edns noted in connection with the *Arcadia* poems, the following modern edns are noteworthy:

Astrophel and Stella, ed. Mona Wilson (London: Nonesuch Press, 1931).

Astrophel and Stella 1591 (Menston, Yorks: Scolar Press, 1970). Facsimile of Q1.

Elizabethan Sonnets, ed. Maurice Evans (London: Dent, 1977, reissued 1992, Everyman's Library).

Textual history

For a complete textual history see Ringler's edn. *AS* was first printed in 1591 in two unauthorised quartos, Q1 and Q2, by Thomas Newman. Both texts are incomplete. The complete text of 108 sonnets and 11 songs was printed at the end of the 1598 *Arcadia*. Sidney's original holograph does not survive; the relationship between it and surviving manuscripts and printed texts is discussed fully by Ring. Probably written November 1581–late 1582.

Copy text

Based on 1598 (hereafter 98), with sources of any emendations recorded in the notes.

Indentation

Ring. has identified various patterns of line indentation according to the rhyme scheme of the octave and sestet of each sonnet. These are not present in 98, which uniformly indents ll. 2–4, 6–8, 10–11 and 13–14, but they are a feature of the quartos (which, however, often get the patterns wrong). I have followed the quartos' guidance over indentation, modifying their practice in accordance with Ringler's analysis where that appeared to be justified. The indentation patterns are clearly authorial.

Title

Apparently Newman's invention for Q1,2 (*Syr P.S. His Astrophel and Stella*), thence taken into 98. But as Ring. and others have noted, Astro*phel* does not make sense, since both Sidney's Christian name and his *Arcadia* persona of *Phili*sides (= star lover) guarantee that the narrator of the sequence should be Astro*phil* (star lover from Gk *aster* + *philos*).

1 An English sonnet in alexandrines (as opposed to the normal

pentameters) is S's innovation; 8 *sunburnt*: parched by his love for sunlike (see 22) Stella.; 9 *Invention*: the finding out and selection of topic(s) (in rhetoric, the first process in creating a work of lit.); 14 *heart*: seat of love, courage, and understanding (*OED Heart* sb 10, 11, 12). It contains the image of Stella (e.g., 4.12).

2 After metrical innovation, thematic innovation: convention dictated that you admitted love at first sight, not 'by degrees'. 1 *dribbed*: random; 3 *mine*: tunnel dug under wall in a siege; 10–11 the Russians (Slavs), currently ruled by Ivan the Terrible, were popularly said to enjoy his tyranny.

3 1–8 catalogue of contemp. rhetorical devices: 1–2 invocation of the 9 Muses; 3–4 imitation of 6th cent. BC rhapsodic poet Pindar (a convention followed by the Pléiade); *pied*: variegated (but since it derives from magpie, suggesting also the stealing of modes of expression); 5–6 rhetorical complexity (*trope* = figurative language, e.g. metaphor); *problem*: question proposed for discussion, suggested by the pseudo-Aristotelian *Problemata*; 7–8: the kind of thing found in Lyly's prose *Euphues* (1578) and its followers rather than in verse.

4 2 *bate*: debate; 5 *Virtue's sceptre* (usually a rod or lance) signifies her fight against vice and also temperance (Ripa (1603), 511–12: but see Tervarent (1958), col. 337); *Cato* the Censor was known for his strict virtue, and for his whipping of slaves: he died in his 80s; 8 *bit*: emblem of virtue and temperance since it controls the tradnlly passionate horse of the libido (Wind (1967), plate 41).

5 The language is neo-Platonic, extolling reason (*inward light*) and acknowledging the identification of beauty and goodness together with recognition of the imperfection of things on earth (made of the 4 elements) which are thus mere *shadows* of true (heavenly) beauty: see, e.g., Spenser's *Four Hymns* for serious application of the doctrine. Platonist thought has the soul imprisoned in the body, sojourning with it until death when it returns to its divine original. The sonnet's wit derives from the fact that Stella (star) denotes heavenly light and wisdom.

6 Catalogue of contemp. Petrarchan sonnet clichés: 1–4, oxymoron as in Petrarch, *rime*, 134 (cf. Wyatt, 8n above); 5–6 mythol. refs (here specifically Jupiter's metamorphosis of himself into a *bull* to rape Europa, a *swan* to rape Leda, and into a *golden shower* to rape Danäe: compare *FQ*, III. xii); 6 *Bordered*: punning on embroidered; 7–8: conventions of pastoral romance, as in S's own *Arcadia*.

7 1–2 Lady Penelope Rich had black eyes: cf. *AS* 9. S's praise of black, formerly 'not counted fair' (Shakespeare, *Sonnets*, 127), draws on Orphic and related tradns that black embodies the ineffable brightness of wisdom: Pico della Mirandola, *Platonic Conclusions*, 6 and *Orphic Conclusions*, 15 (*opera omnia* (1572), 1.96, 107) and Ben Jonson, *Masque of Blackness*, *Masque of Beauty*. The veiling and blackness continue the neo-Platonism of 5.

8 1 *born in Greece* as, among others, Plato's Eros and Cyprian Venus's son. Cyprus was invaded by the Turks in 1573. For Cupid the runaway

see Moschus, *Idyll* 1; 5 *too* (Q1,2): do (98); 6 *clips*: embraces; 13 *firebrands*: cf. the mediaeval and subsequent tradn that Cupid was armed with a torch instead of arrows: Panofsky (1962), 101.

9 2 *chiefest* (Q1 etc.): choisest (98); 6 *porphyr*: see *Arcadia* song 20.57n above, where it appears in another *blason*; 8 *red and white* = the colours of love, their *mixture* symbolising temperate balance; 12 *touch*: shiny black stone often identified as marble: when rubbed its static electricity attracts A's 'straw'. *Touch* also = tinder.

10 2 *brabbling*: disputing; 3 *Muses' hill*: Mount Helicon; 11 *fence*: defensive action in fencing (cf. *foil*); 12 *strake*: streak or stripe (*not* 'strike').

11 1 *kind*: nature; 10 *look babies*: gaze at one's own reflection; 11 *pitfold*: pitfall, trap for birds (i.e. winged Cupid).

12 2 *day-nets*: Ring's reading from Q2 (daunces (98); dimnesse (Q1, etc.)): continuing the idea of Cupid-as-bird, a trap for capturing small birds that used a net (Stella's hair) and mirrors (her eyes); 5 *pap*: baby food.

13 1 *Phoebus*: sun god; *Jove* (Jupiter): king of heaven; *Mars*: warrior god (the contest parodies that between the 3 goddesses Venus, Minerva and Juno and judged by Paris); 2 *arms*: coats of arms; 3 *sables*: black (heraldic); the *eagle* commemorates Jupiter's metamorphosis into that bird in order that he might abduct Ganymede (*Met.*, 10. 161–7); 4–6 commemorate Mars's adulterous affair with Venus (*Met.*, 4.208–28). 8 *thunderbolt*: Jupiter's tradnl emblem; 10 *gules*: red (heraldic): this red and silver (white) of St's cheeks alludes to the Devereux coat of arms, 3 red discs on a silver ground; 14 *scarcely* (Q1): scantly (98).

14 2 *gripe*: griffin or vulture: Jupiter's bird tore at Prometheus's liver in punishment for the theft of fire from heaven (Apollodorus, 1.7.1); 5 *rhubarb*: i.e. bitter.

15 Cf. *AS* 1, 3, 6 with their attacks on imitative love poetry. 2 *Parnassus*: Greek mountain sacred to the Muses; 5–6 *dictionary . . . rows*: cf. S's attack on alliteration in *Defence* (*Misc. Prose* (1973), 117); 8 *denizened*: naturalised; 9 *far-fet*: far-fetched.

16 8 *love* (Q1 etc.): soul (98); 9 *young lion*: Aeschylus, *Agamemnon*, ll. 717ff.: the lion cub which, adopted by a shepherd as his children's pet, grows up to destroy his flock (with ref. to the damage wrought on Troy by Helen).

17 1 *mother*: Venus: see 13n for Venus and Mars; 7 *chafe*: heat of anger: allegorisations of the Venus-Mars relationship require V to assume some of M's wrathful qualities and M to assume some of her gentler qualities (Wind (1967), ch. 5); 13 *wags*: mischievous boys.

18 1 *checks*: reproofs; *shent*: shamed.

19 2 *wrack*: wreck, punning on rack on which torture victim was stretched; 8 *avise*: advise, inform; 11 *skies . . . ditch*: a commonplace deriving from Plato, *Theaetetus* 174A, telling how astronomer Thales fell into a ditch while star gazing.

20 1–3 Cupid in a bush: Theocritus, *Idyll* 15 and Spenser, *Shep. Cal.*,

'March' (Cupid 'in a bush . . . With winges of purple and blewe'); 6 *level*: a place from which you take aim; 9 *passenger*: passer-by.

21 2 *windlass*: ensnare, act circuitously (cf. *gyres*, l. 6); 6 *gyres*: Wilson's (1931) and Ring's emendn (*yeeres*, Q1, 98); 9 *March*: spring equinox and youth but also love's folly (20.1–3n); 10 *May*: greater maturity but also the continuing influence of love because of May observances (Ovid, *Fasti*, 5.185; Spenser, *Shep. Cal.*, 'May', 1–36).

22 2 *Twins*: Gemini, occupied by the sun from late May to late June; symbolic of love and union.

23 2 *Bewray*: reveal; 5 *spring*: S travelled Europe from 1572–5 making political and scholarly contacts; 7 *prince*: Elizabeth I (not that she actually 'tried his service' very much at all).

24 1 *Rich*: i.e. Lord Rich, Penelope's jealous husband: S equates, as was tradnl, avarice and jealousy; 3 *Tantal*: Tantalus, condemned to be surrounded in Hades by fruit and water which he could never eat and drink, because he betrayed the secrets of the gods; also emblem of covetousness (Whitney (1586), 74).

25 1 Plato = the scholar, Socrates the 'wight', adjudged wisest by Phoebus Apollo's Delphic oracle (Plato, *Apology* 21A): it became a commonplace; 3–4: a Platonic commonplace; 8 *inward sun*: reason (described as 'heavenly' in, e.g., Ripa (1603), 424, s.v. *Ragione*); *heroic*: virtuous.

26 3 *ways* (Q1); weighs (98); 7 *brawl*: French dance based on circle; 12 *proof*: experience.

28 7 *slake*: slacken; 10 *to* (Q1 etc.): do (98); 11 *quintessence*: essential meaning (in ancient philosophy the fifth element of which the heavens were supposedly made).

30 Argument topical to the international politics of 1582. 1 *moon*: crescent moon = the Turkish emblem; a Turkish attack on Spain was feared for spring 1582; 3–4 the *right king* = the elected king Stephen Bathory (crowned 1576). His invasion of Muscovy in 1580 culminated in a treaty signed in January 1582; 5 the *three* = the Catholics, Huguenots, and the Politiques struggling for power in France; 6 *Dutch* = Deutsch or German; *diets*: the Diet (Council) of the Holy Roman Empire held at Augsburg, July–September 1582; 7–8: William of Orange lost 5 towns to the Spanish general Parma in 1581–2; 9–10: Sir Henry Sidney, 3 times Governor of Ireland (until 1578), had imposed a tax on landowners to pay for peace-keeping troops; 11 *weltering*: confusion, characteristic result of factioning at the Scottish court from the 1560s to 1586. 98 adds *no* before *weltering*, obviously as a compliment to James VI, the clear heir to the English throne by then.

31 14: i.e., Do they call ungratefulness there Virtue?

32 1 *Morpheus*, son of Somnus, brings dreams, and is *lively* in contrast to his father whose gift of sleep, according to the commonplace, makes one imitate death. Dream lore had it that dreams were either prophetic; born from memory ('historical'); or the product of the over-active imagination (3–4). In the latter 2 cases they were affected by the physiological condition of the dreamer (i.e., the disposition of his 4 *humours*): see *FQ*, I. i. 36–46.

33 6: Paris's abduction of Spartan Helen caused the Trojan War. Apparently an autobiographical sonnet: the dying wish of Penelope's father, the Earl of Essex, in 1576, had been for a match between S and his then 13-year old daughter. S had refused.

34 3 *glasses*: mirrors; 4: Aristotle's *Poetics* 1448B as reported in S's *Defence* (*Misc. Prose* (1973), 92); 8 *close*: secret.

35 4 i.e., Stella is both mortal (child of Nature) and immortal (divine); 5 *Nestor*: the aged Greek counsellor celebrated for his wisdom (Homer, *Iliad*, passim).

36 2 *yelden* (Ring.): golden (98), yeelding (Q1,2). Means *yielded*; 8 *new* (Q1): now (98).

37 5 *Aurora*: dawn goddess (i.e., the east where, at Leighs in Essex, lay Lord Rich's family seat).

38 Cf. *AS* 32. 2 *hatch*: close or (more likely) shade with the lines (bars) of his feathers: but note also that the eyes are eggs which, hatched by Sleep, will give birth to St's image; *unbitted*: unbridled; 5 *error*: straying (Latin *errare*): cf. l. 3; 7 *curious draught*: finely wrought draughtsmanship (cf. l. 2: *hatch* = to shade as in a drawing); 14: i.e., Sleep is killed by St's image.

39 2 *baiting*: resting; 5 *prease*: press; 6 *Despair*: usually portrayed stabbing herself with a dagger (Ripa (1603), 106); 11 *roses* = tradnlly dedicated to Venus and also to Harpocrates, son of Isis and god of silence: Wilkins (1969), 14–15.

41 If this sonnet refers to an actual tournament, it remains unidentified. 7 *sleight*: learned skill; 10 *my blood*: including S's father and grandfather; 12 *shoot* (Q1): shot (98).

42 Cf. **26**. 1 St's eyes are equivalent to the angelic 'intelligences' believed to move the planetary spheres; 14 *Wracks*: defeats, adversities; for the idea of *triumphs* see Petrarch's *Trionfi*.

44 5 *and I no pity* (Q1,2): and yet no pitie I (98).

45 3 *cannot skill*: is unable.

46 12 *this* (Q1, etc.): his (98); 13 *mich*: play truant.

47 12 *Let her go* (Q1, etc.): . . . do (98).

49 Love riding the lover is a common Petrarchan theme: e.g. *rime*, 71, 173. The sonnet also draws on the Platonic idea of the horse of the libido: *AS* 4.8n above; 7 *boss*: knob adorning bit; 9 *wand*: riding crop.

50 11 *those* (Q1 etc.): these (98).

51 7–8 *Hercules, Atlas*: Atlas supported the sky (*Arcadia* poem 20. 103n above), but Hercules held it for him while Atlas helped him in his eleventh labour to get golden apples from the Hesperides. When Atlas returned with the apples he told Hercules to carry on holding the sky because he was tired of doing so, and said that he would deliver the apples to Eurystheus in his place; 10 *cunningest* (Q1 etc.): cunning (98).

52 2 *pretends*: makes legal claim; 12 *demur*: legal objection.

53 Another tournament (cf. **41**). Its basis is the relnship between Mars and Venus (*AS* 13n).

54 4 *point*: stop; 13 *dumb swans*: according to tradn, the swan sang only at the moment of death; *pies*: magpies.

55 4 *skill* (Q1 etc.): grace (98).

56 2: i.e., by heart; 4 *miss*: ignore; 11 *phlegmatic*: dull (disposition derived from the most sluggish of the humours and dedicated to the fourth in 4 ages of man schemes, old age).

58 1–8 allude to the chain of eloquence attrib. to Hercules in his wise old age (the 'Gallic' Hercules: e.g. Alciati (1551), 194). Ref. is also made to the old argument as to whether it is the orator's words or his personality and mode of utterance that have the greater force; 12 *maugre*: in spite of.

59 The lapdog poem is a commonplace: e.g. *Tottel's Miscellany* (1557), poem 202 is entitled 'The lover praieth pity showing that nature hath taught his dog as it were to sue for the same by kissing his ladies hands'. 13 *love*: wish, desire.

61 3 *assail* (Ring.): assaid (98); assaild (Q1,2); 12 *Doctor*: teacher, with special ref. to the mediaeval scholastic tradn and (cf. l. 13) the 'angelic doctor', St Thomas Aquinas. S also puns on the identification of Cupid with Christian angels: Panofsky (1962), 101–2 and *FQ*, II. viii. 5–6.

62 6: *blind Love* would be the opposite of angelic Cupid (61): Panofsky (1962), 125–6.

63 3 *dove*: emblem of Venus, hence love and fidelity; 9 *Io Paean*: shout of praise or triumph. Significantly, dictionaries then as now cited Ovid's *Ars Amatoria*, 2.1 in illustration, where it is uttered on the capturing of a mistress; 12 *weigh* (Ring.): nay (98).

Song 1 4 *begins and endeth*: note the circular structure (almost identical first and last stanzas); 5 *state*: dignity; 10 *decks and staineth*: ornaments and outshines; 12 *crown*: on crowned Cupid, see Panofsky (1962), 101; 13 *steps all* (Q1): step of (98); 16–20: Queen Venus here recalls the tradnl associations of Venus with Eve (Seznec (1961), 213) and reworks her into an *alma Venus* or *Venus nutrix* who undoes the Fall (*tree of life* = from Gen. 2:9). S effects this modulation by also recalling the identification of Venus with Charity, usually depicted suckling her offspring (Ripa (1603), 63–5) and then de- Christianising the image again; 32: i.e., with you wonders aren't miracles, they are perfectly natural.

64 12 *wish* (Q1 etc.): with (98); 10 *bleeding fame*: Julius Caesar was assassinated on 15 March 44 BC.

65 Plays on the ideas of Cupid's nakedness, sight/blindness, and arrows (Panofsky (1962), ch. 4); 11 *tigerish*: an attribute of Bacchus the wine god, tradnl companion of love; 13–14 *arms . . . arrow*: S's own arms comprised a blue arrow head on a gold ground.

66 6 *Fortune* (Ring.): Fortunes (98).

67 4 *time*: opportunity.

68 6 *Amphion*: founder of the art of music who built the walls of Thebes through the power of his lyre (i.e., her voice is soothing, harmonious); 8 *kindled* (Q1 etc.); blinded (98).

69 3 *Envy . . . eyes*: tradnlly squinting and always awake (Ripa (1603), 242; Ovid, *Met.*, 2.970); 11: cf. 63: puns on the cry of joy *io* sung at weddings, etc (e.g., Spenser, *Epithalamion*, st. 8).

72 6 *Venus . . . Diana*: a commonplace (they combine to produce the virtue of chaste love: Wind (1967), ch. 4; 8 *gold . . . dart*: another commonplace (Panofsky (1962), 102). Virtue's gold replaces the gold that tips Cupid's love-inducing arrows: *Met.*, 1.565–8.

74 1 *Aganippe*: fountain sacred to the Muses on Mt Helicon; 2 *Tempe*: tradnlly beautiful valley in Thessaly where Daphne was turned into a laurel (emblem of poetic excellence): *Met.*, 1. 545–707; 5 *poets' Fury*: Ripa (1603), 178–9: personified as a young man with winged head (= swiftness of intellect) and laurel crown (= fame). Implicitly S denies imitating Petrarch's sonnets to his Laura/Laurel; 7 *blackest brook*: river Styx (cf. *Met.*, 1. 216).

75 6: Edward usurped the throne in 1461 after his father, the Duke of York, was killed fighting the Lancastrian forces; 9–11: he invaded France (*flower-de-luce*) in 1474 and was bribed to withdraw by Louis XI (the tradnl alliance between France and Scotland's *red lion* was not in operation at the time); 14 Edward was forced into temporary exile by the Earl of Warwick when his secret marriage to Lady Elizabeth Grey was discovered.

77 5 *Atlas*: see *Arcadia* poem 20.103n; 8 *sublime*: refine and extract.

78 Cf. the attack on Lord Rich in **24**. For Jealousy's *thorns* (11), eyes (12), ears (13), etc., see Ripa (1603), 181–2 and Malbecco, with his cuckold's horns, in *FQ*, III. ix. 7 and x. 54–60; 14 *ill* (Q1): evill (98).

79 3 *consort*: group of instruments belonging to same family (e.g., recorders, viols); 4 *doves*: see **63**.3n above.

80 3 *stall*: official seat; 8 *grain*: dyed scarlet or purple (the latter being Honour's colour: Ripa (1603), 202).

81 5–6 *kiss . . . souls*: a commonplace: Ben Jonson, *Volpone*, 3.2.234–5; Song of Sol. 1:1 (on which see Wind (1967), 154).

82 Plays on the idea of Venus as goddess of gardens, and Song of Sol. 4:12 (a garden inclosed is my sister, my spouse); 2–3: Narcissus, who fell in love with his own reflection (see *Arcadia* poem 7.1–6n); 4: Venus, seen by Trojan Paris and adjudged fairer than Juno or Minerva (cf. *AS* 13.1n above); 6 *Hesperian*: the golden apples in the Garden of the Hesperides, which link with the golden apple given as prize to Venus by Paris (see also *AS* 51.7–8n).

83 1 *Philip*: common name for sparrow, emblem of lechery. Cf. John Skelton, *Philip Sparrow* (?1505) and, in general for S's sonnet, Catullus's sparrow poems, 2 and 3; 8: note the word play (lilies/love . . . lies).

Song 3 1 *Orpheus*, archetypal poet, who could make trees, rocks, etc. move through the power of his harp; 3–4 *Thebes . . . Amphion*: see *AS* 68.6n; 7–10: Pliny, *Nat. History*, 8.22.61 and 10.6.18; 12 *O beasts, O birds*: 98 and Q1; 13 *The birds, beasts* (98): The beasts, birds, (Q1). Text in 98 and quartos only. Ring. reverses the order of *beasts* and *birds* in l. 12; he also adopts 98's reading of l. 13 (in which I follow him). Ring's decision is governed by his reading of the song's chiastic (abba) structure: st. 1 trees, stones, stones, trees; st. 2 beast (lizard), bird (eagle), beasts, birds; st. 3 birds, beasts, stones, trees, trees, stones, beasts, birds. I keep 98's and

Q1's reading of l. 12 because I suspect that the chiasmus operates in sts 1 and 3 only, and that 2 has its own pattern: the order *beasts, birds* is correct because *beasts* (12) looks back to *Earth* (11) and *birds* to *Heaven*, and both repeat the order *lizard . . . eagle*.

85 2 *Beware*: take care; *tottering*: unstable; 6 *pointing*: appointing; 8: i.e., cause nothing but trouble; 13 *weal*: plenty (i.e. breast); *indentures*: contracts sealed between two parties (punning also on Latin *dens-dentis*, tooth).

Song 4 9 *Danger*: Reluctance, Disdain (as in Guillaume de Lorris and Jean de Meun, *Romance of the Rose*, ll. 2823ff. (ed. 1962, 59–64); 15 *flowers*: embroidered, also rhetorical decoration.

86 5 *ermine*: purity (see *Arcadia* poem 20.116n); 14 *one's* (Q1 etc.): once (98).

Song 5. Probably originally written for *Old Arcadia*. 8 *wert* (Q1): art (98); 22 *flewest* (Q1): flew (98); 26 *pap*: nipple or breast, hence baby food; 36 *babies*: dolls; 37–9: cf. *AS* 9 (*blason*); 68 *stain thy white*: *AS* 86.5n (the ermine); 70–1 *Venus-Diana*: not here embodying chaste love (*AS* 72.6n) but abandoning love for virginity.

Song 6 40 *The judgement* (Q1): Eye-judgement (98); 47 *this* (Q1): this side (98); 49–54: for Reason's crown, numbers (which produce the ratios governing musical intervals) and heavenly connections, see Ripa (1603), 424–6.

Song 7 3 *cloyed* (Q1): closde (98).

Song 8 3–4: for May dressed in green and embroidered with flowers, see Ripa (1603), 316–7; 5 *Astrophil* (Ring.): texts have Astrophel here and at l. 73; 10, 12 *yoke*: the marriage yoke, with which Ripa's (1603) *Matrimonio* is weighed down (305–7); 19–20: *arms crossed* as in a tomb effigy; 71 *such wise*: in such a way; 74 *in these effects to prove*: to test in this way; 102 *so* (Ring.): to (98).

Song 9 27 *Astrophil* (Ring.): Astrophel (98, etc.); 49 *blaying*: bleating.

87 8 *sadded* (Ring.): saddest (98).

88 3–4: i.e., another woman offers to yield immediately to him; 8 *cates*: food.

89 The use of 2 rhyme words only may derive from Petrarch, *rime*, 18; but see also *Arcadia* poems 13 and 18.

90 6 *laurel*: see 74 and n; 9 *ne*: nor; *could I* (Q1): I could (98).

91 8 *seeing jets, black* (Ring.): seeing gets blacke (98); seeming iett blacke (Q1,2); 11 *wood . . . skies*: celestial globe.

92 1 *Indian ware*: precious goods from the Indies; 3 *cutted*: abrupt (in speech); 6 *Phoenix*: see *Arcadia* poem 9.102n; 9 *did*: omitted 98.

Song 10 6 *thy* (Q1): the (98); 7 *O if I myself* (Q1): Or if I me selfe (98); 41 *impart* (Ring.): depart (98).

93 5 *might* (Q1); may (98).

95 2 *least* (Ring.): left (98); best (Q1); 8 *mate-in-arms* (Q1,2): mate in arme (98) (i.e., companion in arms).

96 2 *kind*: nature; 8 *express*: squeeze out (as of milk); 9 *mazefull*: perplexing; 11 *ghastliness*: terrible and ghostly; 12 *far*: spelled (and apparently pronounced) *fur* by S: cf. *AS* 102.11.

97 1 *Dian*: moon and hunting deity, sister of the sun god *Phoebus* (5): *Arcadia* song 8.7n; 4 *wight*: person; 8 *dight*: dress.

98 2 *trained*: attracted (Latin *traho*); 4 *lee*: sheltered from the wind; 7 *galled* (Ring.): gold (98); held (Q1); 11 *marks* (Q1): makes (98); 13 *wink*: shut.

99 3 *mark-wanting*: without a target; 8 *mazed*: confused; 9 *charm*: sing; 14 *light in sense*: light perceived by the sense of sight (as opposed to the inner light of reason).

100 9 *conserved*: preserved in sugar; sugared (Q1): surgd (98).

101 7 *inseparate*: inseparable; 10 *runs* (Q1): comes (98); 11 *prest*: prompt.

102 5 *fade* (Q1): vade (98); 6 *engrained*: dyed fast (cf. *AS* 80.8n); 9 *Galen*: celebrated Greek physician, 2nd cent. AD; *sons*: i.e., doctors.

103 9 *Aeol's youths*: Aeolus = wind god: the youths are thus breezes.

104 8 *rigorous* (Q1): rigour's (98); 10 *stars*: S may have worn stars on his armour at tournaments; 11 *empty glass*: drinking glass; window empty of Stella; 12 *moral . . . meaning*: glossing allegorically.

Song 11 23 *they*: thy (98); 42 *Argus*: *Arcadia* poem 2.14–17n; he became an emblem of jealousy (cf. **78**).

105 3 *glass*: eye(s); 11 *whom* (Q1): whence (98).

106 3 *bare . . . hand*: deceived me; 10 *charm*: harmony; 11 *mould*: *Arcadia* song 1.151n.

107 7 *lieutenancy*: delegated authority; 8 *cause*: unidentified.

MARY SIDNEY, COUNTESS OF PEMBROKE

If Gabriel Harvey was right in *Pierce's Supererogation* and Mary Sidney not only could but did 'publish more works in a month than Nashe hath published in his whole life', then much of her output has been lost. From what we have, it is clear that she excelled as a creative translator rather than as an 'original' poet: her transln of Petrarch's *Triumph of Death* is brilliant (if at times obscure); her psalm translns (or metaphrases) – the triumphant fulfilment of a project initiated by her brother Philip – are metrically innovative and metaphorically astute (I have printed 3 which I regard as among the best); of her extant original poems – the dedications to the *Psalms* and the 'Astraea' dialogue – I print both the dedication to her brother's memory (a splendid early example of invocation of a male muse and a fascinating insight into the Renaissance conception of psychological androgyny) and the dialogue which, despite its mediocrity, takes its place neatly alongside Sir John Davies's *Hymns of Astraea*. Apart from the works represented here, Mary Sidney translated Robert Jarnier's play *Marc-Antoine* and Philippe du Plessis Mornay's *Discourse of Life and Death*, both published 1592 (the latter, like the Petrarch, was written under the shadow of her brother's death). The elegy for Sidney, *The Doleful Lay of Clorinda*, printed in Spenser's *Colin Clout's Come Home Again* (1595) has been attributed to her, but the attribution is by no means generally accepted.

Modern editions

F. B. YOUNG, 'The Triumph of Death translated out of Italian by the Countess of Pembroke', *PMLA (Publications of the Modern Language Association of America)*, 27 (n.s. 20) (1912), 47–75.

Two Poems by the Countess of Pembroke, ed. Bent Juel-Jensen (Oxford: privately printed, 1962).

The Psalms of Sir Philip Sidney and the Countess of Pembroke, ed. J. C. A. Rathmell (New York: New York University Press, 1963).

GEOFFREY BULLOUGH, *Narrative and Dramatic Sources of Shakespeare*, vol. 5 (London and New York: Routledge and Kegan Paul and Columbia U.P., 1964); contains the *Marc-Antoine* transln.

The Triumph of Death and Other Unpublished and Uncollected Poems of Mary Sidney, Countess of Pembroke (1561–1621), ed. G. F. Waller (Salzburg: Institut für Englische Sprache und Literatur, Universität Salzburg, 1977).

The Countess of Pembroke's Translation of Philippe de Mornay's 'Discourse of Life and Death', ed. Diane Bornstein (Detroit: Michigan Consortium for Medieval and Early Modern Studies, 1983).

FURTHER READING

COOGAN, ROBERT. 'Petrarch's *Trionfi* and the English Renaissance', *Studies in Philology*, 57 (1970).

ELIOT, T. S. 'Apology for the Countess of Pembroke' in *The Use of Poetry and the Use of Criticism* (1933).

FISKEN, B. W. 'Mary Sidney's *Psalmes*: Education and Wisdom' in M. P. Hannay, ed., *Silent but for the Word: Tudor Women as Patrons, Translators, and Writers of Religious Verse*

FREER, COBURN. *Music for a King* (1972).

FREER, COBURN. 'Mary Sidney, Countess of Pembroke' in K. M. Wilson, ed., *Women Writers of the Renaissance and Reformation* (1987).

HANNAY, M. P. ' "Princes you as men must dy": Genevan Advice to Monarchs in the *Psalmes* of Mary Sidney', *English Literary Renaissance*, 19 (1989).

HANNAY, M. P. *Philip's Phoenix: Mary Sidney, Countess of Pembroke* (1990).

HASELKORN, A. M. AND B. S. TRAVITSKY, eds. *The Renaissance Englishwoman in Print: Counterbalancing the Canon* (1990).

HOGREFE, PEARL. *Tudor Women: Commoners and Queens* (1975).

HOGREFE, PEARL. *Women of Action in Tudor England: Nine Biographical Sketches* (1977).

LAMB, M. E. 'The Countess of Pembroke's Patronage', *English Literary Renaissance*, 12 (1982).

LAMB, M. E. The Countess of Pembroke and the Art of Dying' in M. B. Rose, ed., *Women in the Middle Ages: Literary and Historical Perspectives* (1986).

LEWALSKI, B. K. *Protestant Poetics and the Seventeeth-Century Religious Lyric* (1979).

REES, D. G. 'Petrarch's "Trionfo della Morte" in English', *Italian Studies*, 7 (1952).

ROBERTS, J. A. 'Recent Studies in Women Writers of Tudor England, Part II: Mary Sidney, Countess of Pembroke', *English Literary Renaissance*, 14 (1984).

SMITH, HALLETT. 'English Metrical Psalms in the Sixteenth Century and their Literary Significance', *Huntington Library Quarterly*, 9 (1946).

WALLER, G. F. *Mary Sidney, Countess of Pembroke: A Critical Study of her Writings and Literary Milieu* (1979).

WARNICKE, R. M. *Women of the English Renaissance and Reformation* (1983).

YOUNG, F. B. *Mary Sidney, Countess of Pembroke* (1912).

ZIM, RIRKAH. *The English Metrical Psalms: Poetry as Praise and Prayer 1535–1601* (1987).

(See also *The Sidney Newsletter* and biographical works cited in connection with Sir Philip Sidney.)

1 THE TRIUMPH OF DEATH (PRINTED COMPLETE).

On the vogue for translns of P's *Trionfi*, see Rees and Coogan in *Further reading* above (for the latter 'the accuracy of the transln and the excellence of the verse make [it] the finest transln of this triumph in the English language'); see also D. D. Carnicelli (ed.), *Lord Morley's 'Triumphs of Fraunces Petrarcke': The First English Translation of the 'Trionfi'* (1971) for a thorough background to the triumph genre. MS's adherence to the *terza rima* of the original is a fine achievement, though her insistence on a line-for-line transln leads, on rare occasions, to over-literalism and syntactical obscurity.

Text

Extant in only one version, a transcript for Sir John Harington (early seventeeth century): Library of the Inner Temple, London, Petyt MS 538. 43. 1. First transcribed, with the Italian *en face*, by F. B. Young (*Modern editions*, above) in *PMLA*, also as an appendix to her *Mary Sidney* (1912): both contain inaccuracies. More accurate transcription in Waller (1977).

CHAPTER 1 1 *lady*: i.e., P's beloved Laura, chastely victorious over Cupid; 2 *pillar*: emblem of constancy; 4 *'Turned*: Returned; 11: cf. the tradnl iconography of Cupid: Sidney, *Arcadia* poems 2n: P has the arrows broken as well as the bow; MS's *chaste* arrows remind us that Laura is on the side of the virgin huntress Diana; 14 *chosen mates*: transl. P's *compagne elette* (chosen companions): *mate* = associate, fellow; 15 *squadronet*: P's *drappelletto* (small band); 16 *glory*: P has *gloria* here and *gloriosa* at line 1, but MS adds *glorious* in line 13 to make the word a thematic key: Laura is not just magnificent and exalted but blazing with light (*OED Glory* sb 6): ct. Death's blackness; 19–20: *green* symbolises hope (Ripa (1603), 469–70); the *ermine* signifies chastity as in Eliz. I's 'Ermine' portrait (Strong (1987), 147–9, plate 71): see also Sidney, *Arcadia* poems 20.116n; for the topazes see P's *Trionfo della pudicizia*, 122, where they, too, symbolise chastity; 20 *gold*: not just splendid but also (bec. it was believed by alchemists and others to contain the 4 elements in perfect balance) emblematic of the balanced virtue, temperance; 21 *unfoiled*: never vanquished; *sign*: emblem (cf. *ensign*, l. 30); 25 *seemed*: translating *pareano*. Young and Waller read *send*; *unclose*: reveal (P's *in mezzo, un sole*); 27 *violet, rose*: colours and (as flowers) emblems of chaste love (Sidney, *Arcadia* poems 20.39, 107n); 33 *Phlegra*: the Phlegrean plain, scene of the earthly giants' rebellion against Olympus after the advent of the Iron Age (Ovid, *Met.*, 1. 173ff.); 38: for Death's *blindness* (and black robe) see Ripa (1603), 339 and Panofsky (1962), 110–3; she is *deaf* bec. she refuses to spare those who plead with her (but P has Death being fierce *to* the deaf and blind: MS either misread or indulged in creative iconography); for Death's sword (42) see Ripa, 340; 41: *Trojans* and *Romans* are the same race, of course: Death alludes to the destruction of Troy and the disintegration of the Roman empire induced by the barbarian invasions; 44: it is Death who steals up on the barbarians; 45 *marred*: put an end to; 49 *this*: Morley's transln expands: 'these chaste companyes'; 50: And little to me—you only have an interest in my body (*spoil*); 51 *was one*: was unique; 54 *assoil*: release, with strong overtones of *absolve from sin* (*OED* Assoil v 1.1); 75 *Pestering*: MS's concretisation of P's 'the whole plain was full of dead people': the primary meaning *encumber, overload* (*OED Pester* v 1) picks up *pest* = plague, deadly epidemic; 85 *affy*: trust; 89 *mother*: i.e., Earth (the phrase is tradnlly used of the earth mother Cybele); 103–7: i.e., Laura is dying, and a group of women comes to see her; 107 *lade*: burden; 113–14: cf. Dido's release (Surrey's transln of *Aen.* 4. 938–43 above); 121 *For*: As for; 126 *forslow*: impede, delay; 133 *one o'clock*: P's *L'ora prima*; 134 *tied*: i.e., bound P to love her; (see *rime*, 3, 211); 135 *Changing her copy*: altering her behaviour (*OED Copy* sb VI. 11); 141 *quailed*: withered, destroyed; 154 *enemies*: P's *avversari* (devils); 157: i.e., when plaint and fear were past; *they*: the grieving women.

CHAPTER 2 1 *hap*: unfortunate event, mischance; *ensue*: follow; 5 *Tithon's bride*: the dawn goddess Aurora: see 178 below and Drayton, *End.*, 188n; 7 *tide*: season (i.e., spring, assoc. with love in tradnl personificns; Ripa (1603), 473–4; Botticelli's *Primavera*); 8 *orient*: bright (specifically, *eastern*, coming from the dawn) and denoting pearls (cf. the dew at line 5): P has *gemme orientali*; 17: MS suggests that Laura overgoes Venus's handmaids, the Graces, uniting 3 in 1 (see Drayton, *End.*, 863–4n); 18 *bay*: P's *un bel lauro* (laurel/Laura, emblem of chastity bec. of Daphne (Ovid, *Met.*, 1. 565ff.) and of immortality bec. evergreen); *beech*: sanctified as the tree of the lamenting lover by the opening of Virgil, *Eclogues*, 1 (*Tityre, tu patulae recubans sub tegmine fagi*); 19–20: i.e., how can I but know you?; 27: P's questions have to be asked before daylight (see 178n); 36 *mud*: P's *fango* (signifying worldly dross and the mortal body); 40–1: the tradnl posture of Hope (Emile Mâle, *The Gothic Image*, tr. Dora Nussey (London: Collins, 1961), 114); 42 *rosy*: P's *rosate*: not just *red* but suggesting the *rose* of love (Wind (1967), 145n and Botticelli's *Birth of Venus*) and of silence: Wilkins (1969), 115; 43 *tyrants*: MS omits P's list: *Silla, Mario, Neron, Gaio e Mezenzio*; 43: P speaks; 45 *Causes*: Are causes . . .; 48 *loss*: damnation (P's *danno*); 52ff: Laura tells how, as she was dying, she heard the voices of those around her; 53 *furthest*: utmost limit; 58 *main*: i.e., mainland; 65 *reconsolate*: P's *racconsolato*: comfort; 75 *ruth*: pity; 80–1: MS's literalism leads her here into obscurity. Means: did you ever love me for my pains (though that love would have to be compatible with your love of Honour)?; 90 *cheer*: countenance (P's *viso*): i.e., she used her severity of look to temper his ardour; 98: cf. Wind (1967), plate 41 (bridled horse symbolising control of lust); 116 *tookest . . . toy*: continuing the horse metaphor, means *to shy, take fright at* (*OED Toy* sb 4b); 122 *meed*: recompense (Waller reads *meede*; Young *neede*); 128 *fain*: glad; 132: i.e., his love was excessive, intemperate; 138: the reconciln of Love and Virtue was a favourite Ren. theme: cf. Jonson's masque, *Pleasure reconciled to Virtue*, and Wind (1967), ch. 5; 139 *tried*: i.e. tempered;

150 *My . . . more*: no poem of P's with this line in it appears to have survived; 151–2: obscure over-literalism again: means 'My heart was yours, but my eyes were under my control'; 152–3: you can tolerate (*brook*) your share with difficulty [not realising that] you were deprived of (*leesing*) the lesser by me; 167 *thy nest*: Florence (Laura's *base* birthplace (165) was Avignon – inglorious in comparison); 172 *third*: the sphere of Venus, 3rd in the Ptolemaic order counting outward from earth: cf. Chaucer, *Troilus and Criseyde*, 3, proem 1; 178 *Aurora*: see ch. 2, 5n above: spirits have to depart when daylight comes (*Hamlet*, 1. 1).

2 PSALMS OF DAVID.

Begun by Philip Sidney (who transl. the first 43), the transln was completed by MS, who also revised her brother's versions: see Rathmell's edn, Intro. and Ringler's *Poems of Sidney* (1962), 500–9. The *Psalms* exist in 16 known MSS (Waller (1977), Appendix) and we await an edn with full scholarly apparatus.

(1) Dedic. poem. The second of 2 dedic. poems, the first ('Even now that care which on thy crown attends') being addressed to Eliz. I. Both poems exist in MS only in J (the MS owned by Bent Juel-Jensen). The poem printed here, however, is found in rather different form attrib. to Samuel Daniel in *The Whole Workes of Samuel Daniel* (1623) (this text is repr. by Waller (1977), 190–2). In its J (and presumably later) form it has been repr. by Juel-Jensen (1962); Ringler (1962); and Waller (1977).

Structure

The 7-line stanzas are characteristic of Ren. elegy, as in Spenser's *Ruins of Time* and *Daphnaida* (bec. 7 symbolises mutability, among other things, in Ren. numerology); while the total 13 is assoc. with disruption and Christological suffering (Pietro Bongo, *Numerorum mysteria* (Bergamo, 1599), 401). The early version in 11 stanzas, attrib. to Daniel, was prob. also numerological, since 11 is elegiac on the authority of Ovid, *Fasti*, 2.568 (Henry King's *Exequy* and Milton's *Lycidas* both have 11 stanzas, e.g.)

6 *stuff*: dust (*OED Stuff* sb^2); 7 *lightning*: symbol of divine power; 8–9 *transformed/In substance*: a neat Protestant joke against the Catholic doctrine of transubstantiation: PS has not (priestlike) altered the substance of the psalms; he has merely adorned them (*superficial tire* = surface apparel or ornament); 11 *high tones*: the higher the more joyful: see Francesco Gafurio, *Practica musicae*, tr. Irwin Young (Madison, Milwaukee, London: Univ. of Wisconsin Press, 1969), 1. 1 (low notes are *grave* and closest to taciturnity); 29 *sith*: since; 29 *scope*: goal; 38 *Phoenix*: Sidney, *Arcadia* poems 9.102n (note that it is not only unique but regenerates itself out of its own ashes, as MS sees herself (and the *Psalms*) as the continuation of her brother, however 'maimed' and fragmentary); 43–4: the language of biblical judgment (e.g., 1 Peter 4:5 ('Which shall give account to him, that is ready to judge quicke and dead') and Matt. 18:23–4 ('Therefore is the kingdome of heaven likened unto a certaine King, which would take an account of his servants. And when he had begun to reckon. . . .') (Geneva transln)); 54–6: True Wisdom has

her face elevated heavenward, gazing at a bright light (Ripa (1603), 442);
the syntax is obscure, but it is clear that those who see with Wisdom's
eyes confirm what the best minds approve; *sealed*: attested, confirmed;
63 *Envy*: Sp., *FQ*, I. iv. 30–1; Whitney (1586), 94.

(2), (3), (4): texts from Rathmell (1963), who follows the MS at
Penshurst Place.
(2) Psalm 88. Compare Surrey's paraphrase (Surrey, 39 above). 19
murdered: suggests violent death, even suicide (the standard Sternhold-
Hopkins Psalter (1562) has: 'It were more ease for me to be,/with them
the which were slaine'; the Geneva transln reads 'like the slaine lying in
the grave'); 28 *lightning*: MS's metaphor (but Geneva gloss on verse 7
introduces the concept of storms); 42: i.e., I pray daily; 66 *amazed*:
stupefied, terror-stricken, and with the notion of *maze* (= lostness,
error).
(3) Psalm 130. 10 *cark*: specif. a load weighing some 3 cwt; more
generally, trouble, distress; 21–4: Geneva transln of verse 6: 'My soule
waiteth on the Lord more then the morning watch watcheth for the
morning'; 30 *erst*: first, in preference.
(4) Psalm 148. 5–8: Geneva transln of verse 2: 'Prayse ye him, all ye his
Angels: prayse him, all his armie'; 9–10: *sea*: MS's metaphor; 12
spangles: sequins; 13 *Sphere*: the sphere of the fixed stars; 30 *stones*:
hailstones; 32 *appast*: food; 35–40: Geneva transln of verse 9:
'Mountaines and all hils, fruitfull trees, and all cedars'.

3 A DIALOGUE ... IN PRAISE OF ASTRÆA

.Text: Francis Davison, *A Poetical Rhapsody* (1602). *Title*: possibly
1599 and written to celebrate a royal visit to Wilton which failed to
occur; *Astræa*: see Davies, *H Astr.*, headnote; *Thenot*: cf. Sp., *Shep. Cal.*,
'February', 'April', 'November' (in the last 2 he encourages praise of
Eliz.); *Piers* (i.e., Peter): cf. *Shep. Cal.*, 'May' (where he repres. Prot.
rigour) and 'October' (where he sings in praise of poetry); 4 *plainly*: cf.
the argt of Herbert's 'Jordan (1)': Waller (1977), 62 notes Piers's
Platonist rejection of poetry as untrustworthy; this combines with an
extreme Prot. rejection of allegory and emblem; 15 *Momus*: see Drayton,
End., 1010n; 19 *Wisdom's sight*: see MS, dedic. poem (1), 54–6n; 26
every ill: bec. as the goddess of the Golden Age (and its restoration when
she returns) she is the enemy of vice: Ovid, *Met.*, 1. 169–70; 35 *only she*:
recalling tradnl praise of Eliz. as *semper una* (always one): cf. the name of
the heroine of *FQ*, I and E. C. Wilson, *England's Eliza* (1939); 36
measure: proportion (in relation to your subject); 38: cf. *H Astr.*, 3, 9; 50
palm: emblem of righteousness and strength against vice: Ralegh, 24.9n
and Drayton, *End.*, 25–34n; *bay*: Tr. *of Death*, 2.18n above; 58 *conceit*:
imagination and *construct of images*: Ralegh, 9n; 60 *silence*: the ultimate
expression of mystery and its ineffability: Wilkins as at *Triumph of
Death*, 2.42n above, and Wind (1967), plate 23.

MICHAEL DRAYTON:
ENDYMION AND PHOEBE

Text

Entered in the Stationers' Register 12 April 1595. The title page is undated, but the work was presumably published the same year. It was never reprinted, but D totally recast it as *The Man in the Moon* (1606). Text: 1595.

Genre and circumstances of composition

EP is an early work, preceded by D's biblical verse translns *The Harmony of the Church* (1591); the Spenserian *Idea: The Shepherd's Garland. Fashioned in nine Eclogues* (1593); the sonnet sequence *Idea's Mirror* (1594); and the 'heroic' (or historical) poems *Piers Gaveston* (1593–4) and *Matilda* (1594). It is in the fashionable genre of the epyllion, or brief Ovidian erotic narrative poem. Other examples include: Thomas Lodge's *Scylla's Metamorphosis* (1589), Marlowe's *Hero and Leander* (1593; continuation by George Chapman, 1598), Shakespeare's *Venus and Adonis* (1593), Thomas Heywood's *Oenone and Paris* (1594) and Thomas Edwards's *Cephalus and Procris* (1595). D, however, rather like Shakespeare, modulates his erotic narrative, under the influence of the neo-Platonic concept of love as the pathway to wisdom, into a quest for knowledge: it is in effect a soul journey, and by its end Endymion has attained divine wisdom. In this respect it has affinities with Martianus Capella's *Marriage of Philology and Mercury* and Macrobius's *Commentary on the Dream of Scipio*, though more immediate influences appear to be Du Bartas's *L'Uranie, ou la muse chrestienne* (for the conception of Phoebe) and his long hexaemeral poem *Les Sepmaines* (for the account of the planets, etc.). The story of Diana's love for the mortal shepherd boy Endymion, whom Jupiter had sent into the deepest sleep on mount Latmus because of his attempted violation of Juno, has various fragmentary sources: Apollonius Rhodius, *Argonautica*, 4. 54–61; Pliny, *Natural History*, 2. 6. 43 (which interprets E as an astronomer); Lucian, *Dialogues of the Gods*, 11, and the work of later mythographers, notably Fulgentius, Boccaccio, and Natalis Comes. Edgar Wind (1967), 154–60 notes the neo-Platonic reading of the myth as an image of the soul's translation to the divine through death, a version of the *mors osculi* (death of the kiss); and the tale is the subject of John Lyly's *Endimion* (1591) – a play which, in fact, D's work has no affinities with apart from subject matter.

D seems to have chosen the Endymion myth for two reasons: first, to attract notice by contributing to the cult of Elizabeth as moon queen (as in Lyly's play, Chapman's *Hymnus in Cynthiam* in his *Shadow of Night* (1594), Jonson's *Cynthia's Revels* (1600), Ralegh's Cynthia poems, and Spenser's Gloriana, who appears to the sleeping Arthur as Diana appears

448

to Endymion in *FQ*, I. ix. 13–15, etc.); and second, to register allegorically, through the love of an apparently unattainable immortal for a mortal, the depth and sublimation of his love for Anne Goodere, younger daughter of his early patron Sir Henry. She is the Idea of the *Shep. Garland* and of the Petrarchan-Platonic sonnet sequence of 1594, and his devotion continued after her marriage to Henry Rainsford (1595) for the rest of his life. It should finally be mentioned that *EP* may possibly have been written for the marriage of Lucy Harington to the 3rd Earl of Bedford in December 1594: D was fond of her, and had been 'bequeathed' to her by the dying Sir Henry Goodere for her patronage (see B. H. Newdigate, *Michael Drayton and his Circle* (Oxford: Basil Blackwell, 1941), chaps 4 and 5).

Modern editions

Endimion and Phoebe: Ideas Latmus, ed. J. W. Hebel (Oxford: Basil Blackwell, 1925).

The Works of Michael Drayton, ed. J. W. Hebel, with Kathleen Tillotson and B. H. Newdigate. 5 vols. (Oxford: Basil Blackwell, 1931–41).

Poems of Michael Drayton, ed. John Buxton, 2 vols (London: Routledge and Kegan Paul, 1953).

Elizabethan Minor Epics, ed. E. S. Donno (New York and London: Routledge and Kegan Paul, 1963).

Elizabethan Verse Romances, ed. M. M. Reese (London: Routledge and Kegan Paul, 1968).

Michael Drayton: Selected Poems, ed. Vivien Thomas (Manchester: Carcanet, 1977).

FURTHER READING

BERTHELOT, J. A. *Michael Drayton* (1967).

ELTON, OLIVER. *An Introduction to Michael Drayton* (1895).

ELTON, OLIVER. *Michael Drayton: A Critical Study* (1905).

EWELL, B. C. 'Drayton's *Endimion and Phoebe*: An Allegory of Aesthetics', *Explorations in Renaissance Culture*, 7 (1981).

FINNEY, C. L. 'Drayton's *Endimion and Phoebe* and Keats' *Endymion*', *PMLA (Publications of the Modern Language Association of America)*, 39 (1924).

HARDIN, R. F. *Michael Drayton and the Passing of Elizabethan England* (1973).

HARNER, J. L. *Samuel Daniel and Michael Drayton: A Reference Guide* (1980).

LE COMTE, E. S. *Endymion in England: The Critical History of a Greek Myth* (1944).

NEWDIGATE, BERNARD. *Michael Drayton and His Circle* (1941).

PETRONELLA, V. F. 'Double Ecstasy in Drayton's *Endimion and Phoebe*', *Studies in English Literature*, 24 (1984).

STOPES, C. M. *Shakespeare's Warwickshire Contemporaries* (1907).

Drayton

TANNENBAUM, S. A. *Michael Drayton: A Concise Bibliography* (1941).
TAYLOR, DICK B. 'Drayton and the Countess of Bedford', *Studies in Philology*, 49 (1952).
ZOCCA, L. R. *Elizabethan Narrative Poetry* (1950).

Note: T in the following notes indicates indebtedness to Kathleen Tillotson's notes to *EP* in the *Works*, ed. Hebel.

ENDYMION AND PHOEBE: IDEA'S LATMUS.

Title: *Idea* (D's symbolic name for Anne Goodere) = a Platonic term for the archetype in the divine mind of something which is realised only imperfectly on earth; *Latmus*: the mountain in Caria where Jupiter had placed E in deathlike sleep. *Epigraph*: Phoebus (Apollo) shall be the source and author of our song (Virgil, *Culex*, 12); *Dedicn*: Lucy, Countess of Bedford (see above) became one of the great literary patrons of the seventeenth century. *EP* was also accompanied by 2 other dedic. sonnets, one to D's Muse and Idea by E.P., the other 'To Idea' by S.G. (both authors unidentified); *Text 5 Archelaus*: 5th cent. BC Athenian philosopher who reputedly taught Socrates; 13 *Sylvanus*: wood god whose tradnl companions = fauns and satyrs; 14 *barley-break*: game played in cornfield by 3 couples, the middle position or 'den' in which was known as 'hell'. In view of *EP*'s neo-Platonism, and following Fowler's analysis of the barley-break in Sidney's *Arcadia* (Fowler (1975), 52–6), we may suspect that ll. 13–14 allegorise the sensible world from which Phoebe will elevate E; 15 *Pan*: nature god, the drumming of whose goat's hooves may account for the *tabouret* (drum) which D substitutes for the more usual pipes; 18 *Arabia*: for its connotns see Ralegh, **19**.478n; 21: for the implicns of *Diana* see Ralegh, **6** and **19** and nn; 22 *vestal*: Ralegh, **9**.2n; 23ff: for the topography, cf. Sp's Garden of Adonis (*FQ*, III. vi. 43–5); 24 *clip*: embrace; *welkin*: sky; 25–34: for the tree catalogue as an opening *topos* symbolising the soul's immersion in matter, etc. see *FQ*, I. i. 7–9, Chaucer, *Plt of Fowls*, 176ff., and Dante, *Inferno*, 1 (also Curtius (1967), 194–5); tall *cedar* and fir (*pine*) are paired in Isaiah 37: 24 and signify protectiveness, fragrance and majesty; 30–4: D's attributions to the gods are traditional: for the story of weeping Myrrha see Ovid, *Met.*, 10.327ff.; for the *palm* overcoming hatred and envy, see Whitney (1586), 118 and Tervarent (1958), col. 296; and for the poplar as an attribute of Alcides/Hercules, see Virgil, *Ecl.*, 7. 61; 40 *grapes ... citrons*: tradnl attributes of the earthly paradise: *FQ*, II. xii. 54 and Marvell's 'Bermudas'; *citrons* (oranges and/or lemons) are in alchemy connected with amber (cf. *pine* and *myrrh*) and understood to be solidified sun rays, and *citron* is a well regarded colour in alchemy suggesting the favourable outcome of the work (Chaucer, *Can. Yeoman's Tale*, 816); 42: the golden *Hesperidean* apples, guarded by a dragon (which, however, Hercules managed to vanquish) were emblems of love (Tervarent (1958), cols 311–13) as well as a potent alchemical symbol; 45 *fountains*: another feature of the earthly paradise (Curtius (1967), 195–202); 50

orient: bright, but specifically *from the east* (India) where the best pearls came from according to Pliny and others (*pearl* and *silver* are both attrib. to the moon, as the *golden citrons* and *laurel* belong to Phoebe's excluded brother, Phoebus (Agrippa (1651), 1.22, 23): see Ralegh, 19.97n for another characteristic juxtaposition of Phoebe and Phoebus, and Sidney, *Arcadia* poems 8.7n; 51 *roses . . . eglantine*: the latter is the single hedge rose or sweet briar: both, as roses, are dedic. to Venus and love, and both were also important emblems of Eliz. (Strong (1987), 68–71 and plates 44–9); 52 *crystalline*: common adjectival noun but prob. also recalling the Heav. Jerusalem (Rev. 21:11, 22:1); 53 *birds*: a further prop of the earthly paradise (45n); *purple*: bright, brilliant (a meaning of Latin *purpureus*)); 56 *ouzel*: old name for blackbird; *mavis*: song-thrush; 59 *Zephyr*: the western wind of spring, responsible for the birth of flowers by impregnating Chloris/Flora (itself a neo-Platonic mystery: Wind (1967), ch. 8): see Davies, *H Astr.*, 4.1n, 9; 60 *burden*: bass or accompaniment; 62 *amaranthus*: fabled flower of immortality (name means *unfading*); *gilliflower*: pink or wallflower (common in Eliz. flower catalogues, e.g., Sp, *Shep. Cal.*, 'April', 137); 64 *moly*: Hermes (Reason) gives a branch of this shrub to Odysseus to enable him to withstand the temptations to lust of the witch Circe in *Odyssey*, 10.287ff.; 65 *balm*: the common herb *melissa officinalis*, linked with violets in Chapman's *Odyssey* transln, 5.97; *cassia*: the cinnamon tree or (less specifically) one of several kinds of fragrant shrub; 71 *Impaled*: enclosed, fenced in; 78 *lunary*: could denote an actual plant (moonwort) but is more likely to carry alchemical overtones, as its mention in Chaucer's *Can. Yeoman's Tale*, 800 suggests: for alchemical lunary, which often seems to symbolise the alch. work itself, see C. G. Jung, *Alchemical Studies*, tr. R. F. C. Hull (Princeton, N. J.: Princeton U. P., 1967), ch. 5; lunary appears in Lyly's *Endimion*, 2.3; 79 *Menalus*: Arcadian mount Maenalus, home of Diana (Ovid, *Met.*, 2.520); 86 *hay-de-guys*: see E.K.'s note to Sp's *Shep. Cal.*, 'June', 25–7: 'A country dance or round' (where it is connected with moonlight); 111 *purfled*: bordered; for the description in general T compares Belphoebe at *FQ*, II. iii. 26ff. and Marlowe's Hero (*Hero and Leander*, 1.9ff.). Belphoebe is an iconographical mixture of Diana and Venus, signifying chaste love; whereas Hero (to whom D's description is closer) is a fully-fledged child of Venus alone. Specifically, the *azure* and *rainbows* identify her with the element of air, with which Juno, goddess of marriage, was also associated (Ripa (1603), 123–4) as, too, were Venus and the erotic sanguinic temperament; Marlowe's Hero wears a necklace, but D's *rubies* (118) suggest love and suffering (Ralegh, 24.32–4n) and are the jewel equivalents of the bloodstains of dead lovers which Hero bears as trophies round her 'kirtle blew' (*HL*, 1.15–16); 119 *trammels*: braids or tresses; *pleats*: plaits; 121 *cypress*: a light gauzy material 'resembling cobweb lawn or crape' (*OED Cypress* 1c) (Hero wears lawn: *HL*, 1.9); 122 *lily*: looking back, via Juno, to the milk of l. 114, since lilies reputedly grew from Juno's spilt breast milk (Sidney, *Arcadia* poems 20.6on and *HL*, 5.215–16); 130, 132: probably influ-

enced by the *sententiae* in *HL*, e.g. 1.166, 184, etc.; 136 *roundelay*: tune
with refrain; 140 *her*: Danäe (see 365–8n below); 142 *Aganippe's well*:
sacred to the Muses and located at the foot of Mount Helicon; 143 *Hebe*:
embodiment of youth and cup-bearer to the gods (Davies, *Orch.*, 648n);
152 *Orion*: hunter and companion of Diana killed by a scorpion sent by
Earth because of his boastfulness over his strength: also known as *Diana
comes* (companion of Diana): R. H. Allen, *Star Names: Their Lore and
Meaning* (New York: Dover, 1963), 305; 159: she dresses herself as one
of her own hunting-companion nymphs, thus offering a witty parallel to
Venus's manifestation of herself to Aeneas as a nymph of Diana (*Aeneid*,
1.315); 164 *quavering*: causing to vibrate, with a pun on *quaver* = half a
crotchet and *quaver* (vb) = to trill or ornament; *cittern*: wire-strung
instrument of the guitar type played with plectrum; 166 *Gordian knots*:
an elaborate knot tied by Phrygian king Gordius: the oracle declared that
whoever undid it would rule Asia, and Alexander the Great cut it with his
sword; here simply an emblem of strong union (the interlacing of knots
symbolises marriage); 168 *ranger*: gamekeeper or keeper of the forest,
with overtones of *rake* (*OED Ranger* 1, 2); 172ff.: *fishing*: a contempla-
tive activity that also has strong erotic overtones (cf. Donne's 'The Bait');
181 *nymph . . . blood*: nymphs were technically demi-goddesses who
inhabited water or forests; 182 *Isis' . . . flood*: 'Isis floud' and 'a Popler'
feature at the beginning of Lodge's *Scylla's Metamorphosis*, ll. 2, 79; but
in the late Eliz. period the name of the river suggests the goddess Isis, who
was a form of Diana-Phoebe (Ovid, *Met.*, 1.727–942; Apuleius, *Golden
Ass*, Book 11; Brooks-Davies (1983), Index s.v. Isis (goddess), Isis
(river)); 187 *Oceanus*: god of ocean and father of all creatures; 188
Tithon: Tithonus, son of Laomedon, whose bride is the dawn goddess
Aurora (she fell in love with him, carried him to heaven, and gained
immortality for him: cf the Endymion story); 189 *halcyons*: symbols of
harmony and universal peace, also of marriage: Dolores Palomo, 'The
Halcyon Moment of Stillness in Royalist Poetry', *Huntington Library
Quarterly*, 44 (1981), 205–21; 197 *lunacy*: possibly madness, but more
likely moon blindness (*OED Lunacy* 2); 200 *pomander*: ball of aromatic
substances carried as guard against infection; 204 *Amphion*: Sidney, *AS*
68.8n and Davies, *Orch.*, ll. 141–4 and 637; 206 *manual seal*: autograph
signature (as opposed to wax seal): *OED Manual* A 1b cites *Venus and
Ad.*, 516; 207–24: T compares *Venus and Ad.*, 145–50; 215 *doves*:
symbolising marital fidelity and, as birds of Venus, sensuality and
eroticism: Wyatt, 92.31n; Sidney, *Arcadia* poems 21.6n, and Tervarent
(1958), col. 105; 217 *swan*: emblem of music (picked up in winds, i.e.,
music's element, air); but also signifying the erotic sense of touch and love
generally (Tervarent, cols 138–40 citing Philostratus, *Imagines*, 1.9 and
referring to the Jupiter-Leda myth); 227 *happily*: i.e., haply (by chance);
some: i.e., someone; *Flora*: Davies, *H Astr.*, 4.1n, 9; 232 *in no hand*: on
no account (*OED Hand* sb II 25g); 236 *interdicted*: presumably =
broken, rejected; 236–42: T compares *Venus and Ad.*, 181–4; 251–2
flock . . . gold: hints at the Argonauts' goal of the Golden Fleece, often

interpreted alchemically, and Virgil, *Ecl.*, 4.43–4 (naturally saffron-yellow wool in the restored Golden Age); 253 *bateful*: quarrelsome; *thews*: customs; 255–6: eirenic and apocalyptic again, like 251–2, since they recall Virgil, *Ecl.*, 4.30 (the enduring oak shall distil dewy honey) and thus evoke Eliz. as Golden Age monarch; 257 *tiger*: Bacchic symbol of unrestrained energy (Ripa (1603), 59): cf. *FQ*, I. vi. 26, which also refers to the taming of wolves; 259–60 *spells = words* rather than *magical charms*; but it is worth remembering that *wolves* belong to Hecate, the underworld manifestation of Phoebe as goddess of witches: she tames them here to reverse Matt. 10:16, Luke 10:3, Acts 20:29 and the ecclesiastical pastoral tradn they spawned (e.g., *Shep. Cal.* 'May', 112–31) in the light of the apocalyptic-eirenic texts Isaiah 11:6 and 65:25; 261: cf, *FQ*, I. vi. 25 (where the lion is a symbol of wrath); 262 *boar*: *FQ*, I. vi. 26, where it signifies lust (Tervarent (1958), col. 335); *wrack*: destruction; 263 *bulls*: as in *FQ*, I. vi. 24, lustful and Bacchic (Theocritus, *Idylls*, 20.33) as well as wrathful; 264 *dragons*: symbols of earth (Tervarent, cols 81–2); 265–6: cf. *FQ*, VII. vi. 9, Cynthia 'sitting on an ivory throne'; the ivory is also appropriate bec. of its colour and association with purity *via* the application of Song of Sol. 7:4 to the Virgin Mary. The eagles are stolen from the chariot of Jupiter, king of heaven (Ripa (1603), 53); 268: cf. *Venus and Ad.*, 22–3; 270 *larix*: larch; 271 *teda*: torch pine, so called bec. its resin = partic. good for torches (Pliny, *Nat. Hist.*, 16.43, where it is noted that 'it is a disease of the larch to turn into a torch pine'); 273–6: the *amber gum* suggests that the ref. is to the poplars into which the Heliades were metamorphosed as they grieved for their dead brother Phaethon (Ovid, *Met.*, 2.429–58); 291 *sith*: since; 297 *Cytheron*: see Wyatt, 67n; 298 *Ismaenos*: river in Boeotia; *Thirmodoon*: the river Thermodon in Pontus; 299 *Thetis*: one of the daughters of the sea god Nereus and mother of Achilles; 300 *she*: Ceres-Demeter; 305–8: cf. *Hero and Leander*, 2.271ff (T); 308 *sconce*: fortification (*OED Sconce* v[1], not recorded as a noun); 309–12: for the iconography of Cupid, see Sidney, *Arcadia* poems 2n; 311 *piles*: darts, arrows (Latin *pilum*); 327 *Night*: for her chariot (*chair*) see Ripa (1603), 59 and *Aen.*, 5.721ff.; 328 *cabinet*: chamber, tabernacle; 330 *sunny palfreys*: i.e., the horses which draw the Sun's chariot; 331 *crystal*: symbol of purity and dedic. to the moon (Agrippa (1651), 1.24): Chapman's *Hymnus in Cynthiam* has the moon's 'Christall and Imperiall throne' (116), though Luna's chariot is usually ivory; 332 *pomp*: triumphal display; *rid ... sphere*: followed the path of her planetary orbit; 334 *pearl*: lunar emblem as is dew itself (Ralegh, 6.2n, Agrippa (1651), 1.24, and 50n above); 335 *Zephyr*: see 59n above; he is *hushed* bec. he is the rapist of Chloris (Ovid, *Fasti*, 5.185ff.) and this is a moment when virginal Cynthia prevails; *gale*: breeze; 336–8 *nightingale*: i.e., Philomel, telling of her rape by Tereus (Sidney, *Certain Sonnets* 2 and n); the *thorn* is a common attribute, as in the Sidney instance; 336 *bewrayed*: divulged; 339–44: T compares Rowland's complaint in D's *Shep. Garland*, 9.7–24; 349 *civet*: the musky scent derived from the civet cat;

358 *clip about*: encompass; 361 *Elice*: i.e., Helice, a name of the constellation Ursa Major from the Greek meaning *winding* (i.e., about the pole): the constelln is mythologically the stellified Callisto, a nymph of Diana raped by Jupiter and metamorphosed into a bear by Juno (Ovid, *Met.*, 2.512–602) and cf. Wyatt, 110.23–4n: D may also have in mind that Helice in Arcadia was Callisto's birthplace; 365–8 *Perseus*: for Perseus, son of Jupiter by Danäe, the Gorgon (Medusa) and his beloved (Andromeda), see Ovid, *Met.*, 4.750–908 and Manilius, *Astronomicon*, 5.568ff.; 370–3: *Andromeda*, daughter of the Ethiopian queen Cassiopeia, was bound by nymphs to a rock to be eaten by a sea monster bec. her mother had declared her more beautiful than they were; after rescuing her, Perseus married her, and he, his wife, and her mother were stellified; 372 *transpiercing*: Ralegh, 19.40n; *eyne*: eyes; 377 *wandering*: i.e., the planets, (Wyatt, 110.31n); 385–88: a commonplace, as at *FQ*, I. ii. 1; *hunt's up*: morning call to awaken huntsmen (*OED*); *day star*: the sun; 394 *seld*: seldom; 401ff.: cf. Ralegh, 6, and esp. l. 15n; 417–8: refer to the difference betw. the lunar year of 364 days (13 × the 28 days of the moon's orbit) and the solar year; 421: the moon is the tradnl emblem of fickle (and female) Fortune bec. of its swift orbit: Ralegh, 6; Ripa (1603), 225–6 (*Inconstanza*); 437 *springs*: copses of young trees (*OED Spring* sb[1] 10); 442 *Echo*: Sidney, *Arcadia* poems 7n and 10n; 455–64: for the physiology of love melancholy see Robert Burton, *Anatomy of Melancholy*, 3rd partition; 457 *For why*: because; 470 *ceased*: an alternative spelling of *seized*; 480 *include*: enclose (the eyes are the *looking glass*, as in Donne's 'The Good-morrow'); 484 *lawn*: a fine linen (cf. 121n above); 494 *embay*: bathe; 500 *arew*: i.e., *arow* (one after the other); 501 *galliards*: Davies, *Orch.*, st. 67, 68; 502 *Thyas*: female followers of Bacchus; 508 *heavenly Muse*: cf. 877 and Du Bartas, *L'Uranie*. In Ren. neo-Platonism the Muses had a specific function as inspirers of the first kind of ecstasy or divine impregnation of the soul due to their nature as 'the souls of the celestial [i.e., planetary] spheres'. They illuminate the human soul with divine knowledge using 'natural' things as their medium: i.e., stones, plants, animals, music and words, planetary talismans, numerology and astrology (see Agrippa (1651), 3.46, from whom I have quoted); 510 *kind*: nature; 511 *For why*: because; the whole passage expresses commonplaces: see. e.g., Davies, *Nosce Teipsum*, *passim*; 542 *allayed*: tempered; 569–70: neo-Platonising Petrarchism: E identif. his beloved with the soul, which was tradnlly regarded as the controller (*mover*) of the 5 senses: Davies, *Nosce Teip.*, 357–76, etc.; 572 *impressure*: impression; *conceit*: see Ralegh, 9n and 13.1n; *invention*: the first part of rhetoric, comprising the finding-out of the topic to be treated; 573: cf. *Nosce Teip.*, 495–502, contrasting the nature of the soul with that of the 'vital spirits' (the intermediaries between body and soul that, carried by the nerves, were believed to convey messages from the brain and the soul (*Nosce Teip.*, 1137ff.): 'She is a spirit and heavenly Influence . . . yet not like *aire*, or *wind*,/Nor like the *spirits* about the *heart or braine*'); 578 *touch*: cf. Sidney, *AS* 9.12n;

579–82: T compares Sp., *Shep. Cal.*, 'January', 43, 'April', 12; 'August', 18; 586–610: a characteristically Ovidian tale (cf. *FQ*, II. ii. 6–9) with no obvious source: note the Petrarchan qualities of the women (beautiful but hard) and the way the tale reverses the Narcissus-Echo myth (cf. 442n): for the symbolism of the purple flower (= vanquished lover), see 118n above; 624 *troth*: loyalty, honesty; 631–62: compare the manifestation of Isis-Phoebe to Lucius in Apuleius, *Golden Ass*, Book 11; 636 *three*: a number specifically dedicated to the moon goddess (*Aen.*, 4.511, 'virgin Diana of the triple countenance'; Chapman, *Hymnus in Cynthiam*, 2, 'thy triple forehead') because of her 3 main aspects (Diana-Luna, Lucina (goddess of childbirth), and Hecate); 647 *brave*: splendid; 648 *brother's*: Phoebus Apollo's (cf. Ralegh, 19.250n); 649–50: cf. Jupiter's appearance to Semele (Ovid, *Met.*, 3.385ff.) though T suggests that the ref. is to his manifestation of himself to the island-woman Aegina (*Met.*, 7.671ff.); 653 *Titan*: there were various names for the sun god: Apollo is a Titan by virtue of the fact that his mother Latona was descended from the Titans (giant offspring of Earth and Sky); 653–62: T compares Joshua Sylvester's transln of Du Bartas, *Divine Weeks*, 1.4.762ff.; 663ff.: for the aerial journey, cf. Marlow's *Dr Faustus*, 3; Sylvester, *Divine Weeks*, 1.6. 842ff.; and, among others, Chaucer, *House of Fame*, 2, Macrobius, *Commentary on the Dream of Scipio*, and Martianus Capella, *The Marriage of Philology and Mercury* (Curtius (1967), 359ff.); 670: cf. Wyatt, 110.8n; 674 *First Mover*: both the *primum mobile* and God the creator (Wyatt, ibid., 7ff.); 680: fire is the highest of the elements enveloping the earth; *silver* belongs to Phoebe; 681ff.: instruction in astronomy and astrology features in the works listed at 663ff. n; knowledge of astronomy was believed immediately to precede knowledge of the divine nature (e.g., Eugenio Garin, *Astrology in the Renaissance* (London: Routledge and Kegan Paul, 1983), 65 citing the *Hermetica*): Endymion was often interpreted as an astronomer (head-note above); 689 *mansions*: the zodiacal houses of the planets in which each planet has its greatest influence; 692 *compass*: circle; 693–4: the signs Taurus, Virgo and Capricorn were regarded as earthy; Cancer, Scorpio and Pisces as watery; Gemini, Libra and Aquarius as airy; and Aries, Leo and Sagittarius as fiery; 699–702: i.e., man as microcosm; 704–6: *complexions* = humours and the bodily constitution derived from them (the correlations were: melancholy-black bile-earth; phlegmatic temperament-phlegm-water; sanguine-blood-air; choler-yellow bile-fire). The planets were associated with them thus: Saturn (melancholy); Moon and Mercury (phlegmatic); Jupiter and Venus (sanguine); Mars and Sun (choleric); 720 *starry firmament*: sphere of the fixed stars; 721: i.e., the Milky Way; 722 *Archer*: (i.e., Sagittarius): copy text reads *Archers*; 723 *Dog*: Canis Major, whose heliacal rising (July-August) coincides with the hottest period of the year when the sun is in Leo (Sp., *Shep. Cal.*, 'July', 21–2: 'The rampant Lyon hunts he fast,/With Dogge of noysome breath'); 725–6 *Pleiades*: normally regarded as benign (e.g., Geneva gloss on Job, 38:31); but see Allen (1963), 398 and 402; 731

imped: strengthened (to imp = to graft feathers onto a damaged wing so as to improve flight): cf. Sp., *Hymn of Heavenly Beauty*, 135–6, again in a context of neo-Platonic ecstasy; *736 Muses*: see 508n; *742 bees*: cf. Porphyry's *Commentary on the cave of the nymphs* in *Odyssey*, 13 as a symbol of the soul's condition in the world, where the bee is associated with the moon (since she was denominated a bee by the ancients) and connected with Proserpina, queen of the underworld, who was known as *meltitiodē* (sweet honey) (see 824–8n) and honey is identif. as a symbol of death to the world. More specifically still, those souls were called bees 'who, while residing in this fluctuating region, acted justly; and who, after being in a manner acceptable to the divinities, returned to their pristine felicity. For the bee is an animal, accustomed to return to its former place' (Porphyry, *De antro nympharum*, in *Commentaries of Proclus*, tr. Thomas Taylor (Taylor (1969), 307–8)); *746 fountain*: by the same token this symbolises E's yet-mortal nature: 'Naiads are so called by the Greeks from *namata*, fountains; because they preside over waters: and this term is commonly applied to all souls passing into the humid and flowing condition of a generative nature' (*ibid.*, 303); *757*: i.e., the eagle; *765*ff.: the rest of the poem moves from earth to heaven, starting with the wood creatures (symbolising the vegetative soul and concupiscence), progressing through Phoebe (who, as the planet nearest to earth, marks the entry-point to the spheres of the planets and their astrological and other significances), to the celestial hierarchy; *767*: cf. 87: *fauns*, like satyrs, are goat-legged and represent the lowest appetite, concupiscence, suppressed by E and Phoebe; *768 snakes*: earthy, as at 264n; *769 ivy*: = Bacchic, hence lustful; *770 woodbine*: honeysuckle, dedic. to Venus and thus also signifying lust; *771*: the *cypress* derives from the wood god Sylvanus's (cf. l. 13) beloved youth Cyparissus, in memory of whom the god carried a cypress branch (Virgil, *Georgics*, 1.20; *FQ*, I. vi. 14); *773 Oreads*: mountain nymphs, here combining Venerean qualities with Dianan ones to produce the familiar Ren. composite of chaste love (Wind (1967), 75ff., where it is considered as a neo-Platonic mystery); *774 murrey sendal*: mulberry (purplish red) coloured fine linen or lawn (*OED Sendal*, 2) or 'rich silken material' (*OED*'s sense 1, where the cited examples confirm that it is usually red); red is Venerean (as in Botticelli's *Primavera*, where Venus wears a red robe) and the green is Dianan; *776 fillets*: bands or strings for binding the hair, bound hair signifying chastity; *flaxen* hair is a Venerean detail, since yellow was often attrib. to Venus (Ptolemy, *Tetrabiblos*, 2.9; on this and bound hair, see Fowler and Brooks-Davies, 'The Meaning of Chaucer's *Knight's Tale*', *Medium Ævun*, 39 (1970), 143n); *777 lascivious*: luxuriant rather than lewd (*OED* sense 2, despite its seventeenth-cent. date); *779–80 myrtle*: Venerean (127n above): gilding was ancient triumphal practice; *781 bisse*: fine linen (*OED Byss* sb[1]1); but note *bisset* = lace of gold, silver, etc.; and perh. punning on *bisse* (= a shade of blue or green); *frets*: ornaments of flowers in a network (*OED*); *782 pinks*: emblems of marriage and love (D'Ancona (1983),

74; cf. 62n above); *violets*: chastely retiring but also Venerean (*ibid.*, 94–5); 783: recalling Sp's Belphoebe (*FQ*, II. iii. 27: 'gilden buskins of costly Cordwaine/ Allbard with golden bendes') and *Hero and Leander*, 1.31–2: 'Buskins... brancht with blushing coral': *branched* = decorated with gold or needlework representing flowers or foliage (*OED Branch* v II.6); *buskins* = boots reaching to calf or knee; *cordwain* = Spanish leather (orig. made at Cordova); 784 *spangled*: decorated with metal sequins; *garters*: leg bands; 786 *pennons*: long pointed streamers (pennants); 787 *hamadryads*: wood nymphs; 789 *bulls*: 263n above; 793–4 *dryads*: wood nymphs orig. signifying the life of individual trees, but in practice not distinguished from *hamadryads*; *stags*: emblems of Phoebe (Tervarent (1958), cols 65–6); 795 *palms*: 'the flat expanded part of the horn in some deer, from which finger-like points project' (*OED Palm* sb² I. 3); *dight*: adorned; 798 *Naiades*: river nymphs (and cf. 746n), symbolising the moon's control over the tides (cf. Chapman, *Hymnus in Cynthiam*, 170–2); 802 *Iris*: rainbow goddess, messenger of Juno, queen of heaven: *proud* = magnificent (not pejorative); *control* = used in the sense of *overpowering* or *outshining*: *OED Control* v 5a); the *rainbow* signifies peace (and see also 113n) and connects with the *halcyon* of 189; 804 *tissue*: rich cloth (e.g. satin), often embroidered; 805 *ivory*: Dianan (e.g. 449 above and *FQ*, VII. vi. 9); 806–7: the *unicorns* belong to Diana as emblems of chastity (Tervarent (1958), cols 84–5 citing illustrns of Petr's *Triumph of Chastity*) as do the *pearls* (334n above); but *unicorns* also signify wisdom (Tervarent, *ibid.*) and *pearls* signify divine wisdom (Matt. 7:6, 13:46), thus suggesting the level of initiation E has attained; 811 *crystal*: cf. 331n, but also symbolising attainment of the divine, not only bec. of Jupiter, king of heaven, but bec. of Rev. 21:11, etc.; 814 *emerald*: one of the stones of the Heav. Jerusalem (Rev. 21:19); but since the rainbow, unicorn, crystal, etc. suggest the imagery of alchemical union and the wisdom signified by it (C. G. Jung, *Alchemical Studies* and *Psychology and Alchemy*, *passim*; also Lyndy Abraham, *Marvell and Alchemy* (Scolar Press, 1990), *passim*), the crowning emerald recalls the ancient Hermetic authority for alchemical knowledge, the *Emerald Table*; 816 *helitropium*: i.e., heliotrope, or bloodstone (a green quartz shot through with red veins); 817 *swans*: 217n and also alchemical (Jung, *ibid*, Index, s.v.); 823: this is a literal Triumph of Phoebe, in the tradn of Petr's *Trionfi*; 824–8: the tradnl titles of the moon goddess: as *Diana* she is goddess of the hunt and of virginity; *Delia* = her name when she recalls the Aegean island of her birth (Delos); as *Luna* she = the moon goddess; as *Cynthia* she = the moon goddess commemorating the mountain on which she was born (Cynthus, on Delos); as *Virago* she = the militant female warrior as defender of virginity and wisdom (the epithet was frequ. applied to Minerva); *Hecate* = the Thracian goddess of magic and witchcraft who became identif. with the moon goddess; *Elythia*: from Gk *ellithos*, containing a precious stone (i.e., the moon stone); *Prothyria* = guardian of the threshold (for both see the Orphic *Hymns*, 2.4, and Chapman's gloss on his *Hymnus in Cynthiam*, line 1); *Dictynna*: a name of Diana in Ovid, *Met.*, 2.441, 5.619 (Latin text), etc.; *Proserpine*: daughter of Ceres, abducted by Pluto, god of the underworld, and made his queen (*Met.*, 5.491ff., tr. Golding); frequ. identif. with the dark aspect of the moon goddess; *Latona*: prob. a misprint: Latona was mother of Apollo and Diana, hence Diana was known as *Latonia* (female Latonian): e.g., *Met.*, 1.696 (Latin text), *Aen.*, 9.405; *Lucina*: the moon as goddess of childbirth (she who *brings to the light*): for Proserpina, Diana, Hecate, see the epiphany of the moon goddess in Apuleius, *Golden Ass*, Book 11, which D clearly has in mind here; 830–1: see 811n for the *crystal* and 794n for the deer (also Ripa (1603), 48 citing Boccaccio); 842 *Twenty and eight . . . lamps*: symbolising the days of the lunar month, also the mansions of the moon (Agrippa (1651), 2.46); 853–8: cf. Du Bartas's *L'Uranie*, tr. Sylvester, st. 12, and *Golden Ass*, tr. Aldington (1566) Book 11, descr. the moon goddess: 'her vestiment was of fine silke yeelding divers colours, sometime yellow, sometime rosie, sometime flamy, and sometime . . . darke and obscure, covered with a blacke robe . . . the welts appeared comely, whereas here and there the starres glimpsed'; *FQ*, VII. vi. 8 makes a similar point about Diana-Luna's stasis amid perpetual change, as does Lyly, *Endimion*, opening scene. D alludes partic., of course, to Eliz's motto *always the same* (Ralegh, 6.11, 14nn); 859 *Astræa*: goddess of justice, daughter of Zeus and Themis: see Davies, *H Astr.* headnote for her centrality to the cult of Eliz; 863–4 *Charites*: the 3 Graces, tradnlly companions of Venus: symbols of divine love, they = also signif. in the cult of Eliz: Davies, *H Astr.*, 9; *FQ*, VI. x, etc.; 871–8: the 9 Muses, daughters of Zeus and Mnemosyne (Memory), inspirers of poetry and music among other things, wear laurel crowns as the emblems of artistic excellence and immortality (Tervarent (1958), col. 232): 9, as the square of the *first* (complete) *number* (3, according to Pythagorean-Platonic tradn), shares divinity with it: Pietro Bongo, *Numerorum mysteria* (Bergamo, 1599), 567; Agrippa (1651), 2.6 and 12; 877 *fury*: *furor*, or possession by a Muse (the '*enthusiasmos*' of the Argt to *Shep. Cal.*, 'October'): cf. 508n and 732. D develops the Ren. notion of the *musarum sacerdos*, the poet sacred to the Muses and devoted to the contemplative life (Klibansky, Saxl, Panofsky (1964), 245, 361, and 362n), to whom the Muses are the instruments of revelation concerning 'the last fundamentals of this world and the next', the means of this revelation being a *furor* or *frenzy* (Agrippa (1651), 3.46); *conceit*: the imagination or phantasy; D clearly sees himself as *musarum sacerdos* hymning Phoebe as both Eliz and Idea; 881–4: on the divine signif. of 3, see Agrippa, 2.6; Bongo (1599), 108ff. Odd numbers *include an unity* in the sense that $3 = 2 + 1, 9 = 8 + 1$, etc. and *unity*, in Pythag. and Platonic numerology, 'doth most simply go through every number, and is the common measure, fountain, and originall of all numbers' (Agrippa, 2.4); 887ff.: D outlines the angelic hierarchy as inherited from Dionysius the Areopagite, *Celestial Hierarchies*, ch. 6ff; 892–4 *Epiphania*: those manifesting the divine power and glory. In descending order: *Seraphim*, who burn with the light of

God's love; *Cherubim*, who contemplate God's wisdom; *Thrones*, who in their purity are immovably established in God; *Dominations*, who are the source of lordship; *Virtues*, who are unshakeable in virtue; *Powers* (*Potestates*), who signify the regulation of intellectual and heavenly power; *Principalities* (*Principates*), who embody godlike princeliness and authority; *Archangels*, who are intermediate betw. Principalities and Angels; and *Angels*, who are the divine messengers (*messengers* is also the meaning of *Ephiona*). D's placing of Principalities in the second group of 3 (instead of the 3rd), and his downgrading of Virtues from second to 3rd, is non-Dionysian but not unique: see, e.g., Kathi Meyer-Baer, *Music of the Spheres and the Dance of Death* (Princeton: Princeton U.P., 1970), fig. 97 and *passim*; 902 *particularity.*: i.e., the partic, qualities noted above; 904 *her*: Idea, from whom D had indeed inferred *another order* in *Idea's Mirror* (1594), sonnet 8: 'My Worthie, one to these nine Worthies, addeth,/And my faire Muse, one Muse unto the nine:/And my good Angell in my soule divine,/With one more order, these nine orders gladdeth'; 907 *babes of Memory*: 871–8n; 909: i.e., at Delphi, etc.; 915–20: the Muses were frequ. assoc. with the spheres of the Ptolemaic system, the intervals betw. the spheres (tone or semitone) totalling altogether the 6 tones that comprise the perfect interval of the *diapason* (octave), the whole signifying the descent of the divine spirit from heaven to earth: Agrippa, 2.12; and Martianus Capella, *Marr. of Philol. and Mercury*, tr. Stahl *et al* (1977), 55ff. on the 'celestial tonal intervals'. See also Wind (1967), 265–9 and fig. 20 on the well-known case of the frontispiece to Francesco Gafurio's *Practica musice* (1496), where the cycle emanates from Apollo; D presumably includes *Jove* (919) as king of heaven; 921ff.: the harmonious composition of the soul, which made her partic. responsive to audible music and the visual music of architectural proportion, painting, and sculpture, was a Ren. commonplace: Rudolf Wittkower, *Archit. Principles in the Age of Humanism* (London, 1962); 924–5: D refers to the division of the soul into three faculties (or 'souls'): vegetative (as shared by plants, etc.); sensitive (as shared by animals), rational (possessed by humanity alone), each of which had 3 functions: those pertaining to the vegetative = nutrition, growth, reproduction; and those pertaining to the sensitive and rational involved the powers of apprehension, motion and memory: Davies, *Nosce Teip.*, 937ff., and D's own *Idea* (1619 text), sonnet 12, giving the Augustinian list *Anima, Amor, Animus, Mens, Memoria, Ratio, Sensus, Conscientia*, and *Spiritus*; for 9 as the number of the soul, see Bongo (1599), 567 and *FQ*, II. ix. 22; 929–31: there were various lists of 9 worthies: one comprised 3 classical ancients (Hector, Alexander, Julius Caesar), 3 Jewish ancients (Joshua, David, Judas Maccabaeus), and 3 Christians (Arthur, Charlemagne, Godfrey of Bouillon): cf. *Idea's Mirror*, 8 cited at 904n above; 942 *Eliza's . . . kind*: possibly recalling in part the symbolism of the well-known engraving in John Case's *Sphaera civitatis* (1588), reprod. in Yates (1975a), plate 9c, which features Eliz. as the 9th heavenly sphere (*primum mobile*), embracing all the others; 946 *Orpheus . . . nine*: the strings of O's lyre varied from 7 to 10 in number depending on whether symbologists wished to relate them to the planetary spheres or the OT decalogue (A. D. S. Fowler, *Silent Poetry: Essays in Numerological Analysis* (London: Routledge and Kegan Paul, 1970), 176, and Ptolemy's star total for Lyra was 10 (*ibid.*, 183n). But 9 features in, e.g., Giordano Bruno's reforming astrological dialogue *The Expulsion of the Triumphant Beast* (1584), ed. and trans. A. D. Imerti (New Brunswick, N.J.: Rutgers U.P., 1964), 81 ('There, where one sees the nine-stringed Lyre, ascends the Mother Muse with her nine daughters') and 181. O's lyre was regarded by neo-Platonists as an aid to the soul's return journey to its divine origins and identif. with the spiritual realm in general (J. B. Friedman, *Orpheus in the Middle Ages* (Cambridge, Mass.: Harvard U.P., 1970), 80–2; 949 *man's ... voice*: probably an allusion to Fulgentius's etymology of *Orpheus* from *oraia phone* (= best voice): Friedman, *ibid.*, 89; 951 *instruments*: i.e., strings (instrumental in producing the sound); *ground*: rest, base; 962 *Graces*: 863–4n; their names were Aglaia, Thalia and Euphrosyne. On their number as an adumbration of the Christian trinity, see Wind (1967), 248ff.; 964–6: on the first 3 modes see, e.g., Francesco Gafurio's *Practica musice*, tr. and ed. Irwin Young (Madison, Milwaukee, London: Univ. of Wisconsin Press, 1969), 1.7 (pp. 42–3); the whole chapter describes the 7 modes which were based on the 7 distinct notes of the (non-chromatic) octave; 967–70: i.e., the 12 (3 × 4) signs of the zodiac; 971–4: the 3 *interior senses* of the sensitive soul were common sense, phantasy (imagination) and memory; 987 *thirty years*: a figure from mediaeval and Renaissance mythographers (R. F. Hardin, *Michael Drayton and the Passing of Elizabethan England* (Lawrence, Manhattan, Wichita: Univ. of Kansas Press, 1973), 17, presumably here symbolising the perfect form of the Trinity (and Diana's own triform shape): Bongo (1599), 178 on 30 as 3 × the perfect decad; 993 *Colin*: Spenser's pastoral persona, borrowed from Skelton and used in the *Shep. Cal.*, *Colin Clout*, etc.; 997–1000: the *Musaeus* referred to here (see Davies, *Orch.*, 637n) = Samuel Daniel, whose sonnet sequence *Delia* (a name of Diana) was publ. in 1592. D probably recalls that Musaeus = the 'son of the light-bearing moon' in the Orphic *Testament* (Friedman (1970), 14); 1001 *Goldey*: affectionate anagram of (Thomas) Lodge, writer of prose romances, pamphlets, the epyllion *Scylla's Metamorphosis*, etc.; 1004: cf. 731n; 1010 *Momus*: god of censure and detraction; 1011 *sweet maid*: Idea (Anne Goodere); 1013 *Vesta*: 22n above (as goddess of the domestic hearth she also alludes to Anne's marriage); 1014 *Ankor*: the river Anker, by which the Gooderes' house, Polesworth Hall, was situated (see *Idea's Mirror*, 13, etc.); 1020 *prime*: youth (also spring); 1025: D had already connected Anne Goodere with Phoebe in *Shep. Garl.*, 5.61–5 and 9.19–22 (T).

SIR JOHN DAVIES:
HYMNS OF ASTRÆA and ORCHESTRA

Text

The *Hymns* were published in 1599, probably to gain further notice from Elizabeth after her favourable reception of *Nosce Teipsum* (dedicated to her) earlier the same year. There was a further edn in 1619; the *Hymns* were then published together with *Nosce Teipsum* and *Orchestra* in 1622. There are few textual problems since D seems to have overseen the printing of each edn. Copy text: 1622.

Orchestra, first published 1596, was corrected by D for 1622. A MS of the poem exists from 1592 transcribed by Leweston Fitzjames, a colleague of D's at the Middle Temple (Bodleian MS Add. B. 97). Copy text: 1622.

I have followed 1622 in printing the *Hymns* before *Orchestra*. The full title of 1622 is: *Nosce Teipsum. This Oracle expounded in two Elegies. 1. Of Humane Knowledge. 2. Of the Soule of Man, and the Immortalitie thereof. Hymnes of Astræa in Acrosticke Verse. Orchestra. Or, a Poeme of Dauncing. In a Dialogue betweene Penelope, and one of her Wooers. Not finished.*

Modern editions

The Works in Verse and Prose of Sir John Davies, ed. A. B. Grosart. Fuller Worthies Library. 3 vols (Blackburn, 1869–76).

The Complete Poems of Sir John Davies, ed. A. B. Grosart, 2 vols (London: Chatto and Windus, 1876).

The Poems of Sir John Davies, ed. Clare Howard (New York: Columbia U.P., 1941).

The Poems of Sir John Davies, ed. Robert Krueger, with introd. and commentary by the editor and Ruby Nemser (Oxford: Clarendon Press, 1975).

Orchestra, or a Poeme of Dauncing (1596), repr. and introd. R. S. Lambert (Wembley Hill: Stanton Press, 1922).

Orchestra, or a Poem of Dancing, ed. E. M. W. Tillyard (London: Chatto and Windus, 1945).

FURTHER READING

KRUEGER, ROBERT. 'Sir John Davies: *Orchestra* Complete, *Epigrams*, Unpublished Poems', *Review of English Studies*, 13 (1962).

SANDERSON, J. L. 'Recent Studies in Sir John Davies', *English Literary Renaissance*, 4 (1974).

SANDERSON, J. L. *Sir John Davies* (1975).

SPENCER, THEODORE. 'Two Classic Elizabethans: Samuel Daniel and Sir

Davies

John Davies', in A. C. Purves (ed.), *Theodore Spencer: Selected Essays* (1966).

THESIGER, SARAH. 'The *Orchestra* of Sir John Davies and the Image of the Dance', *Journal of the Warburg and Courtauld Institutes*, 36 (1973).

TILLYARD, E. M. W. *Five Poems, 1470–1870* (1948).

WILKES, G. A. 'The Poetry of Sir John Davies', *Huntington Library Quarterly*, 25 (1962).

HYMNS OF ASTRÆA

Entered in the Stationers' Register on the anniversary of Elizabeth's accession day, 17 November 1599. *Astraæa* = the ancient virgin goddess of justice, the last of the divinities to abandon the earth as it moved from the Golden through the Silver and Bronze to the corrupt Iron Age (Ovid, *Met.*, 1.169–70). Having fled earth for heaven she was transformed into the zodiacal constellation Virgo (now 24 August to 23 September, but anciently and in the Renaissance thought of as governing the whole of August: e.g., Spenser, *Shep. Cal.*, 'August' woodcut). As the constellation of August she became the goddess of harvest, tradnlly depicting holding an ear (*spica*) of corn. As the immortal who reluctantly left a troubled earth she was associated also with spring rebirth; for, it was thought, as the last to leave she would be the first to return to redeem corruption and restore the Golden Age once more. The key text for this concept is Virgil's 4th *Eclogue*, l. 6 (*Iam redit et virgo, redeunt Saturnia regna*: now the virgin returns and now return Saturnian kingdoms). From the medieval period Virgil's prophecy had been associated with Christian reform and the possibility of the accession to power of a just world-emperor; with the accession of Elizabeth in 1558 and the subsequent development of a cult of virginity around her, the mythology of Astraæa-Virgo reached a peak (E. C. Wilson, *England's Eliza* (Cambridge, Mass.: Harvard U.P., 1939); Frances Yates, *Astræa: The Imperial Theme in the Sixteenth Century* (London and Boston: Routledge and Kegan Paul, 1975); Roy Strong, *The Cult of Elizabeth* (London: Thames and Hudson, 1987); James Hutton, *Themes of Peace in Renaissance Poetry*, ed. Rita Guerlac (Ithaca and London: Cornell U.P., 1984)).

Each of D's *Hymns* is an acrostic on *Elisabetha regina*, and there are 26 poems in the sequence because the astronomer Ptolemy's *Almagest* gave 26 as the star-total for Virgo (A. D. S. Fowler, *Spenser and the Numbers of Time* (London: Routledge and Kegan Paul, 1964), 115, 198–200).

1 12 *alchemist*: the identifcn of the Golden Age with pure alchemical gold (symbolic of spiritual purity and enlightenment) and hence of the monarch, restorer of the Golden Age, with the alchemical adept was a commonplace: Brooks-Davies (1983); Yates (1975b).

2 8 *Peace . . . honey*: as Virgo, sign of harvest, Astræa was assoc. with Ceres, the Roman corn goddess and goddess of peace (for the familiar idea of 'Peace the friend of Ceres' (*Pax Cereris amica*), see Cartari (1571),

316–7 and Yates (1975a), 77–8); the *milk and honey* derive from Ovid, *Met.*, 1.127–8 ('Then streames ran milke, then streames ran wine, and yellow honny floude/ From ech greene tree') as well as biblical texts concerning the promised land (Exodus 3:8, Lev. 20:24, etc.).

3 For Astræa and spring see headnote above. The spring-winter debate has particular symbolic point when we recall that Eliz's accession day, the day celebr. by *HA* and on which it was registered, was regarded as a spring rebirth of the nation on the threshold of winter: Yates (1975a), 90 and Brooks-Davies (1977), 127 on *FQ* II. ii. 40–2; 6: characteristic eirenic motifs (Hutton (1984), ch. 7); 7 *balm*: cf. Ovid as in 2.8n above. The word has specific alchemical assocns: as the product of heat and moisture it was regarded as a form of the elixir of life and thus as a cure for the poison released by the serpent at the Fall.

4 1 *May*: named from Maia, daughter of Atlas, at the beginning of whose month the fertility rites of Flora, queen of flowers (who was closely connected with Venus, goddess of love), were celebrated (Ovid, *Fasti*, 5.185): hence harking back to 3.11–16. The connection May-Flora-Venus enables D to identify Astræa-Eliz. as Venerean *queen of Beauty* (5): and see Strong (1987), 47–8; 15: an independent deity named Maia was also worshipped as *Majesta* (Majesty) and sacrificed to on 1 May; 16 *clearness*: brightness and beauty and also fame (Latin *clarus*) (Krueger-Nemser).

5 1 *Lark*: bird of spring, dawn and love, which tradnlly 'at heaven's gate sings' (Shakespeare, *Cymb.*, 2.3); 9 *sphere*: i.e. planetary sphere; so that the *Hymn* becomes part of the music of the spheres. This, together with the quasi-magical notion of *attractive sympathy* (4.12) and the invocation of other symbolic attributes suggests that the *Hymns* were conceived of by D as magical incantations of the powers of Astræa, parallel in effect to the Orphic hymns, etc. (Taylor, ed. Raine and Harper (1969); D. P. Walker, *Spiritual and Demonic Magic from Ficino to Campanella* (London: Warburg Institute, 1958): a hymn = a song in praise of a deity).

6 *Title*: *Nightingale* = nocturnal equivalent to lark as bird of love; 9–10: the idea of the return of Virgo-Astræa to earth (headnote) may also be related here to the notion of reform through the symbolism of descended constellations suggested by the hermetic magus Giordano Bruno: Yates (1978) and Brooks-Davies (1983).

7 *Title*: *Rose*: emblem of Venus (see 9) and of the Virgin Mary as queen of the enclosed *garden* of Song of Solomon 4:12 (for Marian elements in the cult of Elizabeth, see Yates (1975a), 34–5, 78–9, and R. H. Wells, *Spenser's 'Faerie Queene' and the Cult of Elizabeth* (London: Croom Helm, 1983)): for the complex of symbolisms see Wilkins (1969) and Marina Warner, *Alone of all her Sex* (London: Picador, 1985), and for specifically political symbolism (e.g. the union of the roses of Lancaster and York in Eliz.) see Wilson (1939), 133–5 and Spenser, *Shep. Cal.*, 'April': 4 *Hours*: daughters of the Sun who preside over dawn and the seasons, tradnlly 'rosy-bosomed' (Milton, *Comus*, 985) and companions of Venus's graces.

9 *Title*: *Flora*: see 4.1n and Ovid, *Fasti*, 5.183ff. for the legend in full. Strong (1987), 50 compares the flower embroidery in the 'Rainbow' portrait of Eliz.; but floral *motifs* are common in several portrait types of the queen; **3** *Greenwich*: the site of one of the main royal palaces; **6** *Majesty*: see 4.15n; **8** *Hours*: 7.4n; *Graces*: the 3 handmaids of Venus, seen by neo-Platonists as embodying the attributes of divine love: Wind (1967), ch. 3.

10 *Title*: *September*: Queen Eliz. was born on 7 September 1533. But the Marian aspect of the cult of Eliz. (7n) guarantees that D also celebrates the feast of the Nativity of the Virgin Mary (8 September): see Yates (1975a), 78.

11 **1** *Eye*: a commonplace (Pierio Valeriano, *Hieroglyphica* (1602), Book 51, *Osiris*), but influenced in this instance by the Orphic hymn to the Sun (tr. Taylor (1969), 218–9); **9** *Phaethon*: the son of the sun god Phoebus Apollo who stole his father's chariot, lost control of it, and nearly destroyed the earth. D suppresses the tradnl meaning of usurpation and rebellion to suggest that the sun himself is a lesser self (equivalent to his own son) who has been somehow promoted to inhabit the face of Eliz., the emblematic sun queen. Even thus exalted, however, he does not destroy but, rather, inspires love (10).

12 Continues the brightness/blindness idea of **11** (note the pun on *glory* = halo, ring of light, in l.5) modulated into a neo-Platonic mode: Eliz. is the ineffably bright 'one' and her picture a mere shadowy imitation; **6** *red and white*: cf. **9.11** (the tradnl colours of female beauty).

13 At the midpoint of the sequence, D turns from externals (mythological attributes, the picture as manifestation of the external body) to spiritual essence, a move again explained by the sequence's neo-Platonic ideology. *Mind* here = soul, the spiritual entity we share with God (its meaning in *Nosce Teipsum*, 105ff.); **6** *angels' kind*: i.e., spiritual essence (D compares Eliz. to an angel in *Nosce Teipsum*, Dedicn, 30); **11** *sunbeam*: God as light is neo-Platonic as well as Christian: Eliz's soul is the solar manifestation of an ineffably bright source as her picture (12) is a visibly inferior image of her beauty. The soul as sun is an image used in *NT*, Dedicn, 25–9.

15 *Title*: *Wit*: an intellectual power of the soul, identical with understanding, which looks into the phantasy (see 18n below), abstracts thence the 'shapes of things', then 'by discoursing to and fro,/Anticipating and comparing things,/She doth all universal nature know,/And all effects into their causes brings' (*NT*, 1165–8); **15** *policy*: art of government; also statecraft.

16 **1** *Will*: for D's orthodox definition, see *NT*, 1201ff.: will should choose (true) good but is sometimes misled by wit's false data: 'Will puts in practice what the wit deviseth;/Will ever acts, and wit contemplates still . . . Will is as free as any emperor;/Nought can restrain her gentle liberty;/No tyrant nor no torment hath the power/To make us will when we unwilling be'.

17 *Title*: *Memory*: cf. D's description of 'the sensitive memory' (*NT*,

1100ff.), placed in the rear of the brain, as a volume which receives and stores sense impressions; and cf. Spenser, *FQ*, II. ix. 55–8, where Memory is rendered as the psychological equivalent of national history; 16 *Pallas*: Athene, virginal goddess of wisdom.

18 *Title*: I have retained the archaic spelling to distinguish it from the modern word and meaning. *Phantasy* (or imagination) = the recipient of sense data that also has the power to invent its own forms from that data: cf. *NT*, 1085–1100 and *FQ*, II. ix. 50–2; 6 *temper*: temperament, balance of passions, etc.; also *tuning* (as of musical instrument) bec. Apollo the sun god (14–16) is god of music.

19 1 *she*: i.e., Eliz's mind; the imagery of st. 1 is again neo-Platonic; 6 *instruments*: her ministers of state, etc.; also musical; 8 *lute*: instrument of love (see Wyatt, 59n above) but more importantly, bec. of its 7 strings, emblem of the musically-ordered cosmos (strings = planetary spheres). D has in mind something like Eliz. as the prime mover of the sphere of state (where the state is conceived of as the concentric spheres of the Ptolemaic cosmos in its entirety, each sphere producing its musical note) as portrayed in the plate from Case's *Sphaera civitatis*, 1588 (Yates (1975a), plate 9c). Since the body of the lute was tradnlly regarded as feminine, it is a particularly apt emblem of the Elizabethan body politic; 11 *Resolve*: analyse, solve (a problem).

21 15 *beg for*: reckon.

22–25 Praise of Eliz. for her possession of the 4 classical cardinal virtues (Prudence, Justice, Fortitude, Temperance), with deviations as noted below.

22 1 *Wisdom*: Prudence, the primary virtue, = identif. as practical wisdom, and includes judgement and action based on knowledge of the past and anticipation of future consequences (Panofsky (1955), ch. 4). But D amplifies it to include hints of the Judaic Wisdom tradn (see also 23n below): female Wisdom as an aspect of the godhead (Warner (1985), ch. 9). Wisdom was also conflated with Pallas Athene, Greek goddess of wisdom and *Jove's . . . daughter* (l. 3; cf. no. 17 above); 6 *rule*: emblem of rectitude (opposite of wandering *Error*, l.10); 8 *mirror*: emblem of Prudence (Ripa (1603), 416).

23 *Title*: *Justice* = embodied in Astræa (see headnote) and, in the Christian concept of the ideal prince, is tempered with Clemency, the imperial virtue (e.g., *FQ*, V. ix. 30, where Eliz. is described as *Mercilla*, accompanied by the sceptre of 'peace and clemency' and the sword of Justice); 3 *number . . . measure*: Justice maintains balance; but D suggests that Eliz.-Astræa embodies the creative and cosmos-sustaining power of the deity itself, for the phrase comes from one of the apocryphal Old Testament Wisdom books ('Thou hast ordered all things in measure, and number, and weight' (Wisdom, 11:21)), thus linking this *Hymn* with no. 22.

24 *Title*: *Magnanimity* was anciently believed to manifest the cardinal virtue Fortitude (Tuve (1966), 66); 11: the heavens' *axle-tree* = the imagined line forming the axis of the revolutions of the planetary spheres

(cf. Wyatt, 110, 25–31 and n above); the *pillar* of constancy was a common emblem in Elizabethan panegyric: Strong (1987), 75 and George Puttenham, *Arte of English Poetry* (1589), 2.12.

25 *Title*: *Moderation*: a form of Temperance, the rational control of the passions that marked the virtuous person (the subject of Sp's *FQ*, II). Self-government was symbolised by one of the sceptres handed to the monarch in the coronation service (Brooks-Davies (1983), 35–7); so that there is an implied link with no. 23. Temperance displaces *Fortune* (7) because of her traditional instability and unpredictability.

26 *Title*: *Envy*: D banishes the rancorous sin of Envy at the end of his *Astræa* as Sp attempts to banish it, in the form of the Blatant Beast, from the Arcadian pastoral world of *FQ*, VI.

ORCHESTRA

Probably written early 1594. It exists in 3 forms: (1) as found in the Leweston Fitzjames MS, where it comprises 113 stanzas (those numbered 1–108 and 127–31 in the present text); (2) as printed in *1596*, where present stanzas 109–26 were added to produce a 131-stanza poem; (3) as printed in *1622*, where the poem comprised stanzas 1–126 and stanzas 127A to 132A inclusive). (I accept Krueger-Nemser's analysis.) The marginal glosses belong to *1622* only.

The present text follows *1622* wherever possible, while giving the reader the poem in its three forms. The 1622 poem is, however, no more 'unfinished' than its two predecessors, as Sanderson (1975), 68 notes. (For the earlier view, see Tillyard (1945), 13).

The reason for the disruption of the 1596 text in *1622* seems to have been a quarrel with, and attack on, the poem's original dedicatee, Richard Martin, a companion of D's at the Middle Temple, as a result of which D was expelled from the Temple and disbarred (*DNB*; Sanderson, 24–5). In 1622 D replaces Martin as dedicatee and offers the poem to Prince Charles; he also removes an allusion to him in st. 130–31 by the simple device of replacing the concluding stanzas and pretending that the poem is unfinished.

Occasion

Probably written for an audience of lawyers and possibly for the revels of an Inn of Court as a 'disputation' arguing the power of dance (P. J. Finkelpearl, *John Marston of the Middle Temple* (Cambridge, Mass.: Harvard U.P., 1969)) and subsequently modified to appeal to Eliz. and her court, to whom the image of the dance was central (Krueger-Nemser, 358–9). J. R. Brink, 'Sir John Davies's *Orchestra*: Political Symbolism and Textual Revisions', *Durham University Journal*, 72 (1980), argues that the poem is a coded plea for Eliz. to restore order to the kingdom by settling the succession question; and R. J. Manning, 'Rude Order Strange: A Reading of Sir John Davies's *Orchestra*', *English Literary*

Renaissance, 15 (1985), suggests an identification of Antinous with Essex, who is finally led to a vision of Eliz. as supreme monarch.

Title, theme, sources

Greek *orchestra* = space in theatre where the chorus danced and sang. D utilises the commonplace of the dance of the cosmos that is attuned to the harmony of its own planetary spheres. The measure of the dance reflects the divine order and, simultaneously, the political order of a hierarchical state. Sources include Lucian's *Peri orcheseos* (*Concerning the Dance*), Cicero's *De natura deorum* (*On the nature of the gods*) and (maybe) the section on dancing as a courtly obligation in Sir Thomas Elyot's *The Book named the Governor* (1531), 1.20. As a defence of dance it may glance at the attacks by such moralists as Philip Stubbes, who predictably vituperated dancing in his *Anatomy of Abuses* (1583) (Sanderson, 74–6). For general background, see John Hollander, *The Untuning of the Sky* (Princeton, N.J.: Princeton U.P., 1961) and S. K. Heninger, Jr, *Touches of Sweet Harmony* (San Marino, Calif.: Huntington Library, 1974).

Title (1596): *Si vox . . . place*: if you have a voice, sing; if your arms are lithe, dance; and please by whatever means you may give pleasure (Ovid, *Art of Love*, 1.595–6).
Dedication (1596) 2 *capriole*: leap; 7 *Suada*: goddess of Persuasion.
Dedication (1622): *the Prince*: Prince Charles, later (1625) Charles I, celebrated for his dancing in court masques, etc.; 2 *bent*: single-minded, determined; 3 *sadly*: seriously and learnedly; 8 *St George*: patron saint of the Order of the Garter.
Orchestra (note: references are to line numbers) 5: translates *Odyssey*, l.3; 7 *Midland*: literally translating Medi-terranean; 8 *carouse*: drink the health; 16 *man*: i.e. Ulysses/Odysseus; 18 *illudes*: deceives (punning on *eludes*); 19 *ungrateful*: unwelcome; 20 *Fame*: Rumour; 28 *burden*: load, but also musical refrain (cf. 40–2); 29–35: D revises the *Odyssey*, Book 2, inventing an entirely new fiction concerning the Homeric Penelope's main suitor; 36 *Terpsichore*: Muse of the dance, daughter of Jove and Memory (Mnemosyne); 37 *cunning*: learned, skilful; 40–3: i.e. sing in the middle of the range of voices available from the various Muses (*mean* = median, also the middle voices – alto/tenor – in music). *Ground* = plain-song or melody (cf. *plain*, line 40) above which a descant is played or sung. D's Muse will not sing the bravura descant. Cf. Spenser, *FQ* I. xi. 7 for an analogous passage; 44 *torchbearer*: the Sun, 'masked' in darkness in order to sport with Tethys, wife of Oceanus; 59 *Phaemius*: *Odyssey*, 1.153ff. (musician at court of Ithaca); 64 *Pallas*: cf. *H Astr.* 17 and 22nn.; 78 *sith*: since; 85 *mover*: leader in the dance; also *prime mover* (*primum mobile*) in the Ptolemaic system, which causes all the spheres to move; 113–9: Love binds the strife of the elements in Plato's *Timaeus*, 32C (for the commonplace see also Spenser's *Hymn in Honour of Love*, 78–91); but the idea of the primacy of Dance recalls the OT

Wisdom tradition, in which Wisdom, present 'from the beginning', plays (Latin *ludeo*) before the Lord (Proverbs 8: 23ff.): for this play and the cosmic round dance, see Wilkins (1969), 81–7; 129 *digesting*: systematising; 132 *music*: thought to be emitted by a daimon seated on each of the revolving spheres; 135 *Morpheus*: god of dreams; 136 *undivided motes*: Epicurus's theory that the universe is formed through the random conjunction of atoms (cf. *Nosce Teipsum*, 215–6); 141–4: *Amphion*: see Sidney, *AS* 68.6n above; 150–4: for the antiquity of Time, see Plato, *Timaeus*, 38B; but D seems to suggest again (see 113–9n) that Dancing is born of Wisdom's play, and was thus present 'or ever the earth was' (Prov. 8:23); 164–5 *Love*: the paradox of his youth and age originates with Plato's *Symposium*, 178 B–C and 195 A–B: cf. Sp, *Hymn in Honour of Love*, 50–6; 170 *subtle*: 'thin', rarefied; 174 *doublings*: sudden turns; 187 *gentry*: rank by birth, descent; 189 *blaze*: adorn (with armorial bearings); 190 *wight*: person, living creature (suggesting Earth as personification); 210 *ring*: cf. Plato, *Timaeus*, 43A, where circular motion is imposed by the Demiurge to establish order; 211 *rarefy*: refine (because the sublunary region is too gross for divinities to inhabit it); 230 *model*: copy; 243 *great . . . year*: attrib. to Plato, the Great Year was the period of time it was thought it would take for the planets to return to their original positions at the creation (figures included 15000 and 36000 calendar years); 252 *axle-tree*: see *H Astr.* 24.11n.; 253 *fire . . . flames*: i.e., the planets (Gk *planētēs* = wanderer): see Wyatt, 110 (Iopas's song), 31ff. and nn.; 259 *galliard*: lively dance in triple time; 260 *bastard Love*: i.e., Cupid as 'common Love' and as 'heavenly Love' (Plato, *Symposium*, 180–1 and commentators following him (Panofsky (1962), ch. 4)); 262–3: allude to the fact that Venus as the morning star precedes the sun's rising and as the evening star succeeds its setting; 263 *her* (1596): the (1622); 270 *leman*: beloved; 274 *he* (1622 errata slip): she (1622 text); 283 *pavan*: slow dance in duple time; 288–94: the two kinds of fire (domestic and vital) are defined in, e.g., Cicero, *Of the Nature of the Gods*, 2.15.40–1. In the Ptolemaic system the source of both was the envelope of fire which lay beneath the sphere of the moon. Beneath that were envelopes of air and water and, finally, the earth; 309 *Echo*: see Sidney, *Arcadia* poems 7n and 10n; 324 *hay*: country dance rather like a reel; 338 *clips*: embraces; 343 *centre*: the earth; 349 *mace*: Neptune's traditional trident; 351–5: D (like many others) rejects Copernicus's still-recent theory; 360 *dugs*: breasts; 365 *Meander*: the serpentine Phrygian river; 456 *dying swans*: see Wyatt, 62n and Sidney, *AS* 54.13n; 368 *creeks*: turns; *wrenches*: sudden twists; 386–7 *vine . . . elm*: tradnl emblem of marital support, the vine signifying the supposedly dependent woman (Wind (1967), 112 and n); in Whitney (1586), 62 it signifies friendship, and love-as-friendship is the mainstay of cosmic harmony in Plato's *Timaeus*; 394 *Jump*: exactly (in time with); 396–406: the *triangular* formation of *cranes* is reported by Cicero, *On the Nature of the Gods*, 2.49.125; 409 *raped*: hurried, hastened; 411 *Chance* (1596): Chaunge (1622); Chance-Fortune's *wheel* is a commonplace (H. R.

Notes

Patch, *The Goddess Fortune in Mediaeval Literature* (Cambridge, Mass.: Harvard U.P., 1927)); 415 *lords*: Genesis 1.28; 419 *vital twist*: thread of life mythologically controlled by the three Fates; 421 *crown*: circular throng; 429 *seven*: codified in Plato's *Timaeus*, 34A and 43B and subsequently a commonplace; 432 *brawl*: i.e., branle, a dance employing swaying movement; 527 *wries*: turns, twists; 440 *traverses*: crossings; 446 *two Bears*: Ursa Major and Ursa Minor, which circle the north pole; 457 *Atlas*: identif. as the first Egyptian astronomer (Comes (1567), *De Atlante*; see also Sidney, *Arcadia* poems 20.103n); *Prometheus* was the first to raise men's eyes to heaven (Comes, *De Prometheo*); 462 *spondee*: metrical foot comprising two long syllables or accents; 464 *he*: she (1596, 1622); 478 *dactyl*: metrical foot comprising one long and two short syllables or accents; 491 *twins*: Castor and Pollux, who became the zodiacal sign Gemini. They taught the Spartans, whose country was bordered by the Eurotas, to dance: Lucian, *Dance*, para 10 (Krueger-Nemser, 370); 499–501: *Venus* and *Mars* were trapped in a net by Venus's husband Vulcan, who summoned the other gods to laugh at their shame; but D praises the harmony of Venus and Mars as a just mingling of opposites (see Wind (1967), 86–96); 512–25: for the three Graces, handmaids of Venus, and their circular dance which symbolises, among other things, reciprocity of benefits, see Wind (1967), chaps 2 and 3; 514 *doth*: did (1596, 1622): I follow Krueger; 530–32: Rhea hid the infant Jove on Crete in order to prevent Saturn eating him, and his cries were drowned by the frantic dancing of the Curetes (Lucian, *Dance*, para 8); 540 *he*: Orpheus, whose lute/lyre tradnlly had ten strings (A. D. S. Fowler, *Silent Poetry* (London: Routlege and Kegan Paul, 1970), 176 and n); 547 *Musaeus*: reputed son and disciple of Orpheus and addressee of the Orphic hymns; *Amphion*: see 141n above; 548 *Linus*: son of Apollo and inventor of songs; 549–50 *he . . . tongue*: Hercules who, in his Gallic form, was depicted drawing people after him with the 'chains' of his eloquence (Alciati (1551), 194); 551 *Theseus*: created Athenian civilisation out of the rudiments of rural Attica; *too*: to (1596, 1622); 554–5 *lyre*: the constellation Lyra (R. H. Allen (1963), 280–88); *Hercules*: stellified after his death (Allen, 238–46); 558 *Ganymede*: cupbearer to Jove and identified with the constellation Aquarius, pourer of water and wine (Virgil, *Georgics*, 3. 304); *Hebe*: goddess of youth and wife of stellified Hercules; also cupbearer to the gods and the female Ganymede; 561 *Proteus*: sea god renowned for his shape-shifting properties; but Proteus as *dancer* may derive from Lucian, *Dance*, para 19; 568 *Caeneus*: according to Ovid, *Met.*, 12. 191–235 (Golding trans.), born a girl and changed by Neptune into a boy; 575 *Tiresias*: changed from man to woman and back again and fabled to know which of the sexes enjoyed greater sexual pleasure (*Met.*, 3. 403–26); 582 *Venus*: *Met.*, 5. 420 ('Venus in the shape of Fish'); 589–75: Bacchus conquered and civilised Lydia, India, etc. Lucian, *Dance*, para 22 suggests that he achieved this through the dancing of the Bacchic mystery religion (Krueger-Nemser, 373); 610: for the cult of Victory, see Warner (1985), 129–31; 612 *Io*:

469

cry of celebration and rejoicing; 632 *Nestors*: the original Nestor was the wise old counsellor of the Greeks (*Odyssey*, 3, etc.); 635–7: *Thessalians*: Lucian, *Dance*, para 14; 638 *Liberal Arts*: D proceeds to list the seven (grammar, rhetoric, logic, music, arithmetic, geometry and astronomy). Through their number they were assoc. with the planetary spheres and thus link with the cosmogony at 232ff. and the seven movements of 429, etc.; 660: the traditional harmonious (non-discordant) intervals, though D omits the fourth (15 = the consonance of the double octave). These were the intervals thought to govern the structures of the earth and heavens, on the authority of Plato, *Timaeus*, 35A–36D and its followers; 671 *character*: emblem; 687–8 *mother . . . blood*: Medea, who killed her children when betrayed by Jason; or Procne (see below, 698–70); 689 *daughter*: possibly Scylla, who for love of Minos cut off the bright hair from her father, Nisus's, head that guaranteed his life, thereby causing his death (Apollodorus, *Library*, 3.15.8; Krueger-Nemser); 691 *brother*: Atreus, king of Mycenae, whose brother Thyestes seduced his wife and gained the golden lamb that was his emblem of kingship. In revenge, Atreus killed Thyestes's sons and served them to him as a meal (*brother* (1622 errata list): brothers (1596, 1622)); 698–70: *Tereus's* wife was Procne, who killed their son, Itys, and fed him to her husband at supper when she discovered that he had raped her sister Philomel (*Met.*, 6. 542– 855); 751 *house*: body, the temple of the soul; 842 *fortunate triangled isle*: Britain (the triangle being formed by the extremities of Cornwall, Kent, and Scotland), the western land founded by Brutus and, since the mediaeval period and through the tale of Arthur's western resting-place, the isle of Avalon, identified with the Graeco-Roman Fortunate Isles, the western abode of the immortals: J. W. Bennet, 'Britain among the Fortunate Isles,' *Studies in Philology*, 53 (1956; 847 *six and twenty*: Astræa's number (*HA* headnote above); 848 *Penelope*, type of chastity for withstanding the importunities of her suitors, now sees in the *crystal* (861) that is at once the mirror of Truth (Ripa (1603), 501) and the magic glass made by Merlin of Sp's *FQ*, III. ii, a vision of Queen Elizabeth as virginal moon goddess (863–8);879 *Who . . . know*: cf. *FQ*, III. ii. 18–21 on the magic looking glass; 884 *Urania*: Muse of astronomy; 892 *Mantua*: Virgil's birthplace; 894 *Geoffrey*: Chaucer, admired and invoked by Spenser (one of whose poetic personae was *Colin* Clout) in *FQ*, IV. ii. 32–4; 896 *Delia*: subject of Samuel Daniel's sonnet sequence (1592); 897–903: I have had no more luck than earlier commentators in tracing these less well-known acquaintances of D's: *shadow* may allude to George Chapman's *Shadow of Night* (1594) or Thomas Campion's *Fragmentum Umbrae* (1595); *Salice's* = LF's reading (1596 has *Salves*) and, Krueger-Nemser suggest, may allude to Fulke Greville's sonnet sequence *Caelica* (in MS in the mid 1590s); *bee*: Krueger-Nemser's conjecture: *Bay* (1596, LF, 1622). Possibly, if we follow Krueger-Nemser, Thomas Cutwode's *Caltha poetarum: or, the Bumble Bee* (London, 1599): *caltha* = marigold (but D would have to have seen the work in MS); 904 *Astrophel*: i.e., Sir Philip Sidney; 907 *swallow*: presumably Richard *Martin*, the poem's original dedicatee.

SELECT BIBLIOGRAPHY

The following books are recommended for their coverage of various backgrounds (musical, visual, historical, religious, sociological, etc.) to the period, as also of wider-ranging literary topics than those covered by the works listed in the author bibliographies printed with the notes, above. Their methodologies range from the traditional to the modern (new historicist, feminist, post-structuralist, and so on) and thus convey a good idea of current trends in Renaissance scholarship.

ACKROYD, PETER. *The House of Doctor John Dee* (1993; novel brilliantly evocative of alchemical/magical background).

ALPERS, P. J., ed. *Elizabethan Poetry: Modern Essays in Criticism* (1967).

ATTRIDGE, DEREK. *Well-Weighed Syllables: Elizabethan Verse in Classical Metre* (1974).

BENDER, R. M. *Five Courtier Poets of the English Renaissance* (1967).

BERRY, PHILIPPA. *Of Chastity and Power: Elizabethan Literature and the Unmarried Queen* (1989).

BROWN, J. R. AND BERNARD HARRIS, eds. *Elizabethan Poetry* (1960).

BUSH, DOUGLAS. *Mythology and the Renaissance Tradition in English Poetry* (1932; rev. 1963).

CRUTTWELL, PATRICK. *The English Sonnet* (1966).

D'AMICO, JACK. *Petrarch in England: An Anthology of Parallel Texts from Wyatt to Milton* (1979).

DUBROW, HEATHER *et al.*, eds. *The Historical Renaissance: New Ideas on Tudor and Stuart Literature and Culture* (1988).

DUFFY, EAMON. *The Stripping of the Altars: Traditional Religion in England 1400–1580* (1992).

EVANS, MAURICE. *English Poetry in the Sixteenth Century* (1967).

EVETT, DAVID. *Literature and the Visual Arts in Tudor England* (1990).

FINNEY, G. L. *Musical Backgrounds for English Literature 1580–1650* (1962).

FORSTER, LEONARD. *The Icy Fire: Five Studies in European Petrarchism* (1969).

FOX, ALISTAIR. *Politics and Literature in the Reigns of Henry VII and Henry VIII* (1989).

FRENCH, P. J. *John Dee: The World of an Elizabethan Magus* (1972).

GOLDBERG, JONATHAN. *Voice Terminal Echo: Postmodernism and English Renaissance Texts* (1986).

GREEN, T. M. *The Light in Troy: Imitation and Discovery in Renaissance Poetry* (1982).

GREENBLATT, S. J. *Renaissance Self-Fashioning: From More to Shakespeare* (1980).

GREENBLATT, S. J., ed. *Representing the English Renaissance* (1988).

HARDISON, O. B. *Prosody and Purpose in the English Renaissance* (1989).

HEDLEY, JANE. *Power in Verse: Metaphor and Metonymy in the Renaissance Lyric* (1988).

HENINGER, S. K. Jr. *The Cosmographical Glass: Renaissance Diagrams of the Universe* (1977).

HOLLANDER, JOHN. *The Untuning of the Sky: Ideas of Music in English Poetry 1500–1700* (1961).

HULSE, S. CLARKE. *Metamorphic Verse: The Elizabethan Minor Epic* (1981).

JAVITCH, DANIEL. *Poetry and Courtliness in Renaissance England* (1978).

KERRIGAN, JOHN. *Motives of Woe: Shakespeare and the 'Female Complaint': A Critical Anthology* (1991).

KING, JOHN. *English Reformation Literature: The Tudor Origins of the Protestant Tradition* (1982).

LEVER, J. W. *The Elizabethan Love Sonnet* (1956).

LEWIS, C. S. *English Literature in the Sixteenth Century Excluding Drama* (1954).

LINDENBAUM, PETER. *Changing Landscapes: Anti-Pastoral Sentiment in the English Renaissance* (1986).

MACLEAN, IAN. *The Renaissance Notion of Woman* (1980).

MARTINEZ, LAURA. *Society and History in English Renaissance Verse* (1985).

MARTZ, L. L. *From Renaissance to Baroque: Essays on Literature and Art* (1992).

MAY, S. W. *The Elizabethan Courtier Poets: The Poems and Their Contexts* (1991).

MINTA, STEPHEN. *Petrarch and Petrarchism: The English and French Traditions* (1980).

MONTROSE, L. A. 'Of Gentlemen and Shepherds: The Politics of Elizabethan Pastoral Form', *ELH: A Journal of English Literary History*, 50 (1983).

NORBROOK, DAVID. *Poetry and Politics in the English Renaissance* (1984).

ORGEL, STEPHEN AND G. F. LYTTLE, eds. *Patronage in the Renaissance* (1981).

PATTERSON, ANNABEL. *Censorship and Interpretation* (1984).

PETERSON, D. L. *The English Lyric from Wyatt to Donne: A History of the Plain and Eloquent Styles* (1967).

POMEROY, ELIZABETH. *The Elizabethan Miscellanies: Their Development and Conventions* (1973).

PRESCOTT, A. L. *French Poets and the English Renaissance: Studies in Fame and Transformation* (1978).

ROCHE, T. P. *Petrarch and the English Sonnet Sequence* (1989).

ROSTON, MURRAY. *Sixteenth-Century English Literature* (1982).

SAUNDERS, J. W. *A Biographical Dictionary of Renaissance Poets and Dramatists* (1983).

SHUMAKER, WAYNE. *The Occult Sciences in the Renaissance* (1972).

SINFIELD, ALAN. *Literature in Protestant England 1560–1660* (1983).

SMITH, B. H. *Poetic Closure: A Study of How Poems End* (1968).

SMITH, HALLETT. *Elizabethan Poetry: A Study in Conventions, Meaning, and Expression* (1952).

STEVENS, JOHN. *Music and Poetry in the Early Tudor Court* (1961).

STRONG, ROY. *The Cult of Elizabeth: Elizabethan Portraiture and Pageantry* (1977).

THOMAS, KEITH. *Religion and the Decline of Magic* (1978).

THOMPSON, JOHN. *The Founding of English Metre* (1962).

TILLYARD, E. M. W. *The English Renaissance: Fact or Fiction?* (1952).

TUVE, ROSEMOND. *Elizabethan and Metaphysical Imagery* (1947).

TUVE, ROSEMOND. *Allegorical Imagery: Some Mediaeval Books and Their Posterity* (1966).

WALKER, D. P. *The Ancient Theology: Studies in Christian Platonism from the Fifteenth to the Eighteenth Centuries* (1972).

WALLER, GARY. *English Poetry of the Sixteenth Century* (1986).

WHIGHAM, FRANK. *Ambition and Privilege: The Social Tropes of Elizabethan Courtesy Theory* (1984).

WIND, EDGAR. *Pagan Mysteries in the Renaissance* (1967).

WILSON, K. M., ed. *Women Writers of the Renaissance and Reformation* (1987).

WOODBRIDGE, LINDA. *Women and the English Renaissance: Literature and the Nature of Womankind, 1540–1620* (1984).

WOODS, SUSAN. *Natural Emphasis: English Versification from Chaucer to Dryden* (1984).

SUPPLEMENTARY AUTHOR
BIBLIOGRAPHY

Sir Thomas Wyatt
DASENBROCK, R. W. *Imitating the Italians: Wyatt, Spenser, Synge, Pound, Joyce* (1991).

MACFIE, P. R. 'Sewing in Ottava Rima: Wyatt's Assimilation and Critique of a Feminist Poetic', *Renaissance Papers* (1987).

Sir Walter Ralegh
CAMPBELL, MARION. 'Inscribing Imperfection: Sir Walter Ralegh and the Elizabethan Court', *English Literary Renaissance*, 20 (1990).

LITT, D. E. 'The Poetics and Politics of Naming: The Case of Sir Walter Ralegh and His Queen', *Names: Journal of the American Name Society*, 39 (1991).

MAY, S. W. *Sir Walter Ralegh* (1989).

Sir Philip Sidney
ALLEN, M. J. B. *et al.*, eds. *Sir Philip Sidney's Achievements* (1990).

BAKER, M. P. '"The Uncanny Stranger on Display": The Female Body in Sixteenth- and Seventeenth-Century Love Poetry', *South Atlantic Review*, 56 (1991).

DUNCAN-JONES, KATHERINE. *Sir Philip Sidney, Courtier Poet* (1991).

HAGER, ALAN. *Dazzling Images: The Masques of Sir Philip Sidney* (1991).

KINNEY, A. F. *et al.* 'New Directions in Sidney Studies: From Here to Where?', *Sidney Newsletter*, 9 (1988–9).

KUIN, ROGER. 'Sir Philip Sidney: The Courtier and the Text', *English Literary Renaissance*, 19 (1989).

MILLER, P. A. 'Sidney, Petrarch, and Ovid: Imitation as Subversion', *ELH: A Journal of English Literary History*, 58 (1991).

STRICKLAND, R. 'Pageantry and Poetry as Discourse: The Production of Subjectivity in Sir Philip Sidney's Funeral', *ELH: A Journal of English Literary History*, 57 (1990).

Mary Sidney (Herbert)
LAMB, M. E. *Gender and Authorship in the Sidney Circle* (1990).

Supplementary Bibliography

Michael Drayton

BRINK, J. R. *Michael Drayton Revisited* (1990).

Sir John Davies

ERLER, M. C. 'Davies's *Astræa* and Other Contexts of the Countess of Pembroke's "A Dialogue"', *SEL: Studies in English Literature, 1500–1900*, 30 (1990).

KLEMP, P. J. *Fulke Greville and Sir John Davies: A Reference Guide* (1985).

INDEX TO FIRST LINES

Index to First Lines

191067273X